Law
for
Business
and
Management

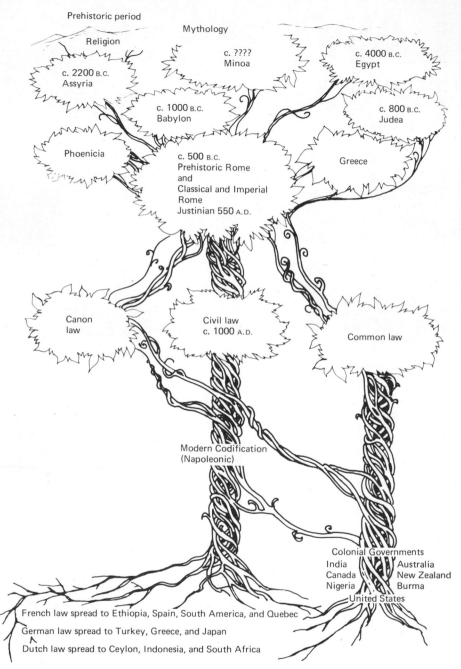

Prehistoric period

Mythology

Religion

c. ????
Minoa

c. 4000 B.C.
Egypt

c. 2200 B.C.
Assyria

c. 1000 B.C.
Babylon

c. 800 B.C.
Judea

Phoenicia

c. 500 B.C.
Prehistoric Rome
and
Classical and Imperial
Rome
Justinian 550 A.D.

Greece

Canon
law

Civil law
c. 1000 A.D.

Common law

Modern Codification
(Napoleonic)

Colonial Governments
India   Australia
Canada   New Zealand
Nigeria   Burma
United States

French law spread to Ethiopia, Spain, South America, and Quebec

German law spread to Turkey, Greece, and Japan

Dutch law spread to Ceylon, Indonesia, and South Africa

The law of the Western world. Law develops with time. Its beginnings are unknown. Much of the first law was interwoven with religion and mythology. Early trade and military conquests introduced an exchange of cultures and ideas, and thus many early cultures contributed to the Roman empire, which lasted over 1,000 years. From Rome developed common law and civil law, each affecting the other.

LAW FOR BUSINESS AND MANAGEMENT

GAIL McKNIGHT BECKMAN, J.D.
School of Business Administration
Georgia State University

WALTER F. BERDAL, J.D.
School of Business Administration
Georgia State University

DAVID G. BRAINARD, J.D.
Business Administration Department
Palm Beach Atlantic College

**McGRAW-HILL
BOOK COMPANY**

New York	Johannesburg	New Delhi	Singapore
St. Louis	Kuala Lumpur	Panama	Sydney
San Francisco	London	Paris	Tokyo
Dallas	Mexico	São Paulo	Toronto
Düsseldorf	Montreal		

Library of Congress Cataloging in Publication Data

Beckman, Gail McKnight.
    Law for business and management.

    1. Business law—United States. I. Berdal,
Walter F., joint author. II. Brainard, David G., joint
author. III. Title.
KF889.3.B346   346'.73'07   74-13709
ISBN 0-07-004136-9

1 2 3 4 5 6 7 8 9 0   MAMA   7 8 3 2 1 0 9 8 7 6 5 4

The editors for this book were Edward E. Byers and Susan L. Schwartz, the
designer was Paddy Bareham, and its production was supervised by Richard
Jacobson. It was set in Century Schoolbook by Monotype Composition Company, Inc.
It was printed and bound by The Maple Press Company.

Contents

Preface

American education is undergoing dramatic change. The objectives of urban universities, two-year colleges, and adult programs are becoming more relevant to people's lives. The study of law has taken on new importance because of its potential as a means of social change and its value as an administrative-managerial tool. Yet few students preparing for careers in business can devote the time and effort required to make an intensive study of law. They can obtain, however, a basic awareness of business law and its influence on the functions and operations of business.

Law for Business and Management is designed to satisfy the business law needs of students who plan to enter the business world as supervisors, managers, and small business proprietors. Its compact coverage takes a managerial approach to law, dealing with the legal aspects of starting a business, staffing it, acquiring assets, and entering into contracts with suppliers and customers. Selected cases are introduced at the end of each chapter for the purpose of providing the reader with opportunities to apply prudent business and legal considerations to making sound business decisions.

Law does not operate in a vacuum. Thus many practical illustrations such as business ratios and causes of business failures are given. Practical suggestions have been inserted to guide prospective business people in the pursuit of their career objective. Tables, legal forms, drawings, and occasional cartoons are introduced throughout the text to reinforce basic legal concepts and aid reader comprehension.

We wish to express our debt to the influence of our instructors, our professional colleagues, and the unceasing flow of continuing-education materials we have received over the years. More specifically, we are grateful for the assistance of General Motors Corporation for permission to make reference to the Wankel engine and the use of the name "Chevrolet"; Humble Oil and Refining Company for permission to refer to the development of their trade name "Exxon"; the Association of American Railroads and Southern Railway System for supplying us with blank bills of lading and waybills; Dun & Bradstreet, Inc., for permission to use Key Business Ratios, Causes of Business Failure, and Cost of Doing Business illustrations; the Atlanta Real Estate Board for furnishing lease and sale forms (not to be reprinted without permission of the Real Estate Board); the Fulton County Licensing Bureau for allowing use of the Business License form and information on requirements; the Small Business Administration for permission to use illustrations from *Starting and Managing a Small Business of Your Own* by W. O. Metcalf; the Social Security Administration for information concerning Social Security and Medicare; Richard D. Irwin, Inc., for permission to quote from Mehr and Hedges, *Risk Management in the Business Enterprise*; Delta Air Lines, Inc., and Sears, Roebuck and Co. for permission to use their names in an illustration; Hauser Associates Inc. for assistance in preparing the trademark application form; John Hart and Field Enterprises, Inc., for permission to use *The Wizard of Id* cartoon; Publishers-Hall Syndicate for permission to reprint the *Grin and Bear It* cartoon; Morgan, Lewis & Bockius for permission to use the stock certificate for the Philadelphia Suburban Corporation in an illustration and their materials on corporate bylaws; Dr. Leslie Rood and Dr. William Rutherford for reading selected chapters of the manuscript; our colleagues for many helpful ideas on developing some aspects of the materials; and other friends who offered ideas and counsel as the work progressed.

Gail McK. Beckman
Walter F. Berdal
David G. Brainard

Introduction

The Attorney-Client Relationship

The legal profession is composed of persons who are trained in the law. Every state has an interest in protecting the public from untrained and unqualified people giving legal advice to the general public for a fee. Therefore all lawyers must meet minimum state requirements by passing a bar examination and obtaining a license which entitles them to hire themselves out as lawyers and charge a fee for their services. A lawyer is frequently referred to as an *attorney at law*. A person who consults a lawyer for advice or services is called a *client*.

Sooner or later, nearly everyone has occasion to seek legal advice. This is particularly true of the business person. Therefore, it is important that people in business recognize when they should seek legal advice. All lawyers have had a business client come to them with the story of signing a contract and then finding that it was a mistake. It may be too late for a lawyer to do much for a client after the client has been acting as his or her own lawyer in the case. There is an old saying: "The man who acts as his own lawyer has a fool for a client

"I thought I didn't need a lawyer when I bought . . .".

The man who was his own lawyer

and an ass for a lawyer." It is much easier, and cheaper, to prevent trouble than it is to correct someone's mistakes. Therefore, a lawyer should be consulted before a serious mistake has been made. Just as preventive medicine can discover and treat conditions before they become serious, so preventive law can help people in business avoid trouble and protect their rights.

WHEN TO SEE A LAWYER

Sometimes the need for a lawyer is quite obvious. When people are being sued, they generally do not need to be told to see a lawyer promptly, for the time to respond in court may be short. Also, if there is a decision to sue someone, a lawyer is obviously needed. But there are many other situations when a person should seek the advice and counsel of a lawyer. These include when:

1. A business is being organized, no matter how small or what the form of its organization will be
2. A transaction, even an apparently simple one, concerns real property (land and buildings), especially land purchases, sales, and leases
3. A transaction of any kind involves a great deal of money in relation to the total worth of the business
4. A business arrangement is for a relatively long time
5. The other party to a transaction has legal advice
6. The other side to the transaction insists on an unusual arrangement
7. Any tax return, with the exception of the most routine, is being submitted
8. Any government agency begins an investigation or shows unusually great interest in the business
9. A deal that both sides want to transact breaks down for lack of agreement on details
10. Someone threatens to do acts that would harm the business person or the business

In short, a lawyer should be called in whenever a transaction is other than simple and routine. A lawyer should not be thought of only in terms of suing or being sued. Most lawyers work hard to keep their clients out of *litigation*, that is, a legal contest in a court. Perhaps 95 percent of the lawyers' work is done outside of the courtroom. They spend their time researching the law, noting how various courts have ruled in similar situations, and analyzing how best to handle their clients' problems in the light of the law.

Regulatory Bodies

In recent years a large body of law has developed that is known as *administrative law*, containing the rules and regulations which apply to procedures and enforcements of various regulatory bodies set up by the state legislatures or Congress, such as the Securities and Exchange Commission, and the Interstate Commerce Commission. Thus the business may need a lawyer for representation before the labor mediation council, tax boards, occupational safety boards, and many others. Although these do not involve litigation in the traditional sense, the consequences of uninformed appearance before such boards can be disastrous.

Arbitration

Instead of litigation, the business may be confronted with a request for *arbitration*. This involves the submission of a dispute to an umpire or a panel of umpires. The persons selected to settle the dispute are usually people who are specialists in a particular field. Frequently they are lawyers.

Arbitration is often preferred to litigation because it encourages compromise. Generally an arbitration hearing is speedy, lacks the formality of a court, costs substantially less, and avoids the technical rules of evidence. However, these qualities should not blind one to the realities of the situation. The ruling of an arbitration panel is just as effective and final as any ruling of a court of law. Therefore, business people must exercise the same care in dealing with matters before an arbitration panel as they do with matters coming before courts of law or regulatory bodies.

ESTABLISHING A LEGAL RELATIONSHIP

Most established businesses have had contacts with a lawyer. A business person who has not established a contact may wish to do so in anticipation of needing one in the future. Or a new lawyer may be needed to tackle a new type of problem which the present lawyer cannot handle. Whatever the reason, there are four common approaches to securing a lawyer:

References

The usual way to secure a lawyer is through a reference from a friend or an acquaintance who has retained a lawyer and been pleased with the result. Professional contacts are another source of references. Colleagues who have experienced similar business problems may be able to recommend lawyers. In this way the business person may be able to obtain the names of several lawyers and compare their reputations.

It is a good idea to secure more than one reference. If a particular lawyer's name shows up more than once, it may be wise to consider this individual further for possible selection.

In selecting a lawyer through references, one should always find out what areas, if any, he or she specializes in. Some lawyers have specialties such as wills and trusts, bankruptcies, commercial paper, or real estate which should be kept in mind. It would not be wise to employ a lawyer with one of these specialties if the problem concerned a patent.

It is also a good idea to find out the type of clients the lawyer represents. One would not want to select the lawyer who already represents one's principal competitor; a situation might develop in which the newer client would have to find another lawyer. A lawyer is usually not permitted to represent hostile parties. The same principles apply to the work of partners in a law firm.

Professional Reference Books

There are several directories of lawyers practicing law in various cities or states of the United States. Among the most comprehensive of these is the multivolume Martindale-Hubbell, which is a standard reference work in many major libraries. It covers all the states and lists lawyers according to city and county, the educational qualifications of lawyers, and other data about the practitioners listed in it. There are similar directories of trial lawyers, Harvard Law School graduates, lawyers in a specific city, and so forth.

Bar association directories usually give the names of members in alphabetical order without reference to other criteria, such as areas of specialization. Thus such a list should be considered only a starting point. A given lawyer may or may not be particularly satisfactory for the job. The cautious business person should use these reference works judiciously to supplement other sources of information.

Lawyers' Reference Services

Metropolitan centers may have lawyers' reference services to assist those of moderate means who need legal advice and do not already have a lawyer to whom they can turn. People go to a central bureau where they are interviewed and their legal problems are evaluated. The service then recommends an appropriate attorney.

Lawyers' Professional Contacts

Sometimes a legal problem crosses state lines. Thus a client and a lawyer in New Jersey may be involved in a case requiring legal action in Illinois. The client could ask the lawyer to recommend an attorney in Illinois, assuming that the New Jersey lawyer does not practice there. The first lawyer's firm may already have made such a selection in other cases. Professional colleagues and reference volumes are other sources that the lawyer may consult. It would be unusual for the New Jersey lawyer to be unable to establish contact through bar association activities or even through a law school. Professional contacts are seldom a problem.

CONTACT WITH LAWYER

The business person who has selected a likely lawyer should call the lawyer for an interview and explain whether special help is needed for some particular problem or the establishment of a more permanent legal relationship is intended. The fee for the brief interview will usually be quite nominal, or there may even be no fee at all, but it should be clearly specified beforehand.

Preparing for the Interview

If the interview is for a particular problem (for example, a debt owed by a customer), all correspondence, account cards or books, and some other details should be taken to this session. This saves time in establishing the facts. The lawyer will also want these documents or copies of them for the files.

If, on the other hand, the interview is for the purpose of establishing a long-term relationship, the lawyer may want to see many records of the business, including its documents of formation, all corporate records, accounts, correspondence, personnel records, and tax returns. These may be so bulky that the lawyer will have to come to the business premises to see them all. At least, the prospective client should ask the lawyer to specify the necessary materials so that they can be readied and some of the more important ones can be brought to the initial interview.

The Interview

Lawyers are bound by a code of professional responsibility in much the same way as doctors. There are nine basic principles forming this code of ethics. For example, lawyers must represent their clients faithfully and render independent professional judgment, and they must treat all communications from clients in the strictest confidence. The law protects both the lawyer and the client. The lawyer cannot be forced to tell what the client disclosed *as a client*. The reason for the principle and the law is that a lawyer cannot fully represent a client unless there has been a full disclosure of all the facts.

At the interview, the business person should decide whether the entire problem, without reservations, can be disclosed to the lawyer. If he or she should find a lawyer to whom everything can be told, it is as unwise to withhold information from a lawyer as it is to withhold symptoms from a doctor. Without accurate facts, in neither case can the treatment cure the disease.

The fact that the individual finds it difficult to talk about a problem indicates that the problem is troublesome. It calls for prompt disclosure and a thorough exploration. The more troublesome, negative, or embarrassing a fact seems, the more important it is to tell the lawyer about it. Sooner or later it will come out, and the lawyer must know about it to be prepared to deal with it. It is far less damaging to tell the lawyer promptly about this fact than to have it come out as a surprise during a trial or under other equally unfavorable circumstances.

Before concluding the first interview, the business person should also find out how the lawyer computes fees. If a lasting legal relationship is intended, a retainer may be agreed upon. The client should know whether payment will be a percentage of what is won through litigation, a flat fee, or an hourly rate. Whatever the basis of the lawyer's fees, all questions about payment should be settled during the first interview.

LEGAL FEES

No one enjoys paying bills. Hence it is not surprising that fee disagreements can give rise to some very bitter disputes between lawyers

THE WIZARD OF ID   by Brant parker and Johnny hart

and clients. Because there is such a wide range of billing practices that may be followed, the business person and the lawyer should establish the ground rules at the very beginning of their relationship. It is much more difficult to ask the reason for a particular charge once it has been billed than it is to discuss it ahead of time. It is quite common for a lawyer to persuade a client not to pursue a matter because the legal fees are so high that the reward is not considered to be worth the cost. However, if a unique point of law is raised, an unusual lawyer may undertake the assignment as a matter of professional satisfaction regardless of the sum involved or the expected fee and treat it as a test case of the applicable law. This is admittedly rare.

Hourly Rate Basis

Just as it is important to know what the first interview will cost, it is essential to find out how much the lawyer will bill for future services and when payment is expected. Lawyers usually bill on an hourly basis for their work. The rate may vary from as little as about $12 an hour up to $100 or more per hour, depending on local customs, the age and experience of the lawyer working on the matter, the importance or difficulty of the matter, how much money is at stake, and how successfully the matter is concluded. The lawyer will usually volunteer an estimate, but if not the client should ask for one. On some complicated matters, the lawyer may feel unable to charge as much as a strict accounting of time and work would seem to call for; he or she may make up for this by charging more on a relatively simple legal matter which will produce large profits for the client.

Contingency Fees

Some matters, particularly lawsuits that have as their object the collection of money, may be handled on a *contingency* basis. This means that the lawyer will charge the client nothing if the case is lost, but that if it is won the lawyer will keep a percentage of all collections, sometimes as much as half.

This arrangement is not rare. Personal injury suits are often handled this way. Someone who is severely hurt in a car accident may sue to recover medical and other expenses, sharing part of the realized sum with the lawyer. A more common example in business is the collection of moneys owed a business. A business person who has given up trying to collect a debt by friendly means may ask a lawyer to bring suit, offering to pay the lawyer a fourth to a half of the amount collected.

Retainer Fees

Some lawyers ask for a retainer fee for an individual matter or, more often, for a continuing legal relationship. The amount of the anticipated legal work is estimated, and the retainer is based on this estimate. The client is then billed for any excess over this amount. If the lawyer incurs unusual expenses, such as filing fees or posting bonds, the client may also be asked to advance these expenses.

In the event that a continuing relationship is anticipated, the lawyer may suggest that certain work be done at a flat rate, that collection work be done on a contingency basis, and that all other legal work be billed at an hourly rate, with a monthly retainer of a certain amount. It is entirely appropriate for the business person to suggest lower fees or altogether different arrangements.

Fee Schedules

In many communities, local bar associations or courts issued fee schedules that described certain frequently performed tasks and established a minimum fee for them. For example, the minimum fee for setting up a simple corporation might be $250, or the minimum fee for drafting a will might be $25. The motive of the legal profession for establishing such schedules was often to prevent price cutting, which might be considered a form of advertising or unfair competition and hence forbidden by the code of professional responsibility. These schedules could benefit clients by telling them in advance what they could expect to be charged, and they could provide reasonable guidelines for lawyers. However, a number of state bar associations have abolished fee schedules following a decision that they constitute price fixing.

Fee Disputes

When controversies do arise, the business person should know how to handle them. The great majority of legal cases are handled smoothly and without problems involving fees; unfortunately, it is not unknown for unpleasantness to arise regarding the fee. This is one of the major causes of friction in lawyer-client relationships today.

Private Discussion

If a business person—or anyone—is confronted with a lawyer's bill that seems unreasonable, what course of action should be taken? First, the client should get in touch with the lawyer and discuss it. The bill may not appear so bad once a misunderstanding has been cleared up. Of course, it is best to reach a clear understanding at the very outset of the relationship.

Litigation or Arbitration

Sometimes the situation becomes more serious. The client is outraged and wants to sue. Usually this is not a good idea because the chances of success are small. The prudent business person, after vainly attempting to resolve the disagreement with the lawyer, should get in touch with the local bar association and explain the situation.

Many bar associations have set up machinery for handling such fee dispute problems peacefully lest the adverse publicity of a lawsuit reflect on the entire legal profession. This procedure may involve arbitration. A panel of several disinterested members of the profession hears all the facts as stated by the parties and their witnesses. Then they reach a decision which everyone may have agreed in advance to accept as binding or without appeal. Fee disputes are regrettable but perhaps inevitable. It is in the interest of the legal profession to have a chance to keep its own house clean.

UNETHICAL CONDUCT

As we have stated, lawyers are bound by a professional code of ethics. Unfortunately, some lawyers forget or subvert their ethical principles out of a desire for money. On discovering this unpleasant fact of life, the client may become disillusioned or irate. What should he or she do—act or forget it? The good business person knows that a lawsuit is a last resort. In a case where a lawyer has violated ethical principles it might be better to turn to the bar association. All states have organizations known as *bar associations*. States that have an *inte-*

grated or *compulsory bar association* require that every practicing lawyer belong to it. Almost every bar association has a grievance or ethics committee to handle disagreements between lawyers and clients. These committees investigate charges of unethical practices and, when appropriate, bring disbarment proceedings to prevent repetition of improper activity. Therefore, a business person who feels a lawyer's conduct is improper can usually bring the matter before the local bar association's ethics or grievance committee. If it finds that unethical practices have been followed, the association will probably initiate its own disciplinary or disbarment proceedings. The client will not have to bear the burden and expense of litigation. In serious cases, the state attorney general may begin an investigation and, when necessary, take similar disciplinary action.

Remember that the lawyer-client relationship is contractual in nature. After compensating a lawyer for work performed, a client can discharge the attorney and contract with another.

PREVENTIVE LAW

It is still not a widely accepted practice for the average business person to consult a lawyer regularly in order to prevent trouble from occurring, yet this is exactly what a prudent executive should do.

In running the day-to-day affairs of a business, everyday concerns often seem far more important than distant, future legal problems. Besides, many legally significant events may not be recognized as such by the business person and thus ignored.

Many business people use lawyers in much the same way people use fire fighters, that is, after trouble develops. This is not good business and often very costly. Consequently, another important segment of the first interview may be a general discussion of the problems of the business. The lawyer may be able to provide some guidelines and to suggest areas that call for consultation with the lawyer. For example, the client and attorney may decide that all contracts of a value of more than $1,000 should be reviewed by the lawyer, that all communications of any kind with competitors or franchisees should be made in the presence of the lawyer, and that the price schedule of a business that could be subject to antitrust laws should be seen by the lawyer before it goes into effect.

The lawyer may not know very much about a particular business, and then the business person must teach the lawyer the necessary details. The more the lawyer knows about this particular business, the better lawyer the business person will have.

Consultation with a lawyer about the details of a business does not necessarily mean that the organization is in trouble. In fact, such precautions very likely will indicate good management and a thriving business.

THE LAWYER IN PERSPECTIVE

The work of the lawyer involves many problems that are handled outside of the courtroom. The lawyer negotiates business deals, organizes businesses, drafts documents, manages the formalities of a real estate transaction, draws up wills, sets up trust estates, and performs many other transactions in addition to trial work. With the trend toward specialization, many lawyers call in other specialists to handle particular parts of a client's business. For example, the lawyer may want the help of a specialist in matters concerning real estate, accounting, or taxes.

Despite the broad area of activity designated for the lawyer, the leading authority in a business is still the person heading it. The lawyer is an aid to, not a substitute for, good business judgment.

PART ONE

CONTRACTS AND SALES

Chapter One

Conducting Business through Contracts

Business law is based on the right of an individual to own, buy, and sell property. *Property* is the entire grouping of rights or assets, both tangible and intangible—for example, leases, notes, negotiable instruments, stocks, bonds, land, and jewelry.

Most business is established for the purpose of handling goods. This may mean buying, selling, holding, or otherwise using goods. Generally, the company will be concerned with making a profit from that endeavor, for without profit, a business cannot long exist.

That which is sold is not necessarily restricted to tangible goods. It may involve intangibles, such as stocks and bonds, or it may consist of services. A large percentage of our population sells services rather than goods. Physicians, lawyers, barbers, dry cleaners, TV repairers, and many other business people market their skills. However, at least half of all business transactions involve goods, ranging from small items for individual consumption to electronic computers, space vehicles, and heavy industrial equipment.

The law of contracts is concerned with the process by which people can undertake the many transactions necessary for the establishment of a business, the production of goods, and the transfer of property rights. It is not easy to define the word "contract." To put it most simply, a contract is an agreement between parties that is enforceable in a court of law. What makes up the agreement and how it is treated in law is the subject of the balance of this chapter.

SIGNIFICANCE OF CONTRACT LAW

Contract law specifies how and when people and businesses must live up to agreements. One person might hire employees, buy raw materials, and borrow money to manufacture a product, because another person has agreed in a legally binding contract to buy the product. The employees, too, rely on a contract with their employer to assure that they will be paid; thus, they can incur obligations through contracts to purchase homes, cars, and television sets with relative safety.

The entire structure of the business community is dependent on the law of contracts. In view of its importance, everyone should have some basic knowledge of contract law.

Making a Contract

Before signing any contract, everyone should take the time to read it, understand its terms, and resolve any serious questions. There are very few worthwhile deals or contracts that need to be seized without thoughtful perusal of the terms. The business person should beware of any situation requiring a prompt decision involving substantial assets of the firm. (Traders in special commodities must often act quickly, but these are professional people in a highly specialized enterprise.)

Anyone signing an important contract is certain to wonder whether the bargain is good and whether the other party will live up to the agreement. These are natural questions and may be very important if large sums of money are involved. If there is any doubt about the correctness of the contract provisions, the individual should see a lawyer. However, the lawyer can only assist in clarifying the terms of the agreement; no lawyer can guarantee that the bargain will be carried out.

SOUND CONTRACTUAL RELATIONSHIPS

Almost every lawyer gets a client who asks for a contract that "cannot be broken." A lawyer cannot make such assurances. The key to sound contractual relationships can be summed up by *the three C's: character, capability,* and *capital.* Although the words may seem self-evident, it is worthwhile to examine them.

Character

Character means integrity. What is the other party's reputation? Is he or she known for fair dealing? Has he or she been contentious and involved in numerous lawsuits? Does he or she default on payments? The answers to these questions should indicate the degree of assurance one can have about the proposed agreement. If the other party has a poor reputation and is frequently involved in litigation, one has little guarantee that the proposed contract will not end up in the courts. In every agreement there is much that cannot be spelled out in detail. Cheerful performance with a friendly spirit, a sense of honor, and an effort to please cannot be regulated by either contract or law. A person who lives up to only the letter of the contract or the law may be giving a pretty bad bargain.

Honor and integrity are commodities that cannot be purchased in the marketplace. Therefore, the business person will be wise to avoid making contracts with someone whose reputation is subject to criticism, since the most carefully drawn contract cannot anticipate every question that may arise. Contracts look to the future, and the future is always unknown.

Capability

Assuming the individual meets the qualifications of character, the next problem is that person's capability to perform. Many a contract breaks down because the parties are too optimistic about their ability.

For example, if the proposed contract is for building a simple fence, generally one need not be too concerned about the ability of the builder to perform. However, if the propsed contract calls for the construction of a large office building, the situation is entirely different. Here one must consider the technical competence, managerial ability, and adequacy of the equipment of the builder. In the area of capability the greatest failure usually comes from overestimating the capability of equipment that is too small, too light, or worn out. Technical competence was probably demonstrated on prior projects. Therefore, in evaluating the individual's qualifications, the capability to perform takes on added significance.

Before one signs a contract involving a large sum of money, one must be sure that the capability is adequate and that the parties are not looking at the prospective performance through rose-colored glasses.

Capital

Capital is closely related to capability, specifically the capability to pay. Money is needed to pay wages, buy materials, and hire and pay subcontractors. Unless this capital reserve is adequate, one can expect countless troubles and delays—even insolvency and bothersome litigation.

CLASSIFICATION OF CONTRACTS

There are many ways in which contracts can be classified. For convenience, they can be differentiated according to the manner in which they were made or carried out. Some contracts are classified by the way in which courts will enforce them or the defenses available to the parties. Another method of classification is by the manner the reasonable expectations of the parties are obtained through the contract and the equities shown in the contractual relationship.

Formal and Simple Contracts

A *formal contract* is a solemn agreement, usually written, sometimes with a seal affixed to it. Originally, only the formal contract, or covenant, could be enforced in a court of law; an agreement without the seal was unenforceable under early common law. A seal was originally a wax impression made by the signer's signet ring or some other instrument.

The significance of the wax seal has diminished, and now contracts under seal also include those containing the word "seal" or the written letters "L.S." (*locus sigilli*) after the signature. Today contracts under seal include documents for conveyance of land, stock certificates, testaments, and leases. In most states a contract need

Fig. 1-1. The promise in the unilateral contract flows in one direction only. In the bilateral contract the promises flow in two directions.

not be under seal to be enforceable. The three kinds of formal contracts are *covenants*, *negotiable instruments* such as checks, and *recognizances* (undertakings in court, often used in lieu of bail).

The *simple* or *informal contract* is not under seal and does not require any particular form. It may be oral or written. Our courts enforce simple contracts as long as they contain the elements described in the next chapter. Most of our concern will be with simple or informal contracts.

Unilateral and Bilateral Contracts

A *unilateral contract* is an offer or promise made by one party for an act to be done by another party. In other words, the first party makes an offer and the second party tacitly accepts the specified terms by performing the requested act. A typical example is the reward case. Individual A offers $5 to anyone who will return the dog Spot; B finds Spot, delivers Spot to A, and claims the $5.

A *bilateral contract* exists when both parties have made an agreement or a promise. In this type of contract both parties exchange promises binding themselves to certain performances. For example, A promises to pay B $10 and B promises to mow A's lawn.

Executed and Executory Contracts

An *executed contract* is a contract whose terms have been completely carried out by the parties. A typical one involves the sale of a house and the payment of the money by the purchaser. When the seller moves out and the buyer moves in, there is nothing further to be done by either party, and the contract is executed. Nevertheless, the contract remains important because the buyer will trace title to the home through it.

In an *executory contract*, at least one of the parties still has something to do to complete the agreement. For example, A goes to the local department store and pays for a refrigerator. The department store promises to deliver it the next week. Clearly, A's obligation under this agreement has been carried out. The department store must make the delivery before the bargain is complete.

Some contracts, like a fire insurance policy, can be both executed and executory. When the policyholder pays the premium, the contract is executed insofar as the policyholder is concerned. Yet the insurance company has an executory contract. It has to perform certain acts if a certain event happens; however, it has no obligation to make any payment until that event occurs.

Express and Implied Contracts

An *express contract* is one in which the terms are spelled out. A normal agreement for the sale of goods is such a contract. For example, A offers to sell one keg of nails for $10; B agrees to buy them and asks A to deliver to B's place of business; when A agrees to do so, an express contract exists.

An *implied contract* is one in which the parties engage in activity without spelling out their respective understanding or agreement; however, their acts imply an agreement. For example, A gets into a taxi and is driven home by B. Although nothing was said about payment, the law will hold that there was an implied agreement to pay the metered rate.

The implied contract is important most often when parties deal with each other over a period of time and suddenly find themselves in disagreement over their respective rights. In the absence of an express contract, the court is likely to find that they have an implied contract. It may be a contract that neither party expected or wanted. Therefore, it is always wise to have all business arrangements clearly spelled out to avoid subsequent disputes and disappointments.

Valid, Invalid, and Void Contracts

The majority of contracts entered into by people are valid. A *valid contract* is one that is recognized by the courts and will be enforced if the parties apply for relief to the courts. An *invalid contract* is one that has an essential element missing. Such a contract is unenforceable.

Occasionally, one will encounter contracts that are illegal and hence *void;* that is, they have no legal force. They may be illegal for a variety of reasons. Some may be against the law, while others may be against public policy. For example, a contract to commit murder is both against the law and against public policy. It is against the law because the state legislature has passed a specific law prohibiting murder. It is against public policy because it violates fundamental principles of ethics, morality, and social behavior; courts simply will not allow themselves to become a party to enforcing such contracts. A contract of insurance would be void unless issued by a state-licensed insurer. A contract to remove someone's tonsils by an unlicensed individual would also be void and against the law.

Voidable and Unenforceable Contracts

Some contracts are perfectly legal unless one or both of the parties wish to exercise a right to avoid the results reached by the agreement. The law grants a person the power to disaffirm a contract if it was obtained by fraud, duress, or undue influence, if one of the parties was an infant (under legal age), or if one of the parties did not have the mental capacity to know what was happening. Such a contract is known as a *voidable contract*.

Within the last few years, several consumer protection laws have been passed by states, and the Congress allowed certain contracts to be automatically rescinded if the buyer notifies the seller within a specified time—usually 48 to 144 hours. For example, under 15 U.S. Code sec. 1645, a buyer of an appliance that is built into a home has "until midnight of the third business day following" to rescind the contract.

Unenforceable contracts are valid contracts that become unenforceable because of some legal obstacle that can be raised by one of the parties. Often this involves the statute of frauds. The *statute of frauds* does not say that a contract is fraudulent but that if certain conditions are not met the court will not enforce it. For example, contracts conveying real estate must be evidenced by writing. Contracts that require a long time to perform (usually over one year) and contracts involving large sums of money must also be in writing before the courts will enforce them. Of course, if the parties wish, they may still carry out their agreement. The statute of frauds is for the protection of the party against whom the enforcement is attempted.

Other contracts may be unenforceable under the statute of limitations, which puts a time limit on bringing lawsuits. If the delay between the cause of action and the trial is too great, witnesses can forget, disappear, or die, and therefore proving the alleged facts becomes difficult or even impossible. If a cause of action based on a contractual arrangement lies dormant for a number of years, the law deems the contract to be abandoned and the parties cannot come back at a later date to demand enforcement. The time is usually six or seven years, depending on the state. In cases other than contracts, rights may be barred by the passage of only one year.

Quasi Contracts

Sometimes a *quasi contract* is imposed by law to prevent an injustice even though the parties have not made any attempts to enter into a contractual agreement. Quasi contracts differ from implied contracts in that the parties to an implied contract usually anticipate that their acts will lead to an obligation enforceable at law. In the case of quasi contracts, there is no formal agreement or understanding between the parties. The measure of damages will depend on what the court considers reasonable. For instance, young people who have not yet become of legal age cannot be held liable on a contract for food and lodging they have signed or agreed to. However, the persons furnishing the goods to them may be able to recover for their reasonable value under the doctrine of quasi contract. The courts use this doctrine to prevent unjust enrichment.

UNIFORM COMMERCIAL CODE

The law is a living thing; it changes to meet the needs of people. Thus the law of contracts has continued to change to meet the needs of people who are engaged in the business of sales and services.

Because of the independent development of laws among the states, many obstacles arose to the smooth transaction of business. For example, one state might have made a law that passed title to the buyer when goods were delivered to the railroad or common carrier. Another state might hold that title does not pass until the goods are delivered to the destination of the buyer. Transactions were further complicated when credit was part of the purchase. As a result the law became highly complex and confusing, leading to much litigation.

Meanwhile, lawyers, jurists, and scholars were aware of the problem and undertook studies to determine what could be done to improve the situation. It was clear that some type of uniform code or act was needed, but the history of getting uniform legislation through the legislatures of all the states was not encouraging.

In 1940, the Commissioners on Uniform State Laws agreed to prepare a proposal which would bring commercial law up to date and repeal all existing laws. The work was first issued in the early 1950s, and in 1962 an official text known as the Uniform Commercial Code was published. Adoption of the code started as soon as the work appeared. At present almost all states have adopted the code. In further discussions on the law of contracts, references will be made to the various sections of the Uniform Commercial Code, or U.C.C.

Highlights of the Code

The code was prepared for business people who buy and sell merchandise. It recognizes their need for a law that is easily understood, widely applicable, and easily administered. The code abolishes many of the old distinctions in the law of contracts pertaining to the sale of goods between merchants. For example, the seal has no real significance under the code.

The U.C.C. was prepared with uniform section numbers for easy reference throughout the country. Alternate sections have been prepared in a few cases to permit states to adopt alternate provisions where special problems existed. Thus, even though there have been some amendments by some of the states, the sections remain numbered the same and the amendments can be recognized as variations without destroying the symmetry of the entire code.

Considerable care was used to achieve clarity in the code. Many of the drafting deliberations of the committee have been preserved and made available to the courts to enable the courts to determine the intent of the language used.

The code provides clear and explicit rules under which title to goods passes. This had been an area of litigation, because under the previous rules there were a number of special situations governing the transfer of title; unless the parties were clearly aware of them, misunderstandings could easily develop. Under the code, business people have an easy reference to the applicable rules. They can make the necessary arrangements for payment and insurance while the goods are in transit with comparative safety.

In succeeding chapters, frequent references will be made to the U.C.C. to enable the student to become familiar with it.

INVOLVEMENT AND STUDY MATERIAL

Understanding Terms

Property	(page 14)	Valid contract	(page 19)
Contracts	(page 15)	Invalid contract	(page 19)
Formal contract	(page 17)	Void contract	(page 19)
Simple contract	(page 18)	Voidable contract	(page 20)
Unilateral contract	(page 18)	Unenforceable contract	
Bilateral contract	(page 18)		(page 20)
Executed contract	(page 18)	Statute of frauds	(page 20)
Executory contract	(page 18)	Quasi contract	(page 21)
Express contract	(page 19)	Uniform Commercial Code	
Implied contract	(page 19)		(page 21)

Questions and Problem Solving

1. Discuss the importance of the three keys to sound contractual relationships and give examples of each.
2. What is the purpose of the Uniform Commercial Code?
3. Explain the significance of the law of contracts in business transactions. Is it possible to do business without contracts?
4. What is the significance of a contract that is voidable?
5. How does the law arrive at a quasi contract? Give an example of one and compare it with a unilateral contract and a bilateral contract.
6. List the classes of contracts and give an example of each.
7. Describe how an insurance contract is an executory contract.
8. Are implied contracts frequent in business situations? Explain your answer.

Cases for Discussion

1. Williams told his neighbor Rivera that he was planning a vacation and would be away about five weeks. Upon returning home, Williams found that Rivera had watered and cut the grass for him. Does the service performed by Rivera constitute a contract? If so, what type of contract is this? Why?

2. Angstrom was employed by Sarkesian at a salary of $10,000 per year. Angstrom worked one year and one month, and then was terminated owing to lack of work. The original contract called for a settlement of the salary at the end of each year. Do the parties have a contract here for the second year? If so, what type of contract?

3. Harrison leased a building to Pinelli for six months for the purpose of running a bookmaking business during the racing season. Pinelli paid the rent at the end of each month but did not pay the rent for the third month. In the middle of the fourth month the building was raided by the police and Pinelli was arrested. Harrison thereupon brought a suit for the four months' rent. Is he entitled to collect? What type of contract is this?

4. Nebel contracted with the Luster Carpet Company to install a new carpet throughout her house. The Luster Carpet Company drove to the correct neighborhood, but went to the wrong house and installed the carpet, discovering the mistake several days later. Luster Carpet Company is now seeking to recover the value of the carpet installed in the neighbor's home. Is it entitled to collect? What type of contract is this?

Chapter Two

Elements of a Contract

As we have seen, commercial transactions depend on contracts. Without contracts, a person cannot sell goods and services. Everything else a business does is secondary to the primary goal of making a sale. No one can maintain a factory, employ workers, or carry on a business without the ability to sell what is produced, and each agreement to sell requires the existence of a contract.

We have said that contracts are negotiated agreements that are enforceable in court. However, the parties who have reached an agreement may later discover that other considerations affected the bargaining process and render the bargain unenforceable. Therefore the process of reaching an enforceable agreement can be viewed as follows:

Existence of the contract		*Validating factors*
Offer		Statute of frauds (writing)
Acceptance	*Meeting of*	Duress, undue influence
Consideration	*the minds*	Mistake, misrepresentation
		Fraud, illegality, capacity

Let us first examine the primary elements that make up an agreement (offer, acceptance, and consideration) and demonstrate a meeting of the minds. In the following chapter, we shall examine the secondary considerations which determine the enforceability of the contract.

NEGOTIATIONS

The process of reaching a contract generally begins with informal negotiations. A seller may not know the exact price to charge for a product and the buyer may not know what to pay for it. Even if they have an idea of the price, they may want to be sure they get a good bargain. Therefore, the parties may enter into preliminary negotiations or maneuvers having no legal significance. The seller may suggest a price of $50 for a necklace for which he or she is willing to take $10, and the buyer may start with an offer to pay $.75. During the preliminary negotiations they gradually converge on a mutually agreeable price.

The next step will be for one party to make an offer. Thus, the seller can open the proceedings leading directly to a contract by promising to sell goods for a specified amount. If that arrangement pleases the other party, the third step will be for the buyer to accept the offer, thereby promising to pay the amount requested.

In the typical American contract such an exchange of promises is called *consideration*. It is a type of legal glue to make both parties adhere to their agreement. In fact, both "contract" and "obligation" are derived from words meaning to draw together and to bind.

Although our courts stress the need for consideration to be present as an objective test of whether a contract exists, they do not entirely neglect the subjective side. When the parties have emerged from the entire bargaining process, they should have reached a meeting of the minds without which no valid contract can come into existence.

It is possible to conceive of the sequence of preliminary negotiations, offer, and acceptance as being a line with the various stages marked off as follows:

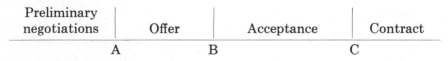

Preliminary negotiations	Offer	Acceptance	Contract
A	B		C

The problem arises over the placement of line A, which can be shifted to the left or right by the court, thereby shortening or prolonging the negotiation stage. This in turn determines whether an offer was made. Troubles begin when the offeror insists that he really did not mean to make an offer, but was only starting the bargaining process. There is no simple formula to tell whether a statement is an offer or only a preliminary negotiation.

OFFER

An *offer* is a tentative promise to do something which may induce a corresponding promise from another person. If an offer is accepted, the one making the offer is legally bound to perform in accordance with its terms.

A group of legal scholars have defined an offer and acceptance as a "manifestation of mutual assent" which "almost invariably takes the form of an offer or proposal by one party accepted by the other party or parties." Each situation must be considered individually, but if a proposal constitutes "a promise which is in its terms conditional upon an act, forbearance or return promise being given in exchange for the promise or its performance," then there probably was an offer.

Determining whether an offer has been made is not always easy. Whether words constitute an offer, a price quotation, an invitation to make an offer, or some other form of preliminary negotiation can depend on very subtle distinctions of words or circumstances.

If the discussions amounted to an offer, did the offer lapse because it was not accepted in a reasonable time? If it did not, was the response a rejection? Even if the offer was rejected, it may have been renewed. Was the response a request for a change in terms or a counteroffer? If the response was a counteroffer, was the original offeror's reply an acceptance of the counteroffer? Situations can become complex. If in doubt, having a lawyer analyze the situation should not take long and will be safer in the long run.

Making an Offer

It would be a happy world if all offers were simple, straightforward communications which everyone understood. Unfortunately, we are dealing with language, and words may have different meanings to different people. At auctions, professional buyers may signal the auctioneer by means of a raised eyebrow, a wave of the hand, or some other gesture; yet the meaning is quite clear to the individuals involved. Some offers are made by means of a large poster or a circular or through mass media. However in all cases when the offer is made, two things must be clear: the offeror must be aware of making an offer, and the offeree must realize it also. These are two factors essential to a meeting of the minds.

An offeror who says, "I offer to sell you this car for $1,500," has clearly made an offer. If the person being addressed then replies, "I accept," the two have concluded a contract of sale. The first person must sell the car and the second person must buy it, assuming that either of them insists on carrying out the transaction. If all transactions were this simple, there would be no need for further discussion.

In view of uncertainties in the past, offers are treated by the Uniform Commercial Code with primary emphasis on how they are to be interpreted. According to sec. 2-206(1)(a), "an offer to make a contract shall be construed as inviting acceptance in any manner and by any medium reasonable in the circumstances." There is a rather new tendency under the code to construe any ambiguity against the offeror. If the parties do not intend to abide by the U.C.C., they must make that intention clear.

Offers can be made orally or in writing, by mail, telephone, telegraph, and any other means which conveys the intent to bargain. There is no set form. Thus the first problem is to determine whether an offer has been made.

Advertisements

Frequently, one advertises to the entire reading public of widely circulated newspapers, and television broadcasts are regularly interrupted by advertisements for the sponsor's products. Are these advertisements offers? They may be, under certain circumstances. A definite offer to sell (or buy) goods can be made by advertisement if the wording clearly indicates it is intended to be an offer. A common example is one containing the words "first come, first served." Otherwise, such an advertisement is generally construed to be no more than an invitation to consider and to negotiate a sale. Because of this, the situation in which an advertisement carries the wrong price for an expensive item gives rise to no great windfalls to a customer who runs in and cries, "I accept your offer of a Mercedes Benz for $9.95!" (If the mistake is too absurd, courts are likely to hold that no reasonable person could consider that an offer was made, anyway.)

The usual result of using mass media is the general rule that an advertisement is only an invitation to make an offer and that sellers are not contractually bound to furnish the advertised goods. This makes commercial sense. A seller has no idea how many people will respond to an advertisement. If a seller were legally obligated to furnish goods when an unknown number of persons accepted the offer, it would be much more difficult to conduct business.

Mail Order Catalogs

Circulars and mail order catalogs are yet another common way of soliciting business by wholesalers and retailers. These can be sent out to tens of thousands of potential customers. Suppose one-third or even one-half of the recipients sent in their orders and checks, but not enough goods had been produced to fill all the orders. Was a legally binding offer made which was accepted to make a valid contract? No, this form of solicitation, even though it is addressed to a specific group of individuals, does not constitute an offer. Although confined to a specific group, an invitation to prospective buyers to negotiate and to trade with the seller imposes no obligation on the sender of the invitation to accept any subsequent offer.

A contrasting situation is presented by offers of rewards to performers of a certain act, such as locating a missing child. These bounties have been held to constitute offers enforceable at law.

Auctions

These are advertised in newspapers and also by circulars. The announcement will usually describe the merchandise, location, terms of sale, and perhaps some dates and other information. Yet this is only an invitation to negotiate. So, too, is the auctioneer's request for bids on the particular object. The bidder is considered to be the party making the offer at an auction sale.

Requests for Bids

Similarly, a contractor can ask for bids in conjunction with a construction project. This advertisement is to be regarded as a solicitation of orders, or offers, on the part of another. Thus, the announcement that bids will be received can usually be considered part of the preliminary negotiations since the request for a bid has no legal effect.

Duration of an Offer

Once an offer has been made, the next question is to determine the length of time the other party has for its acceptance. Many offers stipulate not only the time for acceptance but also the means of acceptance. For example, the offer may be made by mail and the stipulation will state: "reply by return mail." If the offeree accepts the offer by letter as instructed, the reply is an acceptance when it is mailed even though the offeror never receives the letter of acceptance. The U.C.C. sec. 2-206(1)(a) also alters this rule. The offeree might have accepted the offer by telegram rather than by letter, but until the U.C.C. there had been no acceptance until the telegram was received by the offeror. Furthermore, the acceptance by telegram must reach the offeror no later than the letter would.

A frequent question deals with the length of time an offer remains open. The U.C.C. sec. 2-205 adopts the general rule of law that the offer will remain open "for a reasonable time" never exceeding three months in the absence of a period stated in the offer itself. A merchant who does not want an offer to stand for three months should clearly specify its duration.

Problems develop regarding goods that fluctuate wildly in price. If the matter involves large quantities of such goods, the U.C.C.'s "reasonable time" will be relatively short without a deadline being set in the offer itself.

Offers may be regulated by custom and previous dealings. For example, in commodity trading, offers are frequently relayed by telegram and the custom is to accept immediately by return wire in order that the acceptance reaches the offeror the same day before the close of the commodity exchange. Moreover, commodity traders are experienced market people and usually carefully set out the duration of the offer and deadlines for acceptance.

Delays

What happens if the communication is delayed? The transmitting medium is considered to be under the control of the offeror. If the offeror was responsible for the delay, the deadline may be extended. The offeree's state of mind is decisive. If the offeree knew about the offer despite the delay, the deadline for acceptance is not extended; if the offeree was unaware of the offer due to the delay in transmission, the offer will remain open for the time it would have been valid had it been intended to arrive when it did in fact arrive. In other words, if an invoice was mailed to a buyer on Monday, January 11, which should have been accepted before Friday, January 15, but the buyer did not even receive the offer until Monday, January 18, then the buyer does not need to accept before Friday, January 22—providing he or she was not personally responsible for the delay and had no knowledge of the contents of the offer.

Death of a party or delay in acceptance can cause the offer to expire. Thus, it must be accepted within a reasonable time, the duration of which depends on the circumstances—type of commodity, purpose, distance, custom, and means of communication. A telegram would indicate the need for a quicker acceptance than would a letter, perhaps several hours for deliberation rather than one or even several days. Once again, any express provisions in the contract on this issue will prevail. Otherwise duration of an offer can become a question for a court.

Revocation and Modification of Offers

The offer is usually a personal arrangement between offeror and offeree. Generally the offeror can withdraw the offer at any time until it is accepted. A withdrawal should usually be communicated in the same manner as the original offer. One does not need to use any particular words to revoke an offer, and it may in fact be implied from acts such as sale to another. However, revocation in any form will not usually be legally effective until the offeree has had reasonable notice of it.

Counteroffers and Rejections

An offeree who rejects an offer outright destroys or terminates the original offer. If agreement is eventually reached on the terms originally offered, it means that the offeror subsequently renewed the original offer.

Frequently, the offeree makes a counteroffer. If tires have been offered at $50, the offeree may say, "I'll give you $30." Legal theory treats this statement as a rejection of the first offer at $50 and a new offer to buy for $30. The original offer has been destroyed by the rejection; the counteroffer is open and subject to the same rules as any other offer.

As a general rule the offeree's indication of willingness to do something different from the original offer is a rejection or a counteroffer.

One major, but rare, exception which prevents termination of the original offer occurs when the offeree includes in the counteroffer a specific undertaking to "keep the original offer under advisement." Otherwise, the imposition of conditions and counteroffers terminates the original offer.

A request for a change in the terms of the offer is different from both a rejection and a counteroffer. A request like "Will you throw in the air pump with the tires?" is bargaining; it neither rejects the offer nor amount to a counteroffer. The request for minor adjustments in terms, delivery dates, or packaging may be insignificant insofar as the transaction is concerned. Similarly a request for further information is not a rejection.

Still another response to be distinguished from an outright rejection is something called the "grumbling acceptance," which sounds a little like a rejection but a little more like an acceptance. It does not terminate the offer.

ACCEPTANCE

Acceptance is a response to the offer. It should not be surprising that the process of acceptance is very similar to that of the offer. One cannot accept something that was never offered.

An acceptance has to be communicated in order that there can be an eventual meeting of the minds. This means that the parties have to be talking about the same thing at approximately the same time. As an illustration, an offer to sell sand and gravel does not result in the acceptance of a grain transaction.

Means of Acceptance

"I accept" is a clear and common way of accepting an offer. Unless the offeror requires unambiguously that an offer be accepted in some particular way, the offeree can accept "in any manner and by any medium reasonable in the circumstances" (U.C.C. sec. 2-206).

Silence and Retention of Goods

Buyers of goods frequently request shipments of goods for inspection. The U.C.C. sec. 2-327 provides that the buyer's failure "seasonably to notify the seller of election to return the goods" constitutes an acceptance. A different problem exists where sellers ship unsolicited goods to homeowners. The federal government passed a law stating that unsolicited merchandise sent through the mails by other than charitable institutions shall be considered a gift.

Performance As Acceptance

An acceptance may be made by actual performance. Under U.C.C. sec. 2-206, one can accept a buyer's order of goods for prompt or current shipment either by making a promise to ship or by actually making such a shipment, taking care to ship goods conforming to those ordered. If one has to ship "nonconforming goods," one can avoid problems by notifying the buyer it is being done as an accommodation.

Knowledge or Notification of Late Acceptance

When the offer expressly states the time within which an acceptance should be made, the acceptor is expected to know that any acceptance made later will not result in the formation of the contract. No notification is necessary.

Should the offer fail to state the permissible period for acceptance, then it is assumed that it will be a "reasonable" time. Yet people may disagree as to what is "reasonable"; someone may consider it

TABLE 2-1

Responses to Offers

Terms of acceptance	Formation of contract
Simple acceptance	Yes
Acceptance but with request for nonmaterial modification of terms	Yes—may lead to extended bargaining and offeror may ignore additional terms
Acceptance but with material alteration of terms	No—in effect, a counteroffer
"Grumbling acceptance"	Yes
Acceptance after offer has expired	No—in effect, a new offer
Conditional acceptance with request for clarification	No—situation still in bargaining stage

two days, whereas a person who is a procrastinator by nature may figure on at least two weeks in which to act. If the offer is not accepted within a reasonable time, the offeror may withdraw the offer and notify the offeree that it is too late to accept.

CONSIDERATION

There are many definitions of *consideration*. It may be an act or a forbearance or an exchange of promises. Fundamentally it involves an exchange of values. It connotes a *quid pro quo*, that is, something for something. Generally, consideration must have been bargained for by the parties to the contract. For example, Marcia bargains with Joe to sell him a secondhand car for $900. The $900 constitutes sufficient consideration to make the contract enforceable. It need not represent the exact value of the car.

Consideration must involve a present or future exchange of values. A past obligation is not sufficient to support a contract. For example, Wold entered into an agreement to paint a house for Zabrecki for $500. After Wold started painting he refused to complete work unless Zabrecki agreed to pay an additional $250. Zabrecki signed a new agreement for $750 and, when the work was completed, tendered the original $500 to Wold. Wold demanded $750 and brought suit. The court will not enforce the new agreement because there was no exchange of values for the second agreement.

Consideration is basic to our law of contracts. However, it is not always essential. A contract under seal and certain partly performed contracts will be recognized and enforced by the courts even without consideration.

Detriment and Benefit

Another concept is that there be an exchange of legal values. This involves an idea of *detriment and benefit* for both parties; that is, each gives as well as receives something which has commercial worth. The values exchanged need not be identical or even equal. It is sufficient that the parties wanted the exchange.

In determining the existence of a binding contract, the courts consider the act of bargaining and the idea of detriment and benefit. For example, Ann has a gun that she is willing to sell for $100; Harry has the $100 and is willing to buy the gun. Getting $100 is a benefit to Ann, and giving away the gun is a detriment to her; getting the gun is a benefit to Harry, and giving away the $100 is a detriment to him. Now suppose Ann decides that the bargain is not as good as she first thought; she refuses to deliver the gun. Harry comes into court and argues that he relied upon the agreement and that Ann's refusal has caused him further detriment because he has found a customer willing to buy the gun from him for $125. The court could find that a contract exists.

Meeting of the Minds

The whole process of preliminary negotiations, offer, acceptance, and bargaining for consideration should clarify the respective positions of the parties until each understands the other. Their understanding and agreement is called a *meeting of the minds*. One cannot determine whether it exists simply by looking at the offer and the acceptance; one must consider the whole process.

As can be seen, the problem of communications is the principal problem in determining the establishment of a contract. Yet, it cannot be said that the parties have reached a bargain or an agreement unless both agree on what was said and what was intended. In other words, there is no bargain unless both parties are satisfied that they sold or purchased a particular thing for which they bargained. This agreement on the subject matter, or meeting of the minds, is an important element in contract law. Other problems in interpreting the meaning of a contract can arise subsequently and lead to litigation, as discussed in the next chapter. Remember, though, that the basic agreement should be reached during the bargaining process preceding execution of the contract. What the parties understand at the time they enter the contract determines whether there is a meeting of the minds.

INVOLVEMENT AND STUDY MATERIAL

Understanding Terms

Offer	(page 27)	Consideration	(page 34)
Counteroffer	(page 31)	*Quid pro quo*	(page 34)
Acceptance	(page 32)	Detriment and benefit	(page 34)

Questions and Problem Solving

1. Describe the bargaining process through which a contract is reached.

2. What is the significance of a counteroffer?

3. Distinguish between an offer and an invitation to make an offer. Describe a situation which could produce an invitation.

4. Discuss the problem of accepting an offer by letter when the letter is never received by the offeror. What is the effect of acceptance by letter when the offer was received by telegraph?

5. What contractual obligations are incurred by a business when it advertises merchandise for sale?

6. Explain the term "meeting of the minds" and its importance in the law of contracts.

7. Explain how the law treats shipment of unsolicited goods to home-owners.

8. If the parties stipulate that the U.C.C. will apply to their contract, how will ambiguous terms be interpreted?

9. How does the concept of detriment and benefit influence the bargaining process leading to a contract? Which particular element does it affect?

Cases for Discussion

1. The White Department Store placed an advertisement in the newspaper to sell TV sets for $39. Stewart ordered one of the sets. The White Department Store failed to deliver the set, whereupon Stewart brought an action for breach of contract. Is there a valid contract here? Why or why not?

2. Brill came into Smith's Bike Shop and looked at various bikes. Among the bikes available for sale were several specialty bikes that had been slightly used. Brill asked Smith what the price was for X-Brand model and Smith replied that he had just gotten it in, but that he was thinking of asking $85 for it. Brill did not respond, but continued looking at other models and eventually left the shop. Later on Brill was in another shop and came across an X-Brand model bike identical to the one in Smith's shop, but it was priced at $225. Brill hurried back to Smith's Bike Shop and offered to pay Smith $85 for the X-Brand model bike. Smith replied that the price for that model was $175. Brill tendered the

$85 and demanded the bike saying that he had accepted Smith's original offer which Smith had never withdrawn. Is Brill's contention correct? Why or why not?

3. Tagart told Nelson that she would buy all the melons Nelson produced that year for $1 per basket. Nelson said nothing at the time. Later when he had a record harvest of three times the usual amount of melons, he delivered them to Tagart and demanded the $1 per basket price. Was there a valid contract? Why or why not?

4. The Acme Wholesale Company sent out its circular which listed various items for sale. Holden sent in an order which Acme failed to fill. Holden brought suit for damages for breach of contract. Judgment for whom? Why?

5. The Brooks Construction Company advertised for bids for the supply of iron girders. The Ace Steel Company sent in a bid for supplying Brooks with all the iron girders they might want. Brooks placed an order for 20,000 girders which Ace refused to deliver. Brooks sued for breach of contract. Judgment for whom? Why?

Chapter Three

Drafting and Interpreting Contracts

Whether a contract is executed or executory, simple or formal, it will be of little use either to the parties or to outsiders unless they can understand its terms. They must know what the agreement means before they can either perform or determine whether any performance has been made.

FORM OF THE CONTRACT

The form of a contract is totally important. A well-drafted document will cover most contingencies. An inadequate one can fail to make sufficient provision for penalties and damages in case of breach. The dramatic bankruptcy of Rolls-Royce, Ltd., of Britain in 1971 was attributed to a poor fixed-price provision in a contract with Lockheed Aircraft in the United States. Contracts with enterprises in the developing nations are examples of contracts that require particular care; they must be carefully drafted to protect the American investor against losses if the foreign state takes over business properties. No matter how simple or complex the content of a contract may be, its form and interpretation are of the greatest importance to its ultimate success or failure.

Form Contracts

A large part of modern commercial trading uses standard printed forms. Generally, the forms are prepared by the business firm in language selected by the firm's lawyers. Many years of business experience are reflected in the language of these forms. A business firm probably cannot be expected to draft a separate contract for each transaction. Printed form contracts have considerable merit for the preparer, because they are standard and do not require expert preparation each time they are used. However the fact that they are almost always drawn by those with greater power leaves room for abuse and leaves the other party little or no choice in the selection of terms. This is particularly true in leases, franchises, and purchases of large items such as automobiles, machinery, and heavy equipment.

If the form contract contains terms that are objectionable, some of the terms may be subject to negotiations. A large-scale purchaser may be able to get special terms, but a single order does not carry much weight, and will not usually change operating practices. In such a case, it may be possible to find another company that will make satisfactory arrangements and thus avoid an undesirable contract. All this presupposes that the buyer is aware of the contents or terms of the form contract. Unfortunately many unsuitable terms do not come to light until after the contract has been signed and performance started. The courts and legislatures have come to the aid of those who have not drafted the contract. A form contract is considered to be a contract of adhesion, as shown below, and will be interpreted against the party that drafted it. If it should be considered unconscionable, the court has authority to refuse to enforce it under U.C.C. sec. 2-302.

Trade practices may be assumed and thus not mentioned specifically in the form contract. Therefore, someone new in business should become familiar with local trade practices before attempting to negotiate business contracts. It is always wise to examine a new form contract carefully.

Contracts of Adhesion

The *contract of adhesion* is a standard form contract used by a large institution in connection with all its business transactions of one type. Insurance policies, auto purchase orders, leases, and franchise agreements are typical contracts of adhesion. The reason these standard forms are called contracts of adhesion is that they are drafted by one party—generally the seller, which is often a large institution—and the buyer or the other party must adhere to the terms. The contract of adhesion is a comparative newcomer to the contract world; the courts are inclined to give these contracts strict interpretation and resolve all ambiguities against the preparer of the contract.

A business person who examines the form contract and finds its terms are not satisfactory can attempt to negotiate more desirable terms. In sending back an acceptance with a notation that "this acceptance is conditioned on your agreeing to the terms set out here," one simply makes a counteroffer (see Chapter 2) and there is no substitution of terms. The parties will probably go ahead and perform anyway. If the offeror accepts the counteroffer, provisions of the documents containing the original offer that conflict with the notation on the documents of acceptance will drop out so that the terms actually governing the transaction will be those on which the two documents agree, or those provisions of the Uniform Commercial Code that can be substituted for the omitted terms. For this reason, one should examine carefully the applicable sections of the Uniform Commercial Code.

Unconscionable Contracts

Many contracts for the sale of goods contain terms that favor the seller. For example, some time-payment contracts give the seller the right, on default, to seize the goods without notice. Some contracts provide for special charges in the event of default and ignore the rights of the purchaser. Other contracts contain confession-of-judgment clauses which permit the seller to appear in court without notice to the buyer and obtain a judgment in the event of the buyer's default. The judgment will include court costs, attorney fees, and perhaps other charges. By the time the buyer becomes aware of the judgment, it is usually too late for him to do anything about it except pay.

The Uniform Commercial Code sec. 2-302 provides the court with justification not to enforce such unconscionable contracts. Today, many of these one-sided contracts that fail to treat both parties equitably are unenforceable.

Statute of Frauds

Our law has roots in the Middle Ages, when the kings of England set up royal courts administering a law common to all. This is the origin of the term *common law*. At that time, few people could write so the chances of perjury and fraud in connection with contracts were great. Often parties to contracts used their signet rings or seals to indicate their assent to the bargain. The royal courts recognized the validity of these sealed documents or covenants.

For this reason, early common law contracts eventually required the seal before a contract could be enforceable. This practice became too cumbersome for merchants, and so contracts not under seal also became enforceable. Various forms of contracts could be used without any requirement that they be in writing.

Since few people could read or write, many abuses developed that forced the government to intervene. In 1677 the English Parliament passed a statute that is known today as the statute of frauds. It specified, among other things, the types of contracts that must be in

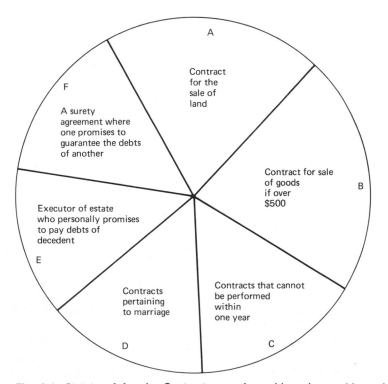

Fig. 3-1. Statute of frauds. Contracts unenforceable unless evidenced in writing.

writing. Not all contracts that fail to meet the requirements of the statute are fraudulent, but they are unenforceable in a court if there is no written memorandum in support of them. All modern statutes of frauds follow the general pattern of the 1677 statute, although they may differ concerning categories of contracts subject to it.

Six major categories are recognized by most states:

1. Contracts pertaining to interests in land, such as mortgages, easements, long leases, and recorded documents, must be evidenced by writing.
2. U.C.C. sec. 2-201 requires a written memorandum for sales of goods exceeding $500 in value.
3. Contracts which cannot conceivably be performed within a year are unenforceable unless evidenced by writing.
4. Contracts pertaining to marriage must be reduced to writing. These are not promises to marry. Originally they were dowry arrangements, but now they could be antenuptial agreements.
5. An executor's individual promise to pay a debt of the estate will be only a moral obligation unless written.
6. Similarly, a surety agreement where one party promises to guarantee the debt of another must be evidenced by writing to be legally enforceable.

Lest these requirements prove to be a trap for the unwary, modern courts are willing to accept almost any form of written memorandum signed by the person obligated. Contracts falling under the statute of frauds today are often unenforceable for other reasons.

INTERPRETING THE CONTRACT

There are innumerable rules for interpreting agreements. Some are general in nature; others are more specific.

Technical Rules

There are certain technical rules of construction, among which two important ones are *expressio unius exclusio alterius* and *ejusdem generis*. The former means that if an item is expressly mentioned (without using any general term), other items that are not specifically mentioned are excluded even though they are similar. The latter phrase signifies that if a general term is accompanied by a more specific one, the general term includes only what is similar to the specifically named term.

Needless to say, many other rules of interpretation have evolved over the centuries and are still used by the courts to justify their decisions. However, good judges now avoid invoking these mechanical rules and read documents as a whole to ascertain what the parties really intended.

General Rules

When there is no evidence concerning how a term is being or has been used, the court has considerable power to interpret the meaning of a contract before construing its legal effects. That interpretation which favors a reasonable, rather than an unreasonable, meaning and which upholds the validity of the agreement will be the one favored by the courts. Moreover, the whole intent of the document will influence the meaning of any specific part.

Often contracting parties make no provision at all for some term, or they may use standard forms with conflicting terms in them. In either situation, the Uniform Commercial Code automatically provides or selects the terms to be used. For example, a contract can be concluded even though the price is not settled. In such a case, the price is a reasonable price at the time of delivery.

The code expects the person charged with the interpretation of a contract to look first to any previous contracts between the parties in deciding how certain terms or provisions were intended. If there were no previous similar contracts, one looks to *trade usage*—patterns of conduct common throughout the industry to which the parties belong. If that is not possible, the code then fills in the gaps in the contract with its own provisions. In other words, the code looks first to what the parties expressly provided, then to what they provided in the past, then to what their business practices have in common which would apply to the case, and finally to its own terms for want of anything more specific.

Surrounding Circumstances

Even if no real ambiguity exists, courts can look to the surrounding circumstances as aids to the interpretation of contracts. The judge charged with the task of interpreting the contract examines the relationship of the parties. If they have dealt with each other on previous occasions, the nature of the prior transaction may indicate what was intended in the disputed transaction. Customs of the community or trade may also reveal the intent of the contract. The knowledge and business experience of the parties will weigh heavily in the final decision. The judge will be inclined to interpret the words used in the contract against the more experienced person and in favor of the one less experienced.

Statements of the Parties

Few words can be fully understood in a vacuum. When a business person uses a term, it must be understood in the light of how he or she has previously used it and what someone in that particular business field usually means by it. The court will be interested in the extent to which a party used a specific term in question. Was it daily or only very seldom? How did the party intend the term to be interpreted and what kinds of actions related to it on the other occasions? The answers to these questions may well indicate what meaning was intended this time. They might also illustrate the interpretation the other party would expect.

Admissions

Self-serving statements uttered to third parties in support of one's position cannot be introduced to prove the meaning of disputed terms. Thus, in a dispute over quantity of goods, a statement like "I just sold 2,500 pounds of Idaho potatoes" made to a friend cannot be used to prove that the stated amount was actually delivered. But statements against one's interest can be used by the other party to show a position that is inconsistent with a later denial of a contract term. If the seller of the potatoes later claims that 2,500 pounds were not sold, and the buyer knows about the conflicting statement to the friend, it can be introduced by the buyer to prove that the seller did sell that amount.

In another example, after signing a contract for a shipment of furniture which did not specify type of upholstery, the buyer discovered that a competitor was selling the same furniture for the same price with nylon instead of cotton upholstery. The buyer confessed disappointment to a friend and later entered into a dispute with the seller taking the position that the contract called for nylon upholstery and that there was never an intention to take the cotton upholstery furniture. The statement made to the friend is an admission against interest; if the case goes to court and the seller finds out about the statement, it can be introduced as evidence to show the true nature of the contract.

Omitted Terms

In analyzing a contract with gaps in it, one should pursue a similar course. If a party has been behaving as though a particular term existed (for example, the goods were always delivered without charge), no one should be surprised to find that such a term has become part of the contract. Furthermore, if the seller wants to change the kind of contract that the buyer and seller have always had in the past, the seller should not rely on a contract that is silent about the matters to be changed. Instead the change should be expressly stated to be sure that it takes effect and thus avoid disagreements.

Terms Supplied by U.C.C.

The Uniform Commercial Code has attempted to supply many terms that previously created disputes or that were too rigid in application. Thus, there are sections in the U.C.C. concerning delivery, quantity, and duration of contracts.

Delivery

Single delivery is common, but circumstances may justify delivery in lots under U.C.C. sec. 2-307.

Quantity

This term is most likely to be left indefinite in requirement contracts. An estimate is often treated solely as a maximum limit to the liability of the seller in the absence of bad faith. Now the U.C.C. sec. 2-306 permits the requirement to be satisfied by actual output or requirements occurring in good faith, if a quantity not unreasonably disproportionate to the stated estimate is chosen.

Duration

The common-law rule that a contract provision for continuous performance can be terminated at the will of either party has given way to U.C.C. sec. 2-309. Now it is considered to be valid for a "reasonable time" (under the circumstances) but can be terminated at any time by either party. Reasonable notice of termination must be given in good faith so that the other party can make a substitute arrangement.

A business person who does not want the provisions of the U.C.C. sec. 2-306, 2-307, and 2-309 to be read into a particular contract should be sure it is carefully drafted and the desired terms included.

Current Trends

In summary, the old common-law rule requiring the terms of the contract to be complete and definite no longer applies in all its rigidity. Now even if several material terms are left indefinite, the U.C.C. provides by sec. 2-204 that the contract will not fail for indefiniteness if there is a reasonably certain basis for the appropriate remedy and if the parties intended to make a contract.

The current emphasis has been on saving the contract whenever possible and on looking to the intent of the parties. Traditional, mechanical rules of interpretation are yielding in importance to the context, the entire document, the acts of the parties, the customs of the community, the trade usage, and the circumstances of the individual case. While retaining the basic contractual forms, this area of law is becoming more flexible to accommodate commercial needs.

MODIFYING THE CONTRACT

After a contract has been executed, many things may happen which alter the situation for either or both of the parties. There may be strikes, storms, floods, earthquakes, or other disasters which neither party had foreseen but which can destroy the subject matter of the contract and hinder its performance. Few contracts make provisions in advance for such situations. Yet, sometimes changes have to be made, and modifying a contract is a process with its own set of rules.

Time for Modifications

The best time to modify a contract is when it is being initially negotiated. That is the time to think of the future. Yet the performance of many a contract is in the unknown future. Therefore, one ought to make provision for changes in circumstances that affect contract performance.

There is considerable political and economic turmoil in the world that may produce a sudden change in the business environment. A business person contracting on the basis of a stable commodity price in a period of inflation would be unwise to plan performance far into the future without a provision for some type of price increase. If one is doing business in an area of political instability, one should be aware that the right to do business may be taken away without notice. The cost of transporting goods increases substantially if shipping canals are closed—such as happened when the Suez Canal was blocked in 1967. A business person's failure to anticipate changes in circumstances may mean the difference between solvency and insolvency.

The Parol Evidence Rule

Once a contract has been written, the terms of the agreement should be derived from within the document itself. No matter how informal a contract is, the parties are presumed to have given some serious consideration to the writing of it and to have intended its terms to take effect. Thus, they cannot subsequently offer verbal testimony (*parol evidence*) to refute the written document by showing that another meaning was intended. However, parol evidence can be used to explain ambiguous terms in the written document. Thus, terms such as "regular shipment," "prompt payment," and "regular credit," may require an explanation in that particular setting.

Although courts are reluctant to accept parol evidence to vary the written document, verbal testimony will be accepted if there is evidence of fraud, duress, mistake, illegality, or insufficient consideration.

Rescission and Reformation As Remedies

The courts are reluctant to change terms of a contract. Where there is a disagreement about a contract and the parties have not materially performed their part of the bargain, the courts are more likely to grant a *rescission*, that is, to treat the contract as though it had never existed and put the parties into the position they held before the contract. Yet there will be times where one of the parties has performed part of the bargain and the second then does not want to go through with the other part. At this point the second party has two choices: bring suit or wait for the first to do so. If the second brings a suit that raises defenses, and if the court finds the defenses valid, it will either strike down the entire contract or *reform* the terms, that is, alter them.

Reformation is most frequently found in real estate transactions. Land titles are complex, and mistakes are sometimes made in descriptions. Thus, although payments have been made and the property transferred to the new owners, the description of the property may have to be changed. If the seller refuses to do so voluntarily, the court will order it done.

In other sales contracts the remedy may be either rescission or reformation, depending upon the circumstances. For example, assume that a buyer accepted an offer to sell a new car which was mistakenly listed at $60 when the price was intended to be $6,000. If the car was delivered, the seller would sue for the entire $6,000. Normally, the court would reform the contract and change the price to $6,000. It would then allow a rescission and permit the buyer to return the car; however, if this was no longer possible, the buyer would be required to pay the $6,000. If it was the buyer who sued for delivery of the car at the price of $60, the court would alter the terms to $6,000 and allow the buyer to rescind.

DEFENSE TO CONTRACT

Although an agreement should normally be interpreted according to its written terms, the court is entitled to look beyond the document when asked to define the nature of the transaction. By doing so, the court can determine whether the agreement even exists. An agreement which seems valid can be ruled either void from the outset or subsequently voidable by either party if certain defenses are raised. Their existence eroded the necessary meeting of the minds at the time the parties executed the contract.

Errors Resulting from an Oversight of the Injured Party

A *mistake* is an error made by the party who raises it as a defense to a contract. It is often caused by oversight. The other party may or may not know of the mistaken belief. However, not all human errors are legally recognized mistakes affecting a contract's validity. The mistake must be so important that it goes to the essence of the agreement. Moreover, it must normally involve a question of fact, since citizens are presumed to know the law of their country and their state.

Mutual Mistake

If both parties are mistaken about the nature of the transaction or subject matter involved, the courts are likely to grant relief. In fact, neither party may be anxious to perform. Suppose an art dealer auctions off a modern painting for $200. While it is still in the auction room, the paint peels and a Titian is discovered beneath it. The buyer may not like Renaissance art, but may know a bargain. The seller, recognizing the value of the painting, may now feel that the $200 price is inadequate. A dispute arises; they will not be forced to execute their contract fully.

Unilateral Mistake

When only one party is in error, the mistake is a unilateral one. A buyer purchases a zircon thinking it is a diamond. Another may purchase land believing incorrectly it has oil on it. Unless the seller purposely misleads or knowingly takes advantage of the error, the buyer cannot get out of the contract by pleading mistake.

On occasion, a salesman may mistake the price of an article and give a particularly attractive quotation. Since the low price undoubtedly induced the buyer to sign the contract, the seller usually cannot disaffirm. If the mistake in price is obvious and grossly disproportionate, for example the sale of the new car for $60 instead of $6,000, there has been no meeting of the minds and thus no contract.

Mistake is not a clear-cut area of the law. Not all mistakes are acceptable reasons for breaking a contract. To justify invalidating an agreement, the mistake should be mutual, material, and related to a matter of fact rather than a question of local law. If one party obviously tries to take advantage of the other, the courts are more likely to intervene than if the mistake is unilateral and caused by the individual's own carelessness. Since this is a technical and often confusing topic, any specific questions on mistakes arising from a contract should be referred to an experienced lawyer.

Consent Wrongfully Induced by the Other Party

Carelessness on the part of the injured party is not as likely to play a role in the other defenses as it does in mistake. Of course, any reliance on statements of the other party must be reasonable. The essence of these other defenses is that there was an intentional attempt by the stronger one to mislead, persuade, or threaten the weaker party.

Duress and Undue Influence

These defenses are related to each other. *Duress* implies the use of a threat to overcome another's will, whereas *undue influence* is persuasion which takes advantage of close personal relationships. One might think of duress as an aggravated form of undue influence.

Duress exists when a party is threatened with force, legal action, or imprisonment without cause. It does not matter that the threat is obviously unfounded if it persuaded the party to enter into the contract. Economic pressure may also constitute duress.

Undue influence can be a factor when someone persuades an elderly person to transfer title to a home under some pretext or when that older person is simply incapable of understanding the full significance of the transaction. Often the two parties stand in a *fiduciary relationship* (that is, one involving trust or confidence), such as doctor to patient, parent to child, or lawyer to client. In these cases, the court will look very closely at such a transaction, and if it finds that an unfair contract resulted, it will declare the contract void *ab initio*—in other words, void from the beginning.

Fraud and Misrepresentation

Fraud is an intentional false statement or concealment of a fact to the injury of the other party. It may be considered a more serious form of *misrepresentation*. The various manifestations of fraud and misrepresentation can arise from a failure to speak when there is a clear duty to disclose information to the other party. Misrepresentation must be distinguished from the normal "puffing" or exaggeration that is common to many sales. Thus, the statements "This is the best little car on the floor," and "This is the best house on the street," are mere opinions that do not carry any significance. After all, one cannot expect the seller to say, "This is a poor buy at any price."

Much depends upon the status of the parties. If the seller knows that the buyer is ignorant about certain products and is relying on the seller for guidance, the seller has a duty to reveal material facts. Statements made under such circumstances become representations. If they are untrue, they are misrepresentations and may even be fraudulent as long as reliance on them was reasonable. Obvious defects such as a bad paint job on a car do not become representations since a simple inspection would disclose the defect.

When one encounters language that is new or strange, it is wise to consult an experienced attorney to help in the interpretation. Courts are not always sympathetic to people who assume knowledge they do not in fact possess. Courts are not a refuge for those that are simply foolish. Nevertheless, if fraud exists, the contract is either void or voidable at the option of the deceived party. If the rights of an innocent third party become involved, damages may be recovered. However, the aggrieved party has the problem of developing evidence to convince the court that it is entitled to damages or other appropriate relief.

Capacity

An individual who is under the legal age, intoxicated, or insane may not have the legal capacity to enter into a binding contract. Contracts with such individuals are voidable at the option of the person with limited capacity, unless they are for necessities of life.

Minority

Persons who are under age are considered infants or minors by law and protected by law from their own improvidence. If minors are parties to a contract, they can deny the contract during their minority or within a reasonable time after they become of age. In cases dealing with land, they can do so only after they become of age.

Minors who misrepresent their age and indicate that they are at or over the legal age may be guilty of misrepresentation and fraud. This is a *tort*, that is, a civil wrong, and they may be liable for damages.

What happens to the article purchased by a minor? When he or she disaffirms the contract, the minor is required to return the article in whatever condition it may be at the time. Of course, this rule cannot apply to such consumed items as dancing lessons. The minor who has sold something can demand the return of the article or its equivalent.

The law does not require that the minor place the seller in the same position as before the transaction. However, there is an exception to this freedom from liability: the minor is responsible for buying the necessities of life. Anyone furnishing necessary food, clothing, or shelter to someone under age can recover the reasonable value—not the contract price—of the items sold.

Insanity

Mentally unstable people are treated similarly to infants. If someone has been officially declared insane, everyone is on legal notice that that individual lacks the mental capacity to contract. However, there are many instances where the insanity has not been recognized officially and is either partial or temporary. In such cases the individual wanting to deny a contract has the problem of proving the lack of capacity at the time the contract was made. The consideration exchanged at the time of the contract generally must be returned unless the other party to the contract clearly knew the individual was insane. In such a case the other party could be guilty of conduct closely resembling fraud and not entitled to the return of consideration.

Intoxication

Contracts made by intoxicated persons can be disaffirmed in the same manner as those made by insane individuals. The intoxication does not have to be total. It only has to affect one's ability to have a meeting of the minds, but not all drinking produces this result.

INVOLVEMENT AND STUDY MATERIAL

Understanding Terms

Contracts of adhesion	(page 39)	Rescission	(page 47)
Unconscionable contracts		Reformation	(page 48)
	(page 40)	Defenses to contract	(page 48)
Statute of frauds	(page 41)	Mistake	(page 48)
Expressio unius		Duress	(page 50)
exclusio alterius	(page 42)	Undue influence	(page 50)
Ejusdem generis	(page 42)	Void *ab initio*	(page 50)
Trade usage	(page 43)	Fraud	(page 50)
Parol evidence rule	(page 47)	Misrepresentation	(page 50)

Questions and Problem Solving

1. Explain the importance of the contract of adhesion.
2. Describe the importance of the statute of frauds to the enforcement of certain contracts.
3. Why is the parol evidence rule invoked in the interpretation of a contract? Does it provide any protection to the parties to the contracts? Explain. What does it suggest that the parties should do when executing a contract?
4. What is the meaning of the two technical rules of construction— *expressio unius exclusio alterius* and *ejusdem generis.*
5. Give an example showing the role of trade usage in relation to contracts.
6. How do courts interpret language used by the parties when the contract terms are a subject of dispute?
7. Distinguish between duress and undue influence used to secure a contract.
8. Give an illustration under fraud, misrepresentation, and intoxication where a party might merely have been unwise or foolish and therefore not really entitled to be relieved of his bargain.

Cases for Discussion

1. Jordan sued Beecher for possession of a farm that Jordan had purchased from Henderson-Powell Co. The defendant responded that the deed from the Beechers to the company had been obtained by duress and was therefore void. The evidence disclosed that Beecher had become indebted to the Henderson-Powell Co. and, when payment was not forthcoming, the president of Henderson-Powell Co., who was also a justice of peace, issued a warrant for the arrest of Beecher and placed him in jail for nonpayment. Mrs. Beecher was told that if she wanted her husband out of jail she would have to sign the deed to the farm, which was in her name. After the deed was signed, Beecher was released from jail and the Beechers continued using the farm for several years. Henderson-Powell did not have the property transferred on the tax rolls, and the Beechers continued to pay the taxes. The purported consideration shown on the deed was $275 but the admitted value of the land was $1500. At the trial, Jordan claimed that he had good title because he was a good faith purchaser for

value although he knew that the Beechers continued using the land. Judgment for whom? Why?

2. Andora had very little business experience and for many years had been accustomed to rely in business matters on Bellini, a man of many business interests. Bellini, without making any false representations of fact, induced Andora to enter into a contract with Bellini's confederate, Perez, that was disadvantageous to Andora, as Bellini and Perez well knew. Andora sues to rescind the contract for undue influence. Judgment for whom? Why?

3. Redding purchased a used car from Bargain Motors for $2,000. The salesman told Redding that the car had been driven about 16,000 miles; actually, it had been traded in with 60,000 miles and required major engine repairs. Redding drove the car only a few miles before the motor developed trouble requiring additional expensive repairs. Redding brought suit against Bargain Motors for fraud. Bargain Motors claimed the salesman's words were merely puffing. Judgment for whom? Why?

4. The Crown Steel Company posted a notice on the employees' information board to the effect that the company was adopting a profit sharing plan for the employees. At the time of the notice Miller was an employee in the Plating Department. Later Miller was terminated because his department was discontinued. Miller brought suit to collect from the profit sharing fund. Crown Steel Company contended that there was no contract between the company and Miller which obligated it to pay this money. Judgment for whom? Why?

Chapter Four

Contracts and Third Parties

THIRD PARTIES

The law recognizes the interest of certain third parties in contracts executed by others. If a manufacturer sells a car to a local retailer, a contract exists between these two. Also affected by that contract will be the consumer who purchases the car from the retailer. If that car has a defective brake, its owner has the right to sue the manufacturer directly in contract for the resulting damage, even though the owner never bargained with the manufacturer.

When a company promises to supply goods to a customer, the employee of the company is a third party who is greatly affected by the contract. If the agreement is not carried out, there may be no further contracts and no more work. The employer will depend on the employee to meet deadlines, achieve the quality required, and assure the fulfillment of many other contract terms. It is a rare business whose employees are not aware of the employer's contracts and affected by them.

Third parties often pay for others' contracts. After a manufacturer signs a contract agreeing to a substantial increase in wages for its employees, the price of its product invariably reflects the increase. Thus, the costs are passed on to the consumer, who was not a party to the contract.

Assignments

An *assignment* is the transfer of a right by a party to the contract. Assume that a buyer and a seller have made an agreement. Later the buyer assigns the right to purchase the goods to a third person, who is the *assignee*. Although not a party to the original contract, the assignee subsequently acquires rights under it which can be enforced at law.

Nonassignable Contracts

Not all contracts can be assigned. Someone who has relied on the credit of the other in negotiating the agreement will not necessarily want to accept anyone else as assignee. Output contracts, in which the seller agrees to sell all he or she produces, and requirements contracts, in which the buyer purchases as much as he or she needs, cannot be transferred to an assignee because an important term, the quantity, is left open and contingent on the performance or needs of the original parties alone.

Contracts that are personal in nature are not assignable. Thus, a contract to marry could not be performed by another. If personal skill, such as that of an artist, is involved, the contract is not assign-

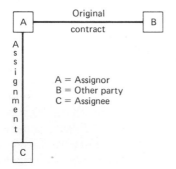

Fig. 4-1. Assignment of a contract. C's position is entirely dependent upon A's rights and duties. C stands in A's shoes.

able because not everyone is equally endowed with creative talents. Many insurance contracts contain specific prohibitions against assignment in order to assure that their standards of insurability are met. Therefore, it may be necessary to obtain the permission of the company before making an assignment. An assignment that would materially alter the nature of the contract and its performance is not binding on the other party to the contract unless that party consents to it.

Delegation of Performance

Many contracts concern performance that one party can make as well as another. U.C.C. sec. 2-210 states:

(1) A party may perform his duty through a delegate unless otherwise agreed or unless the other party has substantial interest in having his original promisor perform. . . . No delegation of performance relieves the party delegating of any duty to perform or any liability for breach. . . .

(4) An assignment . . . is a delegation . . . and its acceptance by the assignee constitutes a promise by him to perform those duties. This promise is enforceable by either the assignor or the other party to the original contract.

(5) The other party may treat any assignment which delegates performance as creating reasonable grounds for insecurity and may without prejudice to his rights against the assignor demand assurance from the assignee.

It is evident from these provisions that the inability of the assignee to perform does not excuse the original party or assignor. The assignee merely steps into the shoes of the assignor and is authorized to perform with the same effect as if the assignor had acted. All rights and duties of the assignor are transferred to the assignee, who can be penalized by the assignor or by the other party to the original contract for a failure to perform.

The U.C.C. gives the other party to the contract additional protection in the case of a question concerning the ability of the assignee to perform. The other party does not have to wait to see whether the assignee can perform but can without prejudice to any rights under the contract, demand assurances that the assignee is capable of performance. If those assurances are not satisfactory, the assignor may be requested to provide additional assurances or else the contract can be considered repudiated.

Future rights under a contract can be assigned as well as present rights; for example, if a garage decides to go out of the business of repairing automobiles and restrict its activity to selling gasoline, it may assign a servicing contract with the distributor to another garage. It is possible to assign a contract either orally or in writing. The assignment may cover the whole obligation or only part of it; a partial assignment in an auto parts supply contract might permit the assignee to deliver tires to the dealer while the assignor retained a duty to supply the other auto parts.

Assignee's Rights and Duties

After the assignment, the assignee remains subject to any defenses the other party to the contract may have had against the assignor even though the assignee has fully performed the assigned part of the contract. Thus, an assignee who sues the other party for the value of the services performed may find that the other party is raising a *setoff* against the amount claimed by the assignee. The other party may have made prior payments or had some other adjustments agreed to by the assignor in the particular contract involved. If the assignor has not completely performed the contract, the other party may also raise a *counterclaim* alleging damages for incomplete performance despite the fact that the assignee has fully completed the assigned part. The validity of the assignment may also be attacked because of gratuitousness, insanity, mistake, fraud, and other reasons.

In connection with assignment, the assignor warrants not to interfere with the rights of the assignee and also warrants that the document (contract) is genuine and that the assignor had a right to make the assignment. There is no guarantee that the other party will perform the contract.

It is important for the business person to understand whether assignment can extinguish rights and duties under a contract. The prospective assignee ought to know how much the assignor's warranties protect, which defenses are retained against future actions by the buyer, and what duties are assigned. The assignor and assignee should find out whether contracts are capable of being assigned before they attempt to do so.

As a matter of precaution, it is wise for the assignee to notify the other party to the contract promptly of the assignment. This ensures that if the other party makes any payments, the money will go to the proper person. After such notice has been given, the other party is obligated to render performance to the assignee. Notice also prevents the possibility of an additional assignment by a dishonest assignor. Under U.C.C. sec. 2-403, if there are two innocent purchasers for value, the first to take possession gets title to the property.

Many consumers discover after they enter into a contract with another party that the right to payments under the contract can be assigned to a third party while the performance is being executed by the assignor. If such an assignment is taken by the assignee in good faith and without any knowledge of impropriety on the part of the assignor, the consumer may lose all rights of setoffs or counterclaims. For example, a home remodeling contractor sells the contract of a collection agent while agreeing to make repairs. A problem arises if the repairs are shoddy, since the owner's only recourse is against the worthless repairer. The financing institution demands its money on time. Investigation of the reputation of the repairer *before* entering into the contract is prudent. Courts have given these assignments close scrutiny to see if the purchase of the notes or payment schedules was in fact in good faith. If the assignment of the contract to the financing institution was in good faith, the assignee cannot be denied the right to collect the contract payments.

Third-Party Beneficiary Contracts

A comparatively new development in contract law is the recognition of an agreement in which someone is designated as the ultimate recipient of contractual benefits although that person is not a party to the contract. The recipient can be considered a *donee beneficiary*, a *creditor beneficiary*, or an *incidental beneficiary* of the contract.

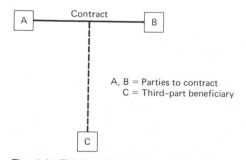

Fig. 4-2. Third-party beneficiary situations. The third party C is not dependent on either A or B alone. Instead, C benefits without any burdens from the contractual relationship between A and B.

Donee Beneficiary

A *donee beneficiary* is the recipient of a gift. A typical third-party donee beneficiary is the widow of an insured man under a life insurance contract. The insured has paid the premiums to the company and specified that payment of its face value be made upon his death for his widow's support. This arrangement between the insured and the insurer represents a gift to the wife.

Creditor Beneficiary

The parties to an agreement may create a situation where the benefits of the contract accrue to a third party. The simplest example of such a case is the resale of an automobile that is mortgaged to the finance company. The owner resells the automobile with the understanding that the buyer will pay off the debt still outstanding. When the finance company learns of the transaction it may still look to the original owner for the balance, but it also acquires the right to make a claim against the buyer. If the buyer fails to meet the payments, the finance company (now the *creditor beneficiary*) can bring suit against the buyer for the full amount of the debt. It could also bring suit against the original debtor, the owner-seller. In most cases it would bring suit against both, but the seller may be out of the jurisdiction of the local courts.

Incidental Beneficiary

If two parties enter into a contract for their own benefit, the arrangement may result in some incidental benefit to a third person whom neither party is considering at the time; this person becomes the *incidental beneficiary*. If a homeowner enters into a contract to enclose his or her backyard, the fence may keep a dog in and benefit the entire neighborhood. However, if the parties agree to cancel their contract, no one can insist on its performance. Similarly, there could be contracts for planting shade trees, landscaping, or other improvements that might enhance the neighborhood but that effect would be incidental to the real purpose of such a contract. In these cases the third, or incidental, parties cannot acquire any interests or complain about the failure to perform.

Municipal contracts often appear to be beneficial to third parties. These arrangements include street paving, sanitation, road improvements, landscaping, parks, and other public facilities that are necessary and desirable in a city. However, if the contracts are breached by the contractors, citizens of the city are not considered donee or creditor beneficiaries who are entitled to legal remedies. The only exception is when a specific municipal contract is intended for a particular person. An example would be a contract by the city to run a water line to a particular business. In that case the enterprise could be considered a donee beneficiary and would be entitled to sue.

AGENCY

Not everyone can personally perform all that is necessary to operate a business. Sometimes a business person must appoint people to act as agents. The law of agency concerns one method of assigning tasks to another. An *agency* relationship is established by means of an agreement between the *principal* and the *agent*. Although the law of contracts may control the relationship between the principal and agent, the concern here is with the acts the agent performs for the principal and how those acts affect others who are not parties to the agreement.

The Creation of an Agency Relationship

Agency does not arise spontaneously except in a few cases of emergency. It is artificially created by word, document, or act. The agency agreement can be written or oral. Often agency will be a subject of a formal agreement detailing its powers, rights, and duties, but it can equally well be informal. The important element is the consent of the principal and the agent to enter into a relationship. The agent acts for the principal. Outsiders need not care whether the arrangement is gratuitous or for compensation. Their concern is whether liability rests on the principal, when they deal with the agent.

Capacity of the Parties

There are few restrictions on persons who can enter into an agency relationship. The agent can be almost any human being, including a minor or a lunatic, if the principal so chooses. There are more limitations on the principal, who must be competent to transact business.

A person of limited legal capacity cannot enlarge this capacity

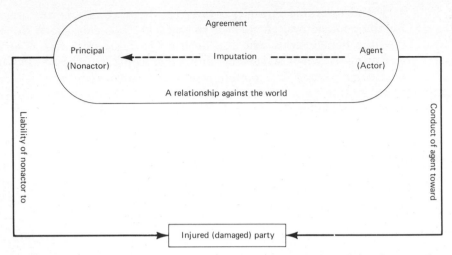

Fig. 4-3. Agency (vicarious liability). The principal can be held liable for the misconduct of his agent committed during the course of agency.

by employing an agent. Infants or insane persons will be bound by their agents only if they were capable of obligating themselves. One principal can hire any number of agents who can do more together than the principal could alone. A principal may not know anything about explosives but can hire an expert as an agent to do the necessary blasting. Of course, if damages result, the principal can be held liable.

The key to the agency relationship is the amount of *authority* granted to the agent by the principal. If the third party justifiably relies upon the authority given the agent by the principal, the principal cannot later deny that relationship to escape liability.

An agent differs from other types of workers (the servant, the employee, or the independent contractor) by having the power to alter the legal position of the principal. The extent of an agent's authority to change another's legal relations through the agent's transactions will depend on the circumstances of the particular case.

Types of Agency

Agency is created by an agreement between two persons who can negotiate powers ranging from very restricted to very broad. One should note what kind of agency is involved and then observe any acts or statements of the principal concerning the agent's authority.

Universal Agency

This relationship gives the agent the broadest powers. The agent is authorized by the principal to do every act which can be lawfully delegated during the period of the agency. In other words, the agent really acts for the principal in all lawful respects. The power is similar to an unrestricted power of attorney.

General Agency

This relationship is not quite as unlimited as the universal agency. It simply authorizes the agent to transact all the principal's particular kind of business at a given place. A general agent has the power to act for the principal in a series of transactions, involving a continuity of services. For example, the agent who is in charge of a grocery store in St. Louis, Missouri, can transact any business involving food orders within that locality but he cannot engage in a nationwide postal sale of shirts as well.

Special Agency

This type of agency involves an agent authorized to conduct a single transaction or series of transactions not involving continuity of service. Examples of such agents are a bill collector for a public utilities firm and a real estate broker for the sale of one house. Each is appointed to do specific acts.

Agency by Necessity

Not all agency relationships receive prior authorization from the principal. If a tornado damages the home of an absent neighbor or an alcoholic neglects his or her family, an outsider can act as an *agent by necessity*. The very name indicates that there is an emergency and it is essential for such an agent to exist in order to prevent the principal from suffering a loss.

Authority of an Agent

The authority of an agent to make the principal responsible for the agent's acts will depend largely on the nature of their relationship. If the agency is created formally, the agent's powers should be specifically stated. Unfortunately, many agency situations are informal and leave much room for later disputes.

Express Authority

This represents the authority given when the principal specifically appoints an agent and gives orders or fails to object to the agent's proposals. It can be either written or oral in form. The power of attorney is a typical example of detailed, written, and express authority.

Implied Authority

Authorization is not always spelled out. Implied authority is the authority to do anything which is necessary or customary to carry out the expressly authorized duties. For example, a business person tells a secretary to buy some shares of oil stock as the business person's agent. Since a secretary cannot be expected to have a seat on the stock exchange, the duty to exercise the express authority to buy stock also carries with it an implied authority to hire a broker who can transact such business in accordance with legal regulations.

Apparent Authority

The situation becomes less clear when apparent authority is involved. It is created by written or spoken words or any other conduct of the principal which would cause a third person to believe the principal has consented to have the act done by the person purporting to act as the agent. For example, if a person customarily takes charge of a store as a manager and the owner learns of it without making any objection, a customer is entitled to assume that the purported agent has the authority to do what a manager usually does.

Sometimes apparent authority is called *perceived authority*, that is, the authority that is perceived by the third person. The principal has led someone to believe that authority has been conferred upon the agent. Apparent authority can be conferred by the behavior of the parties.

Authority by Estoppel

If the principal creates a situation whereby an outsider acts on the reasonable belief that a particular individual is an agent, the principal cannot later deny the existence of the agency. The agent is said to have *authority by estoppel* in such cases. After permitting someone to be in charge of a store, the proprietor could not later say that the agent had no authority to sell merchandise to an innocent third party.

A prior unauthorized act which was not legally binding but which was done or professedly done for an individual can be ratified, or affirmed, by the principal afterwards. The effect of the ratification is the same as if the agent originally had the authority to do the act. A principal who learns of an unauthorized act can choose to disaffirm or to ratify it. Ratification transfers responsibility for the act to the principal; disaffirmation leaves responsibility with the agent.

The need for ratification will not arise if an agent is previously empowered to do the act in question. Authorized acts of an agent are valid from the beginning and binding on the principal. However, in a real situation it is not always easy to determine the scope of the agent's authority.

Subrelationships of Agency

Since there are at least three people potentially involved in each agency relationship—the principal, the agent, and the third party— several major subrelationships arise. These involve the rights and duties of the various parties in relation to each other.

The Principal and the Agent

Since the principal commissions the agent to perform, it is only just that the principal should be required to pay for the agent's services as well as compensate for any payments and losses the agent has made or sustained, unless, of course, the agent has acted wrongly or both have expressly agreed that there will be no payment.

Moreover, the principal is expected to furnish the agent with an opportunity to work, must maintain satisfactory working conditions, and may not interfere with the completion of the service requested. If the principal receives information pertaining to the performance of the delegated duties, the agent must be told.

TABLE 4-1

Liabilities of Principal and Agent to Third Parties in Contract

	Disclosed principal	Partially disclosed principal	Undisclosed principal
Principal	Principal is liable provided agent acted within scope of express, implied, or apparent authority or principal ratified acts of agent.	Principal is liable if agent acted within authority or if principal ratified acts.	Unsettled. Under contract law principal is not liable because no privity of contract. Under agency law principal is liable if agent intends to and does act for principal. Third party can elect to hold either principal or agent liable—not both. If principal settles account with agent, principal may still be liable on basis of apparent authority.
Agent	Agent is liable unless unauthorized act is not ratified. Agent is liable as co-party, surety, or joint obligor of the contract.	Agent is liable as if a party to the contract, a guar-antor, or a co-promisor unless expressly excluded by contract.	Third party can elect to hold either agent or principal liable once principal becomes disclosed.

The agent in turn should perform with reasonable skill, care, diligence, loyalty, and confidentiality. The principal's business or trade secrets may not be divulged to outsiders. If the task requires personal performance, only the authorized agent can render that service. There need be no attempt to do what is obviously impossible or impractical, and the agent should not exceed the authority granted. An agent can act for only one person unless the principal knows about and consents to a dual agency.

With respect to the principal, the agent owes obedience, undivided loyalty, and good faith. No agent may use a principal's business secrets for personal benefit. Furthermore, there is a duty to account periodically to the principal and convey information concerning the authorized activity. The individual to whom duties are delegated can be held liable for civil wrongs, misuse of property, subagent's conduct, and breach of contract. A prudent agent keeps assets associated with the agency in a separate account and does not mingle them with personal property.

The Principal and the Third Party

The agency is established in order that the agent can act on behalf of the principal. Therefore, the acts of an agent, within the scope of the agency, are the acts of the principal. Should the agent be involved in an auto accident while on the business of the principal, the principal can be held liable. If the agent warrants an article and does so in the scope of the agency, the principal will be required to honor that warranty.

Where the agency is obvious, the agent simply acts as a go-between for the principal and the third party. The third party, in effect, is dealing with the principal, bearing the same responsibility to the principal as if dealing face to face.

A different situation can arise if the agency is not disclosed. Sometimes the principal uses an agent to avoid disclosing his or her existence or identity. If a potential buyer is known to be wealthy, the price may increase. When the existence of the agency relationship is concealed, it is generally held that the third party is dealing directly with the agent and cannot rely on the principal to perform. The situation becomes far more complex if the third person subsequently discovers that a principal is involved, because the law varies from jurisdiction to jurisdiction. Some states allow the third party to rescind an executory contract because anyone has a right to choose the people with whom to do business. Others let that person select whether to hold the principal or the agent responsible for the contract. Should this situation arise, it is time to consult a lawyer who will be familiar with the local law on the subject.

In conclusion, agency is a working relationship based on a contract between the principal and agent. It differs from other employment arrangements in the degree of control retained by the principal over the agent's actions and in the authority of the agent to change the legal situation of the principal. Agency is another important area in which third persons who are not party to a contract can be affected by it.

One should not analyze a contract solely in terms of who signs it. No contract exists in a vacuum. There can be a buyer and seller, an assignor and assignee, a principal and agent, and of course there will also be the outside world.

INVOLVEMENT AND STUDY MATERIAL

Understanding Terms

Assignment	(page 56)	Principal and agent	(page 61)
Counterclaim and setoff		Universal agency	(page 63)
	(page 58)	General agency	(page 63)
Donee beneficiary	(page 60)	Special agency	(page 63)
Creditor beneficiary	(page 60)	Agency by necessity	(page 63)
Incidental beneficiary	(page 60)	Authority by estoppel	(page 64)
Agency	(page 61)	Ratification	(page 65)

Questions and Problem Solving

1. Explain the rights of an assignee to a contract. How does an assignment affect the rights of a buyer who purchases merchandise that is later found to be defective?

2. If the assignee stands in the shoes of the assignor, how can the third party raise defenses of setoffs or counterclaims?

3. How does the assignment of credit contracts differ from an assignment of performance contracts?

4. Explain how the principle of agency operates in a business situation. Identify a business situation where agents are usually employed.

5. What protection does the U.C.C. offer the assignor in regard to the ability of the assignee to perform?

6. The acts of the person acting as agent are considered to be the acts of the principal under agency law. If the agent damages a principal's business or property, can the principal sue the agent and recover damages? Explain your answer.

7. Explain the source of the agent's authority. In what ways can the principal's conduct affect an agent's relationship with third parties?

8. A passenger injured while riding in an automobile insured by the driver is entitled to medical payments provided in the driver's insurance policy. Under what contract principle does this protection come? How can this be explained in terms of bargaining between the parties to the contract?

9. If an agent performs an unauthorized act, can the principal be bound by it? Would it make a difference if the act was beneficial

to the principal rather than detrimental to the principal? Explain your answers.

10. If the principal accepted the acts of an agent for several months even though they were beyond the explicit authority of their agency agreement and then decided to repudiate them, would a third party have any recourse against the principal? If so, under what principle?

Cases for Discussion

1. Davis contracted with Duke, a well-known glass cutter, to make an ornamental mirror. Duke found that he was too busy to do the job and assigned the contract to Miller to complete. Upon completion, Davis refused to pay for the mirror. Duke brought an action to recover the price of the mirror. Judgment for whom? Why?

2. Pritchard represented one kind of silk cloth as another and sold it to Myers. Pritchard was acting as agent for Youngblood at the time of the deal. Upon discovering that the silk was inferior, Myers brought suit against Youngblood to recover the purchase price, claiming Youngblood's agent, Pritchard, was liable for deceit. Is Youngblood liable for deceit on the part of the agent? Why?

3. Hiram Wilson Company hired Kinger to act as its selling agent. Kinger was instructed to sell the merchandise at a 5 percent discount. If customers paid by check at the time of the sale, they could have a 6 percent discount. Kinger sold some merchandise to Walters, who paid by check payable to Kinger in order to gain the 6 percent discount. Kinger cashed the check and left town. Hiram Wilson Company brought suit to collect from Walters the price of the merchandise sold by Kinger. Walters claimed to have paid by check drawn to Kinger. Hiram Wilson Company claims Kinger had no authority to collect payments personally and that the check should have been drawn to the order of the Hiram Wilson Company. Judgment for whom? Why?

Chapter Five

Business Accountability

A century ago, the "robber barons" were generally indifferent to the needs of the public, which had to take what was offered. Most manufacturers were far removed from the ultimate consumers, and geographic and jurisdictional problems put many manufacturers practically beyond the reach of the law. Thus, the public was left without effective remedies in the event of poor merchandise.

A common-law doctrine of *caveat emptor* ("let the buyer beware") applied to most sales transactions. If the seller furnished goods corresponding to a particular description, the buyer took a risk as to their quality and condition. Although this doctrine may still apply where the buyer has had a chance to inspect the goods and discover their defects, its harshness has been mitigated by the developing law of warranties. State and federal consumer protection laws have also helped to control sharp practices.

Early consumer protection consisted of warranties given when the sale of the product was made. However, the concept of warranties was rooted in the law of contracts: the warranty was given only to a purchaser who was a party to the exchange of promises. This doctrine was known as *privity of contract.* If anyone was harmed who was not in privity, or connected with the original agreement, that person was without a remedy.

Advertising, sales promotions, and oral and written statements made to induce the purchase of a product, are embraced in the law of warranty. So are guarantees about performance, safety, and quality of the product. All these are the topic of this chapter.

WARRANTIES

Many stores now maintain a policy of "satisfaction or your money back," sometimes called a "money-back guarantee." However stated, such a policy has nothing to do with the quality of the article sold. It is merely an understanding that if the product does not meet the personal tastes of the buyer, it may be returned to the store. It permits people to examine the merchandise at home away from the high-pressure sales tactics of some merchandisers. That the policy pays off is evidenced by the number of large stores that have prospered by using it. However, this practice has no relationship to the quality or performance of the article, which is dependent on warranty and contract.

Warranties arise as an issue when buyers attempt to use a product for its intended purpose and something unexpected happens. The question then involves what was said about the product, where and when it was said, what the parties meant when saying it, and whether any of this conversation was communicated to ultimate consumers even though they themselves had no direct contact with the original seller.

Express Warranties

Express warranties are statements that are made concerning a product. For example, a buyer wanting to purchase a truck asks a sales person for a truck with a 2-ton rated capacity, that is, with a manufacturer's rating that the truck will be able to regularly haul 2 tons of cargo without incurring excessive wear. Assume that the sales person does not have a 2-ton truck available, but fearing a lost sale, tells the buyer that the truck on the floor has a 2-ton capacity. The invoice lists the sale in the same manner. In fact, the truck has only a 1½-ton capacity. The buyer, after discovering the deception, can demand damages to compensate for the excessive wear. Of course, if the cargo being hauled is substantially below the 2-ton level and there is no excessive wear, the buyer has no complaint, unless the price paid was for a 2-ton truck.

Suppose, however, that the purchaser asks for a truck that can haul a bulky cargo requiring 1,000 cubic feet of space. He inspects the vehicles on the floor after the sales person directs his attention to a particular truck. Later the owner discovers that the capacity purchased is slightly under 1,000 cubic feet. In this situation there is no warranty since the buyer inspected what he was getting. He could have measured the hauling space and insisted the sales person sell him a truck meeting his exact space requirements.

Nature of the Express Warranty

The principle behind the law of warranty is that people who sell goods should come close to telling the truth about what they sell. If the article is available for inspection by the buyer and the seller does not wish to make any warranties, he should say nothing. Even in that case, the courts can find that a warranty is implied by law because of the circumstances surrounding the sale. If, however, the seller expressly guarantees his product then it must conform to the warranty. Otherwise, he can be forced to pay damages, take the goods back, or both.

Affirmation

U.C.C. sec. 2-313 states that any *affirmation* of fact or any promise made by the seller to the buyer which relates to the goods and becomes a basis of the bargain creates an express warranty. This means that the buyer must rely on the statements of the seller if the affirmation is the basis of the bargain. As a matter of common sense, one should look at the statement and see whether it was important to the buyer. Thus, an affirmation such as, "This is a new car," together with the price of a new car, would be important. The same comment when the car was being sold at only half price could indicate that the price was the greater inducement. Nevertheless, if the buyer was rather unworldly and did not know about the prices, makes, or models of cars, a court might consider any such statement a warranty.

Descriptions

A statement akin to an affirmation is a description. The U.C.C. sec. 2-313 holds that if the description forms a basis of the bargain, it creates an express warranty that the product will conform to the description. The buyer does not have to accept the goods unless they conform to the description.

The distinction between an affirmation and a description is not always clear. Generally, a description deals more with specifics. For example, an advertisement that "all upholstery in the car is genuine leather" is a description. If the representation was likely to influence the buyer, the courts are inclined to side with the purchaser and find that a warranty exists.

Privity

Privity of contract has already been mentioned. However, the doctrine is now almost completely eliminated from the law of warranties. As a result, manufacturers now recognize that any statement made about a product may be a basis of a warranty action against the manufacturer by any consumer if damages result.

Creating an Express Warranty

This is the age of consumerism. Business people must be aware that today's buyers are more sophisticated than their predecessors were and also more likely to seek relief. Therefore, sellers should know how a warranty is created.

Use of Samples and Models

An express warranty can be made by showing the prospective customer a sample or a model. A *sample* is a part of the goods to be sold; for example, a sample of upholstery material would represent the material for furniture to be manufactured, sold, or reupholstered. A *model* can be a miniature representation of a large item, like an architect's scale model of a building.

The U.C.C. says, "Any sample or model which is made part of the basis of the bargain creates an express warranty that the whole of the goods shall conform to the sample or model." Of course, it recognizes that sometimes a sample or model is not intended to be exactly what the goods are. If they are merely intended to give the buyer a general idea of the goods, they will not necessarily create a warranty of conformity.

To be on the safe side, the business person should make sure that any samples or models shown are substantially like the product to be sold or else should make it clear to the buyer that the goods will not be exactly like the model. Unless this disclaimer is strong and specific, showing the sample will very likely create a warranty.

Puffing

There are things that sellers can say about goods without creating a warranty. They are entitled to their own opinions about their goods. Most people are proud of their ownership, craftmanship, and association. Therefore, a boastful statement about the quality of an article is simple evidence of a human trait and not the basis of a warranty. When auto makers say that their Panda model is the "best," this is what the law calls *puffing*, in other words, a forgivable exaggeration.

People are not expected to rely on these self-serving statements. Thus, a buyer who finds that some other car has greater acceleration than the Panda cannot claim a breach of warranty. But when an architect claims that a garage can hold two Pandas side by side, this is a factual statement. It is a representation by the architect that becomes a basis of a bargain and, therefore, a warranty.

The buyer can do nothing if purchased goods do not live up to puffing, except to transact future business elsewhere. If the statement is a warranty and the goods are not as warranted, the buyer can force the seller to take them back, pay damages, or both. The difficulty comes in deciding whether a statement is puffing or a warranty.

The U.C.C. does not offer much help. It simply states (sec. 2-313) that if the seller makes an affirmation of the value of the goods or merely renders an opinion of the goods, that is not a warranty. If a statement does not seem to fit this formula, it may be a warranty. A comment of the drafters of the U.C.C. seeks to explain what the code language means by saying that the question is "what statements of the seller have in the circumstances and in objective judgment become part of the basis of the bargain."

Deciding Legal Significance

Hundreds, perhaps thousands, of words may be exchanged by the parties in negotiating a bargain. When the transaction is completed, the buyer may have a question about what was received and what was expected. At this point, the customer must examine the statements made concerning the goods and decide which of them have legal significance. To summarize:

1. If the statement is an affirmation of a fact or a promise, and if it is the basis of a bargain, it is an express warranty.

2. If the statement describes the goods in specific terms, such as by serial number, and if it forms the basis of a bargain, it is a warranty that not only describes the item but identifies it as well.
3. However, a statement is not a warranty if it was not persuasive to the buyer. For example, if the buyer is seeking a razor blade and the salesman tells him a certain blade was made in Sweden, but the buyer is merely interested in getting a blade to fit his razor, the salesman's statement obviously is not persuasive. In contrast, if the buyer insists on blades made of Swedish steel, then the statement is material and hence persuasive to the consummation of the bargain.
4. A statement that is merely an expression of opinion about value or in praise of the article is not a warranty. For example, a statement such as, "This is the finest car you can buy," is merely puffing and places no obligation on the seller.

Implied Warranties

An *implied warranty* differs from an express warranty because it arises by law as a result of the conditions surrounding the sale. It is not created by the explicit agreement of the seller and the buyer.

An implied warranty could arise when a person who is not familiar with the product tells the seller that he knows nothing about it and describes his needs; if the seller recommends a specific brand, he implicitly warrants that it will meet those needs. Assume that a buyer tells a salesman that he needs a car to take him from New York to California and back. When the salesman sells him a car, an implied warranty is established that the car will be fit for the particular purpose of the buyer. A point often missed by inexperienced people is that in the assumed case the buyer will have to prove he stated his needs to the salesman. If the salesman denies that such a conversation occurred, it becomes a problem of proof of facts rather than a question of law.

Types of Implied Warranties

There are six implied warranties at common law. These are:

1. The warranty of title when the seller guarantees that he has the right to sell or transfer title to property.
2. The warranty against encumbrances, indicating that there are no outstanding claims against the property in question. However,

caution must be used in certain types of transactions, since the purchaser cannot claim to be a buyer in good faith if the encumbrances are recorded.

3. The warranty of fitness for a particular purpose, when the buyer relies on the seller's skill and judgment in selecting the proper item, and when the seller knows what the buyer's purpose is.
4. The warranty of merchantability, indicating suitability of the property for normal use. It also suggests average quality, labeling, or packaging.
5. The warranty of fitness, involving goods fit for human consumption.
6. The warranty of conformity, meaning that the goods sold will conform to the sample, model, or description on which the buyer based his choice.

Implied Warranties under the Uniform Commercial Code

The U.C.C. left the law on express warranties essentially unchanged from the common law, but its provisions concerning implied warranties have produced a considerable amount of streamlining. They are contained in Secs. 2-312 to 2-317.

Elements

For a warranty of merchantability, the code requires (1) a valid sale (including, incidentally, the consumption of food and beverage on the premises) (2) by a merchant (3) of goods which are "of fair average quality . . . and are fit for the ordinary purposes for which such goods are used" and which "conform to the promises . . . made on the container or label." Thus, not only does the code broadly and carefully delineate implied warranties but it also limits the protection that selling name brands formerly gave to the retailer. These warranties may be excluded expressly at the time of the sale.

Disclaimers and Inspections

Unlike the express warranty, the implied warranty can be waived by the use of expressions like "as is" or "with all faults," or other such language which calls the buyer's attention to the exclusion of warranties. Then if the buyer has inspected or refused to inspect the goods, there is no warranty in regard to defects which a reasonable inspection would have revealed. An implied warranty can also be excluded or modified by the course of dealings or the usages of the trade. Warranties of title and warranties against encumbrances cannot be excluded.

Language excluding warranties of merchantability must mention "merchantability." Exclusion of warranty of fitness must not only be in writing, but also must be *conspicuous*, so that the consumer is adequately warned.

It is almost impossible to disclaim an express warranty, but many attempts have been made to do so. One example is the sale of pesticides and fungicides. Almost all manufacturers state: "Notice: Neither the manufacturer nor the seller makes any representation or warranty, express or implied, and shall not be held responsible in any manner for any personal injury, property damage, or other type of loss resulting from the handling, storage, or use of this product." Yet, when the customer has asked for the product for a specific purpose, the disclaimer frequently is not effective because it is lost in a maze of fine type and an implied warranty may have been established.

Contracts of adhesion sometimes have pages of provisions including a clause that no warranties are included, "express or implied." The code, however, requires fair play. It prohibits unconscionable contracts and requires that written disclaimers be in conspicuous type (U.C.C. secs. 2-302 and 2-316). Courts give these two code provisions liberal interpretation.

TRUTH IN ADVERTISING AND MERCHANDISING

Many sellers advertise and merchandise their goods in ways that are at least reasonably close to being truthful. Others persist in making claims for their goods that they know or should know to be untrue. In so doing, they are treating consumers unfairly.

The law of warranty is not enough to control such sellers. Generally, the public is ignorant of its rights or apathetic. Even when consumers know they have a cause of action, the cost of litigation often outweighs its advantages. To control this situation, it has been necessary to enact special legislation invoking criminal penalties for bad trade practices.

State Regulations

Every state has passed consumer protection laws. The state inspects scales to be sure the public is not cheated on weights. Gasoline pumps and the octane rating of gasoline are checked periodically. Many states inspect sanitary conditions in slaughterhouses, and they test the quality of meat sold in stores. Following the lead of the federal government, states have recently passed truth-in-lending laws requiring the disclosure of interest rates and credit terms before the sale. All these state laws are important as long as they are properly enforced.

Federal Regulations

Supplementing the state regulations, the federal government has enacted similar laws and more. Federal inspectors can inspect meat-packing plants that ship goods across state lines. The U.S. Food and Drug Administration has broad powers for policing merchandising practices relating to food and drugs.

Since federal jurisdiction usually depends on interstate shipment of goods, an important supervisory agency is the U.S. Postal Service. It can regulate everything that goes through the mails.

Perhaps the regulations that get the most publicity are the ones that affect television advertising and those that deal with drugs, medicines, and activities relating to health. For instance, the Federal Trade Commission ruled that an advertiser who represented sandpaper was being shaved clean by using a particular shaving cream was acting improperly by using a piece of plastic with loose particles sprinkled on top instead of sandpaper for the demonstration. In such cases, the FTC can issue a cease and desist order enforced with fines or jail sentences.

A controversy between the Food and Drug Administration and a seller culminated in the 1966 trial in Chicago of the makers and sellers of an alleged cancer cure. After a trial that lasted many months with testimony for both sides by experts, federal prosecutors succeeded in obtaining jail sentences for the drug makers. The court also ordered that they stop advertising and selling the alleged cure. Fraud, or quackery, in medicine is abhorrent because the people who are tricked into thinking they are being cured may refrain from getting proper treatment that could have been effective.

The list of regulations that govern the sale of certain kinds of goods is extensive. Table 5-1 indicates the kinds of goods, the types of regulation, the regulating agency, and the limits of its jurisdiction which are particularly important for truth in advertising and merchandising today.

TABLE 5-1

Regulation of Goods and Practices

Goods and practices	Regulatory agency	Regulation	Jurisdiction	Type of business
Food and drugs	Food and Drug Administration	Sets purity, quality, and inspection standards; fixes labeling and advertising practices	Transactions in any way related to interstate commerce	All
All goods sold by mail	Postal Service	Forbids deceptive and fraudulent claims or misrepresentations in advertising by mail	Any user of the mails	All
All goods and marketing practices	Federal Trade Commission	Forbids deceptive practices	Interstate commerce	All
Stocks, bonds, and other securities	Securities and Exchange Commission; state securities commissions	Regulates all phases of business in interstate transactions, varying from complete to slight regulation	Interstate commerce transactions within states	Stock and bond sellers
Meats and other agricultural products	Department of Agriculture	Sets quality and labeling standards	Goods in interstate commerce	Food sales
All goods— exporting and importing	Department of Commerce	Maintains licensing system	Any exports and imports	All
All goods— radio and TV advertising	Federal Communications Commission	Requires decency and honesty	Any broadcasting	All
Public accommodations	Department of Justice	Forbids racial and other discrimination	Interstate commerce and other areas covered by Civil Rights Act	Hotels, motels, restaurants, etc.

Table 5-1—Continued

Goods and practices	Regulatory agency	Regulation	Jurisdiction	Type of business
All goods sold with weighing and measuring devices	Various state agencies	Require accurate weights and measures	Transactions within state	All
Retail credit sales	Federal and state laws	Require statements of credit terms	Transactions within state	Retail sellers
Automobile sales	Federal and state laws	Requires pollution controls and posting of price on new cars	New auto sales	Auto dealers

INVOLVEMENT AND STUDY MATERIAL

Understanding Terms

Caveat emptor   (page 70)   Affirmations   (page 72)
Consumer protection laws   Descriptions   (page 72)
                         (page 70)   Puffing   (page 74)
Privity of contract   (page 71)   Implied warranties   (page 75)
Express warranties   (page 71)

Questions and Problem Solving

1. It is generally agreed that today's buying public is more literate and more aware of business practices than the buyers of 100 years ago. If this is so, why has the doctrine of *caveat emptor* been preempted by consumer protection laws?

2. How has the doctrine of privity of contracts changed in modern business practices?

3. How can a seller, who has made no positive statements concerning the product sold, be charged with an express warranty?

4. Distinguish the express warranty of question 3 from an implied warranty.

5. Distinguish between puffing and express warranties, and explain the rights of the buyer in regard to these terms.

6. There are six types of implied warranties. Under what circumstances would a buyer not be entitled to the protection of an implied warranty when making a purchase? Give specific example.

7. What is the effect of a disclaimer of a warranty of the sale of a product "as is"?

8. List the various government agencies that are concerned with truth in advertising and with deceptive practices. Name at least five areas that are given government protection.

Cases for Discussion

1. Frontera contracted with the Ajax Machine Company for the purpose of buying several grinders. He was assured that the grinders would grind products to the specific measurements described by Frontera as necessary in the manufacturing of his products. After the grinders were delivered, Frontera discovered that they would not grind his products to the required specifications. Frontera brought suit against the Ajax Machine Company on the express warranty. Ajax Machine Company defends on the grounds that there was no warranty in the contract. Judgment for whom? Why?

2. Clearmont Co. advertised new color television sets with statements that its sets would give the best and sharpest pictures of any set made. Larson, a customer, came into the store and was assured by the salesperson, Sikes, that the sets were the best. Sikes reaffirmed that Larson could expect the sharpest and best color reproduction of any television set made. Larson purchased a set on the basis of these representations. After the set was installed, Larson found that she could not get a clear picture. She brought the set back to Clearmont Co., and they refused to accept the set or refund the money. Larson brought suit against Clearmont Co. for breach of warranty. Judgment for whom? Why?

3. Economy Motors guaranteed its used cars for thirty days against mechanical defects. Johnson, a customer, came onto the Economy lot and looked over various models. The salesman assured him that the auto Johnson selected was in good mechanical condition, that he had made a good selection, and that the salesman con-

sidered the car to be in top condition. Five weeks after the purchase, when Johnson was rounding a curve, the front wheel fell off and the car was wrecked. Johnson brought suit against Economy Motors under implied warranty because of the statements of the salesman. Economy Motors denied any warranties beyond the thirty days and claimed that the salesman's statements were mere salesmanship. Judgment for whom? Why?

4. Evans, a reupholsterer, ordered several hundred yards of upholstery material selected from a sample book shown him by the sales representative for the Moon Fabric Company. When the material arrived, Evans examined it, found that it was not of the same quality, and refused to accept the shipment. Moon Fabric Company then sued for the purchase price of the material. Assume that Evan's contention is correct. Judgment for whom? Why?

5. Walker, a salesman for the By-Products Steel Co., sold a carload of steel plates to the Harrison Stamping Co. He represented the steel plates as being cold drawn when they were actually hot drawn and of a different gauge than originally ordered. The Harrison Stamping Co. brought suit against the By-Products Steel Co. to recover for damages, claiming a breach of warranty. Judgment for whom? Why?

Chapter Six

Performance

Parties who execute a contract often assume that the future will be much like the past. However, the future is always unpredictable. Sellers who expect to move goods and make a quick profit may find that styles have changed and so no one will buy. In that event, they may be faced with breach or failure of contracts.

CARRYING OUT THE CONTRACT

When a seller and a buyer execute a contract for the sale of goods, the buyer is often just as intent on getting that commodity as the seller is on selling it. Performance is the goal of their transaction.

Performance of the Contract

Every sales transaction involves payment, delivery, inspection, and conformity to the description of the goods. Yet payment will not be required if the goods are not delivered, and acceptance can be refused if the goods do not conform to the description given at the time the bargain was made. Frequently, it happens that the seller's goods are not exactly as described in the contract but they are nearly the same. The problem then shifts to the extent of the difference.

Substantial Performance

This is a bona fide attempt to perform the agreement literally and exactly. It is a common problem in contracts for construction, where slight imperfections may appear before completion. For example, the buyer discovers a minor contract violation and immediately complains that the builder has failed to perform the contract according to specifications. Examination may reveal that the violation is due to the soil conditions and is not the fault of the builder.

Slight deviation from literal performance can be overlooked as not affecting substantial performance. In a landmark New York decision by Judge Cardozo, a contract was not invalidated simply because Cahoes drainage pipes, rather than the Reading pipes specified in the contract, had been set in the floors and foundation of the building. Replacement of the pipes would have meant the practical destruction of a $77,000 building. Instead, the court ruled the contract had been substantially performed.

Almost all construction contracts leave the standard of performance to the discretion of the building's engineer or architect. If the architect finds the work is adequate, he or she will issue a certificate. Then payment will be made. Minor deviations will lead to a reduction in compensation unless the contractor is willing to make the corrections. However, if there is substantial performance, the builder is entitled to the contract price less the damages suffered due to lack of performance. This is a sensible approach and gives each party the benefit of the bargain. If the cost of additional work runs to more than 10 percent of the entire price, it is generally agreed that the performance is not substantial.

When the performance is not substantial, the builder generally cannot recover even the cost of the materials because damages begin to run high. If the contract is a large one, some recovery may be allowed to the builder since the construction increased the value of the land.

Satisfactory Performance

Occasionally, the test is not substantial performance but rather *satisfactory performance*. This means that the work must be done to the satisfaction of the one who contracts for it, or his representative, providing his approval is not dishonestly withheld. For example, a party may refuse to accept or pay for his portrait if he is not satisfied. Satisfactory performance is a more difficult test to meet than is substantial performance.

Conditions of Time

Performance of a contract may be contingent on certain conditions, such as time. Business people often have to meet deadlines. A condition that must be fulfilled prior to performance is called a *condition precedent*. A contract provision that water will be piped to a house before the first payment is due represents a condition precedent. A *condition subsequent* operates to suspend completion of the contract after performance has begun. An example of a condition subsequent would be a provision in a lease stating that the lease is terminated if a fire destroys over one-half of the building.

Changing the Contract

Even when they are performed, contracts do not necessarily conform with the original expectations of the parties. Sometimes even the identity of these persons will be subject to change.

Novation

Often the parties to the contract encounter an unexpected situation. The promisor, for one reason or another, cannot or does not want to complete the contract. A substitute may be willing to do so. If the other party is willing to accept the substitution, the new arrangement is a *novation*. The original party is released completely, and the other party will look to the substitute to complete the performance.

A novation is distinguished from a straight assignment (see Chapter 4) because it involves the agreement of the other party to the original contract. In the absence of a specific prohibition in the contract, an assignment of an assignable contract does not need the agreement of the other party. Therefore, if there is an agreement about the substitution, it suggests that the parties intended a novation.

This situation is encountered frequently where a debtor is in financial difficulty. This individual may attempt to sell his or her business to a person who has better financial resources. The new party, after examining the situation, agrees to take over the business and the debtor's obligations. Contact is then made with the creditors. The creditors will usually demand that the new party assume all the debtor's obligations in the form of notes or a renewed mortgage. There very likely will be an exchange of correspondence leading to substitution. The final result will be that the new debtor takes over and the creditors release the old one.

Accord and Satisfaction

An *accord and satisfaction* is a compromise of an honestly disputed claim. Many times parties to a contract find themselves in disagreement over the extent of the contract and the amounts owed. A dispute may arise over the amount of work originally estimated and the compensation actually required; for example, a simple excavation may unexpectedly require costly demolition work. A difference over the amount owing on the contract can be troublesome. It is generally better to attempt a compromise rather than to litigate. Usually, an agreed figure will be made payable immediately, and this itself may have considerable value.

Accord and satisfaction is an agreement concerning a disputed claim. If the amount is not in dispute, the parties cannot exchange promises for a reduced amount without special precautions.

Rescission

A situation can arise so that neither party is happy with the way the contract is going. If they agree, they can terminate the agreement. To *rescind* the contract, it is necessary that both parties be restored to the status quo, that is, to the condition they were in before they entered the bargain. The parties can also modify, release, surrender, or cancel the contract. This can be done orally or by a formal written document. All that is required is that the parties mutually agree to the change.

UNINTENDED DISCHARGE OF CONTRACT

Even when the persons entering into a contract have the best of intentions—as is usually the case—the contract can fail before performance has started.

Reasons for Failure of Contracts

A great variety of problems can intervene—some may preexist, whereas others arise later. Some unexpected situation may arise after the contract is negotiated, such as the death of one of the parties or the destruction of the subject matter of the contract, which will prevent complete performance. Moreover, a condition existing at the time the contract is made but of which one party is unaware can have the same effect. For example, lack of legal capacity to contract can prevent the necessary meeting of minds.

Minority

As was discussed in Chapter 3, infants, or minors, are people who have not reached legal majority. Minors are protected by the law from becoming involved in financial transactions without recourse. There are different legal ages for different purposes in different states. For example, there is a legal age for securing a driver's license, another for buying intoxicants, and still another for voting. Many states now provide that the legal age for entering a contract is eighteen years.

The legal age of majority can be modified by emancipation, that is, when the young person ceases to be under the control of his or her parents. Usually, such an individual is working and self-supporting, possibly living in the parents' home and paying board and room, but not dependent upon the parents for support. Whether one is emancipated or not is a question of fact. In some states young people are emancipated when they get married; they can enter into contracts in the same manner as adults.

Contracts made by unemancipated minors are voidable at the option of the minor. Some states hold that the sale of real estate by minors is completely void. The minors can perform or disaffirm their contracts at any time until they reach majority. After reaching majority, they have a reasonable time to make up their mind, get legal advice, and determine whether they want to honor their contract. Any act by which they enjoy the benefits of the contract can constitute ratification. If a minor should die before reaching majority, a personal representative can disaffirm in the minor's place. This rule applies to executory, partially executed, or wholly executed contracts.

The minor is required to return the consideration that he or she still possesses when disaffirming the contract, even if it has been damaged, partially dissipated, or even destroyed. Suppose that the minor in turn has sold the articles to an innocent third party. Does that person have to return the goods? What if the article has been burned through no fault of the minor? A few states require full restitution; most, however, just provide for the restoration of whatever is still in the possession of the minor.

Favorable treatment by the law does not give the minor a license to buy property recklessly and then simply repudiate the contract after using the property. A minor's limited incapacity to contract does not permit intentional fraud and deceit. Generally, the courts have been reluctant to apply sanctions in such a case if the seller is aware of the age of the buyer, but there have been cases where the minor has been treated harshly.

The minor is obligated to pay for the necessities of life, such as food, lodging, clothing, medical attention, and school. It is doubtful that sending a minor to college would also be a necessity, but it could be considered one depending of the family's socioeconomic circumstances. Payment for necessities is based on their reasonable value rather than on the contract price.

Minors can hire agents to work for them. However, when the agent is working for a known minor principal, the contracts negotiated by the agent are voidable at the option of the minor.

Insanity

Legal insanity creates a situation similar to legal minority, as we discussed in Chapter 3. Contracts made during a period of insanity are voidable by the insane party. The insane person would be liable only for the reasonable price of any necessities furnished. If the seller knew that the buyer was mentally incompetent, the seller might even be guilty of fraud.

If the insane person is legally ruled incompetent and has a legal guardian appointed, any contract with the insane person is void and the guardian can recover any consideration given to the seller by the insane person.

Intoxication

Intoxicated people are regarded in almost the same way as the insane. However, the intoxicated person must show that there was lack of mental capacity to reach an agreement. Restitution is generally different. Presumably, the intoxicated person sobers up some time after the transaction and realizes what has happened. Therefore, restitution of consideration is almost always required. If the person is a confirmed alcoholic, the situation is different. In such a case, the seller may be guilty of fraud by knowingly taking advantage of the condition.

Illegality of Subject Matter

There are several major areas where the law steps in to avoid performance of a contract on grounds of public policy and illegality. A contract may be against public policy because it violates fundamental principles of ethics, morality, policy, and social behavior. The contract may be so repugnant to the court that it will not allow itself to become a party to its enforcement. It may also be illegal because the legislature has passed laws against it.

One cannot enter into an enforceable contract to perpetrate a fraud, to murder, or to engage in activity which would defame a third party. Many attempts have been made to contract away liability for a civil wrong. Property owners in many states cannot avoid the public duty to clear ice off the sidewalk outside their buildings so that pedestrians will not be injured.

Contracts can be invalid because they violate statutes such as the Sunday closing laws or the licensing laws. A corporation that operates in a state without obtaining a state business license generally cannot use that state's courts to obtain any judicial relief on its contracts. An unlicensed architect may be unable to collect a fee. The courts have sometimes been harsh in these cases to enforce revenue laws.

Contracts against public policy include those that tend to obstruct justice, illegally influence public officials, fix prices, and obtain other special treatment. Prominent figures have been indicted and sentenced to prison terms for some of these offenses.

A contract may be perfectly valid when signed but then become invalid when a law is passed prohibiting the activity called for in the contract. This has been demonstrated in the drive for pollution control and the banning of dangerous drugs or improperly canned food.

The U.C.C. sec. 2-302 states that unconscionable contracts will not be enforced. An example would be the sale of a $515 stereo set to someone with seven dependents who earns only $218 per month. In such a case, the court held that the sale was unconscionable and declared the contract not enforceable. Another common example of unconscionable and unenforceable contracts arises from the practice of adding amounts of new sales to previous balances of sales that carried security or mortgage interest. Thus, the buyer never pays off any purchase, and in case of default the seller is able to repossess all the merchandise. In one case in point, the first purchase was in 1957 and the last was in 1962; when the default occurred in 1962, the consumer lost everything purchased since 1957.

There are many types of contracts that the courts are inclined to scrutinize closely because of the disproportionate bargaining power of the parties. For example, a buyer may be asked to waive certain laws for the protection of the public. Usury laws may be circumvented by other complex charges, and borrowers may be unable to complain since they need the loan. Yet, if they later complain to a judge, the court may find the particular contract at least partially unenforceable.

A person who finds a contract containing unusual or incomprehensible clauses should consult a lawyer before signing it, thus avoiding subsequent litigation.

Impossibility and Disability

People often enter into contracts because they have special equipment or talents that will enable them to perform. An owner of a bulldozer may agree to grade a particular site, but after the contract is signed a fire destroys the bulldozer and so it becomes impossible for the owner to perform. In this case, it is important that the contract specify the use of the individual's present equipment; otherwise, the owner of the bulldozer may be compelled to go out and buy another to complete the job.

The same problem can arise whenever parties later disagree about the original assumption or something prevents the anticipated performance. Suppose a singer loses her voice. It is obvious that the audience is not paying the price of admission just to see her dress, nor is a substitute performer always acceptable. Therefore, the contract between theater owner and singer cannot be performed. The objective test of impossibility is "it cannot be done" rather than "I cannot do it."

Death

If the contract is personal in nature, it is obvious that the party's death terminates it. In contrast, contracts for general performance (sale of merchandise, construction, and the like) are not dependent upon the individual's skill or credit, and so the estate can be expected to complete performance. If one wants the particular contract terminated at death, this should be stated in the contract.

Destruction of Subject Matter—Failure of Consideration

If one enters into an agreement to buy a certain antique car which is to be placed in a museum of locomotion, the destruction of the vehicle is a defense if the buyer demands performance. The consideration, or the car for which payment was to be made, no longer exists; therefore, the contract cannot be enforced. One unique item cannot be substituted for another, and so its destruction terminates the contract.

Similar treatment can be accorded situations where the purpose of the contract is frustrated. Some of these cases arose from lawsuits to collect rental for window seats along the coronation route of Edward VII. When the ceremony was postponed, the reason for the lease was frustrated and the contracts served no purpose. The court did not permit the owners of the space to collect future rent, but they were allowed to keep the downpayment.

Strikes

Strikes are a major disruptive force in the modern economy. A contract with a deadline for delivery of certain parts is dependent on prompt shipments of those parts. Should a strike delay production until the deadline for delivery is past, performance may become impossible and the duty to pay for the goods is excused. The law usually places the risk of loss on the party who can best anticipate or prevent the disruption.

Breach of Contract

Failure to perform one's contractual obligation is known as *breach of contract*. When does the breach occur? One party may realize in February that he will not fulfill his bargain, but the other may have to wait until December to discover this breach. When there is *anticipatory breach*, the innocent party can act at once to reduce his damages. Sometimes anticipatory breach occurs because the breach-

ing party notifies the other of his intent or misses several installments; other times, discovery of his insolvency has the same effect.

Upon discovering that the other party will not perform his bargain,
one has a duty to *mitigate damages*. In sales contracts one can reduce
the loss by buying the goods elsewhere even at greater price. When a
construction company breaches its contract, the other party should
get another to complete performance. Finally, if a person loses his
or her job, he or she should seek work of a similar type in that general neighborhood instead of sitting back and waiting for damages
in the form of the entire lost salary. The measure of recovery is the
difference between what one could have received before the breach
and what one in fact gets. The doctrine of mitigation of damages
does not allow the injured party to rely passively on assistance from
the court.

REMEDIES FOR NONPERFORMANCE OF CONTRACT

If performance of the contract cannot be achieved, the parties will
want to know what alternative rights and remedies are available to
them. When a contract has been either intentionally or unintention-
ally terminated, the aggrieved party can seek damages or equitable
remedies like specific performance or an injunction.

Specific Performance

Specific performance is performance of an agreement according to the
original terms. If, for some reason, one of the parties has stopped
performance, can the other insist on performance as originally agreed
upon? Usually damages are considered sufficient remedy, but sometimes money alone will not make good the loss and the party will be
satisfied only with what he bargained for. If it is a physical performance, such as manufacturing or building, the courts may allow
damages only, but land or a work of art is considered unique, and so
a contract involving either may be specifically enforced.

A problem arises in regard to services that are personal. For example, if an opera star feels indisposed some evening, the court
would not specifically force the star to perform because that is close
to compelling one to work in peonage, and slavery is against public
policy. However, the court may enjoin (forbid) performance
elsewhere.

Injunction

An *injunction* is an order issued by a court forbidding or command-
ing the performance of some act. The opera star who is indisposed
cannot be compelled to sing, but the real reason the star is indisposed
may be a substantially higher offer made by a rival theater. Sometimes a court can be persuaded to forbid the star to perform in the
competing theater by issuing an injunction.

Companies also utilize injunctions against former employees who
had been given access to company secrets, formulas, customer lists,
and future plans. Such employees usually sign a contract stating
that upon retirement or resignation they will not work for a rival
company for a stated period of years or within a limited geographic
area. The courts have enforced such agreements if the specified time
and space restriction is reasonable.

Injunctions are frequently used as remedies in areas other than
contracts. For example, an injunction may be obtained to prevent a
factory from dumping waste into the local river. Landowner A may
enjoin neighbor B from diverting a water course, committing a
nuisance, or performing some activity which interferes with A's
rights. Injunctions are often invoked by companies and the federal
government to prevent an unauthorized strike or to provide for a
cooling-off period in the face of a threatened strike.

Damages

The assessment of damages is a very difficult problem in any breach-
of-contract situation. The damaged party is under a legal duty to
minimize damages, and the defendant in a lawsuit is likely to challenge the amount claimed.

The courts use various criteria to fix the amount of damages.
Damages may be set at the difference between the contract price and
the cost of goods on the open market, or they may be set at the
added cost of the products or services supplied by another source. A
situation may involve only the loss of anticipated profits. For example, if the buyer backs out of a car sale, the seller is forced to
expend additional energy to sell that car to another customer. Therefore, the seller may be entitled to what would have been the profit
had the sale been consummated, if those profits are not too speculative.

Many business people have learned the value of specifying damages
in the contract. If both parties agree to a specific and reasonable

amount that will serve as damages, this amount can be written into the contract in the form of a *liquidated damages clause*. When the amount is fixed, the expensive litigation that often follows a breach is avoided. U.C.C. sec. 2-718 provides a limitation on the amount of damages and liquidated damages for nonperformance. Thus, before engaging in any agreements, every business person should be aware of both potential remedies and penalties in case a contract is breached. The court will choose the remedy unless the parties have the foresight to anticipate future problems. In antitrust cases, damages may even be punitive to serve as a deterrent.

The Uniform Commercial Code

Article 2 of the code devotes considerable space to the problem of nonperformance in sales contracts. Anyone entering a business involving sales would do well to become familiar with this part of the code. In brief, a seller faced with a breach can resell the goods; if they cannot be resold, the seller can demand damages (U.C.C. secs. 2-706, 2-709, 2-710). The buyer also may decide to accept delivery of goods that do not accord with the terms of the contract and then demand damages (U.C.C. secs. 2-714 and 2-715). He can reject the goods and then obtain what he needs elsewhere, charging the difference in price to the seller. If he cannot obtain the goods elsewhere, he may be forced to sue for specific performance or for regular damages. It should be noted that the code attempts a reasonable approach and that the parties must minimize the damages involved.

A seller who suspects that the buyer may not be able to pay for the goods does not have to deliver and can stop the goods if they are in transit. He can recover any reasonable charges that were incurred until the goods are returned.

The majority of contracts are completed in an orderly manner to the satisfaction of the parties. The fact that remedies are available in the event of a breach encourages the parties to avoid a breach. Thus, the business person should anticipate performance with confidence but be ready to utilize alternate courses of action if a problem develops.

INVOLVEMENT AND STUDY MATERIAL

Understanding Terms

Substantial performance		Status quo	(page 86)
	(page 84)	Impossibility of performance	
Satisfactory performance			(page 90)
	(page 84)	Breach of contract	(page 91)
Novation	(page 85)	Anticipatory breach	(page 91)
Accord and satisfaction		Specific performance	(page 92)
	(page 86)	Injunction	(page 93)
Rescission	(page 86)	Liquidated damages	(page 94)

Questions and Problem Solving

1. Explain whether substantial performance is a sound concept for most contract situations and why. Would it be suitable in the purchase of precision machinery?

2. Why is satisfactory performance more limited in application than substantial performance?

3. Freedom to contract is an important concept of law. How and why does incapacity due to minority, insanity, or intoxication affect this concept?

4. Courts treat certain contracts as unconscionable. Yet people are perfectly free to enter into bargains for things they want. Why should courts upset the original arrangements? Give several illustrations.

5. What is the key factor that renders a contract impossible to perform? Distinguish this concept from frustration of purpose. If one were engaged to climb a flagpole at a state fair and the fair was canceled because of severe flooding of the fairgrounds, which doctrine would best excuse the nonperformance?

6. Why is the remedy of specific performance limited to unusual situations?

7. Why is the remedy of granting an injunction more suitable than money damages in certain situations? Give several examples.

8. Why is the remedy of money damages generally more suitable than an injunction or specific performance? Is the principle of *mitigation of damages* sound when a breach of contract occurs?

Explain your answer and illustrate how one could minimize or mitigate a loss.

9. Why is a liquidated damages clause valuable in a contract and when is it valid?

Cases for Discussion

1. Parker contracted to build a garage for Naugle. After the garage was partly constructed, Parker abandoned the project without just cause and without the permission of Naugle. Parker then brought suit against Naugle to recover for the cost of labor and materials used. Judgment for whom? Why?

2. Baker agreed to work for Lane for one year at a salary of $1,100 per month. At the end of the first month, Baker left Lane's employment without cause and against Lane's wishes, and Baker now seeks to recover the reasonable value of the services rendered for the month. Judgment for whom? Why?

3. Lesiak was indebted to Khoury in the amount of $1,000. Lesiak entered into a contract of settlement agreeing to pay Khoury $100 and the balance in the form of 500 board feet of lumber. After receiving the money and lumber, Khoury brought suit against Lesiak on the $1,000 debt. Lesiak set up the defense of accord and satisfaction. Judgment for whom? Why?

4. Bruner agreed to build a warehouse on Wear's land and to deliver possession by September 1. After Bruner had completed 98 percent of the warehouse, it was destroyed by accidental fire. Bruner then brought suit to collect for the work done before the fire. Wear contends that Bruner is not excused from the contract by reason of the fire. Judgment for whom? Why?

5. Allen agreed to render personal services to Barber for one year at the rate of $100 per week. Allen died three months later and his estate now seeks to collect the back salary due him. Barber insists that Allen's estate is still liable on the personal contract. Judgment for whom? Why?

6. Durant contracted with the owner of the El Cid Cafe as bartender for one year. Three months later the cafe lost its liquor license and was not able to serve alcoholic beverages. Durant brought suit to collect for the entire balance of his year's salary. Judgment for whom? Why?

7. Pace owned a paper mill in which he manufactured paper by a secret process. Pace sold the mill and machinery to Williams. The contract provided that the seller was to procure for the buyer the exclusive right to manufacture by the secret method. The contract called for the payment of $40,000 worth of paper which the buyer was to give to the seller within a reasonable time after the sale. Pace brought suit for breach of contract against Williams for failure to deliver the paper as agreed. Williams defended by stating that Pace never taught him the secret manufacturing process. Judgment for whom? Why?

Chapter Seven

Carrying Out the Transaction

A contract is often intended as an indication that the parties want something done. It is not self-enforcing. Listing the details of an agreement will not be very useful unless the parties take steps to execute its provisions concerning delivery, inspection, and payment. Under normal conditions, the seller will be obligated to deliver the merchandise specified in the agreement at the time and place chosen. The buyer will be expected to pay for it according to the terms of the contract.

DELIVERY

When the buyer has agreed to purchase some merchandise, it is reasonable to assume that he counts on getting it at the time specified. For example, the merchant who agrees to buy 500 pairs of men's summer trousers is interested in getting them in time for the summer trade. They will not do much good if they are delivered in November of the following year. Time is extremely important in the clothing business, and this year's styles may not sell next year.

The Uniform Commercial Code

To the lawyer, delivery is not a simple question with clear, short answers. The number of cases involving delivery is so great and varied that complex rules have developed to deal with these situations. Most states now look to provisions of the Uniform Commercial Code in such matters.

Delivery by Lot or Singly

There are three basic provisions concerning delivery in code secs. 2-307 to 2-309. The first deals with delivery of lots singly or in installments. Unless otherwise agreed, all goods called for by the contract must be delivered in a single lot. Payment is due only on such delivery.

In some cases, there may be circumstances whereby the parties can demand delivery of the merchandise by lots. If the price can be apportioned by lots, the seller can demand payment with each lot delivered. This can be the arrangement in contracts involving large quantities of goods, such as wheat or coal. The average sale of a car to an individual customer will not involve this practice, yet a car dealer may utilize lots in selling a fleet of automobiles to a newly established taxi company.

Place of Delivery

The place of delivery is a far more complicated matter. Most of us go to a store, purchase an article, and take it with us. Even if we buy an auto, we generally drive it away from the dealer's lot. But in commercial matters things are not always so simple.

The code says that, unless otherwise agreed upon, the place of delivery is the seller's place of business. If there is no place of business, the seller's residence is the place of delivery. But in a contract for the sale of identified goods (generally goods existing at the time the contract is made), the place of delivery is the location of those goods, or if they are to be prepared for shipment, it is the place of such preparation. If the transaction deals with documents of title, title may be delivered through customary banking channels. These arrangements generally involve large shipments of goods.

Suppose the transaction involves the purchase of a used car in reasonably good condition. The seller lives in South Suburbia, and the buyer lives in Center City. It will be up to the buyer to go to South Suburbia and pick up the car. According to the code, the buyer must literally go to the place where the identified goods are kept to exercise ownership over them. The delivery here consists of action of the buyer; the seller plays a passive role.

Time of Delivery

Many purchases involve goods that are needed for a specific purpose at a particular time. Wise merchants will spell out delivery deadlines in order to protect themselves. Yet, many contracts do not have any clear delivery dates. The code says that under such circumstances, delivery shall be within a "reasonable time." In practice, this means that a purchaser of a car can expect delivery within a month or two. The word "reasonable" invites disputes and interpretation. It is generally better to spell out time expectations rather than suffer disappointments and resort to litigation.

If the contract involves sale of a fleet of taxis, the delivery time might well extend over an indefinite period, and the criterion of reasonableness can be applied. A duration of twelve months might be considered quite reasonable under the circumstances.

Suppose too many families own their own cars in the neighborhood where the taxis operate to justify such a large fleet. Can the company rescind or get out of its contract? No simple answer is possible; it depends upon the circumstances. An agreement stretching over an indefinite but reasonable period can be terminated by either party at any time. Yet the terminating party has to give reasonable notice of termination and would not be permitted to take an unconscionable advantage of the other party. For example, in the taxi case, the buyer could not wait until the cars were delivered at the seller's place of business and then cancel the order, because the dealer might have no way of disposing of the specially designed taxis.

Right to Insist on Delivery

In the ordinary course of events, parties contemplate performance. The seller wants to sell goods, and the buyer wants to get them. Delivery schedules are not much of a problem. Shipments arrive to the satisfaction of both parties. Sometimes, however, their plans go awry. As our society increases in complexity, strikes, power blackouts, and technological breakdowns may prevent the smooth flow of goods.

Is one entitled to insist on prompt delivery when the automobile manufacturer's plant is virtually closed as a result of a strike? "Prompt" delivery may be too much to expect, but the code specifies that delivery shall be within a "reasonable time" as determined by trade usage and the circumstances of the contract. The anticipated duration of the strike would play a significant role in the court's decision. Nevertheless, the buyer can utilize a provision of U.C.C. sec. 2-609 which permits either the demand of adequate written assurances of due performance "when reasonable grounds for insecurity arise" or the repudiation of the contract within thirty days.

A related issue is whether the buyer is obligated to pay the full specified amount for the goods whose delivery has been so delayed that the buyer suffers a financial loss. A buyer who can prove a financial loss which is not purely speculative has the normal contract remedy for breach.

PAYMENT

Payment is the opposite side of the coin from delivery. For every seller who delivers the purchased goods, there is a buyer who must pay for them. Receiving payment is the primary aim of the seller in entering a contract of sale.

Amount of Price

Usually the price to be paid is so important to at least one of the parties that it will be carefully governed by the terms of the contract. These terms will prevail. Nevertheless, drafters of the U.C.C. felt compelled to insert adequate provisions on this vital topic by indicating that the buyer can pay either with money or with goods. For example, part of the cost of a new car may be paid with the trade-in value of the buyer's old car. Payments can also be made by checks, letters of credit, drafts, or promissory notes. Thus, arrangements between the individual parties can be flexible and varied.

Unascertained Price

Even the price, important though it is, may not always be settled by the terms of the contract. In sec. 2-305, the U.C.C. accepts the fact that:

(1) The parties if they so intend can conclude a contract for sale even though the price is not settled. In such a case, the price is a reasonable price at the time for delivery if
    (a) nothing is said as to price; or
    (b) the price is left to be agreed by the parties and they fail to agree; or
    (c) the price is to be fixed in terms of some agreed market or other standard as set or recorded by a third person or agency and it is not so set or recorded.

(2) A price to be fixed by the seller or by the buyer means a price for him to fix in good faith.

(3) When a price left to be fixed otherwise than by agreement of the parties fails to be fixed through fault of one party the other may at his option treat the contract as canceled or himself fix a reasonable price.

(4) Where, however, the parties intend not to be bound unless the price be fixed or agreed and it is not fixed or agreed there is no contract. . . .

In such a case the buyer must return any goods already received or if unable so to do must pay their reasonable value at the time of delivery and the seller must return any portion of the price paid on account. Once more the tests of reasonableness and good faith must be met.

Is the buyer always obligated to accept the delivered goods and pay for them? In the normal course of events, yes. Suppose, however, that the delay in delivery has been so extreme that the buyer no longer has any real need for the goods. For example, the summer trousers are delivered in November. Possibly, too, the goods are not those which had been ordered or are so defective that they are useless. Then the duty of payment in full may be avoided.

RIGHT TO INSPECT

Experienced business people will want to see or inspect whatever they plan to buy. But should the buyer inspect the goods before delivery, upon receipt, prior to payment, or at some subsequent time? Is there an unlimited right of inspection, or must the time and place be reasonable?

Examination on Delivery

The prudent purchaser will inspect on delivery. In so doing, one can usually detect any apparent defects. In fact, the law assumes this will be done. For example, if a car lacks the lights required by state law, a reasonable person who drives could be expected to notice that defect. Suppose, though, that an equally serious defect lies in the brake lining. Such a problem would not readily be noted by the average person; its detection would require the skill of a trained mechanic, and the law provides accordingly.

Surprisingly, the U.C.C. says little on this subject, but sec. 2-316 (3) does hold that

> (b) when the buyer before entering into the contract has examined the goods or the sample or model as fully as he desired or has refused to examine the goods there is no implied warranty with regard to defects which an examination ought in the circumstances to have revealed to him. . . .

This rule does not materially alter the position stated above. When receiving goods, the buyer has a chance to inspect them, and therefore, there is no implied warranty covering obvious defects which can be readily seen on inspection.

Examination Where Payment Must Be Made Before Delivery

Situations exist where the buyer cannot see goods until after paying, as in shipments. In such a case, U.C.C. sec. 2-512 provides:

> (1) Where the contract requires payment before inspection non-conformity of the goods does not excuse the buyer from so making payment unless
> (a) the non-conformity appears without inspection; or,
> (b) despite tender of the required documents the circumstances would justify injunction against honor under the provisions of this Act (Section 5-114).
> (2) Payment pursuant to subsection (1) does not constitute an acceptance of goods or impair the buyer's right to inspect or any of his remedies.

Thus, if the buyer must make payment before inspection, no right of inspection is waived. However, the buyer is bound to honor a check or other instrument he issued in payment unless he discovers a fraud or some major discrepancy. Then his remedy would be to ask the court for prompt relief before the seller has an opportunity to use up the money.

Defects Turning Up After Inspection

No implied warranty covers defects of property that are so obvious as to be discoverable by ordinary inspection when (1) there is no fraud or justifiable reliance by the buyer on the seller, (2) the parties deal at arm's length and are on equal footing (since both parties have equal knowledge, one does not owe a duty to explain and the other is not justified in relying upon the statements made), and (3) there has been an inspection before the sale. Yet in a case involving damage to a house trailer after the explosion of a gas cook stove, inspection alone did not preclude an implied warranty against defects which were not obvious on inspection. If the stove exploded after delivery, acceptance, and inspection, the injured buyer might still sue and hope to recover.

The buyer has to act promptly on discovering the defect. According to comment 8 of U.C.C. sec. 2-316, if one unreasonably fails to "examine" (rather than inspect) the goods before using them or uses them anyway after discovering defects, one forfeits any legal rights of recovery. One cannot complain about defects and continue to use the goods; one must reject and refuse to use the goods.

Even after the buyer has rejected delivery of goods on the grounds they do not conform, the seller has a chance to cure the defect by making a conforming delivery within the contract time. This right is guaranteed by U.C.C. sec. 2-508.

PRODUCT LIABILITY

Particularly in the case of potentially dangerous instruments (e.g., cars), but to a lesser extent with respect to all sales, the buyer has a right and a duty to inspect the goods for defects. The discovery of defects may in turn materially alter the customary rules about delivery and payment. It can and does lead to liability on the part of the seller or the manufacturer for damages arising out of those defects. The disappointed buyer will want to know any rights in this regard.

An important and growing area of law regulates the circumstances under which liability can be imposed on various persons for damages due to defective equipment. The parties involved are the retailer, the manufacturer, the processor, the subassembler, the wholesaler, the distributor, the contractor, and even the importer. Depending on the situation, any or all of these persons can be sued. In the case of products which are inherently dangerous special rules may apply because of the extreme damage which may result from the use of such defective equipment.

Breach of Warranty

Damages for breach of warranty have been discussed in Chapter 5. Breach of warranty is an important basis for recovery of damages under the concept of product liability. When the car manufacturer puts a product on the market, he is guaranteeing first that it is merchantable, or in a salable condition, and second that it is reasonably fit for its intended use. Moreover, an express warranty can be breached if the car manufacturer has specifically guaranteed that the product is a sports car appropriate for racing if that does not prove to be true.

When a product is defective, a lawsuit can be brought against the manufacturer for damages on the basis of breach of express or implied warranty. The problem is that the warranty depends on a privity-of-contract relationship, and so a third party cannot recover damages.

Misrepresentation

Just as the retailer can be guilty of misrepresentation in a sales talk, so too can a manufacturer be liable for reckless, intentional, or even negligent material misrepresentations. This traditional rule has been expanded to include false representations no matter how innocent the intent when the statements were made. Suppose a manufacturer's brochure warrants that the car's brakes are so good it can stop on a dime, and that this statement is issued in ads by the dealer. Such a statement can be recklessly misleading when the buyer tries in vain to stop on short notice to avert an accident. Liability can be imposed on the manufacturer who originally issued the brochure to its sales outlets.

If potential defects cannot be entirely eliminated (owing to technological limitations) but can only be minimized, the manufacturer may be obligated to warn potential buyers of the anticipated danger. These notices should be of ample size and in such a conspicuous position that the average person would be put on guard. Packages of cigarettes now caution smokers of possible ill effects. Similarly, the day may come when new cars have to have labels on the windshield warning of potential dangers.

Negligence

Negligence is the failure to exercise the care that a reasonable person would use under the circumstances. The doctrine of negligence has been used where warranty did not form a basis of recovery. Early cases confused privity-of-contract and negligence rules in refusing to recognize a duty on the part of a manufacturer to outsiders. In 1916, Justice Cardozo struck down that doctrine in *McPherson v. Buick* and held the Buick Motor Company liable for the negligent manufacture of an article which was inherently dangerous to human life. He extended the duty of the manufacturer to cover any user of the product. This still left victims of product injuries with the formidable task of proving negligence against a remote manufacturer. The courts solved this problem by allowing the warranty to travel with the product and eliminating the privity-of-contract principle. Therefore, suits were allowed on the basis of either breach of warranty or negligence.

Negligence as a ground of action can be broad. To minimize extraordinarily heavy liability, the manufacturer must check, recheck, and check again at every stage of the manufacturing process.

Strict Liability

A comparatively recent reemergence in the field of litigation is the doctrine of *strict liability*, which holds generally that the manufacturer of a defective product can be sued for injuries caused by it. The doctrine is not yet uniform in all states. Under the doctrine an injured party can sue the manufacturer without regard to warranties or negligence. All that the plaintiff has to show is that the article was improperly designed when sold to the consumer. In a recent case, a man who lost a hand in a commercial meat grinder recovered damages from a manufacturer that had made the product many years before. The basis of his recovery was a defect in design that allowed the removal of a safety device by an unknown person and permitted insertion of the plaintiff's hand into the mechanism.

Most of the cases of strict liability have involved automobile manufacturers. A car can be found to be unreasonably defective in view of its great potential for doing harm to the public. The specter of strict liability looms so large over the auto industry that thousands of cars are recalled whenever any model proves defective.

The automobile manufacturer is not the only target of suits under this doctrine. Architects have been sued for defects in buildings designed as long as twenty-five years before. Construction contractors and manufacturers of other products are also susceptible. One case concerning a defective lifting mechanism resulted in a verdict of $3.5 million. Products like dynamite that are inherently dangerous require the greatest care on the part of the seller to prevent injury to the user as well as to a bystander.

There is some evidence that the manufacturer may now be held responsible under the doctrine of strict liability even when the product is misused, since the manufacturer has to foresee a certain amount of misuse. Hence the designer of the product must keep in mind that the product may be improperly used. In a recent case, a car crossed over into the opposite lane and hit another car head on. The impact pushed the steering shaft into the chest of the driver who crossed lanes. The injured driver sued the manufacturer. The court put the question to a jury, and after a three-week trial, the jury brought in a verdict for the defendant. Nevertheless, the court may have tried to place a new duty upon the manufacturer.

In all these lawsuits, the most obvious plaintiff is the buyer or the consumer. This is the person most likely to be harmed when the automobile crashes and thus most concerned with whom can be sued and for how much.

At one time the buyer could sue only the seller—in this case the automobile dealer. Now the situation has changed. The buyer can sue any number of persons, from the local seller to the original manufacturer. This allows far more likelihood of recovery for the consumer. If the buyer sued the local retailer, the retailer can then sue the wholesaler or manufacturer.

INTERPLAY OF DELIVERY, PAYMENT, AND WARRANTY

Delivery, payment, and warranty have been portrayed as separate concepts. If the goods are not delivered or are delivered late or do not conform to what was ordered, the buyer can be excused from paying. Conversely, failure to pay may stop delivery or subsequent deliveries. Damages recovered for breach of warranty, negligence, strict liability, or misrepresentation can be set off against the amount of payment due and may even exceed it.

Product liability is an important field today, even though it seldom looms large in the negotiations of the average buyer and seller. They are often more interested in the provisions concerning delivery and payment. Only later, if something goes wrong, may they be concerned about liability.

INVOLVEMENT AND STUDY MATERIAL

Understanding Terms

Reasonable time	(page 100)	Breach of warranty	(page 105)
Reasonable price	(page 102)	Negligence	(page 106)
Inspection	(page 102)	Strict liability	(page 106)

Questions and Problem Solving

1. Describe how trade usage and circumstances surrounding the sale affect delivery.
2. Discuss the effect of the Uniform Commercial Code on delivery.
3. Discuss the methods available for the buyer and seller to resolve conflicts when price has not been settled.
4. Explain how the right of inspection can affect delivery.
5. List the remedies available to the buyer upon delivery for defects in the product purchased.
6. Explain the use of the doctrine of negligence as a basis for recovery in the absence of warranties.
7. Discuss how the present concept of product liability differs from the past concept.
8. Discuss the effect that inspection has with regard to the warranty of the product. Cite several examples in which the right of inspection may alter or affect the warranty on the product.

Cases for Discussion

1. Singleton Nurseries ordered tulip bulbs from Van Oster, a tulip grower in the state of Washington. The tulips were to be delivered

the following year. No price was mentioned. Van Oster shipped the requested number of tulip bulbs on the date requested, but the nursery claimed that it had no contract since no price had been agreed upon. However, Van Oster pointed out that trade practices left the prices open until catalogs were printed just before shipments were made. Van Oster also pointed out that the nursery was fully aware of this practice since it had made similar purchases from other growers in previous years. Van Oster finally brought suit. Judgment for whom? Why?

2. The Pacific Woolen Mills ordered two bales of khaki worsted material from the Westover Rag Company, agreeing to send for them. Westover Rag Company tagged the bales and set them aside. The Pacific Woolen Mills driver called for the material during the lunch break, was unable to find the bales, and left without picking them up. Upon failure of the Pacific Woolen Mills to pay for the bales, Westover brought suit for the purchase price, claiming title had passed to the Pacific Mills. Judgment for whom? Why?

3. The Atlas Appliance Company purchased some electric stoves from the G. N. Stove Company and used them as demonstrators for six months. Then Atlas notified the G. N. Stove Company that the stoves contained defects and offered to return them. The G. N. Stove Company refused to accept the stoves and sued for the purchase price. Judgment for whom? Why?

4. While shopping at the Fastway Grocery Store, Jacobs purchased a bottle of cola. Later as he was trying to open the bottle, it exploded and injured him. Jacobs sued the Cola Bottling Company for breach of warranty. Judgment for whom? Why?

5. Dexter purchased a bottle of ginger ale. After opening it and drinking some of it, she discovered a foreign substance in the bottle. She became ill immediately. Dexter brought suit against the bottler, claiming a breach of warranty. Judgment for whom? Why?

6. Amper Corporation agreed to buy ten milling machines from the National Machinery Company. Later Amper defaulted on the contract and refused to buy the machines. Upon learning of the default, National sold them to the Woolright Corporation at a much higher price. Amper then sued National for the difference in price. Judgment for whom? Why?

Chapter Eight

Financing the Transaction

Nearly everyone has seen freight trains or trucks loaded with cars being shipped from the manufacturer to a local dealer. Few, however, understand fully the business transactions that control such a shipment.

DOCUMENT OF TITLE: THE BILL OF LADING

The physical shipment of cars is generally made by a common carrier —often a long van on which the gleaming new cars are stacked in double decks bumper to bumper. In legal terms, as opposed to physical terms, the shipment is made by means of a bill of lading.

The *bill of lading* is "a document evidencing the receipt of goods for shipment issued by a person engaged in the business of transporting or forwarding goods" (U.C.C. sec. 1-201). The bill of lading represents:

1. A contract between the shipper and the transportation company in which the terms of the shipment are spelled out
2. Title to the goods in the hands of the holder
3. A receipt acknowledging that the goods have been received for shipment

724—SOUTHERN RAILWAY SYSTEM—724

STRAIGHT BILL OF LADING—SHORT FORM ORIGINAL — NOT NEGOTIABLE

RECEIVED, subject to the classifications and tariffs in effect on the date of the issue of this Bill of Lading.

5 FORM 407-C-6 PT. REV. 11/72

STOP THIS CAR | AT | FOR | LENGTH OF CAR: ORDERED | FURNISHED | MISC. PRO. NO.

CAR INITIALS AND NUMBER	TRAILER INITIALS AND NUMBER	CHASSIS INITIALS & NUMBER	PLAN	WAYBILL DATE	WAYBILL NUMBER
SOU 61234					
CAR TRANSFERRED TO	**TRAILER INITIALS AND NUMBER**	**CHASSIS INITIALS & NUMBER**	**PLAN**	2/9/73 WB	21056
				TIME:	BY:

TO STATION: ELKHART, IND. STATE

FROM NO. STATION STATE

BILLED AT NO. STATION STATE: 1111 ATLANTA, GA

ROUTE: SRS CINTI C&O

ROUTING SHOW "A" IF AGENT'S SHOW "S" IF SHIPPER'S: S

FULL NAME OF SHIPPER AND ADDRESS: BIRMINGHAM STEEL

CUSTOMER CODE NO.: 3456

RECONSIGNED TO STATION STATE

RWC

PER

ORIGIN AND DATE, ORIGINAL CAR, TRANSFER FREIGHT BILL, AND PREVIOUS WAYBILL REFERENCE AND ROUTING WHEN REBILLED.

AUTHORITY

CONSIGNEE AND ADDRESS: INDIANA CONSUMER CO, 2640 MAPLE AVE.

CUSTOMER CODE NO.

BILL OF LADING DATE

WEIGHED: AT; GROSS WT AGMT.; TARE; ALLOWANCE; NET

BILL OF LADING NO.: 96041

INVOICE NO.

FINAL DESTINATION AND ADDITIONAL ROUTING

SPECIAL INSTRUCTIONS — C. L. TRAFFIC

If charges are to be prepaid, write or stamp here, "TO BE PREPAID"

Subject to Section 7 of Conditions: ☐ YES SIGNATURE OF CONSIGNOR

NOTE—Where the rate is dependent on value, shippers are required to state specifically in writing the agreed or declared value of the property. This agreed or declared value of the property is hereby specifically stated by the shipper not to exceed

PER

DATE REV. W/B PREP.

COMMODITY CODE NUMBER: 33 124 33

FOR THE CARRIER

PER

NO. PKGS.	DESCRIPTION OF ARTICLES SPECIAL MARKS AND EXCEPTIONS	WEIGHT	RATE	FREIGHT	ADVANCES	PREPAID
28	LIFTS, BAR STEEL	140180	58	813.04	COLLECT	

DESTN. AGENT'S F/B NO.

Fig. 8-1. Bill of lading.

4. A notice to the buyer that the goods have been shipped and that the buyer is to pick them up

A copy of the bill of lading known as a *waybill* is kept by the carrier and forwarded with the rail car to its agent at the point of destination so that he can handle the shipment when it arrives. The original

T-19851

PLACE SPECIAL SERVICE PASTERS HERE

724 — SOUTHERN RAILWAY SYSTEM — 724
FREIGHT WAYBILL

FORM 2262
REV. 2/72

STOP THIS CAR | AT | FOR | LENGTH OF CAR: ORDERED | FURNISHED | MISC. PRO. NO.

CAR INITIALS AND NUMBER: SOU 61234
CAR TRANSFERRED TO
TRAILER INITIALS AND NUMBER
TRAILER INITIALS AND NUMBER
CHASSIS INITIALS & NUMBER
CHASSIS INITIALS & NUMBER
PLAN
PLAN
WAYBILL DATE: 2/9/73 WB
TIME:
WAYBILL NUMBER: 21056
BY:

TO STATION: ELKHART, IND. | STATE
FROM NO. | STATION | STATE
BILLED AT NO. | STATION | STATE: 1111 ATLANTA, GA.

ROUTE: SRS CINTI C&O
ROUTING SHOW "A" IF AGENT'S SHOW "S" IF SHIPPER'S: S
FULL NAME OF SHIPPER AND ADDRESS: BIRMINGHAM STEEL
CUSTOMER CODE NO.: 3456

RECONSIGNED TO | STATION | STATE
RWC
PER
ORIGIN AND DATE, ORIGINAL CAR, TRANSFER FREIGHT BILL, AND PREVIOUS WAYBILL REFERENCE AND ROUTING WHEN REBILLED.

AUTHORITY

CONSIGNEE AND ADDRESS: INDIANA CONSUMER CO
2640 MAPLE AVE.
CUSTOMER CODE NO.

BILL OF LADING DATE
BILL OF LADING NO.: 96041
INVOICE NO.

WEIGHED
AT
GROSS WT AGMT.
TARE
ALLOWANCE
NET

FINAL DESTINATION AND ADDITIONAL ROUTING

SPECIAL INSTRUCTIONS — C. L. TRAFFIC

If charges are to be prepaid, write or stamp here, "TO BE PREPAID"

Subject to Section 7 of Conditions:

☐ YES SIGNATURE OF CONSIGNOR

NOTE- Where the rate is dependent on value, shippers are required to state specifically in writing the agreed or declared value of the property. This agreed or declared value of the property is hereby specifically stated by the shipper not to exceed

PER

FOR THE CARRIER

PER

DATE REV. W/B PREP.
COMMODITY CODE NUMBER: 33 124 33

NO. PKGS.	DESCRIPTION OF ARTICLES SPECIAL MARKS AND EXCEPTIONS	WEIGHT	RATE	FREIGHT	ADVANCES	PREPAID
	28 LIFTS, BAR STEEL	140180	58	813.04	COLLECT	

DESTN. AGENT'S F/B NO.

Outbound Junction Stamps Here. Yard Stamps on Back.

FIRST JUNCTION | SECOND JUNCTION | THIRD JUNCTION | FOURTH JUNCTION | DESTINATION AGENT STAMP

724 — SOUTHERN RAILWAY SYSTEM — 724

Fig. 8-2. Freight waybill.

is retained by the shipper. The *consignee*, that is, the person to whom the goods are being shipped, may also get a copy of the bill of lading which serves as a notice that the goods have been shipped and that he can expect them in due time.

Meanwhile, the seller sends the original bill of lading and a bank draft received from the buyer to his bank for collection. This bank will then transmit the draft through banking channels to the buyer's bank. It will be up to the buyer to make arrangements about final payment of the draft through his bank. When it has been paid, the original bill of lading is delivered to the buyer so he can present it to the transportation company and receive his goods. The buyer's bank transmits the money to the seller's bank, and the transaction is completed.

NEGOTIABLE INSTRUMENTS

There are several ways to pay for a shipment. Basically, it can be either prepaid or paid for at a future date. Payment can be made in cash, by means of a negotiable instrument, or through a credit arrangement. As a practical matter, cash is used in very few commercial transactions today. Most business is conducted by means of negotiable instruments with which business people should become familiar.

Types of Negotiable Instruments

Negotiable instruments substitute a transferable written memorandum for cash. There are many kinds of negotiable instruments. One common type is the *promissory note*, which is a written undertaking to pay a designated sum of money at a specific time, or on demand, to the bearer. A less familiar negotiable instrument is the *certificate of deposit*, which represents a bank's acknowledgment that it has received money and will undertake to repay it.

Two other kinds of negotiable instruments are readily recognizable. A *draft* is an unconditional promise for payment of money either on demand or at a specified time. A *check* is also a draft payable on demand but a more limited one because it is drawn on a bank to the order of a specific person.

What makes these negotiable instruments different from any other written memoranda of indebtedness? According to sec. 3-104 of the Uniform Commercial Code, the four elements which must be present in a negotiable instrument are that the writing:

(a) be signed by the maker or drawer; and
(b) contain an unconditional promise or order to pay a certain sum in money and no other promise, order, obligation or power given by the maker or drawer . . . ; and
(c) be payable on demand or at a definite time; and
(d) be payable to order or to bearer.

The Parties and Their Respective Legal Position

Basically, a negotiable instrument involves two or three parties. First is either the maker of a draft or the drawer of a check—the one who executes the negotiable instrument. This is done to benefit a second party, the payee, to whom the sum is to be paid. Finally, there may be a drawee, which in the case of a check is the bank holding the funds from which the sum is to be drawn.

An individual who writes a check is interested in having it honored through payment of the specified sum to the named individual. As

Fig. 8-3. Parties to a negotiable instrument.

long as there are sufficient funds in the account and the check is properly executed, there is no reason why it should be dishonored or why the bank should not pay damages if it is dishonored. However, there may be occasions when the drawer will want to stop payment on an already executed check. If so, written instructions can be given to the bank to issue a stop order to prevent payment of the check.

A payee who does not wish to cash the check may transfer it to another person by an appropriate endorsement. In Figure 8-4(*b*), John Hudson is the payee who had endorsed the check so that Barbara Rock becomes his endorsee and is entitled to payment provided there has been no forgery, illegality, or fraud. She will be a *holder in due course* if she has acted in good faith and in ignorance of any defenses, adverse claims, or dishonoring of the instrument. As such, her rights could be greater than those of John Hudson. Subsequent transferees who are also innocent of wrongdoing and have given *consideration* are called *purchasers in good faith*, and their rights are similarly protected.

The bank is primarily concerned with the detection of forgeries. Its cashiers are trained to notice defectively executed and altered negotiable instruments. They compare signatures with those of their customers which they have on file. Now many banks rely on protective devices such as preprinted checks and use of special codes which can be identified by computer, and they may protect themselves by requiring an additional endorsement from the bearer of the check.

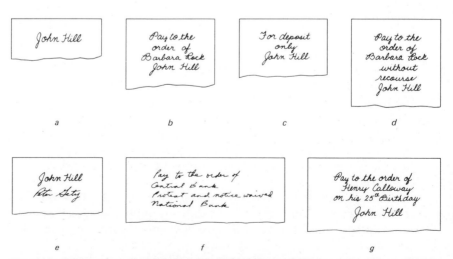

Fig. 8-4. Types of endorsements. *(a)* blank; *(b)* special (or full); *(c)* restrictive; *(d)* qualified; *(e)* accommodation; *(f)* waiver; *(g)* conditional.

Endorsements

There are at least seven recognized types of endorsements. The most common, but the least safe, is the *blank endorsement*. It means that anyone—even a thief—attaining possession of the check can present it for payment by signing on the instrument. A blank endorsement is the simplest kind because it requires only one element—the signature of the bearer.

Two elements make up the *special* (or *full*) *endorsement:* the signature of the endorser and the designation of the party to whom the money can be paid. Only the party designated can demand payment.

Banks prefer use of a *restrictive endorsement*, particularly when the customers send in their deposits by mail. On mail deposit forms they often ask depositors to write "Pay to Bank for deposit only" above their names. This restriction limits risk in case the check miscarries in the mails.

The *qualified endorsement* begins like a blank or special endorsement, but adds a new factor in the words "without recourse." It limits the endorser's responsibility for payment if the check is dishonored and others default. Qualified endorsements are normally restricted to cases involving collateral security of agents who have no personal interest in the transacted business.

Less commonly used is the *accommodation endorsement*, which provides greater security through the added signature of another person with good credit. *Waiver endorsements*, which contain the words "protest and notice waived," are used mainly between banks. There is, in addition, a *conditional endorsement*, which restricts payment until the occurrence of a given condition or event. One does not see many of these.

Negotiation of a check not only makes the endorser liable for payment of the negotiable instrument if others default (unless it is a qualified endorsement), but it can also create certain warranties. Among these are the warranties of good title, rightful transfer, genuine signature, lack of defenses good against oneself, no material alteration in the check, and ignorance of any insolvency proceedings against the maker.

Should there be any doubt about payment, one can always use a *certified check*. The bank sets aside the sum of the check and thereby guarantees that it can and will pay the amount of the check on demand.

Negotiable instruments are important in financing many sales transactions.

SHIPMENT OF GOODS

Let us return to the auto manufacturer and the consumer. How much each pays and what duties each assumes will depend on how the shipment is to be made.

Shipping Arrangements

Goods can be shipped C.O.D., ex, F.O.B., F.A.S., C.I.F., C. & F., or ex dock. Of course, there are other arrangements and refinements, but the following are the major ones with which a business person should be familiar.

Collect on Delivery (C.O.D.)

One of the commonest forms of shipment is C.O.D. Housewives ordering dresses from mail order houses, and business people ordering heavy office equipment can both arrange for shipment to be made C.O.D. The buyer pays the shipper for the goods on arrival in order to receive possession. Although the buyer cannot inspect the goods before payment, they can be rejected later.

Ex

This designation refers to the point of the shipment's origin, such as a warehouse in "ex standard warehouse." Payment is figured on that place of origin. The key date is the time agreed upon for delivery from the warehouse. Until that date, the seller bears all costs (storage, servicing, etc.) and any risk of loss if the building is destroyed.

At the specified time, the seller places the goods at the disposal of the buyer, who simply goes to the warehouse or factory to take possession of them. If export taxes, fees, and charges are to be paid, or if documents relating to exportation and importation must be obtained, the buyer is responsible, though the seller can assist. For example, if John Lerski buys a car at a Volkswagen factory in Germany, the costs and risks shift to his shoulders on the day he takes possession. He has to pay the shipment costs to America, but he can expect the Volkswagen representative to aid him in procuring and filling out the various forms necessary for transatlantic shipment. When he drives away from the factory, all the rights and burdens of being a car owner will be his.

Free on Board (F.O.B.)

A better known shipping arrangement in the commercial world is F.O.B. The seller's obligations last only until the goods are loaded onto the carrier. For example, "F.O.B. *S. S. Vulcan*" means that the seller has to arrange for the goods to be loaded onto that particular barge for shipment and that the price is computed to delivery onto the barge. Thereafter the buyer assumes the costs and the risks of shipment. F.O.B. contracts were originally associated with shipments by sea, but they are now commonly used in rail and truck carriage.

Free Alongside (F.A.S.)

Another less known type of shipping arrangement which used to be confused with F.O.B. is governed by commercial practices. Whereas F.O.B. requires placement of goods on board the shipping vehicle, F.A.S. means placing goods on a dock or loading platform within reach of the loading tackle. The loading then is at the cost and risk of the buyer. This arrangement almost always involves shipment of lots that are less than a carload. In transportation, it permits delivery to the dock or loading platform without waiting for the arrival of a particular ship. In land transportation, it permits accumulation of shipments until a carload is made up.

Cost and Freight (C. & F.)

Under most F.O.B. arrangements, the obligation of the seller stops when the goods reach the carrier. This is not true of C. & F. shipments. For example, "C. & F. Erie" simply means that the price quoted by the seller includes the cost of transporting the car to Erie as the ultimate destination. Thus, C. & F. is somewhat less extensive than its cousin, C.I.F., because it does not include insurance.

Cost Insurance Freight Coverage (C.I.F.)

The C.I.F. shipping arrangement is frequently used in international commerce. The price includes everything (cost, insurance, transportation) from the point of shipment to the place of destination.

There is considerable latitude in C.I.F. arrangements. Consequently, it is prudent for the parties to agree in advance on troublesome details: the type of insurance; the interest charges; the responsibility of each party for any additional expenses, like inspection or weighing; the division of risks between the parties; and, of course, the quantity of goods to be shipped. Such foresight can spare litigation later.

Ex Dock or Ex Ship

This is the last type of shipping arrangement to be discussed here, although these seven do not exhaust all the possibilities. "Ex dock Norfolk" means that the quoted price includes the cost of the goods, any additional costs required to unload the goods on the dock at Norfolk, and payment of any duty. The seller must pay the freight to that port and release the shipowner's lien. It is unquestionably the most extensive of the shipping methods described herein.

"To Arrive" or "No Arrival, No Sale" Contracts

On occasion one will see documents containing the terms "goods to arrive" or "no arrival, no sale." These terms mean there is ordinarily no contractual obligation until the goods have arrived, since their arrival is a condition of the contract. The seller may be liable for damages if they do not arrive. Merchants and courts usually interpret such contracts as imposing on the seller a duty to ship goods conforming to the contract and to assume the risk of loss during shipment. The seller is not, however, liable for nondelivery if the goods are destroyed due to transportation hazards or an act of God.

U.C.C. sec. 2-504 provides that the seller must obtain and deliver promptly to the buyer any documents needed to obtain possession of the goods. The seller must also put the goods in possession of the carrier and promptly notify the buyer of the shipment. If the seller's failure to give prompt notice results in material loss or delay, it can become a ground for rejection of the shipment.

INTERPLAY OF TIME AND TITLE

Time is often the essential factor in a transaction. The execution of every contract for a shipment of the goods involves change of title from the seller to the buyer. When does that change of title occur? The answer to this question resolves some basic issues: who is liable for insurance and risk, how soon the goods can be delivered, and when payment must be made for the goods. These are essential problems for the buyer and the seller alike.

Time of Payment

Payment can be made on the spot. Someone can go to a store, buy a tie, and hand the clerk cash for it. Alternatively, the purchaser can buy on credit or pay C.O.D.

The seller must anticipate a variety of times, either immediate or postponed, when payment will be made. Paying in advance or on the spot is not common in commercial transactions because raising sufficient capital is not always easy, but it is by no means unknown. Installment payments are common when successive shipments are made. Usually the contract will specify not only the amount, but also the time and place for making payments. Sometimes it does not.

U.C.C. Provisions

U.C.C. sec. 2-310 makes elaborate provision for situations when the time clause is left open. If documents like bills of lading are involved, payment should be made where and when the buyer gets those documents. The place where the goods themselves are to be received is not important and can be elsewhere. Hence, a shipment of cars can be made to Duluth, but if the documents of title are to be received by the buyer at Ann Arbor, then Ann Arbor is where payment must be made.

In the absence of documents of title, payment is due at the time and place the buyer is to receive the goods (U.C.C. sec. 2-401). In the above example, this would be Duluth.

When goods are shipped on credit, the credit period begins with the date of shipment. Postdating the invoice or delaying its dispatch may delay the beginning of the credit period and the time of payment accordingly.

Passing the Title

Traditionally the moment title passes is important. It determines who bears the risk of loss if the goods are destroyed, who has to carry insurance upon them, and who pays property taxes. At common law and under early statutes, the intention of the parties was significant. Yet, who could determine intent in every case? The Uniform Commercial Code has brought substantial changes in the law to eliminate the problems created by the old rules.

Unless otherwise agreed upon by the parties, in C.I.F. shipments U.C.C. sec. 2-320 requires the seller at his or her own expense and risk to put the goods in the possession of the carrier. If a "where-on-board" bill of lading is involved, the seller also is responsible for loading them. Unless otherwise agreed, title and risk of loss passes to the buyer at the time and place at which the seller completes the physical delivery of the goods (U.C.C. sec. 2-401). Thus, if the price indicates delivery to the buyer, the risk of loss would be retained by the seller until delivery.

Yet, just because title passes does not mean that the seller is without interest in the goods. U.C.C. sec. 2-510 provides that if the buyer rightfully refuses or revokes acceptance, the risk of loss rests with the seller from the beginning. Further, the seller may wish to retain a security interest in the goods until receiving payment. For this reason the seller will want to insure the goods even though the buyer also insures them. The code subdivides the complex issues into different sections. It treats insurable interest in sec. 2-501, risk of loss in secs. 2-509 and 2-510, and right to damages in sec. 2-709. It isolates these problems from ownership and title. For instance, in determining who bears the risk of loss when a contract is breached, one goes to U.C.C. sec. 2-510, which places liability on the party who has breached the contract. Even sec. 2-326 concerning sale-on-approval and sale-or-return transactions does not basically alter the prevailing legal situation. Unquestionably, the code is deemphasizing passage of title. What happens to the concept of title when the prospective buyer has a right to return the goods after taking possession of them? Consider the following situations:

1. Consignment: ownership remains with the seller (or principal), but an agent has a right either to sell or to return the goods.
2. Sale or return: ownership of merchandise rests in the seller, but the buyer has an option either to return it, assuming the expense and risk, or to pay for it when it is delivered to him.
3. Approval: the seller retains ownership of the goods, but they are delivered to the buyer to try them in anticipation of subsequent sales negotiations.
4. Sale on approval: the seller retains ownership (according to the intention of the parties), but the prospective buyer obtains an option to buy and acquire ownership by signifying approval of the goods.

Under U.C.C. sec. 2-401(2) title passes when and where the seller delivers the goods. The buyer's refusal to receive the goods revests title in the seller. The presumption is against interpreting a delivery to a merchant for resale as a sale on approval or against seeing delivery to a consumer as an application of sale or return.

IMPORTANCE OF FINANCE

The name of the game is the orderly transfer of merchandise from the seller to the buyer and of money from the buyer to the seller. Admittedly, financial transactions involve paperwork. The language of such transactions is filled with strange terms that make dry reading. Yet here the business knowledge of the seller and buyer determines the success or failure of the entire venture. If the business fails to take into account the dry detail of finance, it is headed for financial disaster. It will fail not because the product involved is inferior or because the person in charge lacks ability, but because the importance of finance in every business situation has been ignored.

Thorough knowledge of finance is as important as technical product knowledge, yet many business people are inclined to treat it as unnecessary. Successful individuals have discovered the importance of this aspect of business. It is very likely that the booming enterprise became successful because the financial side of the business was not ignored. It is for this reason that so much space has been devoted in this chapter to the Uniform Commercial Code and the impact of finance on the law of sales.

INVOLVEMENT AND STUDY MATERIAL

Understanding Terms

Bill of lading	(page 111)	Check	(page 113)
Freight waybill	(page 112)	Endorsements	(page 116)
Negotiable instrument		C.O.D.	(page 117)
	(page 113)	F.O.B.	(page 118)
Promissory note	(page 113)	Consignment	(page 121)
Certificate of deposit	(page 113)	Sale or return	(page 121)
Draft	(page 113)	Sale on approval	(page 121)

Questions and Problem Solving

1. Explain the purpose and implications of a bill of lading for the buyer.

2. Describe the various types of negotiable instruments used in business today.

3. Compare and contrast the various types of endorsements and cite examples of each.

4. Define and explain the four elements that must be present in a negotiable instrument.

5. Distinguish between the terms "C.O.D." and "F.O.B." and indicate their relationship to the passage of title to the goods.

6. Explain the status of title to the goods in the following situations: consignment, sale or return, approval, and sale on approval.

Cases for Discussion

1. Goldman gave a note to Holt in payment for a debt. It read: "I promise to pay Holt on order $1,000 or deliver a 1969 Ford automobile." It was signed by Goldman. Is this a negotiable instrument? Why?

2. Martinez delivered a check to Smythe made payable to the order of Smythe in the amount of $500 and drawn on the Capitol City Bank. Smythe lost the check, and his name was forged and the check presented to the Capitol City Bank for payment. The bank paid the check and deducted the amount from Martinez's account. Martinez now brings suit to recover the $500 paid by the bank from his account. Judgment for whom? Why?

3. Jackson obtained a note by fraud and negotiated it to Ernest, who knew of the fraud. Ernest negotiated the note to a holder in due course who had no knowledge of the fraud. Later Jackson reacquired the note from the holder in due course and presented the note for payment to the maker, who refused to pay. Jackson sued on the note. Is the maker liable to Jackson on the note? Why?

4. Mayahara notified his bank to stop payment on a check. The bank required Mayahara to sign a stop-payment order stating that the bank would not be held responsible if it should pay the check inadvertently or through oversight. The bank later paid the check by mistake. Mayahara brought suit against the bank for the amount paid. Judgment for whom? Why?

Chapter Nine

Protected Marketing of Ideas

Monopolistic business practices are harmful to society. To discourage such practices, antitrust laws have been enacted that prohibit acts in restraint of trade. Free competition is encouraged.

At the same time, individuals with creative ideas about products or marketing have to be protected. Therefore, a form of monopoly is allowed for the innovative individual, because it permits innovators to develop their own ideas without exploitation by others. In the end all of society benefits.

SAFEGUARDING IDEAS AND INVENTIONS

So long as an idea remains just an idea, it has very little commercial value. It cannot be patented until it is expressed by some symbol or transformed into a product. Inventions, copyrights, and trademarks were recognized at common law.

When the United States Constitution was written, its framers stressed in Article 1, Section 8, the necessity "To promote the progress of Science and useful Arts, by securing for limited Time to Authors and Inventors the exclusive Right to their respective Writings and Discoveries." That original provision has been strengthened by subsequent detailed provisions for the protection of patents and copyrights. The Lanham Trade-Mark Act of 1946 controls trade names and trademarks. Other titles of the U.S. Code cover copyrights and patents.

Trade Names, Trademarks, and Collective Marks

Great sums of money are spent each year in extolling the virtues of a particular product. The public is exposed to an assortment of goods and told that Brand A is superior to Brand X. Whether or not this is true is not important to us here. What is significant is that comparisons can be made and choices are available in the selection of goods.

The law protects the developer from the unfair competition of one who seeks, through using a similar mark, to pass other products off as those of the owner of the trademark. It is also concerned with protection against confusion of the buying public. Therefore, before issuing any registration, the Patent Office examines the proposed use of the trade name or trademark. It considers use, appearance, and structure of the articles; similarity of packaging; and place of sale. It also determines whether the goods are of the same character as other similar goods before approving the trade name or trademark registration. Similar trademarks may be registered by different people if the articles do not compete in the same market area.

Trade Names

A *trade name* is a distinctive title that identifies a business, a product, or a person. The trade name becomes associated with a business and its reputation. "Bird's Eye," "Hershey," "Citgo," and "Exxon" are trade names serving to promote the reputation of a line of products and suggest uniformity in quality.

A mobile society can expect to find a certain brand of product anywhere and depend on that trade name to guarantee quality. Acceptance by the buying public signifies trust in the quality and reliability of the product. The owners of the trade name are assured of a dependable market and, in turn, are careful to preserve the quality of the product. Airlines, auto rental agencies, railroads, insurance companies, and other business organizations that are anxious to project good public images spend large sums of money to identify their line of products or their companies. National retailers may develop uniform outdoor signs that are placed in front of their stores to help the public identify the type and quality of business represented.

Trademarks

Trademarks include any word, name, symbol, or device used to identify goods sold by a person and to distinguish them from goods made or sold by others. Similar marks may be used by different companies if their products do not compete with one another; thus, the name "Atlas" identifies an automobile tire as well as cement, a noncompeting product. Trademarks frequently feature a pictorial symbol, such as the Rock of Gibralter used by an insurance company and the white owl used by a cigar maker. Many trademarks identify a product with some quality in nature, such as strength, fleetness,

Fig. 9-1.

grace, or durability. Automobile manufacturers often name some of their models after animals. Many trademark commodities, particularly tools, carry manufacturer backing in the area of performance or satisfaction. A trademark cannot consist of the flag or coat of arms of the United States, any state, or any foreign government. A trademark will not be registered if it leads to confusion—unless the confusion is unavoidable.

Collective, Service, and Certification Marks

A distinctive mark need not belong to an individual; it can apply to a company or even to a group of persons as a collective mark. Many clothes have a label to show that they have the endorsement or approval of the International Ladies Garment Workers Union (ILGWU), by which they were produced.

Other special marks are service marks that advertise the type of service being offered. The three balls before a pawnshop are derived from the coat of arms of the Medici, a famous Renaissance banking family. Because this symbol is associated by long tradition with the financial transactions of a pawnbroker, the public would not generally assume it signifies a toy shop. Similarly, a red-and-white-striped pole traditionally indicates the presence of a barber. (Early barbers performed surgical operations which are represented by the blood and bandages symbolized in the barber pole.) A notary's seal or the wing emblem worn by stewardesses and airline pilots can also be considered a symbol for a particular official or position.

Trademark Registration

Trademarks, as distinguished from copyrights, are registered in the U.S. Patent Office. Trademark registration is fairly simple. The necessary form can be secured from the Patent Office. Five specimens of drawings and the submission of the filing fee, as indicated on the application form, are all that is required.

Many states also have trademark laws. Of course, a registration within the state will not protect the owner against infringements outside of the state. However, if the business will not operate in interstate commerce, state registration might be adequate for its purposes. Generally, if one takes the trouble to register a trade name or trademark, it is sensible to register it with the U.S. Patent Office just in case one may later wish to expand the business beyond the state borders.

A certificate of registration can remain in force for twenty years and can be renewed for an additional twenty years if application is

---

(FORM FOR USE OF CORPORATION)
(Instructions on reverse side)

APPLICATION FOR TRADEMARK REGISTRATION
(DECLARATION)

Mark ....**CE**...................................
(Identify Mark)

Class No. ....
(Insert number, if known)

TO THE COMMISSIONER OF PATENTS:

1 Consolidated Earmuffs, Inc.

2 a corporation of the State of Georgia

3 1800 Ricardo Blvd., Sequoia, Georgia 33780.

4 Same

The above identified applicant has adopted and is using the trademark shown in the accompanying drawing for 5 earmuffs

and requests that said mark be registered in the United States Patent Office on the Principal Register established by the Act of July 5, 1946.

The trademark was first used on 6 July 7,   , 1972   ; was first used in 7 Territorial   commerce on 8 October 26   , 1972   ; and is now in use in such commerce.

The mark is used by applying it 9 to tags or labels affixed to the products.

and five specimens showing the mark as actually used are presented herewith.

10 C. B. Jones declares that he is 11 President   of applicant corporation and is authorized to make this declaration on behalf of the corporation; he believes said corporation to be the owner of the mark sought to be registered; that to the best of his knowledge and belief no other person, firm, corporation, or association has the right to use said mark in commerce, either in the identical form or in such near resemblance thereto as may be likely, when applied to the goods of such other person, to cause confusion, or to cause mistake, or to deceive; that all statements made herein of his own knowledge are true and that all statements made on information and belief are believed to be true; and further, that these statements were made with the knowledge that willful false statements and the like so made are punishable by fine or imprisonment, or both, under Section 1001 of Title 18 of the United States Code and that such willful false statements may jeopardize the validity of the application or document or any registration resulting therefrom.

.....May 8, 1973.........
(Date)

12 *C. B. Jones*
(Signature)

[Enclose Filing Fee of Thirty-Five Dollars]

POL-304(c) (10-65)

Fig. 9-2. Application for trademark registration.

United States Patent Office

928,194

Registered Feb. 1, 1972

PRINCIPAL REGISTER
Trademark

Ser. No. 313,694, filed Dec. 5, 1968

Laugh-in

George Schlatter-Ed Friendly Productions (joint venture),
and Romart, Inc. (joint venture)
111 Pearl St.
Hartford, Conn.   06103

For: INFLATABLE AND MOLDED TOYS—
NAMELY, FIGURES, DUMMIES, GAVELS, PUNCH-
ING BALLS AND PUNCHING BAGS—in CLASS 22
(INT. CL. 28).
First use on or before Oct. 1, 1968; in commerce on or
before Oct. 1, 1968.

The registered trademark shown above is currently
in use in the George Schlatter-Ed Friendly Productions and Romart, Inc. It will be used in all
promotion and advertising of our products in the
foreseeable future.

George Schlatter
George Schlatter
President

Fig. 9-3. Trademark registration certificate.

made prior to expiration. However, the certificate is automatically
canceled unless the registrant files an affidavit at the end of five
years that the trademark is still being used. If it is merely suspended
temporarily, the affidavit must tell why. The registrant must state
that there is no intention to abandon the mark. This ruling was
instituted to eliminate unused trademarks in the Patent Office.

Copyrights

Copyright protects the owner's creative expression of emotions or
ideas. Books, pamphlets, newspapers, architectural plans, maps,
dramatic compositions, choreographic works, musical compositions,
works of graphic art (both original and reproductions), and motion
pictures are all covered by copyright protection. An artistic invention

is often put under copyright, whereas the mechanical invention of an engineer will be placed under a patent.

It is the act of publication with the copyright notice, following application and payment of a fee, that actually secures copyright protection. This simply means placing on the publication the word "copyright" or the symbol © followed by the year of copyright and the name of the owner, for example, "Copyright 1973, John Smith." In case one changes an original copyright, the new material should contain the original copyright date followed by the new copyright date, for example, "Copyright 1970, 1973, John Smith." The year of the first publication need not be given on a label.

If something is published without the required notice, the right to secure copyright is lost and cannot be restored. To make this notice valid, an application is filed to register the copyright with the Register of Copyrights in Washington, D.C., and accepted by it.

Publishing means communication to third parties. Setting an idea down on paper and leaving it in the writer's desk drawer is not publication. However, showing it to a third party is publication. Therefore, to protect the material, one should publish the material with the proper copyright notice.

Infringements

The granting of a copyright gives its owner an exclusive right to print, reprint, translate, publish, and sell the creation for twenty-eight years. Under certain circumstances it can be renewed for an additional twenty-eight years. Like the owner of a trademark, a copyright holder can sue anyone who substantially reproduces the protected work (either in whole or in part). The court can award damages for past injury and issue an injunction forbidding future violations.

Students, educators, and business people often want to reproduce a portion of an article or book. If the user merely copies the material once for personal convenience, it is believed that this is not a violation of copyright laws since the user is not publishing. If a duplicating machine is being used and the material is not republished in a periodical or book that gets some circulation, the difficulty of proving damages and the cost of litigation pose formidable problems for the copyright owner. Nevertheless, business people should take care to comply with copyright laws.

One who copies the work of another and presents it as one's own is guilty of plagiarism. The careful writer acknowledges sources and obtains permission where necessary.

Patents

A *patent* gives the inventor the exclusive right to use, make, and sell an original, useful, and novel invention for seventeen years. The law is designed to stimulate the new technological developments which are so essential to a thriving industrial economy and to encourage the investment of capital in the manufacture of such inventions.

The filing of the patent application is obviously done after the patent idea or process has been developed and probably tested with a working model. This may involve months and even years of work. Therefore, it is necessary that the matter be protected in the meantime. Further, the developer often wishes to discuss the idea with someone before finalizing it and before filing for a patent. It is felt that such discussion can be held safely only with a lawyer or a most trusted friend to guarantee confidentiality. The lawyer will generally recommend that some immediate steps be taken to record the existence of the idea or process by means of statements, drawings, models and descriptions. These will be dated and authenticated by reliable witnesses.

Anyone who may be contemplating the development of an idea that might eventually be suitable for a patent would find it profitable to write immediately to the U.S. Patent Office for information concerning the manner in which the developments of patented items can be protected and the steps required in patent applications.

An invention is the development of a product or a process. It can involve the improvement of an established article or the development of an entirely new article that is novel, different, useful, not previously obvious to anyone having ordinary skill in the field, and not already patented. The Patent Office determines whether these prerequisites are met when it receives an application. It can issue the patent to one person or to several.

Many times it is the accomplishment of something that forms the basis of a patent that is important; the actual mechanics may be of secondary importance. For example, in the field of atomic energy, it was the successful detonation of the atomic bomb and not the method by which it was achieved which was significant. In other words, the realization that atomic fusion was possible encouraged nuclear physicists around the world to attempt to duplicate the process. Similarly, competitors are constantly on the alert for the development of new products in an effort to exploit the market. For this reason some people do not wish to patent their inventions until they have completed all their arrangements for production and marketing. An early patent application makes the development public knowledge and sometimes discloses the details of manufacturing. This may allow the duplication of the product by a slightly different process, and the benefit of the entire invention is lost to its originator.

Application

In filing a patent application, the inventor gives an exact description of the invention, specifies its purpose, and states that he believes himself to be the first inventor of the object of the patent. The Patent Office then searches its records for earlier patents involving the same ideas and objectives to determine whether the current proposal is original and patentable.

If the proposed invention has been anticipated by another patented device or if it lacks novelty, is inadequately described, or does not work, the Patent Office can reject the application. The rejection letter specifies the reasons for the rejection. The decision is subject to reexamination, and the applicant is entitled to legal representation.

If the patent proposal has any real commercial potential, the inventor should consult legal counsel early. The lawyer will know the Patent Office requirements and can also help in the preparation of the application, designs, drawings, and statements of objectives. If a reexamination is called for, the lawyer can assist in the preparation. The records of all actions taken by the Patent Office, together with any correspondence with lawyers, are kept for a period of five years. A rejection following the reexamination is final.

Interference

A situation known as *interference* occurs when two applications for the same invention are filed by different persons. When interference occurs, a Patent Office proceeding is held to determine who invented the item first. That person will be entitled to the patent.

Patent Pending

Until the patent is granted or refused, the applicant can safely utilize the invention under the designation *"patent pending."* Although competitors may try to exploit the invention by imitating it or copying its usefulness, the inventor is protected by having filed the application.

Effect of a Patent

During the period of patent protection, the owner can make, sell, license, franchise, or use the invention, and can enforce ownership rights against all others in court. The owner may be entitled to treble damages or an injunction to prevent the continued use of the product.

After the patent expires, the invention becomes public property and anyone can make use of it. Even if the owner of the patent has developed an extensive marketing program, others can then make exact replicas and sell them in the same marketing areas. Even local or state unfair-trade-practice laws cannot protect the inventor. To do so would be to make the state laws superior to the United States patent laws.

Assignments and Shop Rights

An inventor's patent rights may be assigned to another individual or a corporation. The assignment should be recorded in the Patent Office within three months to protect the assignee. Assignments are often used where the inventor does not wish to develop the product, does not have the finances to do so, or has an invention that involves a major industry.

A corporation may obtain the patented invention of its employees through shop rights. When employees develop new processes or machines in the course of their employment, using time, materials, and other innovations that they developed in the course of their employment, the patent belongs to the employer. In one case an employee of a major tire manufacturer discovered a new method for manufacturing tires. The new process meant a saving of over $1 million annually. Because the employee used his employer's time and materials, the new process belonged to the employer. The reason for this rule is that the employee acts as an agent of the employer. The agent has a duty to further the employer's business, and therefore the patented item, which the agent developed while on a salary, belongs to the employer. Any other rule could encourage disloyalty, cheating, and perhaps outright thefts of employers' secrets.

Many companies have elaborate plans to encourage their employees to contribute their ideas and knowledge to the improvement of the company product. They offer to share the benefits with the employees. Whether or not they share the benefits, the invention legally belongs to the employer.

MARKETING THE INVENTION OR IDEA

The cost of patenting an invention is relatively minor. The expense begins when the inventor is secure in the knowledge that the proposal is protected by the government and begins to exploit the monopoly. Of the thousands of inventions patented annually, very few are successfully marketed. Although a great deal of money may be spent on product development, the eventual success of the product is not assured.

Development of a Brand Name

Many companies go to great lengths to develop brand names and advertising symbols. An example is Humble Oil Company's expenditure of large sums of money merely to test the sound, appearance, recognition, and recall of proposed names for its service stations. The company was searching for a name that could be used in the United States and foreign countries; therefore it was necessary to test the name in foreign languages as well as in English. An initial list of approximately 10,000 names was narrowed to 200. These were researched further and finally reduced to about 10. The company had to be sure other trade names or trademarks were not infringed upon. The names were tested in the United States and elsewhere. A name that is perfectly acceptable in the United States might have an undesirable connotation in a foreign setting. The final choice was Exxon, but this was only a beginning. The next step involved the installation of signs at the company gasoline stations across the country in states where Exxon operates. By the time the signs were installed, the company had spent millions of dollars on the project.

Exploiting a Patent

Despite the excellence of a patent proposal, it is of little value unless its use can be successfully demonstrated. Many people lack the knowledge to appraise the value of their inventions realistically. Too frequently, they overvalue the inventions and thereby hamper negotiations with people who are willing to help in development. An invention, like any other product, has no value unless it can be sold. This may not be a simple task, because one cannot just go out onto the street and offer the article for sale.

The public is accustomed to making purchases through stores, dealers, and sales people. This suggests a marketing organization. To develop one from the beginning can be a gigantic task that is usually beyond the capacity of the inventor. Therefore, it may be necessary to explore the possibility of licensing a manufacturer who will market the product and give the inventor compensation.

Licensing

Licensing is a way of permitting another to make use of the patented article in return for a royalty. A license may give its holder exclusive rights, or the owner of the patent may wish to license it to other manufacturers. Royalties are usually higher when the holder has exclusive rights to a patent. Franchising agreements are often executed in connection with licensing arrangements. A franchise agreement allows the franchisee to use the inventor's name, trade name or trademark.

A dramatic example of an invention and licensing arrangement involved the Wankel engine, invented by a German, Dr. Wankel. He recognized the potential of his engine, but he knew that it would take time and funds to test and refine it before it could have commercial usefulness. He obtained help from German industrialists and Curtis-Wright, an American corporation which bought the Wankel rights, to improve the designs. The engine was then licensed to a Japanese automobile manufacturer that made further improvements and produced a model for sale.

Meanwhile, in the United States, environmentalists protested the pollution generated by the reciprocating gasoline engine. Congress passed strong laws; the Environmental Protection Agency ordered automobile manufacturers to clean up the exhaust emissions of automobiles. Confronted with the requirements of the federal and state governments, automobile manufacturers began searching for a substitute engine. The Wankel engine, with its different operating principle, offered great potential if it could be developed to meet the needs of the American automobile. General Motors obtained licensing rights to the engine for five years at a cost of $50 million. It is expected to spend several hundred million dollars on engineering work in an effort to put the engine into production. Meanwhile, just about every automobile manufacturer in the world may have obtained some type of licensing agreement on the engine.

Not all inventions are of such proportions. The average inventor is fortunate to make a small discovery that is useful and can be purchased by the public. The inventor may start manufacture either personally or with the aid of a few backers. The market may be held to the local community at first. If the product starts selling, modest expansion will permit increased manufacture. Investors will recognize the potential of the idea, and a larger infusion of capital will enable the product to secure a wider market. The inventor may choose to give over control to a successful manufacturer who wants the product as a part of a large line. Often the decision on whether to release control will depend on the individual's age and resources and on the success of the product.

INVOLVEMENT AND STUDY MATERIAL

Understanding Terms

Trade name	(page 125)	Patent	(page 131)
Trademark	(page 126)	Interference	(page 132)
Copyright	(page 129)	Patent pending	(page 132)
Infringement	(page 130)	Licensing	(page 135)

Questions and Problem Solving

1. Why has the government decided to grant monopolies to business people and inventors?
2. Distinguish between trade names, trademarks, and collective marks and cite examples of each.
3. Describe the procedure for the registration of a trademark.
4. What is the first step that a writer must take to protect a copyright?
5. What is meant by publication?
6. Discuss the problems concerning the use of modern duplicating machines and the copyright laws.
7. What problems confront the owner of a copyright in attempting to prevent unauthorized use of his or her material?
8. Discuss the relative merits of the shop rights of an employer and the work of an employee developing an invention. Does it make

any difference if the employee does not know about the shop-rights laws?

9. When should inventors market their own patented inventions and when should they attempt to secure licensing arrangements?

Cases for Discussion

1. Polyethylene manufacturers encountered difficulty in moving poly-ethylene pellets in conveyer tubes, because they would rub against the pneumatic tube lining leaving a residue that would later dis-lodge and foul the tubes. Large sums of money had been spent by the industry in an attempt to solve the problem.

   Pneumatic conveyance of material is not new. The problem was attacked by making the inside of the tube smoother. Some were highly polished but the problem remained. Schneider, a plaintiff employee, tried to solve the problem by making the inside of the tube rougher. This idea worked and plaintiff ar-ranged to have the process patented. The defendant adopted the idea and sold over 40 systems using this principle. The plaintiff sued for infringement.

   The defendant claimed that the idea was not patentable be-cause it merely described a new use for old apparatus and that it lacked novelty. Furthermore, there were numerous patent ap-plications for pneumatic tubes. The plaintiff relied on the fact that his process and patent involved a deliberate design of rough-ness inside the tubes, and, though roughness may have been a feature of other tubes, the roughness was an unintended result of fabrication and not intended by design. Judgment for whom? Why?

2. Denker was a machinist at the Foremost Machine Company. He noticed that the device used to mount parts for machining did not hold the parts completely secure at all times. He decided to work on a solution to this problem, and using some of the material lying around the shop, he was finally able to make a device to solve this problem. He then filed for a patent on his invention. Denker con-tacted several other machine companies in the area to sell them his invention. The Foremost Machine Company brought suit to prevent Denker from manufacturing and selling this clamping device, claiming that the patent belonged to it under the rule of shop rights. Judgment for whom? Why?

3. Hays invented a bronchial asthma spray and brought suit to have the commissioner of patents issue him a patent on the composition

of his product. Hays's invention was similar to one invented by Keating, on which a patent had already been issued. The inventions use a particular pharmaceutical composition. Hays claimed that since he was using different proportions of drugs in his product, his product was different, and he was thereby entitled to a patent. The commissioner claimed that the invention or product must be distinct and not just different from the Keating invention and that mixing the drugs in different proportions did not make it distinct from Keating's. Judgment for whom? Why?

4. Corcoran brings suit against Montgomery Ward and Company for infringement of the copyright on his poem "Plain Bull," which is thirteen four-line stanzas describing a cowboy's attempt to put his brand on a maverick bull. Montgomery Ward is selling recordings of the poem set to music without Corcoran's permission. Corcoran claims this is an infringement of his rights, since the poem is protected by the Copyright Act. Corcoran claims that his poem has been recorded in the form of a drama using the characters, action, plot, and dialogue from his poem. Montgomery Ward claims that all it did was reproduce the words of the poem in combination with music, and Corcoran has no right to copyright protection of the music. The copyright law allows composers the exclusive right of recording their copyrighted musical compositions as well as dramatic works. Judgment for whom? Why?

PART TWO

BUSINESS ORGANIZATIONS

Chapter Ten

Sole Proprietorship

Before starting a business, one must first determine its form, its organization, and the nature of its operations. Will it be individually owned and operated, or will it involve others? To answer that question, one must become familiar with the types of business organizations that can be chosen.

To own and operate one's own business is the goal of many individuals. The prospect of success so excites the imagination that reality can become a little blurred. Often decisions about the form of the enterprise are overlooked because the prospective business person has not realized their importance.

Basically, there are three forms of capitalistic enterprise: the *sole proprietorship*, the *partnership*, and the *corporation*. We shall consider them in that order, beginning with the sole proprietorship because this is the form of most new businesses.

ADVANTAGES OF SOLE PROPRIETORSHIP

There is nothing formal about a sole proprietorship; it simply means that a person has set up a business in which he or she alone has an interest. As a form of business, it has definite advantages for the owner. At least four of these will be discussed here.

Freedom of Action

Being one's own boss has great appeal for the starting entrepreneur. One can set one's own standards of performance and rules of behavior, theoretically at least. If one wants to sleep late or take a day off to go fishing, there will be no one to prevent it. One can work as late as desired and maintain the hours of one's choice. If one wants to change some line of business, one can do so without consultation and without concern for what others may think. The absence of restraints and the great independence inherent in the sole proprietorship make this form of business very attractive.

Ownership of the Net Profits

The sole proprietor knows that he or she alone will enjoy the profits of the business. There is no question of dividing them among several persons. What is earned by the business belongs to the owner. Of course, funds must be set aside for taxes, maintenance, and new equipment, just as in any other business, but the net profits will belong to the sole proprietor alone.

Unified Control

A substantial advantage of the sole proprietorship is the concentration of authority in the owner. This provides the business with unified control and responsibility. The proprietor will often hire other workers but will retain the power to direct the organization. It is the proprietor who decides how many will be employed and the kind of work they will do. The harmony of the workers and the success of the enterprise are determined by the personality, leadership, and drive of the proprietor. Most sole proprietorships are small, which ensures that the work units are also small. This increases the opportunity for closer team work between the owner and the employees, and helps them to identify with the goals of the proprietor. Consequently, there may be fewer labor troubles and less worker dissension.

Ease of Dissolution

The sole proprietor may eventually want to retire or may be forced to discontinue doing business for other reasons. To wind up affairs will be relatively easy, for the proprietor is working alone. True, if employees have been hired, they must now be discharged. Nevertheless, the unified control which characterizes the sole proprietorship simplifies the process of dissolving the business. The sole proprietor can make decisions quickly.

DISADVANTAGES OF SOLE PROPRIETORSHIP

Every worthwhile thing has a price. Occasionally, one may not notice it at first glance, but it is still there. Despite its great advantages, the sole proprietorship has serious disadvantages. Before deciding to embark on the great adventure of establishing a business, one should study some sobering statistics.

The United States Department of Commerce reports that about 50 percent of all businesses are liquidated within two years of their start. Only about 30 percent survive four years, and over 80 percent are out of business within ten years. The high mortality rate of new businesses warrants a sobering look at the problems facing them.

Need for Managerial Ability

The desire to be one's own boss is often so strong that the new sole proprietor fails to recognize the need for managerial ability and a disciplined approach to a new business venture. The idea that it is possible to take a day off, go fishing, or sleep late does not fit the facts of life. The owner who thinks there is no boss will soon find out how wrong that is. One look at the statistics should reveal that only the person who has been forced to liquidate can sleep as late as he desires.

According to Dun & Bradstreet, Inc., lack of managerial aptitude and experience accounted for about 90 percent of the more than one million failures in the space of a century.

Business is a jealous and exacting taskmaster. It does not forgive any failure to attend to its wants and often requires the owner to work harder and longer than any employee. Every customer is a boss far more demanding than most employers.

Lack of Continuity

The ease of making business decisions, which is so appealing to the sole proprietor, may not be as attractive to customers who cannot get goods or to creditors who may not be paid. In the event of failing health or death of the owner, the business may have to be liquidated, and employees do not feel secure in a business that has made no provision for continuity. The value of continuity and stability cannot be ignored in deciding upon the form of the business enterprise.

Handicap of Size

The small size of the beginning venture creates difficulties in securing adequate and competent labor. Many people will not be attracted to such an enterprise because it rarely offers the opportunity for promotions or attractive fringe benefits. It may not be able to provide group insurance programs unless it can do so through some trade association. Once the business succeeds in getting employees, it has to provide steady work and avoid seasonal fluctuations. To do so, it may be necessary to stockpile products, which requires capital that could be used for other purposes. A small business may find such a situation extremely difficult.

PREPARATION FOR BUSINESS

Starting a new enterprise deserves serious thought. A business will never begin unless an idea is put into action, but every new business needs the right kind of action. There will be employees to be hired, payrolls to be met, and equipment and building facilities to be secured. Most important will be the development of the managerial approach.

Functions of a Business

Every business involves the following basic functions:

General management

Finances	Sales advertising	Planning
Accounting	Production	Record keeping
Purchasing	Personnel	Risk management (insurance)
Inventory	Shipping	Tax analysis
Warehousing	Planning	Controls
Maintenance	Customer relations	

A specific business will have to add other functions that correspond to its particular needs. The individual owner will recognize the need for long-range planning, cost controls, budget preparation, and a system of controls which will inform the owner that the operation is proceeding according to plan. After preparing a list of functions, the entrepreneur must determine individual ability to perform the outlined tasks. Some will be more important and more difficult to perform than others.

Each function should be separately examined. Can the owner perform it? If not, is it possible to employ someone who can? It would be folly to start a sole proprietorship and risk one's time, money, and career without a study of the most important asset: the owner. The analysis should be committed to paper; then faults can be spotted and corrections made on a rational basis. This also gives the prospective sole proprietor an opportunity to display managerial and planning ability. One who is incapable of making a careful analysis of potential may be incapable of managing a business after it is started.

Business Aptitudes

The ability to perform the various functions of a business is essential to the success of the new business. In addition, the personality traits of the owner are important since the owner will be that business's most important employee. The Small Business Administration has prepared a rating scale for evaluating personal traits important to the proprietor of a business.

Personnel departments of many large companies utilize similar charts in evaluating prospective employees. These are in no sense psychological tests but merely devices to help determine the aptitude

TABLE 10-1

What Caused 10,326 Businesses to Fail in 1971?

		Manu-facturers (%)	Whole-salers (%)	Retailers (%)	Con-struc-tion (%)	Commer-cial services (%)	All (%)
Neglect due to	Bad habits	0.3	0.9	0.5	0.4	0.5	0.5
	Poor health	0.4	1.7	0.9	0.8	0.7	0.8
	Marital difficulties	0.1	—	0.2	0.2	0.2	0.1
	Other	0.5	—	0.3	0.3	0.2	0.3
Fraud on the part of the	Misleading name	0.1	0.2	0.1	0.1	0.1	0.1
principals, reflected by	False financial statement	0.4	0.7	0.2	0.3	0.1	0.3
	Premeditated overbuy		0.2				0.1
	Irregular disposal of assets	0.4	0.6	0.5	0.3	0.4	0.4
	Other	0.4	0.3	0.4	0.1	0.5	0.3
Lack of experience* in the	Inadequate sales	47.0	42.7	45.4	40.1	48.4	45.3
line evidenced by inability to	Heavy operating expenses	11.6	9.3	7.0	9.6	9.2	8.8
avoid conditions which	Receivables difficulties	15.6	15.9	3.8	13.7	6.8	9.1
resulted in	Inventory difficulties	3.7	5.8	6.3	0.8	0.5	4.2
	Excessive fixed assets	5.8	1.7	2.4	2.5	6.9	3.7
	Poor location	0.8	1.5	6.9	0.6	2.7	3.7
	Competitive weakness	21.5	25.2	26.8	31.1	24.3	26.0
	Other	6.5	7.8	2.8	3.3	4.9	4.4
Disasters, some of which	Fire	0.3	0.7	0.6	0.3	0.3	0.5
could have been provided	Flood	0.1	—	—	—	—	0.0
against through insurance	Burglary	0.1	—	0.2	—	—	0.1
	Employees' fraud	0.1	0.5	0.1	0.1	0.0	0.1
	Strike	0.0	0.2	0.0	0.3	0.0	0.1
	Other	0.5	0.2	0.7	0.1	0.3	0.5

TABLE 10-1—Continued

	Manu-facturers (%)	Whole-salers (%)	Retailers (%)	Con-struc-tion (%)	Commer-cial services (%)	All (%)
Reason unknown	2.1	2.2	2.7	3.3	3.5	2.8
Total						
Percent of total failures	18.7	9.3	42.9	14.9	14.2	100.0
Number of failures	1,932	957	4,428	1,545	1,464	10,326
Average liabilities per failure	$368,846	$189,083	$100,290	$183,290	$243,800	$185,641

* Experience not well rounded in sales, finance, purchasing, and production on the part of the individual in case of a proprietor-ship, or of two or more partners or officers constituting a management unit.

Classification of failures based on opinion of informed creditors and information in Dun & Bradstreet Reports. Copyright Dun & Bradstreet, Inc. Used with permission.

of an individual to fit into the proposed business atmosphere. In addition to self-rating, the prospective sole proprietor could have a friend ask other acquaintances to evaluate certain qualities anonymously. The result may be startling and give pause.

Evaluation Aids

Because starting a new business is not a simple act, any information which sheds light on the subject should be welcome. There are many sources that can prove helpful. The local bank should be one of the first to be consulted. Dun & Bradstreet, Inc., publishes material that may be particularly useful, such as *Key Business Ratios* and *Cost of Doing Business* for proprietorships and partnerships. Its quarterly analysis of business failures should be examined in order to profit from the mistakes of others and permit the introduction of preventive measures when they can do some good.

TABLE 10-2

Business Aptitudes

Instructions: Place a check mark on the line following each trait where you think it ought to be. The check mark need not be placed directly over one of the guide phrases, because the rating may lie somewhere between the phrases.

Initiative			
Additional tasks sought; highly ingenious	Resourceful; alert to opportunities	Regular work performed without awaiting directions	Routine worker awaiting directions

Attitude toward others			
Positive; friendly interest in people	Pleasant, polite	Sometimes without awaiting directions	Inclined to be quarrelsome or unco-operative

Leadership			
Forceful, inspiring confidence and loyalty	Order giver	Driver	Weak

Responsibility			
Responsibility sought and welcomed	Accepted without protest	Unwilling to assume without protest	Avoided whenever possible

TABLE 10-2—Continued

Organizing ability			
Highly capable of perceiving and arranging fundamentals in logical order	Able organizer	Fairly capable of organizing	Poor organizer
Industry			
Industrious; capable of working hard for long hours	Can work hard, but not for too long a period	Fairly industrious	Hard work avoided
Decision			
Quick and accurate	Good and careful	Quick, but often unsound	Hesitant and fearful
Sincerity			
Courageous, square-shooter	On the level	Fairly sincere	Inclined to lack sincerity
Perseverance			
Highly steadfast in purpose; not discouraged by obstacles	Effort steadily maintained	Average determination and persistence	Little or no persistence
Physical energy			
Highly energetic at all times	Energetic most of time	Fairly energetic	Below average

SOURCE: Small Business Administration, *Starting and Managing a Small Business of Your Own,* The Starting and Managing Series, vol. 1, 2d ed.

The Small Business Administration publishes several useful booklets. For example, one is titled *Starting and Managing a Small Business of Your Own.* A complete list of publications is available from the local office of the Small Business Administration or from the Superintendent of Documents, U.S. Government Printing Office, Washington, D.C.

Another important source of information is the trade association, which can provide useful data about business practices, statistics, and answers to specific questions. Prospective suppliers are also a source of potential information. Finally, one should not neglect friendly local business people. They have a fund of knowledge that they may be willing to share.

INITIAL FINANCING

Although some failures of new businesses are attributed to lack of managerial ability, many others can be traced to the proprietor's inadequate attention to finances. The prospective business person may have enough money to open a business, but having enough to continue until the business becomes self-sustaining is another matter.

It is said that to borrow money, one first has to be able to show it is not needed. In view of the high rate of failure noted above, a starting business is not a bright prospect for a loan. No money should be solicited without first making a detailed analytical plan. The plan will be subjected to review and criticism by prospective money lenders. If the criticisms are valid, changes should be made when they can be made at minimum cost.

Commercial Banks

Banks are not anxious to supply venture capital for a business that does not have a record of success. A new business is an unknown quantity; therefore loans available will probably be short term. The new business generally needs a longer-term loan of a year or more. The local bank should not be neglected, but the business person should also consider other sources of capital.

Government Credit Guarantees

Congress has recognized the difficulties faced by the new business in securing adequate credit. Accordingly, the Small Business Administration helps the new business establish a line of credit until the business can become self-supporting. Various agencies have been set up that may apply to special situations. The local office of the Small Business Administration can give advice about these agencies. The local bank may have had experience with government agencies guaranteeing lines of credit and may be able to assist the business person in making the initial contacts.

Credit from Business Sources

Everyone starting a new business should study the availability of credit from suppliers. Many suppliers are interested in helping a new business become established. It may mean a new outlet for the supplier's product. However, a supplier or seller extending credit performs a service very similar to that of a bank; money is being tied up that could be used elsewhere or invested in income-producing securities. The seller may even have to borrow money to extend credit to the buyer, and therefore will want some assurances from the new business that the venture has a chance of success.

Some sellers can extend reasonably long-term credit to a starting business under various plans: installment payments, deferred payments, charge cards, and charge accounts. The cost of such credit should be examined closely before relying upon it. If the invoice shows that the terms are "Two percent off if paid within 10 days— net due in 30 days," it may seem attractive to take advantage of the free thirty-day credit. However, a closer look will reveal that the buyer is getting free credit for only ten days. After that one is forfeiting 2 percent on the money that is kept for another twenty days. In other words, the buyer is paying 2 percent for the twenty days of extra credit. This amounts to 36 percent annually. (There are 18 twenty-day periods in a year; hence $2 \times 18 = 36$.) Substantially better rates can be secured from other lending institutions.

Installment Buying

The practice of installment buying is popular today. Deferred payment terms can be extended for long periods of time, even beyond the usual charge account time. However, the interest payments can also become substantial. For this reason, people in business should note the installment charges, terms, practices, and interest rates. Although the rate of 18 percent may not seem like much on a small outstanding balance, it can mount up to a substantial sum over an extended period. Many suppliers of equipment will extend credit on much more favorable terms, sometimes on terms that cannot be matched by other lending institutions. Therefore, it pays to examine terms carefully and select the seller who offers the best terms in both initial and final price after the interest charges have been added. The final price will reveal whether a hidden interest charge is included in the quoted price of merchandise. Low interest charges alone do not guarantee favorable credit terms. For example, a machine quoted at $1,000 with three years to pay at 3 percent interest appears to offer very good credit terms. The final cost will be the $30 per year interest plus the $1,000, or a total of $1,090. However, a similar machine quoted at $700 with one-year terms at 7 percent interest will cost only $749 at the end of the one year. Assuming that the buyer had to borrow the money for an additional two years, even if it were borrowed at 7 percent the equipment would have cost only another $98. Thus, total cost of the machine at the higher interest rate would only be $847 against the $1,090 of the so-called easy credit.

Whatever the cost, installment-plan purchasing enables someone beginning in business to start an enterprise before having amassed great amounts of capital. Installment plans require the participant to have the discipline to meet payments on time while enjoying the use of objects so purchased. However, they may foster overoptimism. One may be tempted to buy too much and become overindebted. Consequently, installment purchases should be limited in time, number, and value.

In every installment purchase, a formal contract is involved. It specifies the amount of down payment by the buyer and the security owed the seller for the unpaid balance. In many cases, the purchaser does not really own the goods until the title passes upon making the last payment. The Uniform Commercial Code sets out the manner in which the seller retains a security interest in goods sold on installment plans.

Some installment sales contracts, called *add-on contracts*, have provisions that permit additional purchases after the principal sum owing on the first purchase has been reduced. Failure to pay one or more installments under such a contract may result in forfeiture of everything purchased under the contract. This can cause serious problems for the purchaser, and it is best to insist on insertion of a provision clearing title to any items which are fully paid for. The state and federal consumer protection laws should also be examined when a forfeiture is threatened.

Personal Finance Companies and Credit Unions

The prospective borrower is not restricted to banks in his quest for funds but can also turn to personal finance companies and credit unions. Personal finance companies are organized to lend money at a rate of interest based on the risk. Credit unions are cooperative institutions for money lending. Both institutions require less security than banks, but the interest rates may be higher. These sources of funds should not be ignored when establishing a business.

Interest Charges

In all credit arrangements, the buyer must be particularly careful about the amount of interest that is included in the purchase price or the carrying charges. There may be usury statutes making interest rates over a certain amount illegal. As indicated above, a high interest rate may be disguised in the purchase price with apparently easier credit terms.

In 1968 Congress passed the Consumer Protection Act, popularly known as the Truth in Lending Act, which requires full disclosure of the interest charges, finder's fees, cost of credit investigation, and any insurance charges protecting the creditor against a credit loss. States have enacted similar laws, and generally interest rates cannot exceed 18 percent on an annual basis. The effectiveness of these laws depends upon the awareness of the buyer. Many buyers utilize installment payments in such a manner that they are completely unaware of the charges heaped upon them in their purchase contracts. Instead they are merely interested in the cost to them each month. If an unscrupulous merchant includes usurious interest in his charges, there is little danger that anyone will complain to the authorities unless the buyer examines the charges that are included in the total price. The wise person will examine all costs carefully and recognize the cost of money.

FRANCHISING

One of the fastest growing fields for the individual with small resources is the franchise business. It is estimated that the total number of franchise establishments is approaching one-half million and involves more than $130 billion.

Franchise agreements may not involve patented items but deal with marketing processes. The holder of a particularly successful trade name will agree to allow another to operate a business under that name. This enables a businessman with low capital to engage in a business of his own. Examples of such franchises are familiar to everyone: hamburger, pizza, fried chicken, beverage, and roast beef stands; motels; automobile dealers; and department stores.

Franchising Agreements

The franchiser agrees to permit another to use a trade name or trademark and to guide the business in its operations by providing counseling in the selection of a business site, financing, training of employees, advertising, and product knowledge. The agreement guarantees adequate territory and freedom from other competing identical franchises in the same marketing area.

In turn, the franchisee has to agree to follow the directions of the franchiser and to use the franchiser's products, designs of buildings, business signs, and practices. The franchisee must be prepared to secure the necessary employees, equipment, and financing. The arrangement becomes a type of joint venture because the franchise user is not wholly independent.

Franchises are created by contract. The franchiser may want to include restrictions in regard to the sale or transfer by the franchisee. Most grants are for a fixed term with an option for extension. Permanent grants will not be favored because they can impede ordinary business dealings. Moreover, the typical franchise can be terminated by the parties. This may occur through mutual consent, abandonment, misuse, and nonuse. Arbitrary revocation will be permitted only if the right to do so has been reserved in the contract.

Franchise relationships are subject to the applicability of other branches of the law. Consequently, the court can apply the principles of what is conscionable, or what will protect the solitary or lower-income party, to any interpretation of the franchise agreement. Warranties and antitrust laws also enter into franchising.

Government Regulations

Because of the large sums of money required to start any kind of business, federal and state governments have become concerned about the manner in which the franchise agreements are being secured. Unscrupulous franchisers have attempted to cash in on the popularity of franchising. As a result, advertisements for investors in franchising agreements have come under the scrutiny of the Federal Trade Commission and state securities regulators. At least ten states have enacted laws to protect the new investors against exploitation.

The franchiser is required to furnish state officials with copies of the proposed franchising agreement and a statement of the franchiser's capital structure to ensure that the investor will be able to get the help being promised. State officials are also interested in the number of successful franchises operating under a particular franchiser in the state and in the nation. Therefore, they want to know the number of businesses that have lasted over five years. If these ratios are satisfactory, there is a greater likelihood that the franchiser will provide the one starting in business with the guidance suggested by the franchise agreement.

If the franchiser is selling stock to the general public, the Securities and Exchange Commission also investigates the genuineness of the franchise operation. It has taken steps to make the franchiser furnish adequate information to the investor as well as to provide the promised guidance.

The individual starting a business under a franchise should contact the Securities and Exchange Commission and the state securities commissioner. They may have valuable information about the particular franchiser. The business person should also request a prospectus from the franchiser. State regulations also attempt to prevent false advertising and fraudulent or deceptive offers of franchises. These laws empower the securities commissioner to halt illegal promotion and offering of franchises.

Other branches of the government are also concerned with the franchise operation. Antitrust regulations apply insofar as they pertain to prices, restrictions on the activity of the franchisee, and requirements that one buy certain products only from the franchiser. For example, the courts have held that gasoline station franchises which prohibited the operator from buying tires, batteries, and other accessories from anyone but the franchiser were illegal.

Financing

Franchising generally involves an initial fee of perhaps $10,000. Thereafter, the franchisee will be expected to pay royalties or periodic sums for the use of the trademark or trade name, continuing supervision, inspection, and marketing advice. A bookkeeping system must be set up that accords with other franchise operations. Tax services will be offered for an additional fee.

Capital requirements for some franchises, such as an automobile dealership, are often high. However, the Small Business Administration may be able to help one make such necessary financial arrangements as paying the franchise fee and buying equipment and other facilities. Money lenders are more inclined to favor a franchising arrangement than they are an individual venture because of the assurance offered by the guidance of a proven and successful franchiser.

The Socioeconomic Significance of Franchises

Merchants in the deprived urban areas have often been outsiders, and it is against these merchants that much racial hatred and riot destruction have been directed. Through franchising, the individuals from within the neighborhood are now being offered a chance to become independent business people. Of course, they must be prepared to work long, hard hours and to follow instructions. In return, they may find credit easier to obtain because they are associated with a known business rather than starting out entirely on their own.

It should be noted that most franchises deal with service industries or product marketing and that neither services nor sales are self-generating. When considering a franchise agreement, it is well to bear in mind the causes of business failures discussed earlier in this chapter. Although the franchiser arrangement offers some security from poor management, it does not guarantee proper management of one's habits and willingness to work. The advantages and disadvantages of franchising should be carefully weighed.

INVOLVEMENT AND STUDY MATERIAL

Understanding Terms

Sole proprietorship	(page 140)	Add-on contract	(page 151)
Unified control	(page 141)	Consumer Protection Act	
Managerial ability	(page 142)	(Truth in Lending Act)	
Business aptitudes	(page 147)		(page 152)
Installment plans	(page 150)	Franchising	(page 152)

Questions and Problem Solving

1. Why does a sole proprietorship stand a good chance of having less labor troubles than another form of business?

2. Discuss the advantages and disadvantages of the sole proprietorship.

3. What is the biggest single factor leading to business failures according to the Dun & Bradstreet figures? Why is this so? Discuss contributing factors.

4. Explain the statement that the ultimate boss of the sole proprietor is the customer.

5. Why is it necessary to prepare a list of functions in planning a sole proprietorship?

6. How can analysis of personality traits aid in planning for a business?

7. Why are many young people not attracted to a sole proprietorship?

8. Explain why a sole proprietorship may have difficulty obtaining financing and list several sources of possible funds and the advantages of each.

9. Discuss the relationship and function of the Small Business Administration with regard to the sole proprietorship.

10. How can high interest rates be hidden in the cost of merchandise?

11. Describe the advantages and disadvantages of franchising agreements for the sole proprietor.

12. Why has the government become interested in the franchise business?

13. Describe the socioeconomic significance of franchises.

Cases for Discussion

1. Hartley, age 45, had been a construction worker for many years. Several years ago he joined a local group that made ceramics as a hobby. Hartley became particularly good in making fine porcelains and other fine art items. Occasionally the members of the group were able to sell some of their products at high prices. Hartley priced similar products at various stores and was amazed at the retail prices of items that he could make. He estimated that retail prices were marked up as much as 300 percent over wholesale prices. He figured that an investment of $36,000 would enable him to start a commercial operation. He calculated that he could make certain items that should bring him at least $2,000 per month. He had $18,000 in savings. The $36,000 would

allow the purchase of the necessary equipment and a reserve for seven months to permit getting started. The manufacturing process for ceramic objects is relatively short, and Hartley figured he would be able to start selling his products about six weeks after getting started. Should Hartley quit his job and go into the ceramics business? Why or why not?

2. Tarello was a sales manager for a hardware company and earned $15,000 per year. He disliked the amount of travel his job required and he wanted to be able to spend more time with his family. He read an article on franchises in a business magazine and was impressed with the possibility of having a business of his own. He contacted a franchiser of a hamburger chain. A representative displayed figures taken from similar established operations that were producing a profit of $25,000 and more. The franchiser pointed out that start-up costs were at least $35,000. The franchiser would help in the selection of a site and in starting the business. This would include training in food preparation and the like. Tarello discussed the matter with his wife and son, who was in a local college. Both agreed to work with Tarello to help him get started. The son had two more years of college but would be able to work after school and on weekends. Tarello had $22,000 in savings and could borrow $25,000 from his brothers. The business site available was a corner location on a prominent street that was torn up and being widened. The street work was scheduled to be completed at about the same time the hamburger shop construction would be completed. Should Tarello quit his job and accept the franchise? Give reasons to support your answer.

3. Albert Moeller had worked in the foundry of the Able Corporation for 35 years. He was now 60 years of age and the company had a mandatory retirement age of 62. Albert had saved $22,000 and calculated his potential retirement income at about $400 per month. He felt that it would not be adequate to maintain himself and his wife while his youngest son was still in school. Therefore, he looked around for a business opportunity that would provide him with additional income for at least another five to ten years. Besides, he always wanted to be a businessman and dreamed of the independence and security he could obtain if he were in business for himself.

He discovered a food franchiser that offered the opportunity he wanted. It involved an investment of $15,000, and the balance would be financed by the franchiser. The franchiser agreed to select a suitable site, furnish the design of the building, and supply the initial guidance. Albert discussed the project with his son, who was only lukewarm to the idea. Albert's wife was very concerned that the project might prove a failure, and she urged Albert to abandon the idea. She pointed out that both Albert and she were 60 years old and suffered from high blood pressure. She was worried that neither of them could work long hours, and she felt that taking on the franchise would demand at least 14-hour days. It was her opinion that they would be unable to do the required work. She urged Albert to seek some other opportunity which would enable them to finance their son through school.

What advice would you give to Mr. and Mrs. Moeller? What do you think of an individual who is approaching retirement age investing most of his or her savings in a business venture?

Chapter Eleven

Partnership

A *partnership* is an association of two or more persons to carry on a business for profit. When they make no decision as to their form of business, the law presumes that it is a partnership. Much of what was said about the sole proprietorship is true of the partnership, although profits, rights of management, and decision making have to be shared. This is offset by the sharing of losses and a potential additional source of capital.

NATURE OF A PARTNERSHIP

Most states have adopted the Uniform Partnership Act. It defines a partnership, provides rules for those situations where the partners are not covered by an agreement, and extends powers to the partnership that it would not possess under the common law. The act outlines the responsibility of the individual partners, their title to partnership property, the relations of partners to persons dealing with the partnership, the relations of the partners with each other, their property rights, and the provisions for dissolving and winding up the enterprise. However, a partnership agreement should be prepared before beginning the business arrangement.

Types of Partners

There are so many types of partners that a full discussion of all of them is impossible here. However, we shall examine the most frequent partnership arrangements.

General Partners

The most common arrangement is the *general partnership*. A general partner may enter the partnership as a result of a financial contribution, knowledge, or some special asset, with or without taking an active part in the management of the business. A partner will share in the profits according to some predetermined ratio. Usually the partners benefit according to their investment in the business.

The most noteworthy aspect of a general partnership is that there is unlimited liability for the losses of the business. The partnership assets are expended first to cover the losses, but if they are not enough, the personal assets of any partner can be seized by the creditors without regard to the partnership agreement. A general partner may be able to recover a contribution from other solvent partners under their partnership agreement.

Limited Partners

A *limited partnership* enables a person to invest money in a partnership without sharing in its management. Most states have a limited partnership act which specifies that the partners must prepare a formal statement (under oath) which sets out the name, location, and character of the business and other pertinent data. In addition, they must declare the amount of the investment by the limited partner, his or her share of the profits, and the rights of the general partners. This certificate must be filed with the appropriate government office, usually the county registrar of deeds. The limited partner's name cannot be a part of the firm name. Thus, the limited partner avoids liability for the debts of the partnership exceeding the amount invested. Failure to make and file the formal statement makes one a general partner.

Silent Partners

A *silent partner* is one who takes no active part in the business. The limited partner is always a silent partner. However, there may be other partners who are not interested in taking an active role in managing the business; for example, a general partner may be away a good part of the time or have other business interests. Such inactivity makes one a silent partner, but still liable for all debts.

Secret Partners

A *secret partner* is one who is unknown to outsiders but who takes an active part in the management of the business and shares the profits according to some prearranged ratio. The law does not favor the secret partner. If such an individual becomes known, he or she is held liable for the debts of the partnership in the same manner as any general partner.

Dormant Partners

A *dormant partner*, who is both silent and secret, does not take any active role in the business and is unknown to outsiders. Such a partner also becomes fully liable for the firm's debts when discovered.

Nominal or Ostensible Partners

Occasionally a person seems to be a partner but is only a *nominal* or *ostensible partner*, usually to induce a creditor to lend money or extend credit. Of course, if any representation was made in someone's name without the knowledge of that individual, the creditor cannot hold that person liable as a partner. When a person knows that his or her name is being wrongly used in connection with a partnership, there is an affirmative duty to stop it, possibly by a newspaper advertisement which gives notice to prospective creditors. Alternatively, one can bring suit for an injunction against making such false representations. This is probably the most effective way to force the other party to discontinue the unauthorized use of one's name and to avoid partnership liability.

Joint Ventures

These are informal enterprises in which several people may join for a limited purpose and a limited time while continuing their normal business. For example, construction companies form joint ventures for extremely large projects while each carries on its own separate enterprises.

Liabilities of a joint venture are generally governed by the law of partnerships. The joint venturers, like general partners, can be liable for the wrongs committed by the venture's members. Liability for their contracts may not be so clear. Generally, in a joint venture, one of the members is appointed manager. Persons dealing with the venture are expected to check the managerial authority of the person they deal with.

The Name of the Partnership

Normally, partners want to use their own names in establishing the partnership. Thus Hiram White and Abraham Black might call their new business "White and Black Company." Suppose, however, that for some reason they wish to do business under a fictitious name like "Twin Hills." Most states have a fictitious-name statute which requires that such names be recorded with the appropriate government office. The purpose of this act is to permit potential creditors to identify the real parties who are operating the business. If the business arrangement is a partnership, the creditors will be able to identify them, and the assets of the partnership as well as the assets of the individual partners will be available to satisfy creditors.

PARTNERSHIP RELATIONSHIPS

Each partner has a *fiduciary duty* toward the other partners, that is, a duty of good faith and utmost loyalty that the courts enforce strictly. One partner cannot take advantage of another for self-enrichment at the expense of the partnership. If one makes a profit with the consent of the others, it is held as a trust for the partners. In return the partnership owes a duty to the individual partner to allow each a share in the profits.

Management

Unless the partnership agreement provides otherwise, each partner has a right to share in the management of the business. Since the partnership agreement arises from a personal arrangement, partners can make almost any arrangement for managing the business. They can divide the power equally or delegate most of it to one or several partners. If no specific provision is made concerning this in the partnership agreement, article 18(e) of the Uniform Partnership Act states: "All partners have equal rights in the management and conduct of the partnership business."

Article 18 then continues: "Any difference arising as to ordinary matters connected with the partnership business may be decided by a majority of the partners; but no act in contravention of any agreement between the partners may be done rightfully without the consent of all the partners." This, too, is an important ruling. Of course, the partners can provide otherwise in their agreement. They might prefer to give the deciding vote to the senior partner, to an executive committee, or even to their lawyer. If they disagree to an extent where no compromise solution can be reached, the relationship itself may have to be dissolved. The threat of withdrawal leading to the dissolution of the flourishing firm can be a strong card in the hands of any partner in cases of disagreement.

Centralization of management can be a major problem in a partnership. Suppose the number of partners increases steadily as business expands, demanding more skills and more capital. Perhaps they will be scattered in branch offices throughout the country. Yet each has, in theory at least, an equal voice in the conduct of the business of the whole enterprise. How is this best exercised in the interests of the firm? To prevent the arrangement from becoming too unwieldy, the partners may have to delegate certain responsibilities to various committees, including an executive committee, thus undercutting the theoretical equality and personal control of the business which are such favorable features of partnerships.

As was pointed out in the last chapter, every business has specific functions. A well-organized partnership will have studied the strengths and weaknesses of its membership and made provision for the best utilization of its strengths. Thus one partner may become the director of finances; another, production; another, sales; and in that way management duties will become well defined. A business maxim states that what is everybody's business becomes nobody's business. People beginning in business would do well to remember it and provide for a clear assignment of duties before the business is started.

Financial Arrangements

The problem of financing a new partnership is no different from that of financing a sole proprietorship. However, the proposed partnership raises some other financial problems. These concern the expected profits that will be available for salaries of the new partners. The facts, as indicated by the mortality rate for new businesses, indicate that profit is frequently overestimated. This means that partners may be forced to survive on their own capital far longer than they had anticipated. The time to examine this problem is before the prospective partners leave old jobs and cut off all other sources of income. A sole proprietor has to attend to the business. This may be neither necessary nor wise for all the partners.

Partnership Accounting

Each partner has a right to inspect the books of the business and to be kept informed about the state of the venture. If additional partners are contemplated, any partner can object to their admission. Because of the fiduciary relationship between the parties, it would be unfair to force an unwelcome associate upon the unwilling partner.

Each partner is obligated to release any and all information concerning the partnership to the other partners. If a partner dies, the surviving partners must furnish information to the representatives of the deceased's estate. In other words, a fiduciary relationship means that the partners must deal fairly with each other at all times.

When the partnership is dissolved, the partners are entitled to an accounting. If they cannot get one voluntarily, the court will grant a decree requiring it. A partnership which continues beyond its original term without a new agreement merely continues the old agreement at will.

Agency among Partners

The law of agency applies to members of a partnership. Of course, the limited partner does not take any active part in the business and would not be an agent. Other partners are agents of each other when they are acting for the partnership. The partnership agreement may restrict authority to particular individuals, but such limitation would not be binding upon third parties unless they have actual notice of it.

A partner has the express authority conferred by the other partners and, in addition, that implied authority which is reasonably necessary to do whatever is authorized. There may also be apparent or perceived authority resulting from the conduct of the other partners.

The Uniform Partnership Act denies the authority of the partner to do the following:

1. Assign the partnership property in trust for creditors
2. Assign the partnership property on the assignee's promise to pay
3. Dispose of the good will of the business
4. Do any other act which would make it impossible to carry on the ordinary business of the partnership
5. Confess a judgment
6. Submit a partnership claim or liability to arbitration or reference

If real estate is owned in the name of the partnership, any partner may convey the property. The conveyance can be set aside by other partners if they show that the partner did not have actual authority to make such conveyance. This is not a harsh rule since the buyer would have had notice that partnership property was involved and should have verified the authority.

Admissions or statements of one partner, in connection with the business, will bind the other partners. Similarly, if information important to the partnership comes to one of the partners, the other partners are legally bound by such notice.

In general, a partner has whatever authority is needed to conduct the work. If the business is a store, each partner has the authority to sell the goods. A partner has the power to buy merchandise and ask that it be delivered on credit. Normally the authority to buy merchandise not customarily stocked by the business is not within the scope of such apparent authority. Neither can one go to the bank and borrow a sum of money which is proportionately high in comparison to the net worth of the business.

LIABILITY

The normal partnership agreement is generally concerned with a profit in accordance with some predetermined ratio. When the partnership is being formed, liability for the acts of others seems so remote that it may not occur to the parties. Some routine losses in business are expected, but the partners assume that the business will normally show a profit. Often, only when the business gets into serious financial troubles does the partner become aware of the rule that each general partner is individually liable for the full debts of the partnership. Only a limited partner is protected from a levy on personal assets. A new partner becomes liable for the existing debts of the firm only to the extent of that investment made at the time of joining the partnership; however, for all subsequent operations, including debts sustained after joining the partnership, the new member of the enterprise is held to be a general partner.

Liability from Contracts and Torts

A partnership can sustain liability from contracts or from wrongs committed by its members or employees in the course of the partnership business. Even though the partnership agreement may regulate the proportion of individual responsibility, it will not help the individual when the other partners are insolvent and the creditors demand their money from the solvent partner. Moral: Choose your partners carefully!

Breach of Trust

Liability to a partnership may arise from a partner's breach of trust when a third person's money is received and misapplied by one of the partners. Partners are jointly and severally liable. This means that they can all be sued together (jointly) or they can be sued as individuals (severally).

Liability on Retirement

When a partner retires from the firm, the partnership agreement will govern what debts that person will be liable for with respect to the other partners. The agreement will not be binding on existing creditors nor upon new creditors unless notice of the retirement is given to all who habitually do business with the firm.

ADVANTAGES OF A PARTNERSHIP

A partnership, as a form of business, depends upon the choice of the people starting a business. Clearly there has to be a certain amount of mutual respect and confidence for the parties to accept such a relationship.

Many features of the sole proprietorship are included in a partnership. The partnership offers a certain amount of freedom, better resources, and improved chances of financing the business. However, there are other considerations that need further study.

Continuity of Business

The question of the permanence of a business is important to the individual, his or her family, and the customers. A successful sole proprietorship ends if the proprietor dies. In a partnership the business can be continued even though, in theory, death leads to dissolution under the Uniform Partnership Act.

The ending of a partnership does not occur immediately upon its dissolution through the death or voluntary withdrawal of one partner. There will be an intermediate period known as a *time of liquidation* when the remaining or liquidating partners wind up the business. They must pay a portion of the firm's assets, after the debts have been met, to the withdrawing partner or to the estate of the deceased partner.

Other arrangements can also be made. For example, the partnership agreement may stipulate that the share of deceased partners should not go to their estates but instead should remain in the business and be the source of interest, ultimately even of business profits, for the heirs. If, however, it is desired that the partnership continue notwithstanding death, one can provide during one's lifetime that one's capital be left in the company and only eventually repaid to one's executors. The articles of partnership may also give to the surviving partners the right to purchase the share which had belonged to the deceased partner.

Key-man Insurance

This type of insurance on each partner provides that if a partner dies, the amount of the insurance goes to the heirs, and the deceased partner's interest is given to remaining partners. The arrangement assures continuity to the business and does not force either a dissolution or an unwelcome partner on the business.

Taxation

The partnership enjoys certain tax advantages over a corporation, which is an important consideration today. If a sole proprietor incorporates a business, the government will require more taxes than if it were conducted as a partnership, although some corporations may arrange to be taxed as sole proprietorships under the Internal Revenue Code.

For tax purposes, the partnership is disregarded entirely and the tax is levied on the partners as individuals. Thus the partners will be taxed individually on their shares of partnership income as well as on any salary they may get from the firm. Will this put them in an unreasonably high tax bracket? Not necessarily. If a partner is married, such income can be split for tax purposes. Furthermore, income continues to be tax exempt in the hands of the individual partners if it would have been tax exempt in the hands of the partnership, unlike corporate dividends, which lose their tax-exempt status on distribution.

DISADVANTAGES OF A PARTNERSHIP

Many of the disadvantages of the sole proprietorship are also inherent in a partnership. Adding extra people to a new business will not necessarily make it easier to attract larger sums of capital. Other factors may also be examined here.

Lack of Unified Control

As indicated above, each partner has a right to share in the management of the business. The diffusion of managerial control may result in a situation where there is no single direction. The organization may simply drift for a period of time until the differences are resolved. Meantime, important matters may not be handled and employee dissatisfaction may result. Long-term inability to achieve unity in management decisions may ultimately require dissolution of the business enterprise.

Dissolution

As has been indicated earlier, termination or dissolution of a partnership is a relatively easy matter. Such dissolution can occur when a partner voluntarily or involuntarily withdraws from the firm. Partners always have the power to get out of their obligation. This likelihood of withdrawal causing dissolution of the partnership is particularly strong, since the personal qualities of each partner are often essential to its formation. All too frequently, a good working relationship between two or more people in business is the exception rather than the rule. Hence partnership is a relatively fragile form of business organization.

PARTNERSHIP AGREEMENT

The drafting of a good partnership agreement is a serious matter. It is usually a job for a lawyer. Many of the topics discussed here should be considered before consultation with the lawyer. Specifically, the partners should agree in advance on the functions of the business and who will perform them. There should be a clear assignment of duties before the articles are drawn, because otherwise every partner has an equal voice in the management of partnership affairs.

Any differences arising in connection with the business are decided by a majority vote. The partnership agreement should consider the appointment of a referee in the event of deadlock among the partners. Even though there may be an odd number of partners at the beginning (thereby making a deadlock vote unlikely), sickness or death can change the situation.

The drafting of the agreement has been considerably simplified by the Uniform Partnership Act and its companion, the Limited Partnership Act. Anyone contemplating a partnership would be wise to study them in detail or use them as a model for drafting a partnership agreement. Areas of the business that are adequately covered by the acts can be omitted. By limiting the agreement to essentials, the document can be kept relatively brief.

Specific Considerations

Although there will be special requirements of the particular business, some general considerations apply to every business. The most important are (1) who the partners will be, (2) what the scope and nature of the business will be, (3) how much money each partner must invest on entering the partnership, (4) how much time each must spend on the business and in what capacity, (5) who is entitled to make what kinds of decisions that may result in liabilities for the other partners, (6) what share of the profits each partner is entitled to, (7) what happens when one of the partners dies, including the use of key-man insurance, and (8) property rights of each partner in specific partnership property.

Normally partners do not consider their children or spouses when the partnership is being formed. Yet the business arrangement necessarily involves a close relationship that affects the position of the others' families. Will husbands or wives be asked to share in certain duties? Will the sons and daughters be asked or allowed to do minor jobs during weekends or during school vacations? To ensure continuity, will the partnership be prepared to take in family members as it prospers?

All these and many more considerations should be discussed before the agreement is completed. The problems do not just go away if one ignores them. When the partners do not solve these problems at the outset, the law under the Uniform Partnership Act will furnish the answers, which may not be as satisfactory as solutions the partners could have provided for themselves. Hence the partnership agreement is an important document that must be carefully drafted in consultation with a lawyer.

INVOLVEMENT AND STUDY MATERIAL

Understanding Terms

Partnership	(page 159)	Nominal partner	(page 161)
Uniform Partnership Act		Joint ventures	(page 162)
	(page 159)	Agency	(page 164)
General partner	(page 160)	Breach of trust	(page 166)
Limited partner	(page 160)	Dissolution	(page 167)
Silent partner	(page 161)	Key-man insurance	(page 167)
Secret partner	(page 161)		

Questions and Problem Solving

1. Discuss the legal and economic advantages and disadvantages of a partnership.

2. Compare the various types of partners with respect to their authority, responsibility, and relationship to the general public.

3. Compare the beginning partnership with the beginning sole proprietorship, giving similarities and differences.

4. In what way does the fictitious name statute protect creditors?

5. What are the objectives of the Uniform Partnership Act?

6. What are the obligations of the partners toward each other?

7. What authority does a partner have to carry out the business of the partnership?

8. What limitations apply to a partner's authority?

9. Describe the liability of the partnership for debts of judgments against it. If one partner is forced to pay such a debt or judgment, what recourse is there against the other partners?

10. Under what circumstances is a partnership terminated?

11. What measures are available to the partners to avoid unexpected and undesirable terminations of dissolution, and when should these measures be implemented?

Cases for Discussion

1. Newton and Danvers were partners. Danvers wanted to buy out Newton, and so he entered into a secret deal with another party to form a partnership. The third party paid Danvers $10,000, and Danvers then bought out Newton's interest for $900. Later Newton learned of this secret deal and brought a suit against Danvers for an accounting. Judgment for whom? Why?

2. Wilson and Wilcox entered into a partnership with each one putting in $10,000. Wilcox later took $15,000, invested the money in the stock market, and lost. Wilson is now suing Wilcox to recover the $15,000. Judgment for whom? Why?

3. Yee, Lawson, and Ling operated a business as partners for many years. By agreement they dissolved the partnership, publishing a notice to each person they had done business with over the years. Yee continued to seek credit and acquire goods from the former suppliers of the partnership. Upon Yee's failure to pay the suppliers, they brought suit against all three partners. Judgment for whom? Why?

4. Abrams, Cohen, and Evans were partners in the Association Printing Company. They ran up a large bill with the Kraft Paper

Company which they were not able to pay. The Kraft Paper Company brought suit to collect the bill against Evans alone and they secured a judgment. Evans now brings a suit against Cohen and Abrams for reimbursement. Judgment for whom? Why?

5. Nielsen, O'Brien, and Schwartz had been employed as supervisors in a large merchandising organization for twelve years. Although they worked in different departments they saw each other frequently, and their families engaged in joint social activities. Each wanted to start a business that would assure some independence and security. They began looking into franchising opportunities. They were handicapped by limited finances but eventually they came across a food franchiser who seemed to offer the opportunity they wanted. Each would have to invest $10,000; the franchiser agreed to extend credit for supplies and franchise payments.

The three men were elated over the prospect of owning a new business and signed the contract after the franchiser had located a site for the restaurant. Meanwhile they had resigned their jobs to devote full time to building the shop and getting the business started.

The franchiser inquired about the arrangements that had been made for the management of the franchise and discovered that each individual expected to take home at least $1,000 per month. Although the three got along well socially, they had never really worked together and had not made any definite plans about the management of the business.

If you were the franchiser, what would you think about this situation? What recommendations would you make to the new franchisees?

Chapter Twelve

Incorporating the Business

The third type of business arrangement is the *corporation*. Although there are fewer corporations than sole proprietorships or partnerships, the corporation is by far the most important form of organization in the American economic system. The great advance made by the American economy can be largely attributed to this form of enterprise. The corporation has many distinct advantages over the other forms of business and offers its owners an opportunity to participate in ventures they would otherwise not be able to undertake.

The corporation is the favorite of the professional manager, the individual with little investment in a firm, and the comparative newcomer to the business scene. A business person may find that even though the business was started under some other arrangement, it may be wise to change to this form to enjoy its advantages. A corporation is *closely held* when it is owned by only a few stockholders. They may be a family group or friends. A *publicly held corporation* is one whose shares are held by the general public; even here, some individuals may own large blocks of stock, but the corporation is still classified as publicly held.

BENEFITS OF INCORPORATION

The principal advantages of this form of business are limited liability, easier financing, better management, centralized control, continuity, and employee benefits. We shall consider them in that order.

Limited Liability

In a sole proprietorship and a partnership, the owners are responsible for the debts of the firm to the extent of their assets. Under the corporate form of business, liability for the debts of the corporation is limited to the amount of the investment. In other business arrangements, only limited partners can enjoy this advantage, but they cannot take any part in the management of the organization.

The corporation can take substantially more risks than either the sole proprietorship or the partnership. Because of their liability, the sole proprietor and the partners could be ruined if an employee had an accident or caused extensive damage to third persons. Not so with the corporation. It is considered a separate entity from its owners in law. As such it can sue and be sued. It owns its property and it conducts its business through agents. If it suffers losses and no fraud is involved, its creditors usually cannot penetrate behind the structure of the corporation. Their debts must be satisfied from corporate assets.

Financing the Corporation

Ease of financing is the second major benefit of incorporation. Even if the unincorporated business itself does not need a great deal of capital, the fact that it has unlimited liability makes entrepreneurs concerned about the possibility of financial disaster in the event the business fails to prosper.

Under the corporate form of organization, investors can invest as little or as much as they can safely put into the venture, and they rest assured that their other personal assets will not be sacrificed. The chance to invest only small sums of money can be attractive to investors. A new and large group of small investors can support the capital-hungry organization. If the venture succeeds, the investors all profit. If it fails, limited liability prevents the investors' ruin.

The corporate feature of limited liability protects other assets of the individual investors.

The sole proprietorship and the partnership are dependent on their own capital or credit for financing. The corporation can get its capital either through a large number of small investors or through comparatively few large investors. However, this is venture capital; it is neither credit that has to be paid back nor a liability that may threaten to ruin the investor along with the business, if the business fails. Thus the corporation investment philosophy is differently oriented. Capital is put into the business; it does not cost the business anything until a profit is made. It may even be possible to get additional capital, in the form of borrowed money, simply because a corporation does not start its existence badly in debt.

Better Management

Generally, corporations require better management than other types of enterprise. When outsiders are asked to invest in a business, they will demand something more in return than just a gilt-edged certificate. They want to know about the ability of the business to produce a profit, to create a continuing market, and to grow. Mere verbal assurances are not likely to attract many investors.

The investor will want concrete evidence of management ability. This will require planning, objectives, market forecasts, and considerable emphasis on the individual ability of the proposed management team. Once the corporation is formed, the outside stockholders will ask for periodic reports. Management will discover that forming a corporation is only the first step. The second step is to manage it successfully. Almost every decision will be concerned with the effect it will have on the balance sheet to be shown to the investors.

Centralized Control

The control of a corporation lies in the hands of the board of directors. Thus, no matter how many stockholders there may be, the corporation is controlled through a formalized structure.

Partners have an equal voice in the management of the affairs of the partnership. A similar situation may develop in a closely held corporation with few stockholders. Generally, this is true in a corporation with a larger number of stockholders. The board must act as a body; individual directors cannot address themselves to the management of the corporation. Instead, centralized control resides in the officers and a chief executive officer.

Continuity

A corporation is dissolved only by the expiration of its charter, a court decree, a consolidation, or a merger. The death or withdrawal of an owner does not affect the corporation. The corporation exists outside of its owners; it is a creature of the state. Creditors do not need to worry about the death or withdrawal of the participants in the venture.

Insolvency of an individual owner does not affect the finances of the corporation. However, a top manager who is unable to manage personal affairs may alarm creditors by demonstrating poor managerial ability. Nevertheless, most corporations keep personal considerations out of corporate operations, thus preserving their separate identity.

Employee Benefits

Sole proprietorships and most partnerships do not have the capacity to provide their employees with group insurance, retirement, and other employee benefit plans. An important advantage that a broadly held corporation has over other forms of business is the security it provides its employees. Continuity of the corporation gives the employee greater assurance of continued employment. The health of the individual director or officer does not affect the employee in the same manner as would the health of the sole proprietor or partner.

An equally important consideration is that continuity also makes promotions more likely. This, in turn, stimulates competition among employees. There would not be very much incentive to outdo the boss in a sole proprietorship. In fact, the "reward" might be loss of the job. In a corporation, doing a better job generally means promotion. This generates benefits to the corporation.

Recently, states have passed statutes allowing professional people, such as doctors and lawyers, to incorporate their businesses, and this can mean substantial savings. The corporate structure allows implementation of profit-sharing plans, tax-free group insurance, and other benefits. Self-employed persons, such as sole proprietors or partners, do not share these advantages. The professional corporation can have central management, accumulate certain funds, and, in cases where there are few stockholders, avoid the double taxation otherwise levied upon corporate earnings.

DISADVANTAGES OF INCORPORATION

There are two basic disadvantages to the corporate form of business. The first applies to the starting business and the other to taxes.

Starting the Business

Starting a corporation involves a certain amount of expense. These expenses can be justified only if there is a clear advantage for the business. For example, the limited liability feature of the corporation is valuable only if one does not invest all one's assets in the new business.

Outside investors may be hesitant to put capital in the new business. People starting a new business generally need not only what they have saved but borrowed money as well. Initial earnings may be needed for reinvestment into the business rather than for dividends. The untried business is not the best risk in the world; therefore a new small business has little chance of securing adequate financing through the sale of securities.

Creditors can be expected to give the financial structure of a new business a thorough examination. If it is shaky, additional security will be required to guarantee that the creditors will be paid. Further, the organizers of the business will not escape personal liability if they undercapitalize the organization. Limited liability is not a device that permits a business person to entice creditors to extend credit when the corporation is not adequately financed at the outset.

Taxation

A corporation is a legal entity, and so a tax is levied on its profits. Later, each shareholder must pay a personal income tax on dividends distributed out of the corporate profits. Because of this, a corporation is said to be subject to double taxation.

This situation did not always exist. In the second half of the nineteenth century, the partnership principle was applied to the federal taxation of corporations. However, that has now been changed, perhaps because it would not be an administratively feasible practice for the large corporation of today.

Double taxation is an obvious concern for the investor, and corporate management is well aware of its effects. It may influence many financial decisions of the company, such as the decision to borrow needed money rather than try to raise it through the sale of corporate shares. In this manner, the tax burden gets passed to the defenseless consumer. The corporation may even decide not to declare dividends, but to reinvest its profits in the corporation for future expansion. In this way, investors do not get charged the double income tax and yet the value of their shares will be increased, providing the reinvestment is wise and hence profitable.

If the corporation is closely held by a family group or close friends, management may decide to employ the investors at good salaries. Thus, the profits are really paid out in salaries, rather than as dividends, which avoids the double taxation.

If there are fewer than ten shareholders who are resident individuals, the corporation may also elect to come under a special provision of the Internal Revenue Code, as a subchapter S corporation. Special tax provisions permit the corporation to be exempt from taxation so that the income goes directly to the shareholders.

PROCESS OF INCORPORATION

Once a business has chosen to incorporate, decisions must be made about the type of ownership, financing, control, and management the corporation will have. The majority of the states have adopted the Model Business Corporation Act. The corporation is formed when certain procedures specified by the act are performed. An application is made to the state for the issuance of a charter or articles of incorporation, identifying the name of the corporation, its purpose, the number of authorized shares of stock, the number of directors, and other requisites for the establishment of the new organization.

The Organizers

A corporation is formed by persons, generally called *organizers*, who contribute their assets to it in the form of ideas, money, land, or machinery in exchange for shares. The holders of the shares of stock are called either *shareholders* or *stockholders*.

A corporation becomes a legal entity only after the organizers have completed the necessary steps outlined in the statute. Until then the organizers may incur personal liability if they perform any acts on behalf of the yet unformed corporation. Therefore, the organizers should proceed with care and follow the statutory requirements exactly. Decisions have to be made about:

1. The name of the proposed corporation
2. The state where it will be incorporated
3. Its principal place of business and its address
4. Its purpose and extent of business activity
5. The term for which it is incorporated
6. The initial capitalization and the amount of stock to be issued
7. The powers of stockholders to run the corporation, either with or without official meetings
8. The date and time for the annual meeting
9. The number of directors who sit on the board
10. The officers who run the corporation and their powers

For the beginning entrepreneur, there seems to be little difference between the corporation statutes of the various states. However, if a business is to operate across state lines, careful consideration should be given to the state of incorporation. There may be advantages in the taxes of certain states. Some states permit corporations more latitude in corporate operations. No matter which state the corporation is formed in, a lawyer should prepare the incorporation documents.

Articles of Incorporation

The Model Business Corporation Act is an extensive statute covering most details of corporate operations. However, incorporators are allowed considerable freedom either to strengthen the powers of their shareholders where there are few or to give greater control to the directors and managing officers where the number of stockholders is large. Whenever the articles of incorporation have tighter provisions than the statute, the articles will control.

Articles of incorporation can be relatively brief. Functions that are adequately covered by statute need not be included. Only those areas that the incorporators want to vary from the statutory regulations should be included. There are some areas of corporate regulations that cannot be changed. For example, no corporation can pay dividends out of capital when it has no earnings and is threatened with insolvency, except under tightly controlled circumstances.

Bylaws

Bylaws are rules and regulations that guide the day-to-day management of the business. They may outline duties and powers of corporate officers, specify salaries of directors and officers, or permit adoption of additional bylaws by the board of directors to assist them in the operation of the business. The bylaws are adopted at the first meeting of the stockholders. Articles of incorporation, or a charter, will often make a provision that certain bylaws cannot be changed except by vote of the shareholders.

Stockholder Rights

The stockholders own the business. When the articles of incorporation are prepared, certain powers will be reserved to them. In general, the stockholders will insist that the corporation engage in a particular line of business and that any change be approved by a majority, or even a two-thirds vote of the owners of all outstanding stock, not only of those voting. Stockholders usually will reserve the right to dispose of major corporate assets, such as buildings, land, or other major investments of the corporation. Annual and special meetings frequently are specified under the articles. These articles cannot be changed without the approval of the stockholders.

Voting Rights

The Model Business Corporation Act provides for voting rights that accompany certain types of issued stock. These types of stock and their voting rights will be discussed in Chapter 14. Special voting rights are provided for any stockholder group that may be threatened by any action of the corporation. For example, if a particular class of stock has been sold, and the corporation proposed another issue of like stock, the owners of the existing stock could sue to block the new issue because their position would be diluted by sharing future profits with a larger group of shareholders. The corporation cannot issue such stock unless the existing stockholders give their consent.

Election of Directors

A business cannot be run on the basis of one or two meetings a year. Consequently, the articles reserve to the stockholders major protection with regard to a few selected items of corporate affairs.

Beyond that, the major function of the stockholders is to attend the annual meeting and elect the board of directors. We will discuss the duties and functions of that board in the next chapter.

The number of directors can vary to suit the needs and wishes of the stockholders. Many corporations appoint from three to nine directors; large corporations may have fifteen or more. Directors are often appointed by class during the first election. The first class serves only one year; the second, two years; and the third, three years. Thereafter, they are elected for staggered three-year periods, which provides continuity on the board. The corporation does not have a completely new board after each election.

Functions of a Corporation

Once the corporation has a charter and articles of incorporation, it can function in many ways like a person. It can own, buy, and sell property; borrow money; sue and be sued; and conduct business.

The board of directors sets out the objectives of the corporation in accordance with the purposes set out in the charter and the wishes of the stockholders. The board also organizes the business, elects the principal executive officers, outlines their duties, and delegates the authority necessary to enable the company to perform the job for which it was created. Once the organization is set up and starts functioning, the board of directors holds periodic meetings to review the performance, suggest alternatives, and make any other recommendations it deems necessary. They also declare dividends to the shareholders if the corporate earnings warrant, and they instruct the officers of the corporation whom they elect.

The day-to-day management and control of the business is centralized in the officers who run it. These are usually the president, vice-president, secretary, and treasurer. Their respective powers are set out in the bylaws of the corporation. Under these officers are the numerous employees and agents who are hired by the officers of the corporation.

THE BALANCE SHEET

The balance sheet is to a corporation what a medical report is to a patient. It reveals whether the corporation is healthy, ill, or dying. Therefore, every business person should be able to read a balance sheet and understand how it reflects a firm's economic situation.

Assets

A balance sheet is divided into two parts: assets and liabilities. Assets, in turn, are often subdivided into current assets and fixed assets. Cash and inventories are current, or working, assets. They will vary from time to time and can be increased or reduced according to managerial decisions. There is no difficulty in understanding the meaning of "cash," but "inventories" represents a more difficult problem. Here the figures depend on an accounting system which reflects what has happened to the raw materials that have entered into production. The increase in cost of the original material reflects not only the added labor but the expense of electricity, rent, heat, and other costs due to the manufacturing process.

Fixed assets involve the company property, plant, and equipment. They are figured at cost less depreciation. Depreciation is an amount that represents the decline in value of the fixed assets. It is not a sum that is put aside to purchase new equipment but merely treated as an expense for the given year. The amount taken as depreciation is cash that can be used in the business.

Liabilities

Liabilities also differentiate between current and long-term items. The current items are those that have to be paid off within a comparatively short time. Generally, payments are taken out of current earnings or short-term borrowings. Many of these items are invoiced at thirty-, sixty-, or ninety-day intervals. Some carry an inducement to pay promptly by offering a discount of 2 percent if paid within ten days.

A mortgage is shown as the long-term item in Table 12-1. It may have a sinking fund schedule, which is in the nature of a prepayment fund. The sinking fund schedule requires that money be put aside at stated intervals and blocks of bonds retired. This avoids a large payment coming due at one time, when the money market could be unfavorable, thus jeopardizing the company's financial structure. The arrangement encourages sound fiscal practices and serves as a protection to the bondholders.

In the same example, accrued items shown for wages and salaries are the result of the usual delay in salaries earned but not paid. Good accounting practice requires that money be set aside for items that are due and payable, correctly reflecting the earnings of the company. Although taxes do not become due until a given date, an

TABLE 12-1   Reliable Manufacturing Company

Balance sheet: End of current year

Assets

Current assets:

Cash		$ 35,520
Accounts receivable		102,420
Notes receivable		34,250
Inventories:		
Raw materials	$ 46,140	
Work in process	177,680	
Finished goods	96,780	
Supplies	7,780	
Total inventory		328,380
Total current assets		$500,570

Fixed assets:

Property, plant, and equipment	$555,490	
Less depreciation	94,220	
Total fixed assets		461,270
Total assets		$961,840

Liabilities

Current liabilities:

Notes payable	$ 80,100	
Accounts payable	18,680	
Accrued liabilities—wages, salaries, etc.	17,670	
Provisions for taxes	39,280	
Total current liabilities		$155,730

Long-term liabilities:

Mortgage bonds due 1984		$200,000

Stockholder's equity:

Paid in capital (20,000 shares)	$240,000	
Capital surplus and retained earnings	366,110	
Total stockholder's equity		606,110
Total liabilities and capital		$961,840

amount should be set aside each month as if taxes were also charged to the regular business expenses.

The next item, the stockholder's equity, represents the amount of capital stock paid in by the investors and the accrued earnings that have been invested in the business rather than paid out as dividends. This stock originally sold for $12 a share since it brought $240,000 as paid-in capital. It now has a book value of a little over $30 per share (the paid-in capital plus the surplus equals $606,110 divided by 20,000).

Ratios

The balance sheet holds very special information for the business person who knows how to look for it. The net working capital, obtained by deducting current liabilities from current assets, is an important figure because it discloses the liquidity of the business ($344,840 in Table 12-1). In other words, it shows whether the business can pay its bills on time. The current ratio of 3.2:1 is obtained by dividing the current assets by the total current liabilities:

$$\frac{500,570}{155,730} = 3.2$$

For every dollar of current liabilities, the company has $3.20 in current assets to support it. Many market analysts place a great deal of reliance on this particular figure since it discloses the financial position of the company. If this figure is unfavorable, the company may be having financial problems and may not be a good investment risk.

Another figure frequently used is the ratio between "quick" assets (cash, accounts receivable, and notes receivable) and current liabilities. The inventories are not used in the calculation because they are tied up in the manufacturing process and not readily available for a quick conversion to needed cash. This ratio is known as the acid test of solvency, and in our example the ratio is satisfactory since it would be

$$\frac{172,190}{155,730} = 1.1$$

This figure shows that if the company needed emergency cash it could raise it internally and would not be at the mercy of the money market or demanding creditors.

PROFIT AND LOSS STATEMENT

For full information, the balance sheet should be read in connection with a profit and loss statement for the same period.

TABLE 12-2   Reliable Manufacturing Company

Profit and loss statement: End of current year

Gross sales		$1,304,990
Less:		
Cost of goods sold	$841,010	
Selling and administrative expenses	103,780	
		944,790
Net sales		$ 360,200
Other expenses:		
Interest	$12,400	
Consultant fee	17,500	
Trucking expense	22,200	
Attorney expense	1,200	
Freight	8,400	
Insurance	22,200	
Real estate taxes	20,000	
Total other expense		103,900
Gross profit		$ 256,300
Federal and state income taxes		87,400
Net profit		$ 168,900
Dividends paid		60,000
To surplus		$ 108,900

Note that the firm in Table 12-2 had a total of $1,304,990 in gross sales. Assuming that the inventories, shown on the balance sheet, reflect the usual amount for this firm, we can see that the inventory turnover amounts to

$$\frac{1,304,990}{328,380} = 4.0$$

This figure indicates that the goods represented by the inventory were purchased at least four times during the year, on the average. Whether this is a good figure depends on a closer analysis of the business. Comparison to similar businesses might reveal that the turnover ratio should be 5 instead of 4. Successive years of experience may also reveal fluctuations. The sum of money shown represents a substantial investment in inventory. If the investment can be reduced, the money might be used more profitably elsewhere.

There are many other valuable comparisons that can be made from scrutinizing a balance sheet and profit and loss statement. The serious business person can investigate them in greater detail by securing a book on accounting that will explain their value. Figures used frequently in financial statements reflect the health of the organization. More important, they indicate the capabilities of the management team that was responsible for them.

INVOLVEMENT AND STUDY MATERIAL

Understanding Terms

Legal entity	(page 174)	Stockholder rights	(page 180)
Double taxation	(page 178)	Voting rights	(page 180)
Organizers	(page 178)	Balance sheet	(page 181)
Stockholders	(page 178)	Assets	(page 182)
Articles of incorporation		Liabilities	(page 182)
	(page 179)	Sinking fund	(page 182)
Bylaws	(page 180)	Profit and loss statement	
Charter	(page 180)		(page 185)

Questions and Problem Solving

1. Explain why the corporate form of business organization, although less common than the sole proprietorship or partnership, is by far the most important form of business organization in the American economic system.

2. When is it advantageous to incorporate a business?

3. In what way does limited liability make the corporate form of business more attractive than the sole proprietorship or partnership?

4. If individuals invest all their assets, plus whatever they can borrow in a business, is there any particular advantage in incorporating the business? Explain your answer.

5. Outline the steps that must be taken to form a corporation.

6. Distinguish between the functions of the articles of incorporation and the bylaws.

7. Describe the relationship of the stockholders to the corporation, the directors, and the officers.

8. How does double taxation affect the corporation and its stockholders?

9. Distinguish between the profit and loss statement and the balance sheet.

Cases for Discussion

1. The defendants were promoting the organization of a corporation. They purchased some merchandise from the plaintiff prior to the organization of the corporation. When the corporation received its charter, the plaintiff billed it for the merchandise but did not receive payment. The plaintiff now sues the defendants to recover the price of the merchandise. Judgment for whom? Why?

2. The plaintiff was a corporation promoter, and he contacted some prospective incorporators who agreed to form a corporation and to pay him $3,000 per month to manage it. The plaintiff organized the corporation and managed it for five months, whereupon he was fired. He now sues the corporation for breach of contract. Judgment for whom? Why?

3. Patrick was a promoter and incorporator of the Park-Ryan Company. The company received a charter and issued stock. Patrick acquired 100 shares of preferred stock. He executed a contract in the name of the corporation with the Ajax Supply Company for goods. The Park-Ryan Company was issued a bill for these goods, and payment was refused. Ajax now brings suit against Park-Ryan Company. Judgment for whom? Why?

4. The plaintiff is a minority stockholder in the Beckett Corporation. She made a written request to be furnished with a list of the other stockholders and to examine the books of the corporation. The

corporation refused her request, whereupon she now brings suit to force the corporation to open its books. Judgment for whom? Why?

5. A, B, and C are incorporators and have filed articles of incorporation with the state of Florida. They have not been granted a charter, nor have they solicited subscriptions for the sale of stock. They have selected neither the board of directors nor the officers and have acquired only a building and some land. The plaintiff was injured on the premises and brings suit against A, B, and C as individuals to recover the amount of his loss. A, B, and C claim they are not personally liable and that the plaintiff must sue the corporation instead of them. Judgment for whom? Why?

Chapter Thirteen

Managing the Corporation

It is useful for everyone to examine the operations of a large corporation. A discipline that works well in a large business should also be practiced by smaller businesses, since the objectives of both are the same.

Much has been said about stockholders being the owners of the corporation. Yet according to the Model Corporation Act, the corporation is managed by the board of directors and not by the stockholders. The importance, size, and composition of the board depends on whether its stock is publicly or closely held.

BOARD OF DIRECTORS

The right to elect the board of directors is an important right for the stockholders of a closely held corporation. Stockholders who own large blocks of stock in publicly held corporations may get on the board themselves or elect directors who will support their views, but the average stockholder has little influence on the choice of a director. In such a corporation the operating management recommends to its stockholders the choices for the board, and the stockholders rarely disagree. It is doubtful that such a board can effectively oppose the plans and policies put forth by the management that placed them in office. Nevertheless, the board of directors remains an important and integral part of corporate organization.

Types of Directors

Directors who are also company officers are called *inside directors*. In other words, they function in a dual capacity. Such directors are intimately involved in corporate management and are usually thoroughly familiar with the corporate operations. For example, the company whose organization chart is shown in Figure 13-1 might wish to include at least two of the operational vice presidents, the treasurer, and the president as members of the board of directors in order to secure the benefit of their knowledge of the details of company operations. Many corporations also elect *outside directors* to their board to profit from their experience and make wiser decisions in unfamiliar areas. Outside directors are not involved in corporate operations and do not necessarily own stock in the corporation. They are often highly influential in such fields as finance, law, politics, marketing, and other businesses. They can bring new and differing points of view when management decisions are under consideration. For example, in 1965 Sears, Roebuck and Co. stockholders, on the recommendation of their existing board, elected Claire Giannini Hoffman of the Bank of America to their board of directors. Her knowledge of finances was a valuable asset in board deliberations.

Interlocking Directorates

In the past, many companies placed directors on the boards of competing companies. These cozy arrangements, known as *interlocking directorates* enabled the supposed competitors to learn all about each other's operations, plans, prices, and markets. In some cases they led to special agreements to set prices, limit markets, and eliminate competition. Since such directorships were considered to act against public interest and often against the very companies they purportedly represented, they have come under the scrutiny of the U.S. Justice Department. Contracts between companies with such directors may

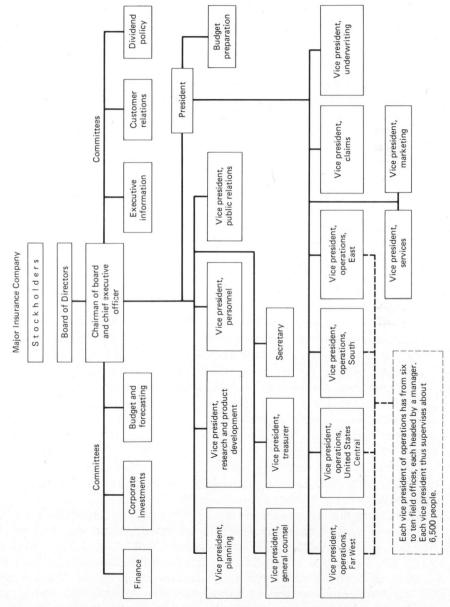

Fig. 13-1. Organization chart of company with short chain of command.

be subject to attack, and the courts will examine the relationship closely.

The Principal Officers

Usually, the title of the company officer will identify that officer's power and duties. Thus, the title "chief executive officer" leaves no room for doubt as to who has the top authority within the company. If the chairman of the board assumes that position, his title will be "chairman of the board and chief executive officer." This occasionally poses a problem for the president of the company, who is sometimes viewed as the top officer of the company. Normally, the president's title will reflect his authority, for example, "president and director of corporate planning." All good corporations have carefully prepared organization charts, and the position of each officer is clearly set out. Such a chart is an important tool in defining duties and responsibilities within an organization.

Other important corporate officers are the vice presidents whose titles are usually followed by a functional designation. Other prominent officers are usually the treasurer and the heads of marketing, operations, and research and development. If the company is small, one officer may perform two or more of the functions assigned to a single officer in a large corporation.

One of the requirements of a functioning corporation is that it comply with the formalities set out by law, by its charter, and by its bylaws. Although the company may be advised by its attorneys and others skilled in corporate affairs, it is important that the records of meetings, resolutions, authorizations, elections, appointments, and other corporate activity be maintained. This duty falls to the corporate secretary, who keeps the minutes of meetings and certifies their correctness. When various executives deal with people outside of the corporation, it may be necessary to produce evidence of authority. The secretary will supply the necessary copies of resolutions or authorizations granted by the directors, the bylaws, or the charter.

Inside directors, who are also officers of the corporation, presumably keep the board of directors informed concerning the problems facing the company. The arrangement makes good sense and generally leads to wiser guidance of the corporate business by the board. A real danger can develop when the majority of the corporate directors are also the corporate executive officers. Obviously, such directors will have great difficulty in divorcing their role as directors from their role as operating officers. Under such circumstances it may be impossible for the board to perform its function as a supervisor and reviewer of company operations on behalf of the stockholders.

ORGANIZATION CHARTS

An organization chart is the best single tool for becoming acquainted with a corporate organization. It is a thumbnail sketch of the position and relation of the principal officers of the company. It informs all interested parties of the lines of authority as well as lines of communication. Two means of giving an employee job security are to tell the employee who the boss will be and to explain what duties are to be performed. An organization chart can help to accomplish both in a graphic manner, and it is useful for the old employee as well as the new.

The organization chart shown in Figure 13-1 illustrates the organization of the executive staff of a corporation with assets of approximately $3 billion. Its structure is sometimes called "flat" because it contains a relatively limited number of levels of authority. In other words, there is a short chain of command or few intervening officers between the chief executive and the operating officers in the field. In contrast, the chart shown in Figure 13-2 depicts a long chain of command in a manufacturing company. Part of the difference may be attributed to the fact that the companies deal in different lines or products. A manufacturing operation may require much tighter supervision than a service organization. The type of the organization may also reflect the personalities of the chief executive officers or its board of directors.

An organization chart can be a useful tool in determining the functions of various personnel. Therefore, no matter how small the organization, a chart should be prepared to clarify lines of authority and individual responsibility. It tends to focus the attention of the individual on personal objectives as well as to identify the objectives of the entire enterprise. It promotes one's sense of belonging. It helps spot awkward situations and avoid conflicts of authority. For this reason no enterprise should ever be planned without the use of an organization chart at every step of the way. It is a most valuable tool to a decision maker in the planning stages as well as in actual operations.

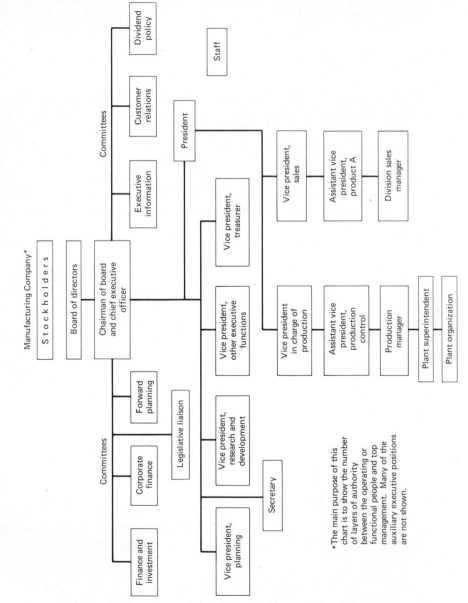

Fig. 13-2. Organization chart of company with long chain of command.

Relative Importance of Corporate Officers

To the casual observer of the corporate scene, the title of a particular corporate executive does not always indicate the relative importance of his office. Below the level of chief executive officer it is usually the circumstances that dictate the amount of influence and power wielded by the particular individual.

As the fortunes of the company wax and wane, so does the relative importance of the various officers. For example, a company that has a healthy cash position can afford to concentrate on a program of sales expansion. The chief executive officer may defer to the vice president in charge of marketing. This does not mean that one can ignore the presence and power of the treasurer; this officer is always concerned with the financial position of the company. The treasurer must zealously guard the financial security of the company and also participate in major corporate decisions. Money greases the wheels of the enterprise. The treasurer's knowledge of the financial affairs guides the company in research, expansion, stockpiling of inventories, and other activities.

DUTIES OF THE BOARD

The formal duties of the board of directors are set out in the charter and bylaws of the corporation. However, the mere following of rules and regulations will not ensure a well-run corporation. This is where the experience and ability of the directors comes in. The manner in which the board fulfills its functions depends, in a large measure, upon the character, interest, and judgment of the individual members. The character and bylaws are designed to protect the interests of the stockholders. To this extent, they serve a very useful purpose. Many functions require formal board action. Formalization, in itself, tends to ensure that the items under consideration will get the board's thoughtful attention. Therefore, it is advisable to have a corporation reserve activities that might have a major impact upon the welfare of a corporation for action by the board or even the stockholders.

In a publicly held corporation effective control is usually exercised by the operating officers. They select the board of directors by proxy solicitations to the stockholders. It is the operating management that sets the overall policy and submits it for review and approval by the board. Clearly, the board is not an independent representative of the stockholders. Nevertheless, the fact that approval must be requested usually results in careful preparation and justification of a proposal. Thus the directors can be viewed as trustees of the company with primary responsibility to the corporation and thereafter to the stockholders, the employees, the customer, and the public. In a closely held corporation the directors may intervene in day-to-day management.

The action of the board of directors becomes most visible when the large publicly held corporation gets into financial trouble. It is usually the board that has the responsibility for replacing the top operating officers. Where many of the board members are also company officers, outside directors may find themselves involved in major reorganizational problems as well. The bankruptcy of the Penn Central corporation illustrates the change in board functions to more control after the existing management led the company into insolvency.

Committees

Of particular importance are the committees shown in the organization chart of Figure 13–1. These are corporate employees that really serve as full-time staffs rather than committees. They are engaged in projects considered important by the chairman of the board and other directors. In a large corporation many of the important board decisions are based upon the studies prepared by these committees and their recommendations. After all, the committee has the time to make a careful study of the particular proposal coming before the board. The board very likely referred it to the committee. Therefore, many of the board decisions are actually committee decisions.

Other executive officers also employ staffs that serve as committees. For example, the vice president of personnel undoubtedly has a committee dealing with pensions, retirement, and employee benefits. The vice president of marketing might have a committee studying product acceptance, promotions, and the benefits secured from advertising.

The average executive is far too busy with day-to-day operations to conduct research or special studies. Therefore, setting up committees to make the necessary studies, preparations, and recommendations is a wise policy to conserve the executive's time. Making more information available to the executive will promote wiser final decisions.

Activities under the Bylaws

In general, the activities of the board of directors are divided by the bylaws into two general categories: *fiscal* and *administrative*.

Under their fiscal powers the directors authorize the issuance of company securities for sale to the public; decide when dividends are to be declared; review and approve operating plans; establish salaries and bonuses for executive and managerial personnel; pledge, sell, or mortgage real estate; and handle other necessary financial affairs of the company. The *administrative powers* involve selecting and controlling corporate officers, fixing their salaries, delegating operating authority, fixing basic policies of the corporation, arranging for annual meetings, observing the rules set out in the charter and bylaws, and such other functions as result from the corporate operations.

The Board Meeting

In closely held corporations all the members of the board may also be operating officers. One cannot review oneself, and therefore a board meeting can serve only to formalize decisions already made. In a publicly held corporation the board almost always has some outside directors. Thus, although the board may be considerably influenced by the operating management, the process of formalization provides an opportunity to review company operations.

This text cannot describe every type of corporate board meeting, but it will be useful to examine a type of meeting common to several large corporations. The necessary painstaking preparations have great value as a technique of self-discipline, and are recommended in almost any business.

The board meeting starts with the directors and all officers being present. Various staff assistants may or may not attend at this time. Usually, the chairman of the board will notify the personnel who are expected to come. A formal agenda normally is prepared in advance and distributed to the people concerned. The agenda provides a schedule of department presentations, and occasionally the planned times are also shown. However, if serious problems come under discussion, the board will not feel bound by time schedules.

When all are assembled, the presiding officer will call the meeting to order and the chief executive officer will very likely open the presentations by discussing the balance sheet, profit and loss statement, cash position, short- and long-term debt situation, sales forecasts, and expected earnings. This presentation will usually be followed by an explanation by the individual who prepared most of the data for the chief executive officer. This assistant will expand on the chief executive's remarks and point out the principal areas of interest as they concern the various departments. The most important part of this presentation is the identification of potential trouble areas that may be showing up in statistical trends. If the corporation follows detailed budgets, the principal variations from the budget are shown at this time also. The introductory presentation sets the stage for the balance of the meeting.

The thoroughness with which the board reviews the company operations determines the importance of a board of directors. The operating executives have thoroughly examined every aspect of their own performance. They may have compared it with budget expectations, and if they are not prepared to defend their position, they must have acceptable plans to make corrections where indicated. In contrast, the board members scrutinize adverse trends and developments; they probe and question. If the answers are not satisfactory, the board may require additional data or study. Experts may be called for supporting opinions and help in developing alternate solutions.

Thus far it would appear that the board of directors can do no wrong, however they can encounter unsuspected danger by being inundated with data and statistics so accommodatingly spewed out by the computer and put together ably, sometimes craftily, by the statistical staff. The very process that enables the corporation to develop current and detailed information may also be the process that obscures the real status of the corporation.

It should be clear that the members of the board are usually fully aware of and, in fact, anticipate human frailties. However, they too are victims of circumstances and might be subjected to the old trick of focusing the attention of the audience—the directors—on unimportant matters. Of course, the presentation will be given in a convincing manner, but its purpose may be to obscure what is really important. Even if the board member avoids this pitfall, can flaws be recognized in an officer's presentation if one is unfamiliar with the intricacies of an operation? Clearly, the answer may be no. It is for this reason that many corporate boards of directors include capable and proven executive officers who are familiar with detailed company operations and who can be depended upon to spot the half-truths in the presentations. This may be a major device to avoid the pitfalls and potential dangers to the corporate welfare as well as to the individual director.

PROBLEMS FACED BY CORPORATE OFFICERS

There has been rising criticism concerning the performance of many boards of directors. Prestigious names and figureheads who do not bother to attend board meetings certainly do not help in directing the affairs of a company needing leadership. In many cases stockholders have been misled into believing they had competent boards looking after the affairs of the company when, in reality, they had boards that were inclined to rubber stamp the actions taken by company officers and operating personnel.

Fiduciary Responsibility of Officers and Directors

The law states that the business of the corporation shall be managed by the board of directors. Thus directors and officers occupy a position of loyalty to the company rather than to the stockholders. As fiduciaries, they must avoid all self-interest and manage the corporation in its best interest. If a director or officer engages in misconduct and, particularly, has secretly profited from that position of trust, the company may be able to recover damages. If the other officers or members of the board fail to demand restitution, a stockholder can bring a *derivative suit* on behalf of the company to compel restitution to the corporation.

A derivative suit must be distinguished from the situation where an individual stockholder feels personally damaged by the action of the directors or officers. The problems facing an individual stockholder in proving damages are formidable, and most such suits are unsuccessful. In a derivative suit, the stockholder intervenes on behalf of all the stockholders to protect the interests of the corporation on the assumption that the officers and directors have failed to act. It is brought only after demands have been made in vain upon the operating officers or directors to make the necessary corrections. An alternative course of action that is open to the stockholders in such a situation is to voice their displeasure at the next stockholders' meeting and to try to elect a new slate of directors.

Inadequate Representation of Stockholders

In the last few years, there has been increasing criticism of boards of directors and executive officers where stockholders' interests have been jeopardized or injured. The courts have also become more receptive to *class actions*, which permit one individual to bring suit on

GRIN AND BEAR IT   BY LICHTY

"I had money, position, power . . . until the annual
stockholders meeting when this little old lady with 2
shares gets up. . . ."

Fig. 13-3.

behalf of others who are similarly affected. Class actions have made
it easier for stockholders to sue the directors for negligent performance of their duty in representing the stockholders' interests.
Court rules permit recovery of costs and attorney fees if the suit is
successful. Until 1974 there was every indication that class actions
would increase in the future, but that year the U.S. Supreme Court
greatly limited their use by imposing on the plaintiff the expensive
burden of notifying all class members of the action.

Liability of Directors and Officers

A few years ago it would have been safe to say that, in the absence
of fraud, a director is not liable to the corporation or its stockholders
for losses sustained by the corporation. The director was only required to use ordinary business judgment; if the corporation suffered
a loss, that was unfortunate. Today the law in this area is uncertain,
and the cases seem to suggest that the director may be held liable
for simple negligence. In any event, some directors have found themselves engaged in very expensive litigation.

There are numerous cases where directors and officers have been held liable to the corporation and stockholders because of misconduct and outright fraud, such as using information secured by virtue of their position for personal gain. In some cases directors have been held liable because they released false information to the public or concealed facts which should have been disclosed. One cannot find fault in placing liability upon dishonest directors and officers, but the cost to the director for simple oversight or inadvertent action can be abnormally high. The courts and stockholders may be taking seriously the statutory directive that the affairs of the corporation shall "be managed by the board of directors."

Many criticize directors for failing to discover in time potential problems facing the company. The directors, in turn, point to the complexity of the data they are being asked to examine and the short time they have to do it. Directors may need a staff to help them understand the data submitted at board meetings. But if the directors are forced to rely on staff committee judgments, is there any need for a board of directors?

In the Penn Central bankruptcy case, not only are the directors being sued for large sums of money because of their responsibility for the bankruptcy, but criminal charges may follow. Consequently many prospective directors are taking a long, hard look at the desirability of being on a board and assuming a liability that may not be discernable until *after* a company gets into difficulty. For example, a new director who had been on the board for two weeks was asked to sign a registration statement for the issuance of stock. He had questioned the company accountants about the accuracy of the statement and, after being assured that the facts represented on the statement were correct, signed the registration. The statement was later proven to be false. The court found the new director guilty of giving a false certification and assessed penalties against him.

Compensation versus Responsibilities

In the early part of this century, board membership was rewarded by nominal compensation at most. Corporations with assets under $100 million frequently paid $100 or less per board meeting attended, and attendance was sporadic. Larger corporations—assets $100 million to $500 million—paid around $250 per meeting. This compensation has been increased by some corporations, and today payments range from $3,000 to $5,000 per year.

In the 1960s, concern was generated about the director's responsibilities and potential liabilities. Corporations began to purchase liability insurance to protect the directors against stockholders' suits. It is clear that in cases where suits are filed mainly to harass the directors, the corporation owes a duty to its board to protect them from the expenses of defending such suits. However, the problem becomes quite different where the stockholders have real grievances and can show substantial damages.

To cope with this situation, two proposals have been suggested for adoption by corporations into their bylaws. The first provides for *indemnification* (payment for losses suffered) with approval of the court trying the case after a finding of no willful misconduct. If the court does not make such a finding, the disinterested members of the board may do so or the matter be given to an independent firm of attorneys for study. If they find, after a careful review, that the mistake of judgment was not willful, the corporation would be authorized to reimburse the director. The matter can be submitted to a general vote of the stockholders; however, it may be difficult to get stockholder approval if substantial losses have been sustained.

The second proposal deals with the advancing of expenses as soon as litigation starts. Such expenses can run into hundreds of thousands of dollars. This proposal assures both the company and the director of securing able counsel at the outset.

Need for Better Reporting

The accounting profession has not escaped untouched. Several large accounting firms are being sued for failure to discover corporate irregularities despite the fact that they did not purport to certify company operations—only records and reports. Accountants are now searching for ways to make accounting reports more meaningful to people like shareholders and outside directors. If a way can be found to make internal reports better and to provoke prompt action by responsible executive officers, so much the better.

A further effort is being made to design a system to give stockholders more frequent reports. An annual report may be too old. A philosopher once remarked that knowledge keeps no better than fish. Certainly one cannot expect a stockholder to remember all the details of a lengthy report that is over a year old.

By being better informed the stockholders in turn may be able to contribute to the welfare of the corporation. By being interested in its activity and developing some contact with its management, they may help the directors make a better analysis of data, which should result in wiser decisions.

INVOLVEMENT AND STUDY MATERIAL

Understanding Terms

Inside directors	(page 190)	Administrative powers	
Outside directors	(page 190)		(page 197)
Interlocking directorates		Fiduciary responsibility	
	(page 190)		(page 199)
Corporate secretary	(page 192)	Derivative suit	(page 199)
Fiscal powers	(page 197)	Class action	(page 199)

Questions and Problem Solving

1. What is the value of an organization chart?
2. In a publicly held corporation, effective control is exercised by the operating officers. Does this mean that the board of directors meetings are useless exercises?
3. Explain the advantages of formalized procedures utilized by corporate officers and directors in examining and approving corporate plans and operations.
4. What is the value of having operating departments defend the results of their operation before a board of directors? Could similar results be achieved if the presentations were made before the superior operating officers?
5. What are the advantages and disadvantages of outside directors?
6. What is the value of having inside directors on the board? Are there any dangers to such an arrangement? Explain your answer.
7. What is the purpose of an annual meeting of the stockholders?

8. Explain the difference between a derivative suit and a class action.

9. Discuss the problem of the director's potential liability for losses to the corporation.

10. How can management practices of large corporations be useful for a small business? Will the formalities observed by a large corporation develop the same care and examination of operations in a small business?

Cases for Discussion

1. The board of directors of the Facit Corporation voted to lease the property to another corporation for twenty years. The stockholders were not involved in the voting. Is this lease valid? Why?

2. The board of directors of the Adamski Corporation voted to increase the number of outstanding shares of stock of the corporation. The stockholders were not informed of this vote. Is this a valid exercise of the board's powers? Why?

3. The Hickel Corporation and the Wyanov Corporation made a contract between themselves. The same directors are on the boards of each corporation. Is the contract valid? Why?

4. The directors of Bonelli Corporation voted to approve a deal that would increase its markets. The business deal resulted in a loss of markets instead of a gain, and the corporation lost $1 million. Are the directors liable for this mistake? Why?

5. The directors of Riehl Corporation passed a resolution to borrow money. The resolution also stated that when the stock was sold to the public, the corporation would pay off the loan out of the proceeds. The board borrowed the money from the First National Bank, but after selling the stock they used the money for other corporate purposes and did not repay the bank. The bank sued, claiming that the directors misappropriated the money of the corporation, and were derelict in their duties as directors. Judgment for whom? Why?

Chapter Fourteen

Financing the Corporation

Although a corporation is a creature of the state, it owes its existence to its incorporators, who have contributed their property, ideas, and money as assets. In exchange, they receive shares of stock in proportion to their investment.

Many corporations require financing beyond that furnished by the incorporators. One method these corporations can use is to "go public" and offer securities to outside investors. This is *equity financing*. Sometimes, however, the owners of a corporation need to raise money but want to avoid bringing in more shareholders, and so they make use of *debt financing*, which we shall discuss later in this Chapter.

EQUITY FINANCING

A common method of raising funds for a corporation is *equity financ-*

ing, that is, issuing stock. The corporate charter must specify the number of shares of stock which the corporation can issue.

More than one class of shares may be sold. Each class must be designated and its preferences, limitations, or relative rights described. If preferred stock is issued, it may be in a single class or a series. If it is issued as a series, each series must have a similar statement of the variations, preferences, and relative rights. The charter should specify any special authority to be vested in the board of directors concerning stock issuance.

Shareholder equity is composed of various types of stock which can have par value or no par value. The presence or amount of the par value has little significance except, perhaps, at the time of issue when the stock is sold at the designated par price. In some states, corporation stock is taxed on the par value, but if none is stated, then a per share tax applies. Tax considerations are the most important single reason for this classification.

The new corporation may decide to issue only a fraction of the total shares authorized in its articles of incorporation. The shares that are not sold are called *nonissued stock.* Those in the hands of the stockholders are known as *issued stock.*

Treasury stock is composed of stock that has been issued to individual stockholders and reacquired by the corporation. The corporation can either retain these shares in its treasury or reissue them. Retained treasury stock does not draw dividends nor does it have voting rights.

The most basic categorization of securities consists of preferred and common stock.

Common Stock

Every corporation issues common stock. The popular notion is that all common stock is the same. However, there can be many classes of common stock. Each has different degrees of voting or nonvoting powers. The voting stockholders elect the directors of a corporation.

Common stock frequently fluctuates in the market. However, it offers a large chance of financial gain if the corporation is successful, because the gains in the value of the stock are considered capital gains when the stock is sold. It also poses greater risk than preferred stock because if a division of corporate assets has to be made between the creditors and the shareholders, holders of common stock are the last to be considered.

Preferred Stock

Preferred stock is more secure than common stock though less exciting to the speculator. It is not as popular as common stock and is used to attract investors when other types of financing become unavailable. It offers a high rate of return with less fluctuation in price. However, sometimes even these features are insufficient, and so others are added.

Preferred stocks have several subclassifications. They may be cumulative, cumulative-if-earned, or noncumulative; participating or nonparticipating; convertible or nonconvertible; and callable or noncallable.

The cumulative feature of preferred stock relates to the payment of dividends. Legally, the board of directors determines the payment of dividends. If the interests of the corporation with good earnings are better served by withholding dividends in a given year, the board may do so. However, holders of cumulative preferred stock do not lose the passed-over dividends as do holders of common stock. Instead, their dividends accumulate and are payable to holders of common stock.

Cumulative-if-earned stock dividends accumulate only for the years in which the corporation earns a profit. To this extent, they precede common stock even if payments are withheld in a particular year.

Owners of preferred noncumulative stock simply share ahead of the owners of common stock when dividends are paid. If the directors decide not to pay a dividend in a given year, even owners of preferred noncumulative stock lose their dividends for that year. This type of stock is not too popular, and so corporate executives will usually pay dividends on it to maintain a good market image.

Participating stock provides for increases in dividends in accordance with some formula. The owners of preferred stock get their dividend, and then regular shareholders get a dividend that may amount to about the same as that of the preferred stock. After this point, both classes of stock share in distributions of further dividends. This can make participating stock quite attractive, and preferred stock is easier to sell if it contains this feature. Holders of nonparticipating stock merely get the specified payment regardless of company profits; this type of stock rarely increases in value beyond the general money rates.

Most preferred stocks carry dividend rates that have some relation to bank rates. For example, if the bank rates are 7 percent, the rate

Fig. 14-1. Common stock certificate (front).

PHILADELPHIA SUBURBAN CORPORATION

The Company will furnish to any shareholder upon request and without charge a full or summary statement of the designations, preferences, limitations and relative rights of the shares of each class of shares of the Company authorized to be issued, the variations in the relative rights and preferences between the shares of each series of shares of the Company so far as the same have been fixed and determined, and the authority of the Board of Directors to fix and determine the relative rights and preferences of classes and series of shares of the Company.

The following abbreviations, when used in the inscription on the face of this certificate, shall be construed as though they were written out in full according to applicable laws or regulations:

TEN COM—as tenants in common   UNIF GIFT MIN ACT—............ Custodian................

TEN ENT—as tenants by the entireties   (Cust)   (Minor)

JT TEN —as joint tenants with right of   under Uniform Gifts to Minors

           survivorship and not as tenants   Act..................

           in common   (State)

Additional abbreviations may also be used though not in the above list.

For value received, _____ *hereby sell, assign and transfer unto*

PLEASE INSERT SOCIAL SECURITY OR OTHER
TAXPAYER IDENTIFYING NUMBER OF ASSIGNEE

(PLEASE PRINT OR TYPEWRITE NAME AND ADDRESS, INCLUDING ZIP CODE, OF ASSIGNEE)

_____ *shares*

of the capital stock represented by the within Certificate, and do hereby irrevocably constitute and appoint

_____ *Attorney*

to transfer the said stock on the books of the within named Corporation with full power of substitution in the premises.

Dated _____

NOTICE: THE SIGNATURE TO THIS ASSIGNMENT MUST CORRESPOND WITH THE NAME AS WRITTEN UPON THE FACE OF THE CERTIFICATE IN EVERY PARTICULAR, WITHOUT ALTERATION OR ENLARGEMENT OR ANY CHANGE WHATEVER.

THIS SPACE MUST NOT BE COVERED IN ANY WAY

Fig. 14-2. Common stock certificate (back).

on the preferred stock will probably be 7 or 8 percent. A required dividend payment, as on cumulative preferred, is a heavy debt, since the corporation pays taxes on the earnings needed to pay these dividends. Unless some provision is made to redeem preferred stock, the corporation can be saddled with an expensive debt-paying requirement without any easy means of retiring it should money rates become easy or the corporation's money requirements lessen. Consequently, corporate management tries to avoid issuing preferred stock that does not contain a redemption provision. Generally, this provision provides a minimum period after which the shares will become subject to recall. Sometimes, the redemption provision includes a sinking fund that will be set up by the company and used to repurchase preferred shares.

The redemption provision also covers any accumulated dividends and describes which block of shares may be called up so the buyer can know what will continue to earn dividends.

Convertibility of preferred shares also makes stock attractive to investors. Convertible shares can be exchanged for a junior security at a predetermined ratio. A junior security is one that has less preference than the one in question, in this case, common stock. The holder of convertible shares will convert the shares only at a time when the conversion ratio is favorable. For example, if the preferred stock is selling at $100 when the common stock is selling at $80, the owner will not wish to convert these shares to common stock. If the common stock increases in value to $110, the additional $10 may induce the owner of preferred stock to convert to the common stock.

DEBT FINANCING

The incorporators who hold the controlling stock may not wish to share their control with others. They may want to finance their corporation through *debt financing*, that is, borrowing money through notes, mortgages, and bonds.

Debt financing provides "leverage" for the stockholders. It is advantageous when the company is successful because it raises money comparatively cheaply without diluting control.

Interest payments on notes, bonds, or mortgages are a deduction from income taxes, yet debt financing is not necessarily the best way of financing an operation. Even if the company falls on hard times, interest must be paid on the debt or it accumulates as an added charge until the creditors may take over the company. However, if the company does well, debt financing is a cheap way of getting money, and because interest payments are tax deductible, it quickly builds stockholder equity.

Other methods of financing also are designed to increase stockholder equity. However, the owners of a new business are not always able to dictate which type of financing is used. Those who lend money may want a share of the profits if the company is successful. They also will be looking for reasonable security.

Debt owed by a corporation can be in many forms, such as convertible bonds or first mortgage bonds. First mortgage bonds claim first priority on the corporate assets; the priority of other mortgage bonds has to be ascertained. Some bonds may be identified with a particular purpose; some, called debentures, are an unsecured obligation of the corporation.

Major newspapers list bond prices. Although bonds are generally sold in denominations of $1,000, prices are given in hundreds; for example, 82 means $820, and 110 means $1,110. The rates of interest, ranging from about 5 to about 9 percent are also given.

Bonds appear to be the most secure of investments. In days of high money rates, they provide a return that is usually higher than that of most stocks. However, no corporation can pay interest or dividends unless it makes a profit. If a corporation is mismanaged or becomes unprofitable for any reason, it will be unable to meet its interest charges. This leaves even bondholders with a bankrupt company and worn out equipment as security for its debts.

Equipment Obligations

Additional debt financing may involve equipment obligations. These are mainly used by railroads and airlines. Through an equipment trust plan a company can buy machinery on installments, technically a lease arrangement, until the machinery is paid for. This method has many tax advantages and avoids the necessity of seeking funds on the general money market.

CHANGES IN SECURITIES HOLDINGS

In a public corporation shares of stock can usually be freely sold on the market. They are sources of capital and are used for investment or speculation. To the outsider, the transaction may seem simple, but behind the scenes it is hedged with intricate bookkeeping devices and legislative restrictions.

Corporate Records

The names of all the shareholders (not bondholders) must be listed in the records of the corporation together with the number of shares they hold. Otherwise, notices of meetings or dividend checks could not be sent to shareholders. Maintaining an accurate list of shareholders is an important duty of the secretary of the corporation, who must be informed when stock shares are transferred.

Stock Transfers

The record of stock transfers can be kept in any or all of several books: (1) the certificate book from which the certificate is removed, while the name of the shareholder is entered on the stub; (2) the stock ledger, indicating all credits and debits resulting from share transfers next to the shareholder's name; and (3) a transfer book, noting that for value received, the stockholder assigns and transfers to the buyer a given number of shares in the capital stock of the company. Thus, the corporation recognizes formally that one party has been substituted for another as the shareholder on its books.

In connection with the transfer, the original stock certificate, duly endorsed, will be delivered to the buyer by the seller. Next, the buyer surrenders the certificate to the corporation, whose transfer agent will issue a new certificate, signed by the transfer agent and countersigned by the registrar. Then the transfer agent accurately notes the transaction as a debit to the seller and a credit to the buyer. The agent can delay the registration long enough to investigate the validity of the transfer, but cannot refuse to register it altogether.

Stock can be transferred by a separate assignment and a power of attorney. The holder can sign and have the stock registered in the corporation's books, but it is not necessary that the transfer be registered for it to be valid.

SHAREHOLDERS' RIGHTS

Shareholders possess powers granted by the corporation charter as well as those included in the bylaws. In addition, state statutes provide them with basic rights. The state is interested in the well-being of the corporation lest a group that is entrenched operate the corporation to the detriment of its investors. Some of the special laws and powers deal with the right to vote; others include agreements and methods of enforcing shareholders' rights.

Shareholders' Meetings

Shareholders are the owners of the corporation, but the management of its affairs rests with the board of directors. The shareholders meet at annual or special meetings to elect the directors and to conduct other business. This does not give the shareholder much influence, except for reviewing corporate affairs.

Shareholders' meetings are important to the stockholder who can demand answers to questions concerning the business. Directors are usually anxious to give good reports to the stockholders. Long-range plans are discussed, and special problems facing the corporation are brought before the stockholders. Charters and bylaws also reserve rights to the stockholders. For example, mortgages, bond issues, new stock issues, and major transfers of assets often require stockholder approval.

Time and Place

The charter or bylaws provide for an annual stockholders' meeting. Generally, the annual meeting is held at the registered office of the corporation. Special meetings of the shareholders may be called by the president, the board of directors, holders of not less than one-tenth of all the shares entitled to vote at the meeting, or other persons designated in the charter or bylaws.

Voting

Each outstanding share is entitled to one vote on every matter submitted to vote at a stockholders' meeting. The shareholder may vote either in person or by proxy. The proxy authorizing another to vote for the shareholder must be executed in writing by the shareholder. A proxy is revocable at will, but the secretary of the corporation must be notified of the revocation. Death or incapacity of the shareholder does not revoke the proxy unless notice has been given to the secretary of the corporation.

Cumulative Voting

The right to accumulate votes is an important minority stockholder right. Some states provide for this type of voting only if included in the charter. In essence, it permits the voting stockholder to cast as many votes for one person as the number of shares multiplied by the number of directors that are to be elected. As an example, if there were three directors to be elected, the person with 150 shares should cast 300 votes for one director or 100 votes for each director. The holder of one-third of the shares of stock can thus be assured of at least one favored director. This right becomes significant in a closely held corporation.

Voting Trusts

Although proxies are a recognized way of choosing another to vote for one at a single shareholders' meeting, voting trusts are more permanent arrangements because they may be irrevocable. The trustees act as owners of the stock, not just as agents for the owners.

Voting trusts can be useful for corporate financing (loans, mergers, reorganizations, etc.), preventing rival companies from getting control, and apportioning representation to protect minority interests. They should not be used to gain permanent control of the corporation or to tamper with salaries, contracts, and benefits.

Beneficiaries

Shareholders are entitled to share in the profits of a corporation as long as they are registered on its transfer books. They receive dividends and participate in the distribution of corporate assets when the corporation is dissolved.

Specific Rights of Class Shareholders

Each particular class of stock has certain basic rights. If the corporation has a class of preferred stock, it cannot issue another such series which would lower the priorities and preferences of the existing share. Even if such an issue would not be a real threat, the corporation will have to get the approval of the owners of the existing shares.

Preemptive Rights

Preemptive rights protect the shareholders from dilution of existing shares. When additional shares are to be issued, owners of the existing shares have the right to purchase a proportionate number of the new shares before they are offered to the public. In the absence of a prohibition in the charter, most states provide for preemptive rights. In theory, if the charter denies preemptive rights, the shareholder should be able to keep a proportionate share of the stock by purchasing it on the open market.

Watchdogs

To ascertain whether the company is being properly managed or whether their economic interest is in jeopardy, shareholders have a right to examine the corporate books at reasonable times and places. Through such inspection, the trained eye can appraise the company's financial position, detect possible mismanagement, determine the number and identity of other stockholders, and assess the value of the shares.

Though this is frequently cited as one of the most important rights guaranteed to every shareholder, few avail themselves of this opportunity, for most are content just to glance at the statements sent out periodically in conformity with the Securities and Exchange Commission rulings.

SECURITIES LEGISLATION

Securities have played a major part in financing American industry. Fortunes have been won and lost in stock manipulations. Fraudulent stock schemes involving watered stock and bucket shops (or brokerage houses dealing in such securities) were prevalent at one time.

State Regulations

State laws regulating the issuance and sale of securities within the state are called *blue sky laws*. The name stems from the attempt of legislatures to prevent the sale of securities that were backed by visionary promises but were in fact worthless.

The problem of security regulation was compounded by the lack of uniform state laws. Delaware was a favorite state for incorporating new businesses until fairly recently because it did not have any regulations concerning the issuance of corporate securities. A Uniform Sale of Securities Act was prepared in 1930, but it was adopted by only a few states. It is now being replaced with a Uniform Securities Act.

Such state statutes as exist regulate the registration of securities and dealers in securities. Their fraud provisions widen the common law remedy of deceit. Under the common law the injured party had to prove that the other party was guilty of fraud which was difficult because it involved intent. Now the laws are inclined to grant relief to the party claiming injury without the necessity of proving fraud. The courts also attempted to make it easier for defrauded persons to get relief, and they give greater power to the attorney general to regulate sales of securities. Broker-dealer registration not only regulates the activities of brokers but requires brokers to register the securities they handle. Registration of securities forces greater disclosure. Many of these state acts parallel the laws of the federal government, but they are concerned with securities that are not traded on national exchanges.

Federal Regulations

The first thorough federal security legislation was the Securities Act of 1933 concerning truth in the issuance of securities by the organization. Small issues under $300,000 can be exempted from some of the requirements of the Securities and Exchange Commission. The act was later amended to increase the powers of the commission.

The Securities and Exchange Commission is empowered to require full disclosure in regard to any sale of securities. This means a thorough disclosure of balance sheets, profit and loss statements, salaries of officers, debt positions, troubles facing the corporation, pending litigation, past profits, dividend payments, names of underwriters, and any other information considered to have a bearing on the issue. The commission also requires the filing of annual statements. This in turn affects statements that are issued to the stockholders.

The SEC does not approve securities. It merely attempts to force adequate disclosure of relevant information to enable ultimate buyers to make wiser selections.

A prospectus must be furnished each purchaser of newly issued securities. It contains most of the information that the corporation was required to furnish to the SEC in order to get the securities registered. If a company engages in transactions that should have been registered, supplies false or misleading statements, or makes material omissions, civil and criminal penalties can be imposed.

Investment capital is necessary for the growth of our economy. Through current national and state efforts, the climate for investors may improve substantially. Greater investor awareness should stimulate corporate management into making greater disclosures and provoke more stockholder participation in corporate affairs.

INVOLVEMENT AND STUDY MATERIAL

Understanding Terms

Equity financing	(page 205)	Bonds	(page 211)
Treasury stock	(page 206)	Proxy	(page 213)
Common stock	(page 206)	Cumulative voting	(page 213)
Preferred stock	(page 207)	Voting trusts	(page 214)
Sinking fund	(page 210)	Preemptive rights	(page 214)
Debt financing	(page 210)	Blue sky laws	(page 215)

Questions and Problem Solving

1. Should a starting business begin its operations with debt financing? What are the dangers of debt financing under the described circumstances?

2. Is the issuing of cumulative preferred stock preferable to debt financing? Explain your answer.

3. There are several classifications of preferred stock. Under what circumstances will a company be able to sell each of the various classes?

4. Compare the rights of a stockholder of a small company to examine the books of the company with the same rights claimed by a stockholder in a large corporation.

5. Explain the value of cumulative voting in a closely held corporation. Why is it less valuable in a large corporation whose shares are widely held?

6. Describe the functions of the Securities and Exchange Commission. Has the quality of investments improved because of the SEC requirements? Explain your answer.

7. What is a prospectus? How does it help the investor?

8. How do state securities regulations help the investor?

Cases for Discussion

1. The Farmington Corporation issued both preferred and common stock. The corporation earned a surplus during the year and the board of directors decided to declare a dividend to the common stockholders. One of the preferred stockholders brought a suit to prevent the payment of the dividends to the common stockholders claiming that the preferred stockholders should be paid first. Judgment for whom? Why?

2. The Baker Cleaning Corporation had no profits or surplus for the year; however, it declared a cash dividend payable out of the assets of the corporation. Is this a proper declaration of a dividend on the part of the directors? Why?

3. The Hytone Corporation sent out a notice of the annual meeting to all stockholders which stated that the meeting would be held in Atlanta, Georgia, at 1:00 P.M. Was this sufficient notice to the stockholders of this meeting? Why?

4. The Fisher Corporation issued stock with a cumulative voting feature. Brown, a minority stockholder, multiplied the number of shares she owned by the number of people to be elected, and then she cast her total vote for one director. The chairman of the board sought to have Brown's vote thrown out, claiming she did not have the right to vote in this manner. Is the chairman of the board correct? Why?

Chapter Fifteen

Changes in the Form of a Business

Very few of the thriving companies of the 1920s are in business today. Technological changes have made many companies obsolete. A business must maintain efficient operations or it may outlive its usefulness and be unable to change.

A prosperous enterprise can be threatened by social changes, and the people who make decisions must determine how best to meet them. Should a grocery chain stay open on a twenty-four-hour basis? Should it add other services to draw new customers? Should it try to eliminate a competitor? Entrepreneurs are always on the lookout for opportunities that will improve the present situation.

CONSOLIDATION AND MERGER

Regrouping of business is the purpose of consolidations and mergers. The terms are not synonymous although both represent a form of corporate reorganization.

Consolidation occurs when at least two companies join in such a way that their respective identities are absorbed into a new company. Thus, Haley's Hi Fi Shop and Tom's TV Repairs can consolidate to reemerge as Electronics, Inc.

A *merger*, in contrast, occurs when one of the converging companies survives and the other disappears. The stronger of several entities will absorb the others, and the new combination will continue to operate under the charter of the surviving company. Thus, a successful chain, American Home, Inc., could take over a number of small, struggling motels across the country by means of successive mergers.

Advantages

There are many reasons for combining several corporations. Let us examine the most important of them.

Economic

Mergers and consolidations are frequently motivated by economic necessity. A company may have to merge with the giant competitor before being squeezed out of the economic picture. Two merchants might consolidate their medium-sized business to form a more powerful and lucrative one. Economic survival, gain, and profit are persuasive arguments.

Taxation

Another important incentive is taxation. It has frequently been noted that the advantages gained under the present Internal Revenue Code through merger and consolidation are by no means the least of the incentives in favor of such moves, but the intricacies of the present tax laws are too complex to cover here. Many combinations ensure substantial tax benefits to the substituting company. Sustained business losses of the merging company can be used by the surviving company as a tax writeoff, and furthermore the survivor usually gets the assets of the old company at a reduced price because of these losses. For example, a company with $900,000 of assets and $500,000 in losses has an equity of only $400,000. The new or merging corporation takes over the ailing company at its net value of

$400,000 but, after the merger, it can utilize the tax loss of $500,000 in reporting its profits.

Transfer of Assets and Liabilities

Without the unwelcome problems of delay and expense, a business reorganization will automatically result in a transfer of all assets, rights, and liabilities to the newly merged or consolidated entity. Debtors and creditors alike must accept this shortcut which substitutes one corporation for several previous ones.

Recapitalization

In a sense, combining and rearranging the assets of the component companies is both a goal and an attribute of corporate reorganization. The financial structure of the business is reappraised and realigned when a merger or a consolidation takes place. Such changes are not always welcome; shareholders may not want an adjustment of their stock and their dividends, but they usually cannot prevent it from taking place.

Stock Adjustments

In the process of reorganization, the classification and the rights of the outstanding shares of stock can be completely changed. The individual shareholders may receive new shares of stock in place of the old certificates issued by corporations that no longer exist, but they may lose their claims for dividend arrears in the process and suffer a real financial loss. Even dividends owing on preferred shares, as well as preferences attributable to them, can be forfeited. In fact, the achievement of this end may be an ulterior motive behind the merger. The elimination of shareholders' rights to preferred stock dividends, which is not an uncommon accompaniment of the merger, is seldom upset in court on the grounds that it is unfair to the stockholders.

Transfer of Assets

Mergers may be preferred to consolidations in some situations. While leases or franchises may not be readily assignable to another in case of a consolidation, they can continue as assets in the hands of the surviving company into which the others have been merged.

Other Considerations

An individual, particularly a sole proprietor, may be swayed by other considerations favoring a merger or consolidation agreement. These may be wanting colleagues who can take over enough days in the year to permit a much-needed vacation, or seeking continuance of the business after death or retirement. The business person may see in reorganization an opportunity for pooling resources, more capital, greater efficiency, and professional cooperation. Often these aims are realized; sometimes, as in the case of the New York Central and Pennsylvania Railroad merger into the ill-fated Penn Central, they are frustrated. Mergers and consolidations can be disappointing in their outcome.

Disadvantages

In the rush to combine enterprises, many overlook the problems. Since these disadvantages are at least equal in importance to any advantages, they too must be considered.

Changes in Employment Practices

Mergers, or even consolidations, may be traumatic to the former managers. Loyalties of years are difficult to change. The sole proprietor and a president of a company, accustomed to dominating, may find it extremely difficult to adjust to new work procedures. It may be difficult for the former president to become a junior officer reporting to a much younger president of the new company.

In one of the nation's largest mergers, employee loyalties were so strong that factions became aligned with their old management teams and defeated the efforts of the new management. Fairly high-placed executives became so frustrated that they refused to cooperate and, perhaps, worked at contrary purposes. It has often been demonstrated that the person who is not convinced that a new way of doing business is the right way will sabotage the job, perhaps subconsciously, to vindicate the belief that the proposal was wrong. Sometimes there is so much division throughout the organization that the conglomerate cannot succeed. Just as "a house divided against itself cannot stand," a merger can fail through lack of cooperation at the executive level.

The lesson to be learned from the failures of others is that a merger must be carefully planned and sold to all the employees. A business cannot operate under two different systems. The consolidation or merger anticipates that there shall be one management and one company. Unless this is clearly understood beforehand, the merger will have difficulties instead of reaping the benefits desired when the reorganization was first undertaken.

Some unusually successful conglomerate organizers follow the practice of acquiring the new business with as little internal disruption as possible. The old management is left intact. The only change is the new direction furnished by the central office of the conglomerate. It, in turn, maintains a relatively small office to direct budget preparation, set profit quotas for the various units, and encourage increased efficiency. Only when the results are less than expected does the conglomerate management intervene in the local operation. Meanwhile, the takeover has been accomplished, and the employees have been conditioned to subtle changes in management philosophy. Resentment is held to a minimum.

Unemployment

Proposed mergers and consolidations can be bad news for the workers. Supervisory staffs are often seriously affected. In some cases, all supervisors of the merged company lose their jobs. Assuming that three companies are being combined, one firm might have 100 employees, another 125, and the third 75. If only 150 employees are needed to run the newly formed business, one-half of the present employees will have to be laid off.

Not long ago, a major merger took place that called for a layoff of over 800 workers. Negotiations concerning the merger were released, but complete silence was maintained about the employment situation. On midnight of the day preceding the merger, telegrams were delivered to all employees of the merged companies, notifying them that they were laid off. Their jobs had been taken over by the employees of the surviving company. Although the laid-off employees were later assured of liberal severence pay, no one can claim that the situation was a happy one. Reorganization is fraught with anxiety, particularly for employees who are loyal and who have given their best working years to the company that will not survive. Few can find new jobs at an advanced age. The merger affects the families of the employees as well. As mergers and consolidations continue, personal disappointments and tragedies rarely seem to be mentioned except as a matter of passing interest.

PUBLIC INTEREST

Considerable emphasis has been placed on efficiency and the need to make a profit. Indeed both are essential if the organization is to survive. However, it is necessary to consider how far the zeal for profit serves the public interest. Is the combination of businesses really a matter of greater efficiency and economy, or is the combination successful in producing a larger profit because it eliminates competitors?

Another question is whether profit should be the sole guide of any business. Is the public better served by a diversity of businesses with several competing entrepreneurs to capture each other's markets? Out of real competition have come many technological advances that probably would never have come from complacent companies that were not worried about inroads into their business.

Antitrust Prosecution

Since the passage of the Sherman Anti-Trust Act in 1890, the federal government has contended that combinations in restraint of trade are against public policy. Government officials, from the United States Attorney General down to local Justice Department officials, will review prospective mergers to determine whether they involve violations of antitrust laws. Many additions to the original antitrust act have been enacted: The Clayton Act, the Robinson-Patman Act, the Celler-Kefauver Antimerger Act, and many state antitrust regulations. The public is well aware of the power of industrial giants and wary of attempts to swallow opposition. Reducing competition may well result in increased cost to the consumer.

Merger statutes of the state of incorporation, as well as the states where the corporation does business, must be observed. The surviving corporation will have to file the amended articles of incorporation with all the states in which it does business. Blue sky laws of the various states must be observed.

Securities and Exchange Commission

The Securities and Exchange Commission may become interested if the filed reports show lack of candor. The Commission has the right to intercede if the proxy law has been violated. It also has power to intervene under the antifraud provisions, the power to supervise the acquisition of new securities resulting from the merger, and the right to object to any prospectus that may be filed in connection with such stock.

Vertical and Horizontal Mergers

Economists recognize the existence of both vertical and horizontal mergers. A horizontal merger involves the situation where two companies that are in the same business are combined. Thus, if one hardware company merges with another, it is a horizontal merger and may be illegal. The vertical merger involves a situation where one company acquires another company that operates in a supporting capacity. Thus, if a newspaper company merged with a newsprint manufacturer to complement its operations it would be a vertical merger and more acceptable, although these too are beginning to be viewed with suspicion. Factors to be examined by the government and the court in reaching a decision about whether the merger or consolidation is to be allowed will be the percentage of the total market the merged enterprise can command and the consequent lessening of competition.

REORGANIZATION PROCEDURE

Once a consolidation or a merger has been decided upon, a special procedure must be followed to achieve that goal. There is a unique pyramid of control within the corporation, and each level of the power structure will play its role in the reorganization procedure.

Action by the Board of Directors

The directors of a corporation have a fiduciary responsibility to act on behalf of the stockholders. They are under a moral duty to ascertain and obtain the best price they can for the corporate assets. Corporate exchanges of stock frequently show little relationship to the market price of the stock. In addition, the directors must negotiate and approve the reorganization agreement. It will be drafted under their supervision in accordance with the statutory requirements.

The Shareholders

There is usually a body of stockholders who take an active interest in the merger or consolidation of their corporation. The courts are willing to listen to complaints and apply a test of good faith or fairness in assessing the proposals put forth by the directors. The courts accept certain *class actions,* in which a group rather than a single individual brings litigation.

The Model Business Corporation Act

The Model Business Corporation Act provides that upon approval of the plan for merger or consolidation, the directors must submit the plan to a vote at a meeting of the shareholders. Written notice must be given not less than twenty days in advance to each shareholder of record whether or not the person is entitled to vote at the meeting. A copy or summary of the plan must be included with the notice. The act requires the approval of two-thirds of the shareholders eligible to vote, not only two-thirds of those voting. Where there are several classes of stock granting voting rights, holders of each class must approve by a similar majority.

Rights of Dissenting Shareholders

The Model Business Corporation Act has extensive provisions for any shareholder who does not wish to consent to the merger or consolidation but does not wish to contest the merger by a class action. The dissenter may make a written demand upon the corporation to redeem his or her shares at a fair value. The corporation then has the opportunity to offer a settlement to all dissenting stockholders at a price it considers fair.

If the dissenters do not accept the offer, the corporation can petition a court to determine the fair value. Any dissenter can also file such a petition, and all the dissenting stockholders automatically become parties to such an action. The court is empowered to appoint appraisers and award a decree that will include interest and assess the costs of the proceedings against the corporation.

Importance of Prompt Action

The Model Business Corporation Act would seem to give the dissenter adequate protection against mergers that are not acceptable. The problem arises not so much from a lack of legal rights as from ignorance of those rights. For example, the stockholder must file notice of dissent prior to the meeting at which the proposed corporate action is submitted for a vote. If the shareholders approve the merger, the dissenter must make a written demand for payment of the fair value of the shares. All this action requires rather precise timing; failing to comply can result in a loss of these rights. Once the procedure to secure a reasonable share for the stock is started and reaches a court, the determination is fairly routine.

The reason for speed is to prevent inconvenience to reorganization proceedings after the majority have consented. Although the law provides the dissenter with clear, ample remedies, there are other interests to protect, and these interests represent the majority of the stockholders. Therefore, it seems only right that the dissenter be required to act quickly.

Exchange of Stock

Two corporations contemplate a merger or consolidation because the directors and stockholders see a way each party can benefit. If their shares have identical market value, it is a simple matter to exchange the old shares for an equal number of new shares. Unfortunately such is seldom the case.

A company that is being taken over by a larger organization obviously cannot just exchange its shares for the stock of the merging company. Some formula must be developed that will allow a fair exchange of the shares of the disappearing company for the shares of the continuing company. The method by which the exchange of assets is figured will be included in the plan. If some stockholders feel that the plan is an attempt to take unfair advantage of them, the courts are willing to entertain a class action and insist that the plans provide for a fair exchange of assets.

Execution of the Reorganization

Before the resumption of operations under the merged arrangements, many preparations have to be completed. Otherwise chaotic events can occur to disrupt the new organization and result in its failure.

Organization Charts

We have emphasized organization charts in connection with the management of the corporation. It may be thought that one sole proprietorship merging with another does not need such a chart.

This can be a serious mistake. If the two proprietors are to work as partners, or in a corporate structure, their respective duties should be spelled out in advance. If there are objections, it is better to find out about them before any irrevocable steps have been taken. A dissolution of a partnership or corporation can be very expensive, even disastrous, for the small enterprise.

Assimilation of Property

The merger of a company involves the use of the properties and facilities of either or both of the entities being merged. A plan of operation should be prepared in advance that will identify operations, tools, or equipment that will be required. Excess equipment should be eliminated beforehand, or some may be kept in reserve until the reorganization is concluded.

Each party to the merger may have rented office or factory space, and rent may have to be paid until the end of the lease. If the property is owned, the organization plan should contemplate its disposition.

Assimilation of Obligations

Most companies have contracts with other businesses. These may be supplier contracts, employee contracts, sales distribution contracts, contracts with distribution agencies, and other obligations. They must be collated and coordinated into an operating plan for the new combined business. If overlapping areas exist, efforts can be made in advance either to eliminate them or to minimize the adverse effect of such conflicts. Franchises that may have been highly beneficial may also conflict with the design of the new business. These problems have to be resolved in advance.

CORPORATE DIVESTITURES

Mergers and consolidations are not always what their planners hoped for. In times of inflation, swollen stocks can be used to purchase sound industries, but a recession may find a conglomerate overextended and in need of ready cash. One quick way of getting it may be to sell one of the companies.

Government policy against mergers may be relaxed in the interest of the national economy. Nevertheless, large mergers can be attacked at any time by the Justice Department, and a *divestiture*—transferring of ownership or interests—may be ordered.

Occasionally a corporation will find that one of its acquisitions was less than anticipated. The product lines may not be compatible; distribution may have become too complicated. Sometimes a corporation develops a profitable line of goods but its major expansion is in another direction. As a result, its distributorship is not equipped to continue handling the line and it may wish to dispose of the division involved.

Methods of Divestiture

If the subordinate company is a wholly owned subsidiary, the parent company may simply ask the stockholders for permission to sell the particular company. Some other company may wish to merge with it. If this is not practical, other methods of divestiture may be used.

Spin-offs

A company may solve its problem by simply setting the other company free by issuing separate stock that represents the company's full value. The new company's stock is issued on a pro rata basis to the existing stockholders.

Split-offs

A split-off is identical to a spin-off, except that the original corporate stockholders exchange their shares for the shares of the new corporation. Stockholders may prefer one of the new companies to the other, but in the exchange of shares they cannot get special treatment.

Tax Problems

Neither the corporation nor the stockholders recognize any loss or gain in these stock transactions. There is no creation of new value even though there may be an exchange of stocks which came about solely by virtue of the separation of the corporate assets. Accordingly, reorganization results in no taxable income for the stockholders. Many such reorganizations are made after consultations with the Internal Revenue Service. If the IRS opposes a tax-free exchange, the corporation may wish to have the matter decided by a court before the transaction is consummated.

Mergers tend to mark periods of inflation and acquisition; divestitures attend financial crises. If the squeeze becomes too tight, it may reach even the parent company which may then think in terms of reorganization, dissolution, or bankruptcy.

INVOLVEMENT AND STUDY MATERIAL

Understanding Terms

Consolidations	(page 219)	Notice of dissent	(page 226)
Mergers	(page 219)	Spin-offs	(page 229)
Recapitalization	(page 221)	Split-offs	(page 229)
Antitrust acts	(page 224)		

Questions and Problem Solving

1. Distinguish between a consolidation and a merger. Cite several examples of each.

2. List several advantages and disadvantages of consolidations and mergers.

3. What has been the effect of the federal antitrust legislation upon mergers? List the guiding rule for the invoking of these laws.

4. What role does the Securities and Exchange Commission play with respect to the merger of corporations?

5. Distinguish between a spin-off and a split-off, citing several examples to illustrate each.

6. Describe the process of reorganization and its effect upon the stockholders.

7. Discuss the rights of the dissenting shareholders with respect to mergers or consolidations.

8. What effect, if any, does a merger have on the general public?

Cases for Discussion

1. The Entron Corporation directors decided to merge with the Atlantis Corporation, but they did not secure the consent of their own stockholders. Ryder, a stockholder in the Entron Corporation, brought a lawsuit to prevent the pending merger. Judgment for whom? Why?

2. The National Steel Corporation and the American Steel Corporation decided to merge. The merger was approved by the stockholders of both. The National Steel Corporation was the third largest steel producer in the United States, and the American Steel Corporation was the fifth largest producer. The federal government brought suit to stop the merger under the Sherman Anti-Trust Act, claiming that the merger would substantially reduce competition. Judgment for whom? Why?

3. The Palace Corporation contemplated a merger, and it secured the approval of the majority of the stockholders. Hilbling, a minority stockholder, did not approve of the merger, and he sought to prevent it through court action. The directors claim that Hilbling's suit is improper since it is not a class action and that his proper remedy was to make a written demand upon the corporation to redeem his stock at a fair value. Are the directors correct in their claim? Why?

Chapter Sixteen

Insolvency and Bankruptcy

A business, like a person, can become ill and die. Despite the best efforts of management, its objectives may not be realized. Corrective action then becomes necessary.

FEELING THE PULSE OF BUSINESS

The manager of a business must know when the business is healthy and when danger threatens. It is vital that the manager not only learn to read business charts, ratios, balance sheets, and profit and loss statements but, more importantly, understand what the various ratios mean. Just as many human deaths can be prevented if early warning signals are recognized, so it is with a business. It is necessary to act while alternatives are available and before the company's financial position is threatened.

To stay in business, one must make a profit. The business that does not utilize meaningful controls is often a sick business. Sometimes the disease becomes irreversible. A business that is over-capitalized cannot compete with other businesses because it must have a return on its investment. The business that is losing money and continues to operate because it still has cash reserves or because the owner works for almost no salary in the hope that things will get better is undergoing slow and painful death. Because their management is unrealistic, many businesses continue operations beyond the point where all signs indicate they should be terminated.

Remedial Treatment

Alert management will be concerned with the health of the business. Although it may concede short-term losses, the long-run operation must eventually reflect profits.

Analysis of the figures needs constant attention. Forward planning should utilize budgets. The first budget may not be perfect, but later ones will improve in both preparation and effectiveness.

A small business may find it difficult to spot problems and remain objective about its own plan. Therefore, an outside consultant should be considered, who should be chosen with care. Local businesses or a local university may be able to provide guidance in this selection. The consultant should have a record of success in directing businesses toward profitable operations.

Insolvency means that the business can no longer pay its debts. Being in financial trouble does not necessarily mean that the business should be declared insolvent. A business may not be able to pay its debts, but may be able to continue operations by persuading creditors to postpone their collections. In such circumstances, careful study is in order. Does the business need to reduce expenditures? If it is in financial troubles, it obviously has creditors. They will be vitally interested in the health of the company, but are they scattered, numerous, friendly, or obstreperous? Will they be willing to help the business? Perhaps contact with creditors can best be made by a specialist in this field. The lawyer or the consultant may be able to direct the manager to such a person.

ASSIGNMENTS AND COMPOSITIONS

If a thorough analysis of the ailing business reveals a reasonable basis for its continuation, its problems should be solved without terminating it. The solution should not merely be a postponement or continuation of the slow process of insolvency.

Assignments and compositions are ways in which a business can be reorganized without declaration of insolvency. However, these plans should not be attempted unless there is a genuine belief that the business can become successful and that continuation will increase the return to both the creditors and the owners.

Assignments

An *assignment* is an arrangement whereby the business, including all its assets, is assigned to a neutral party with the consent of the auditors. Generally, the business cannot succeed in treating itself. If it persists in running as before, there is little chance for improvement. The ailing business needs the aid of an expert. A consultant who has adequate business experience need not be a specialist in ailing businesses, although some are. A person who successfully manages another business can frequently spot trouble areas in the ailing business and recommend corrective action. The outside accountant and lawyer should be present during the preliminary planning of an assignment. The lawyer will be needed to analyze the legal implications and to make contact with creditors later. A creditor may assist in furthering the assignment with other creditors or in improving the plans for continued operation. If major creditors agree, other creditors will usually follow.

After the assent of the creditors has been secured, the business is assigned to the attorney or some neutral party. The assignment must be voluntary with no rights retained by the debtor business, although the assignment can provide for return of the business to the owners after the creditors have been repaid. If the creditors do not agree to assignment, an act of bankruptcy results.

The assignee either operates the business for the benefit of the creditors or liquidates it in accordance with the terms of the assignment. Sometimes, the assignment specifies that the assignee will operate the business for a given period according to a predetermined plan. If the arrangement does not produce the anticipated results, the assignee can liquidate the business.

Composition

Composition is an arrangement with creditors that provides for a legally binding reduction of debts by each creditor. An agreement by all the creditors to reduce their debts might enable the business to recover. As in the assignment, such a reduction has to come by agreement of all the creditors.

The business cannot hope for such a reduction unless there are plans that would show changes in operations and justify the continuance of the business. The business cannot simply seek a reduction of its debts. Creditors will want to see balance sheets, profit and loss statements, ratios, budgets, proposed changes in the business, and other plans lending some assurance that the reduction in debt will have a reasonable chance of returning money to them. If there are many small debts, it may be possible to refinance them after reasonable rehabilitation plans are accepted.

In composition, as in assignment, the creditors will be interested in knowing who will make payments. In an assignment, the assignee is held responsible to the creditors. In a composition, by implication at least, the old, unsuccessful management will still run the business. It may not be a management that inspires confidence about payment of debts. For this reason, the new operational plans should provide some type of watchdog over company operations that would justify the creditors in relying on the new plans and accepting a reduction of their debts.

Other types of compositions countenanced by the National Bankruptcy Act include arrangements, real property arrangements, wage earner's plans, and corporate reorganization.

Arrangements

An *arrangement* is a method by which the business can file a petition in court for acceptance of a plan to settle, satisfy, or extend the time for paying its unsecured debts. The petition is called "an original petition in proceedings under Chapter IX." An arrangement is an alternative to filing bankruptcy. The plan put before the court must be reasonable and fair. It may be instituted before or after a bankruptcy judgment, but it should be accompanied by schedules and statements of the company's affairs, a statement of the debtor's executory contracts, payment of fees to the clerk, as well as a list of the creditors with their addresses, a bond, and a summary of the company's assets and liabilities.

Basically the arrangement is a settlement with one's creditors either for less than the full amount due or for an extension of the time within which payment is to be made. The court will approve such an arrangement as long as it is fair, workable, and in the creditors' interests.

An arrangement is not entirely distinct from bankruptcy proceedings, since it can involve the appointment of a court receiver to supervise the business of the debtor while payment is being made on the debts. In the case of an arrangement under the Bankruptcy Act, that statute cannot have been violated by the debtor nor can anything be done to bar a discharge in bankruptcy. Meanwhile, unliquidated and disputed claims have to be settled and priorities determined. The arrangement must have been accepted by the majority of the creditors, both in number and in terms of the amount of their debt claims.

The debtor will be examined at a meeting of the creditors or in open court and will file a schedule of assets and liabilities just as if full bankruptcy proceedings were to be held. In fact, if the arrangement is not accepted in writing by the required number of creditors, is not approved by the court, or is set aside on the grounds of fraud within six months, the full bankruptcy proceedings will be held.

Real Estate Arrangements

There is a special type of real estate arrangement where the debts are secured by real property owned by a debtor. The debtor in this case cannot be a corporation. The plan must be accepted in good faith by the creditors before confirmation by the court.

Wage Earner's Plans

These also involve insolvent individuals rather than corporations. Here the composition or the extension of time for paying one's debts is based on the anticipated future earnings of the debtor. Such plans too must be accepted by the creditors in good faith and confirmed by the court.

Corporate Reorganization

Another step which falls short of the complete liquidation of an enterprise under bankruptcy proceedings is a corporate reorganization within the protection of the court. This eliminates any interruption of the corporation's business and stays all lawsuits against it while the rights of all its creditors and security holders are readjusted.

Either the company or at least three creditors to whom it owes $5,000 or more can file a petition for a reorganization showing that business is insolvent and cannot meet its debts as they mature. The plan for the reorganization, as included in the petition, must have the approval of the court, those creditors holding two-thirds of the amount of the claims filed, and a majority of the shareholders. It must also be a fair and workable plan.

Initiation of Court Action

Bad news travels fast! If the ailing company does not act swiftly to take action to control the situation, it cannot expect its creditors to cooperate. Creditors appreciate it when management exhibits concern over the business. If the matter is ignored until outside action is essential, the business may be beyond help.

In an effort to protect themselves, creditors may take court action. A writ may be issued to the sheriff that enough property be seized to satisfy the judgment. This is a drastic and costly way to satisfy creditors. Forced sales are notorious for bringing low returns. Thus every effort should be made to stay in control of the situation. The creditors themselves will try to salvage as much as they can. Once suits are filed by a number of creditors, it will generally be too late for any plan to continue business.

BANKRUPTCY

The business that simply cannot continue or cannot get the agreement of its creditors has reached the final stage, bankruptcy. This can be voluntary or involuntary. Although many states have laws dealing with insolvency, most cases are handled under the federal Bankruptcy Act and under the jurisdiction of the federal courts.

Involuntary Bankruptcy

Involuntary bankruptcy is an action brought by third persons (usually creditors) seeking to have the defendant, who can appear and contest the proceedings, declared bankrupt. If the person is declared bankrupt, assets will be seized and distributed to the creditors. In any involuntary bankruptcy proceeding, the defendant can be any individuals or corporation except railroads, banks, building and loan associations, insurance companies, farmers, municipal corporations, and some others, since public policy would have a special interest in protecting the community against their dissolution through bankruptcy.

The Bankruptcy Petition

In order to initiate involuntary bankruptcy proceedings, a creditor must file a petition. If there are fewer than twelve creditors, any one can act alone. Should there be more than twelve creditors, any three or more can file the involuntary bankruptcy petition together if (1) they can prove that they have a liquidated claim for debts totaling $500 more than the value of the securities held by them, (2) the debtor owes a total amount of $1,000 or more, and (3) the debtor has committed an act of bankruptcy no more than four months before the petition was filed.

Acts of Bankruptcy

An act of bankruptcy can be any transfer or concealment of part of the property by the alleged bankrupt in order to defraud creditors. For example, the officers of the troubled company remove goods from the warehouse in the middle of the night and send them to another city. Another such act would be to transfer part of its property to a creditor, because of an earlier debt, in such a way that that creditor would receive a greater share of it than any other creditor of the same class while the company was insolvent. In general, it can be said that an act of bankruptcy results whenever the debtor acts in a way that is prejudicial to the rights of one or more creditors.

A final act of bankruptcy consists of the bankrupt's admission in writing of inability to pay the debts and willingness to be declared bankrupt. At this point, the creditor can file a petition for involuntary bankruptcy and give bond to cover any costs incurred by the debtor.

Bankruptcy Judge

The bankruptcy judge is an officer appointed by the federal district court to perform many of the administrative matters that are necessary in connection with bankruptcy proceedings. The old title to this position was *referee* and still may be used to distinguish this position from that of the district judge. The bankruptcy judge's actions are always subject to a review by the court. The bankruptcy judge makes findings of fact; if the creditors object, the findings may be modified. The lawyer for the bankrupt debtor may make a motion before the bankruptcy judge for the appointment of a receiver or trustee. The trustee will have the power to remove the assets from the premises of the bankrupt to a warehouse in order to cut costs resulting from continued use of the premises and may also conduct the business of the bankrupt in an effort to conserve the assets. Most important, the trustee is authorized to dispose of the bankrupt's assets at either a public or a private sale with the permission of the court. The bankrupt has no personal rights over the property after such a trustee has been appointed, except for any new property acquired after the declaration of bankruptcy.

Schedules

A schedule of assets will have to be drawn up by the debtor listing, in addition, the names of the creditors and the amounts owed to them, specifying whether the debts are secured or unsecured.

Meeting of Creditors

The bankruptcy judge presides over the first meeting of the creditors. This occasion can be used as a chance to see whether any creditor has received preference. Creditors will have a chance to question the bankrupt, spouse, relatives, bank, business associates, accountant, and other creditors to ascertain the amount of assets. Of course, the greater the assets, the more intense is their interest. If a trustee has not been appointed at the request of the lawyer for the bankrupt, the creditors can request that the bankruptcy judge appoint one to administer the assets and wind up the business.

Generally, all the claims are filed within six months of the first meeting. The bankruptcy judge will review the claims and pass on their acceptability. The court may call additional meetings of the creditors at its discretion or on request of creditors.

Voluntary Bankruptcies

A voluntary bankruptcy is instituted by a petition filed by the debtor. Any person, partnership, or corporation—with the exceptions noted above—can file a petition for a voluntary bankruptcy. The ensuing bankruptcy proceedings liquidate the assets of the bankrupt and distribute them to the creditors.

Schedules

The bankrupt has to file schedules similar to those prepared under the involuntary proceedings. The name and address of every creditor should be listed. The burden of proof is on the bankrupt to demonstrate that the creditors had notice of these proceedings. The trustee or receiver must post bond for faithful performance of all duties, such as disposing of perishables or protecting the property. He or she concludes with a final accounting to the court.

Effects

Following the decree in bankruptcy, any legitimate liens on the property of the bankrupt remain in effect. If there are life insurance policies among the bankrupt's assets, their cash surrender value remains for the beneficiary. However, a bankrupt's lease is valid only until the bankruptcy petition has been filed. Thereafter, the trustee can accept or reject the lease, though rent remains due while the tenant is in possession.

Debts

Some debts will not be affected by a discharge in bankruptcy. Certain wages, future alimony, taxes, any unscheduled debts, and claims involving fraud or willful, malicious torts remain liabilities of the bankrupt even after a discharge in bankruptcy.

Provable debts are dischargeable as a general rule. In order for a creditor to share in the distribution of the bankrupt's assets, a claim must be filed within six months after the declaration of bankruptcy. The final court order frees bankrupts of all debts listed. Creditors cannot later recover any part of that debt by an action at law, because the discharge in bankruptcy is a complete defense to it.

Denial of the Petition

Of course, there are certain cases in which a discharge in bankruptcy can be denied, such as when the books and records have been destroyed, falsified, mutilated, or concealed. Other instances arise if the bankrupt has made false written statements about his or her financial condition or has concealed or transferred any property to defraud creditors within six months before the discharge in bankruptcy was supposed to take place.

Limits on Bankruptcy

Some individuals and companies delude themselves into believing that bankruptcy proceedings are a quick and easy "out" if business becomes bad, but bankruptcy should be only a last resort. After a voluntary bankruptcy petition has been filed, a second one may not be submitted by the same individual for six years. Even more important, a decree of bankruptcy does not improve one's credit rating in the community.

The moment financial statements flash a warning, a lawyer should be consulted. If action is taken in time, it may still be possible to arrange for a composition, arrangement, or reorganization. Only if conditions are hopeless should an enterprise be terminated by a decree of bankruptcy.

CREDITOR RELATIONSHIPS

Not all creditor relationships are as drastic as the ones we have discussed. Nevertheless, the options open to the operator of a business should be known. Further, some general credit information will also be helpful to prevent the troubles that arise from unwise credit decisions.

Credit Purchases

Many merchandise sales involve some type of credit arrangement. Merchants who sell large appliances will normally take a security interest or chattel mortgage. A security interest or chattel mortgage is a formal document in which the buyer acknowledges the debt to the creditor and agrees to hold the described property as security for the debt until paid. The creditor next files the document with the proper county official as evidence of the debt and notice to third parties of an interest in the described property. The document is called a *financing statement* and is a binding notice on all prospective purchasers to the property. Some states provide a central filing location. Mortgage interests in automobiles are recorded with the department of motor vehicles and title registrations. Anyone purchasing a mortgaged or secured article is on notice that the title is not clear and ownership is subject to the mortgaged interests (see U.C.C. article 9).

Bulk Transfers

Of equal importance is U.C.C. title 6 concerning bulk transfers. *Bulk transfers* are purchases that are not in the ordinary course of business. A store that sells merchandise can give a clear title to any purchaser who buys an article in good faith and pays the agreed price; however, the moment the owner decides to sell all the store's merchandise, it becomes a bulk transfer under article 6 of the U.C.C. In substance, that article requires the bulk buyer of merchandise or fixtures to get a sworn statement from the seller. The statement lists the transferrer's existing creditors. Any person known to the transferrer who has filed a claim, even though the claim is disputed, must be included. The property to be transferred must be identified on a schedule.

Ten days before accepting or paying for the goods, the buyer must give notice to all the listed creditors. The notice must identify the parties, their addresses, and the manner in which the debts are to be paid and fulfill a number of other requirements. The accuracy of the list is the responsibility of the transferrer but the buyer is responsible for notification. Failure to comply with this section makes the transferrer liable to the creditors except for such sums as may have been paid to other creditors (U.C.C. sec. 6-109).

POST MORTEM

One solution to insolvency is dissolution of the business. The realization that the venture was a failure is a bitter pill indeed. Opportunity for starting a new enterprise will be dimmed because the credit of the entrepreneur has been impaired. Neverthless, bankruptcy and the various creditor plans should be recognized as orderly conclusions of an enterprise with financial troubles. Dissolution is better than letting the venture struggle hopelessly. It lifts the load off of the debtor, who is given an opportunity to start all over without the worry of old debts.

The discussion in this chapter should remind the prospective manager that there are penalties for inattention to the company.

A manager who recognizes a problem and starts doing something about it immediately can avoid the long road to failure.

INVOLVEMENT AND STUDY MATERIAL

Understanding Terms

Insolvency	(page 233)	Reorganization	(page 236)
Assignment	(page 234)	Bankruptcy	(page 237)
Liquidate	(page 234)	Acts of bankruptcy	(page 238)
Composition	(page 234)	Bankruptcy judge	(page 238)
Arrangements	(page 235)	Financing statement	(page 241)
Wage earner's plan	(page 236)	Bulk transfers	(page 242)

Questions and Problem Solving

1. Why is the business that is continuously losing money undergoing a slow and painful liquidation?

2. How does one feel the economic pulse of a business?

3. Why is it important to utilize charts, ratios, balance sheets, and other business data in guiding a business?

4. Explain why a business may sometimes concede short-term losses but in the long run must make a profit.

5. Why and when does it become necessary to have an outsider take over a business in a composition or an assignment? When insolvency threatens, is it unconstitutional to take the business away from the entrepreneur who developed it? Explain your answer.

6. In what way can major creditors be a source of help to an ailing business?

7. Why is it preferable for the business person to initiate remedial action rather than wait for the creditors to do so?

8. Explain the advantages of a wage earner's plan.

9. Describe some acts of bankruptcy.

10. What debts or obligations are not discharged by a decree in bankruptcy?

11. Explain the obligations of the seller and buyer regarding bulk transfers.

Cases for Discussion

1. Sill brought suit to have the Kentucky Coal and Timber Company declared an involuntary bankrupt and to have a receiver appointed to wind up the affairs of the company. Sill was a stockholder in the company as well as one of the creditors. He contended that the company was unable to meet its debts and obligations as they matured. The company denied Sill's contention, stating that this was not a test as to its solvency. Judgment for whom? Why?

2. The Michigan Stove Company solicited orders for stoves from a large number of local merchants. In an effort to get a carload shipment all agreed with Michigan's agent that the carload shipment would go to Cochrane Company who would then distribute to other purchasers. Later the agent directed the local purchasers to make payments for the merchandise to Cochrane who, in turn, would pay Michigan Stove Company for the entire shipment. After the agreement Cochrane was declared bankrupt and Michigan brought suit against the other buyers to collect the remaining money owed on the shipment. The defendants refused to pay saying they owed the money to Cochrane and the receiver in bankruptcy, not Michigan. Judgment for whom? Why?

3. Murray Tool and Supply Company, E. S. Brammer and Dave Maxwell filed a petition in bankruptcy claiming that Arkansas Oil and Mining Company committed an act in bankruptcy when it allowed Troy E. Scott to obtain a lien on its property for $5,013.50 and that Arkansas Oil and Mining Company was insolvent at the time the lien was filed. Arkansas Oil and Mining Company opposed the petition on two grounds: the Murray Tool and Supply Company was not a bona fide creditor but a partner in the business with the Arkansas Oil and Mining Company and at the time the lien was filed Arkansas Oil and Mining was not in fact insolvent. To support the fact of insolvency, the plaintiff introduced a letter from the vice president of the Arkansas Oil and Mining Company who wrote that he was insolvent, and that he was willing to have the company declared

bankrupt. In support of the contention that Murray Tool and Supply Company was a partner, Arkansas Oil and Mining Company introduced a copy of a document which disclosed working arrangements on a project. The court ruled that this contained the essential elements of a partnership. Assuming that the document disclosed a partnership agreement, would the partner then be a proper party to the filing of a petition in bankruptcy? If not, what would be the proper remedy? Was the letter from the vice president of the company, without any further support or documentation, an act of bankruptcy? Why? If the letter did not disclose a partnership, was it sufficient to prove insolvency at the time the lien was filed, and was the failure to contest it an act of bankruptcy?

PART
THREE

EMPLOYMENT

Chapter Seventeen

Employment Liabilities

The decision to engage the services of another is a serious undertaking carrying many economic and legal implications for both the employer and the employee. Poor selection can be costly in time and money to both. Although the employer is normally experienced in selecting applicants, mistakes are possible. If so, both lose, and any waste is unfortunate. Thus it is hoped that this discussion will teach both the manager and the job applicant that executing an employment contract is a serious undertaking which deserves careful analysis of all the factors involved.

PROCESS OF EMPLOYMENT

The process of employment may not appear at first to be very complicated. The employer wants someone to perform a task, and the prospective employee offers to do it. Payment for performance will usually be a part of the arrangement. Neither party may be aware of the legal implications of the relationship that is being established or of the various laws that bear upon the employment process. However, the law of agency, civil rights laws, formalities of the employment contract, fair labor standards, the Wage and Hour Act, and finally, the employer's legal liability for the acts of employees are all involved. Employers should observe certain legal procedures in the employment process. Moreover, the law places additional responsibilities upon them after the contracts of employment have been executed. The application of these laws is not often considered in the initial employment relationship, but it can later loom large to the contracting parties and to third parties.

Preliminaries to the Employment Contract

The preliminary contact between a prospective employee and an employer usually results from some indication that the employer is seeking workers. The prospective employee—the applicant—will usually be required to fill out some form that will be examined by the employer to determine the qualifications of the applicant. This application form is subject to various laws. The Civil Rights Act prohibits questions in regard to race, creed, sex, and national origin.

After the preliminary written information has been examined, an interview may be arranged. Skilled interviewers may test the applicant in various ways. Through analysis of the applicant's appearance, attitude and responses to questions, they form opinions and impressions that will determine whether the applicant will be offered employment.

Employment Records

Prospective employers are frequently interested in information about the applicant's past employment record, reasons for leaving other jobs, possible criminal record, educational background, and references. Sometimes special employment tests are administered. This entire area is extremely sensitive. It affects the applicant's private life and, if handled indiscreetly, can subject the employer to legal liability and damages for invasion of privacy.

It is difficult to verify information furnished by an applicant without some type of investigation, yet contacting a prior employer or reference furnished by the applicant can produce undesirable rumors or comments about the applicant. Even though the prospective employer treats all information received from the applicant in the strictest confidence, there is no assurance that the people contacted will do likewise. Therefore, to protect themselves against the charge of invasion of privacy, many employers request the permission of the applicant before conducting the necessary investigations. Nevertheless, such permission from the applicant is not a license to engage in unreasonable investigations or to volunteer unnecessary, inaccurate, or unwarranted information to other people. This applies to other employees who are not concerned with the employment process. Failure to observe adequate precautions may give the applicant grounds for suit for defamation or invasion of privacy.

Many thoughtful people have expressed fear that placing confidential employee information in a computer can constitute an invasion of privacy. However, computer experts claim that, although misuse of such information is possible, it is not probable because the cost would not justify the results.

THE CIVIL RIGHTS ACT

There is now increasing concern about discrimination in employment on the basis of sex, race, creed, or national origin. Several statutes have been enacted in an effort to give the applicant an opportunity to secure employment on merit. The most far-reaching is the Civil Rights Act of 1964.

Provisions

The Civil Rights Act covers most businesses that employ more than twenty-five persons. It prohibits all discrimination in employment based on race, creed, color, sex, or national origin. The employer can neither refuse to hire nor discharge a worker on the basis of these criteria. Once the employee is hired, no discrimination within the company by such practices as differential promotion criteria or separate eating facilities or other accommodations is permitted.

An individual who feels there has been unlawful discrimination can file a charge of discrimination with the Civil Rights Commission. Once such a charge is filed, an investigation will be made, followed by an effort to eliminate any practices that violate the act. If the Commission finds that discrimination exists and it cannot reach an amicable solution, the matter is referred to the Justice Department for prosecution in a federal court.

(PLEASE PRINT OR TYPE)

CHARGE OF DISCRIMINATION	EEOC CHARGE NO.	FORM APPROVED OMB NO. 124-R0001

INSTRUCTIONS	CAUSE OF DISCRIMINATION
If you have a complaint, fill in this form and mail it to the Equal Employment Opportunity Commission's District Office in your area. In most cases, a charge must be filed with the EEOC within a specified time after the discriminatory act took place. IT IS THEREFORE IMPORTANT TO FILE YOUR CHARGE AS SOON AS POSSIBLE. *(Attach extra sheets of paper if necessary.)*	☐ RACE OR COLOR ☒ SEX ☐ RELIGIOUS CREED ☐ NATIONAL ORIGIN

NAME *(Indicate Mr. or Ms.)*	DATE OF BIRTH
Ms. Rita Valdez	April 5, 1950

STREET ADDRESS	COUNTY	SOCIAL SECURITY NO.
1234 Maple St.	Fulton	332-86-6768

CITY, STATE, AND ZIP CODE	TELEPHONE NO. *(Include area code)*
Atlanta, GA 30303	414-834-6920

THE FOLLOWING PERSON ALWAYS KNOWS WHERE TO CONTACT ME

NAME *(Indicate Mr. or Ms.)*	TELEPHONE NO. *(Include area code)*
Ms. Juanita Jimenez	214-348-7411

STREET ADDRESS	CITY, STATE, AND ZIP CODE
1234 Main Street	Dallas, TX

LIST THE EMPLOYER, LABOR ORGANIZATION, EMPLOYMENT AGENCY, APPRENTICESHIP COMMITTEE, STATE OR LOCAL GOVERNMENT WHO DISCRIMINATED AGAINST YOU *(If more than one, list all)*

NAME	TELEPHONE NO. *(Include area code)*
Terrapin Manufacturing Co.	414-268-1111

STREET ADDRESS	CITY, STATE, AND ZIP CODE
5431 Center St.	Atlanta, GA 30301

OTHERS WHO DISCRIMINATED AGAINST YOU *(If any)*	

CHARGE FILED WITH STATE/LOCAL GOV'T. AGENCY	DATE FILED	AGENCY CHARGE FILED WITH *(Name and address)*
☐ YES ☒ NO		

APPROXIMATE NO. OF EMPLOYEES/MEMBERS OF COMPANY OR UNION THIS CHARGE IS FILED AGAINST 215	DATE MOST RECENT OR CONTINUING DISCRIMINATION TOOK PLACE *(Month, day, and year)* March 7, 1974

Explain what unfair thing was done to you and how other persons were treated differently. Understanding that this statement is for the use of the United States Equal Employment Opportunity Commission, I hereby certify:

I am an employee in the accounting department in pay grade 6. I have been employed by this company for 5 years and am a graduate of a junior college. My immediate supervisor has been rating my work as excellent. When a pay grade 6 vacancy occurred a young man who was hired only six months ago was given the job. When I inquired why I didn't get the job I was told by the department manager that I did not have enough experience. When I checked the qualifications of the person who got the promotion I found that he had graduated from a junior college only a year ago and worked only six months before coming to this company.

I swear or affirm that I have read the above charge and that it is true to the best of my knowledge, information and belief.	SUBSCRIBED AND SWORN TO BEFORE ME THIS DATE *(Day, month, and year)*
DATE March 14, 1974	CHARGING PARTY *(Signature)* *Rita Valdez*	SIGNATURE *(If it is difficult for you to get a Notary Public to sign this, sign your own name and mail to the District Office. The Commission will notarize the charge for you at a later date.)*
Subscribed and sworn to before this EEOC representative.	
DATE	SIGNATURE AND TITLE

(NOTARY PUBLIC)

EEOC FORM JUN 72 5   Previous editions of this form may be used.   U.S. GOVERNMENT PRINTING OFFICE : 1973-728-451/1250 3-1
GPO 871-188

Fig. 17-1. Charge of discrimination.

Impact

The Civil Rights Act has already had an impact on hiring practices in the United States. No brochure or advertisement of job openings can express any discriminatory preference except for "bona fide occupational qualifications." A differentiation can be made in salary based on merit, earnings, or seniority. To avoid difficulty, many employers have developed job classifications through which promotions and pay increases can be given. When such classifications are carefully and fairly administered their use prevents charges of discrimination. It is important that the employees be made aware of company policies in regard to these matters. When salary increases are granted, all employees should know why they are made. Unless employees are told about the basis of promotion, they are likely to suspect that the action of the company is based on caprice or even prejudice.

The National Association for the Advancement of Colored People (NAACP) and the Equal Employment Opportunity Commission (EEOC) have initiated an organized and effective campaign against discrimination in industry. Many of the techniques being used in this effort are reminiscent of those long employed by labor unions: publicity, picketing, and strikes are directed at companies who are charged with discriminatory hiring policies. The courts have also been used in attempts not only to rectify individual cases of discrimination but even to prevent the transaction of business until integration of the workers is complete.

Particularly controversial is the idea of fixing quotas so that the percentage of minority employees more closely approximates their percentage of the total population; for example, perhaps 14 percent of the jobs on a construction project would have to be reserved for minority applicants. Would this employment irrespective of training, ability, and experience in itself be evidence of differential treatment?

Civil rights laws also apply to unions. They too can neither refuse membership to an individual nor discriminate against and expel a member because of race, religion, sex, creed, or color.

Employment Contracts

No matter how informal the agreement is, certain procedures are to be observed. An employment contract should specify the amount of the salary, the type of job, and the immediate superior for whom the applicant will work.

Written or Oral Contracts

Under the statute of frauds, a contract that is to run longer than one year must be in writing. Contracts of employment for specialists or executives often are in writing. Agreements for employment of a group of people through a labor union are also usually written, since they last for a number of years and may affect numerous employees. More informal and oral employment contracts usually involve employment for less than a year or even for an indefinite period of time and can be terminated by either party.

Printed Specifications

Firms that employ a work force of fifty or more often have pamphlets describing various details about the employment, hours worked, rest periods, company rules, and other requirements. Although there may be no formal signed contract, the printed pamphlet serves as a part of the contract of employment since violation of the rules generally means termination of employment.

Compensation

It is a rare contract of employment that does not cover the amount of compensation that will be given to the employee. A salary may be paid by the month, week, or at some other interval. It must comply with the minimum wage law as well as regulations for a regular work week and overtime pay. Accurate records of earnings, hours worked, and overtime must be kept by the employer. These records may be checked by the U.S. Department of Labor under the Fair Labor Standards Act of 1938/1949 and the Equal Pay Act of 1963.

EMPLOYMENT RELATIONSHIP

After a person is hired, a complex set of relationships arises among the employer, employees, and outsiders.

The Persons

Once hired, the employee works for the enterprise. Employees are defined by the National Labor Relations Act as being any who earn salaries, wages, or commissions, except for certain specific exclusions. Thus they are distinguished from independent contractors, who can work as they choose with their own equipment and are accountable only for the end result to the person who originally commissioned the work to be done. The differentiating criterion is the amount of control which the enterprise can exercise over the person doing the job.

The Ramifications

Most cases raising the issue of whether a worker was an employee or an independent contractor arise after injury or death on the job. At that point the injured party or the estate will usually try to establish an employee relationship in order to recover damages from the employer either at common law or under workmen's compensation. In most cases, the independent contractor does not have disability insurance, and so will want to recover under workmen's compensation at least. It is not unusual for common law liability to be substantially greater than the benefits under workmen's compensation, but a common law recovery is more difficult or even superseded by the statute.

The type of working relationship will also be relevant when an outsider wants to sue an employer. Sometimes the employee represents the employer in transactions with third persons. For instance, the sales clerk who sells suits to customers in a store acts as the employer's agent in making the sales. In this capacity the employee can affect the legal status of the employer.

It has been demonstrated in Chapter 4 that a principal is liable for the agent's actions if certain prerequisites are met. This is a serious concern for the manager interviewing applicants who may be accident prone, negligent, or intemperate. An employer who is careless in selecting a worker may be held liable for the conduct of the employee, even if the employee's acts go beyond authorized bounds. Potential liability is the dark side of the employment relationship.

This field of law is currently undergoing relatively rapid and dramatic change. In the Middle Ages, fault was not an important factor: a whole village could be held responsible for an injury if the individual wrongdoer could not be located. More recently, our law has based liability on fault, whether intentional or negligent. The fault of employees, acting within the scope of their employment, is imputed to the employer under the doctrine of *respondeat superior* ("let the superior answer"). Now there are signs that the courts may be extending the liability of the business in areas involving public safety and that legislators are undermining the requirement of fault by enacting workmen's compensation and no-fault insurance. However, until such sweeping changes occur more widely, it is necessary to become familiar with the traditional concepts in this field.

LEGAL LIABILITY

Although it is evident that an individual becomes legally liable to others for his or her own wrongful conduct, what may not be so clear is the extent to which the employer may become vicariously liable for the wrongful conduct of employees. Under the concept of agency discussed in Chapter 4, an employee can impose legal liability to third parties upon the employer either by negotiating agreements or by wrongfully causing damage to such third parties. *Legal liability* may be defined as a state or condition by which the law imposes a requirement on one party to pay damages to another. This situation occurs when the wrongdoer falls short of the objective standard of care presumably exercised by a fictitious "reasonable man" and injury ensues. Damages can be very high in these actions.

This area of law is called *torts* from the Norman French word for "wrong." A tort is doing or failing to do that which a reasonable and prudent man would or would not do under the same or similar circumstances. Although the principles that follow apply to any person acting in relation to third parties, this concise survey is presented here primarily for the benefit of the business which may employ people.

Negligence

The broadest category of tort is *negligence*. It can consist of doing something badly or not doing anything at all. Both driving rapidly through a red light and failing to apply the brakes can be negligent conduct. A person who is adjudged not to have performed with the same amount of care a fictitious reasonable, prudent person would have demonstrated in the same situation is considered negligent.

Almost all forms of negligence can be easily analyzed by visualizing a table with four legs. These legs represent four factors which must exist in order to establish liability on the grounds of negligence. The injured party must prove (1) that the businessman, or the agent, was negligent, (2) that this negligence resulted in an injury for which damages are being claimed, (3) that the negligence was the proximate cause of the injury sustained, and, in many states, (4) that the

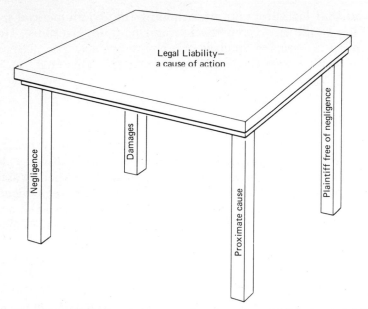

Fig. 17-2. Elements of a cause of action. To establish legal liability, the plaintiff has to prove the elements represented by the four legs of the table. If he fails, the table falls and that is the end of the case. If the plaintiff is not free of contributory negligence, he may be able to restructure that leg with other defenses and still win his case.

injured party was not guilty of contributory negligence. If one of the legs collapses, the table—the claim of negligence—will not stand.

Proximate Cause

The concept of proximate cause is not an easy one. It means that the injured party cannot recover damages unless within the anticipated range of danger. This artificial limit on liability was enunciated in the famous Palsgraf case over fifty years ago. A man carrying a package ran to catch a train which was about to leave the station. An attendant at the station disobeyed company rules and attempted to help the man aboard. In the process, a package the man was carrying was dislodged and fell to the tracks, causing an explosion as the train pulled away. Mrs. Palsgraf, standing at the other end of the platform, was injured by a scale which fell as the result of the explosion. She sued the railroad for the negligence of the attendant but was denied recovery on the grounds of proximate cause. Ever since that time, American courts have distinguished between those like Mrs. Palsgraf to whom injury was not reasonably foreseeable and,

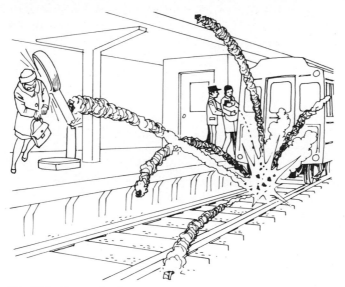

Fig. 17-3. No proximate cause.

therefore, to whom there was no breach of duty and those who can prove a direct cause and effect. In between these extremes are the difficult cases which the jury resolves.

Contributory Negligence

Assuming the injured party, or plaintiff, can establish the existence of the other party's negligence, an injury to himself, and the proximate cause between the two, the defendant will try to topple the table by hitting its weakest leg. The defendant will allege that the plaintiff was guilty of *contributory negligence*, that old common law rule which still prevails in many jurisdictions to prevent any compensatory recovery at all. If this attack is used, the injured party can resort to three arguments: gross negligence, comparative negligence, or last clear chance.

Gross Negligence

If a defendant has been so grossly negligent or reckless that a reasonable juror's conscience would be appalled, an injured person who was also negligent but to a lesser degree may still recover in some jurisdictions. Thus, someone who negligently rolls over onto a railroad siding while drugged might recover from a railroad whose employee neither looked nor sounded an alarm before starting down that siding and severing the plaintiff's legs.

Comparative Negligence

Some states recognize either by statute or by court decision that there is often some fault on both sides in negligence cases. Rather than deny all recovery, they weigh the relative degree of wrongdoing in awarding damages. If the defendant was 80 percent negligent and the plaintiff only 20 percent negligent, the injured party may be allowed to recover compensation for about 80 percent of his or her losses.

Last Clear Chance

A third defense, which is a complicated attempt to avert the injustice of contributory negligence, is the doctrine of *last clear chance*. This principle states that if the plaintiff was negligent but stopped upon discovering the dilemma, damages may still be recovered provided the defendant saw, or should have seen, the situation and had time to avoid the accident. One might say that the defendant's failure to prevent the injury, if there was a chance, amounts to recklessness; therefore, the defendant, rather than the injured person, should be penalized.

Negligence involves behavior which falls short of the standard of reasonable conduct, and it can take many forms. No matter what guise it assumes, the principles stated above apply.

Torts Involving Property

A business person may become involved with other common torts. Some of the oldest of these concern property.

Conversion

If the employer, or the agent, takes, retains, or wrongfully exercises rights of ownership over property belonging to another without permission, that employer can be sued for *conversion*. For example, an employee who has to take an unexpected trip to meet a deadline may borrow the car of an acquaintance without that person's prior knowledge or consent. This would constitute conversion. Similarly, keeping a car longer than one has permission to use it or using it for a purpose not agreed upon could lead to liability for conversion. Conversion is a private action, or tort, which does not exclude prosecution for the crime of theft.

Trespass

A person may *trespass* by crossing the land of another without first obtaining the right to do so. One can even commit this tort by permitting fumes or water to escape from one's property to that of another. Anyone may be subjected to trespass when outsiders cut across one's property without permission and may choose to sue them. The fact that these wrongdoers are trespassers will not necessarily exonerate the owner from liability if they should be injured on that property. If the trespassers are human beings, rather than animals, the landowner cannot wantonly or negligently harm them and may even have to exercise care in remedying known or foreseeable dangers in areas where there is known to be frequent trespassing. The local law should be checked on this point.

Attractive Nuisance

An *attractive nuisance* is a potentially dangerous object—such as an open swimming pool or a turnstile—near a place where children who are too young to realize the danger commonly play. It can attract the children to it like a magnet. Should they be hurt while playing on or in the dangerous object, the owner may be liable for damages, even though the children trespassed, because they were too young to realize either that they were trespassing or that danger existed.

Nuisance

Our law recognizes both *public* and *private nuisances*, depending on the number of persons affected by the situation. One whose factory emits noxious fumes, whose animals resound through the day, or who stages noisy all-night parties may be charged with the tort of nuisance. Recovery of damages depends on the balancing of individual rights: to what extent may the property owner still enjoy unrestricted use of the land and what are the legitimate interests of the neighbors?

Nuisance is undergoing a revival as a tort in this era of environmental law.

Torts against Persons

Shoplifting is a major concern of the modern business. Naturally the manager wants to protect property from theft and avoid heavy losses. In so doing, one may become vulnerable to serious damage claims arising from three torts: false imprisonment, invasion of privacy, and defamation.

False Imprisonment

Assume that a store detective sees someone suspected of shoplifting and detains the suspect in a back office for questioning. If this is done in a reasonable manner, no liability should result. However, if an innocent person is consciously detained despite his or her objections for a relatively long period of time, such as an hour or more, within a restricted area chosen by the other, the business may later be sued for false imprisonment and may pay substantial damages.

Defamation

Other charges, such as defamation or invasion of privacy, may be combined with a false imprisonment in a lawsuit arising out of that suspected shoplifting situation. Suppose the store detective loudly and rudely accuses the shopper of a crime within the hearing of other customers. The accused will probably feel so aggrieved that a lawsuit for defamation or a related tort will result.

Defamation can take two forms: *libel* and *slander*. Both involve the utterance of false and malicious statements injuring the reputation of another. Libel is defamation in written form or through use of the mass media (television, radio, and films). No damages need to be proved to recover in libel, and great sums can be awarded. In contrast, slander is oral defamation, and it is harder to establish, for damages must be shown except in cases where one has imputed the existence of criminality, loathesome disease, unchastity, or business failings to the other. Furthermore, merely telling the aggrieved person something false is not slander; the defamatory statement must be "published," that is, repeated to a third person. The more stringent requirements surrounding slander probably explain why lawsuits for oral defamation are less common and successful than those for libel.

In the case of both libel and slander, the truth of the allegation is almost always an absolute defense to a lawsuit. In other situations, the defendant may have had the right to make such allegations in a courtroom or legislature, or a conditional privilege by virtue of being an employer or a credit bureau. Only if the person so privileged has maliciously abused that right can the other party readily recover for libel or slander. These torts are not so frequently brought to trial, but they can be costly. Every experienced person in business must learn to be discreet in written or oral comments about associates.

Invasion of Privacy

This tort is related to defamation, but its limits are not so explicit. Basically it means an intrusion on one's right to be free from unwarranted publicity. Although public figures whose names appear frequently in the news now have little claim to privacy in the absence of malicious publicity until they retire to private life, average citizens can and do claim this protection under tort law. It may involve cases of unauthorized wiretapping or situations where a person's face or property has been used for advertising or publicity purposes without consent. This is a relatively new and expanding area of potential liability.

Interference with Business Relations

Interference with economic relations is another growing area of tort law. Briefly, the law protects agreements between individuals from unwarranted interference by outsiders. A definite contract must have existed and the interference by a third party must have been wrongfully motivated. These situations can arise with regard to business competition, unreasonably restrictive covenants prohibiting a former employee from using secrets gained in prior employment, and labor unions.

Fraud and Misrepresentation

In our discussion of contract law and warranties, the importance of fraud and misrepresentation as defenses to required performance has been noted. It should not be overlooked, however, that both fraud and misrepresentation can also serve as bases for tort liability.

If the injured party can establish that there has been (1) misrepresentation of (2) a material fact, (3) made with intent and (4) justifiably relied upon to the (5) injury of the plaintiff, it is possible to sue for damages. In practice, proving the existence of all these elements in order to recover is not so simple, but the beginning entrepreneur should be aware that potential liability exists before engaging in "puffing" or making untrue statements to induce performance.

Strict Liability

Most of the torts already mentioned are caused by intentional or negligent misconduct. In some situations, the law imposes a higher standard of duty for certain functions which are sufficiently valuable to society that they are not forbidden but are so potentially dangerous that strict liability is imposed for any resulting injury regardless of fault. One obvious example is conducting a business involving explosives. Other common cases involve manufacturing cars, producing food or drugs, and spraying crops. Owning wild, vicious, or even straying domestic animals has also led to the imposition of strict liability on the wrongdoer.

To date, most courts have been inclined to limit the scope of strict liability to the exceptional situations discussed above. Even the concept of proximate cause represents an attempt to limit liability in tort. However, the situation may be changing, and more manufacturers of articles may be held to strict liability if injury to the consumer results. The employer is therefore placed in the situation of guaranteeing the safety of the user of the article. Not only the employer, but even employees will be required to use greater care in the design, manufacture, and instructions for use of the article.

Ultimately, the cost of this liability will be passed on and distributed to the consumer of the product. However, this will be of little comfort to the individual upon whom liability is first imposed, who must become aware of the potential dangers in this area and take steps to avert the ruinous damages imposed by the courts.

The law of torts is a subject in its own right. Although the principles discussed apply to the individual, for our purposes it is important to recognize that an employer can be held liable not only for personal torts but also for those of others in the scope of his employment.

INVOLVEMENT AND STUDY MATERIAL

Understanding Terms

Employment records	(page 249)	Last clear chance	(page 258)
Civil Rights Act of 1964		Conversion	(page 258)
	(page 250)	Trespass	(page 259)
Employment contract	(page 252)	Attractive nuisance	(page 259)
Legal liability	(page 255)	Nuisance	(page 259)
Negligence	(page 255)	False imprisonment	(page 260)
Proximate cause	(page 256)	Defamation	(page 260)
Contributory negligence		Invasion of privacy	(page 261)
	(page 257)	Fraud and misrepresentation	
Gross negligence	(page 257)		(page 261)
Comparative negligence		Strict liability	(page 262)
	(page 258)		

Questions and Problem Solving

1. Describe the process of employment including the preliminary exchange of information.

2. Discuss the sensitivity of employment records. How do you think they should be handled to protect both the employer and employee?

3. Describe the impact of the civil rights movement on employment practices.

4. Does the concept of quotas solve the employment opportunities of minority groups? What does this suggest to the individual with special abilities?

5. How can an employer become liable to outsiders for the misconduct of any employees?

6. Define negligence. How does the concept of proximate cause affect negligence?

7. What doctrines are available to the plaintiff in the event the defendant raises the defense of contributory negligence?

8. Distinguish between libel and slander and explain the meaning of "publication."

9. How can an enterprise invade the privacy of an individual?

Cases for Discussion

1. The Tri-City Telephone Company was putting in a new telephone line. The line was to run in back of a neighborhood playground. The post hole-digging crew dug holes in back of the playground and the post crew were to install the posts on the following day. The holes were 20 inches in diameter and 4½ feet deep. No covers were placed over the open holes.

   Some time after the hole-digging crew had quit for the day, five-year-old Ellen Hobson fell headfirst into one of the holes in the back of the playground and drowned in the water at the bottom. The father sues the Tri-City Telephone Company for the death of the daughter, Ellen. Judgment for whom? Why?

2. Alfred Pszenny who lives in Redwood City, Montana, was visiting friends in Birmingham, Alabama. Birmingham has an ordinance that prohibits left-hand turns into private driveways or parking lots. Alfred did not know about this ordinance. One day he was driving his Chrysler north on First Avenue and decided to make a left turn into a parking lot. Accordingly, he started a left turn, west, into the driveway of the parking lot. In doing so, he failed to observe a southbound Ford and was struck over the right rear wheel. The impact caused the Ford to go out of control and run up on the sidewalk on the east side of the street where it stopped near a large transformer. The driver of the Ford was not injured by this impact.

   On the previous day the power company crew had worked on the transformer and installed some new lines. A loose line had been left dangling near the transformer. The crew had assumed that the line was dead. Actually, it was live and carried 50,000 volts. The Ford stopped with the wire touching it. The driver of the Ford was not aware of this, and as she stepped out of her car, she was electrocuted as her foot touched the ground. Is Alfred guilty of negligence in making the left turn? Explain your answer. Is Alfred guilty of negligence and liable for the death of the driver of the Ford?

3. On January 10, Jefferson King was on a sales trip for the RX Corporation, working out of the South Bend Office. At 10:00 A.M. he was driving his new Chrysler west on U.S. 66 west of Chicago at about 50 miles per hour. The highway was newly surfaced concrete and freshly marked, with white and yellow (no passing) center lines. The posted speed limit was 55 miles per hour. Traffic

was very light in either direction. There were no cars in sight going west ahead of King. The temperature was below freezing, but the pavement was dry.

As King approached a long curve to his right, an eastbound car was approaching him approximately 200 yards away. The approaching car appeared to be traveling slowly. King started into the curve when the eastbound car was about 150 feet away from him. When King's car was about 50 feet away from the other car, about midway in the curve, his car hit a sheet of ice. He lost control of his car and crossed over the yellow center line and crashed head-on into the eastbound car. The two occupants in the eastbound car were killed.

The driver of the eastbound car was Florence Ashley. The passenger was Alfred Koch. The car belonged to Helen Palmer, Florence's roommate. It was totally demolished. It was discovered that the paving contractor had a water storage tank near the highway. Some unknown person had opened a valve during the previous night and the water drained out into the highway, where it froze. The ice sheet was not visible to motorists until one was about 45 feet away from it. The families of Florence Ashley and Alfred Koch bring suit against the RX Corporation. Judgment for whom? Why?

4. The Equal Employment Opportunity Commission was investigating a sex discrimination charge against Henderson Personnel, an employment agency, in the referral of prospective employees to General Products Company and others. General Products and other companies were engaged in a nationwide recruiting program. Their advertisements and brochures stressed that all supervisory personnel must be male and all nonsupervisory personnel must be female. The EEOC demanded access to information contained in the files of Henderson Personnel including a list of all persons in the files seeking part-time help since May 1, 1971; a list of accounts requesting referral of personnel on the basis of sex; copies of correspondence with General Products and others, including other employment agencies that requested referrals on the basis of sex; and copies of the ads placed in the news media.

Henderson Personnel claimed that there was no basis for the EEOC's charge and that the demand was too broad, bearing no relation to the investigation. The EEOC argued that Henderson Personnel violated the Civil Rights Act of 1964 with its unlawful employment practices and insisted upon access to the information it had requested for its investigation. Judgment for whom? Why?

5. Hester applied for a position as a data typist at the Grand Railway Company's office. This was in response to the advertisement placed in the paper by the railway company. Hester was required to fill out an application and take four tests, all of which she passed. During the interview with the personnel manager, she was asked about night work, and she stated that she would work any shift although she had had no experience with night work. The personnel officer stated that the single most important skill for the job was good typing. Two weeks later Hester received a letter from the railway company stating that she was not hired. Several weeks later she noticed an advertisement in the paper inviting applicants for the same job. Hester filed suit claiming the railway company violated the Civil Rights Act of 1964 by its unlawful employment practices, in that preference was given to white applicants over black applicants. Hester stated that during 1968, the railway hired thirty-eight white data typists and only thirteen black typists and that during 1969 it hired thirty-two white and ten black typists. The 1970 census report showed that over 50 percent of the city's population was black. Hester also claimed that the tests used were not professionally validated for accuracy or relevancy, that the personnel officer did not have any written or formal guidelines to conduct or score the interview, and that his decisions were therefore based upon subjectivity. The personnel officer stated that he had rejected Hester because she had no night work experience. Judgment for whom? Why?

Chapter Eighteen

Employee Benefits

People have many needs. Among them are security, dignity, respect, recognition, and self-fulfillment.

A job may mean different things to different people and different things at different times. For example, in a period of rising unemployment, security may loom most important; in other circumstances, an employee may want personal fulfillment. Let us examine the processes by which employee needs can be met in some orderly manner.

EMPLOYER POLICIES

Almost all employers would like to believe that their employees like them and have been given an opportunity to meet their needs. Various programs designed to accomplish these ends are implemented.

Job Classification

A serious concern to employees is job security. Unless employees know what their jobs are and to whom they report, there may be anxiety. To allay such fears, many employers carefully spell out job descriptions and job classifications stating the qualifications necessary for someone to be appointed to a particular job. For example, a position as a machine operator may require at least two years of some specific experience. This criterion for job selection provides an orderly progression in employee development.

Aside from job descriptions which make clear the duties and responsibilities of the job, pay scales will be assigned to each position. These may be from a range, such as $2.25 to $4.50 per hour or from $450 to $525 a month. Succeeding classifications can overlap in salaries, such as: class A—$425 to $525 a month; class B—$500 to $625 a month. Some jobs may be classified as starting or trainee positions for a given period of time.

Employers realize that salary is not necessarily the most important factor in employee satisfaction. However, money is a measuring device which reveals a great deal about a job. If a job is in classification 6 and its pay scale starts in the upper quartile of the pay scale for job classification 5, everyone knows that management considers job 6 more important than job 5. Thus a promotion from job 5 to 6 has a social significance that may be substantially more important than the simple increase in salary.

Performance Evaluations

Performance evaluation is essential to maintaining a reasonably happy work force. The goodwill of employees cannot be measured, but where it does not exist the employer probably has deep-seated problems that may threaten the entire company.

Employees want to know that they are being treated fairly. The job classification is the first step to assuring the employee of that intention. Periodic job appraisal is the second step. The techniques of such an appraisal can be found in books on personnel management.

Sound and regular appraisals allow variations in salary levels. They are an effective way to recognize the individual's contribution to the company in effort, attitude, and production. There should be no hesitation to assess performance correctly. Personalities should not enter into such evaluations. The company is paying for work done, and so that should be the subject of job appraisal.

Hours, Wages, Overtime

Although most employers announce the hours of work, many questions can develop. For example, what happens if the employee is delayed fifteen minutes by an expressway tie-up? Will a quarter of an hour's pay be deducted? What if a shipment is to be made just at quitting time? Does the employee stop at the appointed time or is the shipment finished?

Much has been written about the place wages play in meeting the needs of employees, and every employment contract should make clear the wage policy. Does the employee get paid for overtime and, if so, how much and when? The Wage and Hour Act requires that employees be paid under specified circumstances or penalties may be assessed for violations. There may be other company policies concerning overtime. Some companies provide a dinner allowance if the employee is expected to work more than two hours overtime. If this is company policy, the employee should be given a clear understanding of it. It is important that each employee know exactly what is due.

There is something pleasant about getting a raise, especially if the employee knows it is based on merit. Raises based on merit encourage increased production, better quality work, and greater effort. However, in today's production-line environment, it is often difficult to recognize individual merit. Therefore, it may become necessary to announce a schedule of raises. Many companies provide automatic raises after the first six months or after the first year. Thereafter the employees go on a merit system.

Vacations

After a minimum period most employers provide vacation time. It may be two weeks of vacation after a year of service, three weeks after four years, and, perhaps, four weeks after eight to ten years of service. In this way, the employee is rewarded for a long period of employment. It demonstrates that the employer appreciates faithful service, and at the same time, encourages younger employees to maintain a long, unbroken, record of employment.

Employee Grievances

One of the most troublesome situations in employer-employee situations is the machinery for handling employee disputes. Most employers are interested in good labor relations, because they realize that disgruntled employees are disruptive and affect those around them. Each employee represents a substantial investment, and so every effort should be made to keep workers satisfied.

Although many people may feel that the corporation is an unfeeling master, many executives have come up through the ranks themselves and know the frustrations of an employee who is denied the opportunity for a fair hearing. Even when it is essential to discharge an employee, most employers are conscious of its effect on public relations. Maintaining good public relations is another reason for an orderly resolution of grievances and disputes.

Where there is a union in the company, its representatives will generally get together with a management group to hear the dispute. In a nonunion company, a similar body may be set up through the personnel department. The employee is given an opportunity to discuss the problem away from any immediate superiors. The grievance committee then handles the matter through established channels.

If the employee is dissatisfied with the results, some companies without unions have a procedure that gives the employee access to the chairman of the board if necessary. If the chairman is a long distance from the location of the employee, transportation is provided by the company. If the employee is represented by a union, an equally detached procedure is established. It too provides for successive levels of review that may take the dispute above the level of the local union.

Employee grievance procedure should be well publicized. If a problem arises, the employee should know exactly where and what can be done. A good grievance procedure is one of the most important benefits available to the employee. It gives the good employer an opportunity to demonstrate interest in the well-being of the employee.

FRINGE BENEFITS

Employer policies are fairly standard in most occupations. Whenever large groups of people are employed, there have to be minimum work rules and generally accepted work practices. Items such as vacations which may not have been common fifty years ago are standard parts of the present-day work package. Since the Great Depression, and particularly following World War II, a number of additional employee benefits have developed that are commonly called fringe benefits but could be more properly called a type of deferred compensation; whatever their name, there should be no mistake that they are something earned by the employee.

Profit Sharing

Profit sharing was introduced fairly early. Charles Babbage wrote about it in 1832. It was started as a genuine effort to share the benefits of a successful operation. In the United States, one of the oldest plans was developed by Sears, Roebuck and Co. in 1916 and is undoubtedly one of the most successful plans today.

Profit sharing means essentially that the company shares part of its profits with employees. To this extent, it has to have the support of the shareholders. Many of the plans supplement the employee's income in such a way that as they approach retirement, profit sharing allocations increase to enable them to retire with substantial savings accounts. Under the Sears, Roebuck plan, a truck driver who was employed by the company when the plan went into effect and never earned much over $35 per week retired in 1952 and collected over $100,000.

Under most plans, employees are required to contribute a portion of their salaries—usually 5 percent—up to a total annual amount. The amount they later collect is determined in part by how much they have contributed. The maximum limit on contributions prevents an unfair share of the profits from going to those with higher salaries. The company matches the employee contributions according to some predetermined formula. For example, the company may allocate 10 percent of its net profit to the fund. The beginning member may share on a per unit basis for every dollar contributed. As the employee gains seniority, the per unit share may be increased. The Internal Revenue Service regulations provide that when employees retire the amount of money they receive beyond what they have contributed is taxed at *capital gains* rates; and that means they pay less in taxes than they would if they had received that extra money as salary. The favorable tax treatment thus encourages personal saving; although some funds are paid for entirely by the employer.

Merit raises, promotions, and other periodic salary increases result from individual activities of the employee. Profit sharing is concerned with a group effort whereby all employees have a mutual interest in the welfare of the company.

Stock Option Plans

Another arrangement to encourage savings is the stock option plan. Employees are permitted to purchase company stock at some predetermined price. An issue may be made available to the employees that will reflect the market price at a chosen time. The option may remain open several years after it is offered to the employees, and thus the employee eventually gets an opportunity to profit. Salary deduction plans usually accompany stock options.

The plans and Internal Revenue Service regulations require that the stock be held for a certain length of time or else any profit on the sale of the stock will be treated as regular income. The employee is encouraged to hold the stock until retirement, when the profit will be taxed as capital gain. More important, if the employee retains the stock, it should provide an extra source of income in the form of dividends.

Special stock option plans are often available to certain executives. Upper-level executives are usually in fairly high income tax brackets. It is difficult to offer monetary incentives to such people if their income is greatly reduced by income tax. Accordingly, some executives are offered large stock options involving several thousand shares that can be purchased over many years. According to Internal Revenue regulations, when these shares are held for a designated period of time, they can be sold and the profits taxed as capital gain.

Although this method of compensating corporate executives is sometimes criticized, the fact remains that capable executives have to be attracted and retained. Stock option plans, coupled with some deferred income, have been the most successful way of getting and keeping them there. Deferred income provides retirement income, whereas stock options permit the development of an estate.

Bonuses

Bonuses are another means to stimulate employees in their work. They are more common in executive and sales jobs but are also used in sharing a profitable venture, or year, with all the employees who made the success possible.

General bonus distribution is not common because the bonus ceases to have its original meaning as a reward for a particularly good result. Instead, it can become a part of the expected salary. Bonuses can sometimes cause wide variations in annual income. For the employee who is earning a lower salary, this may create problems. Therefore, many companies have found that it is better to give a general salary increase, rather than a bonus, except to special employees.

As a practical matter, bonuses are not a particularly attractive method of compensation since they are subject to regular income taxes. Therefore, other forms of benefits are used to give the employee a greater return.

Deferred-income Plans

Most deferred-income plans are forms of pensions. The money is put aside into some fund during the time the employee is earning most and paying high taxes. Deferred income starts to benefit the employee on retirement and is then taxed at a much lower rate. This gives the employee a higher yield on the dollar earned during the years of regular employment.

Many of the deferred-income or pension plans are combined with Social Security payments. Thus they enable the employee to choose early retirement. If the employee retires several years before becoming eligible for Social Security benefits, often payment from the pension or deferred-income plan will be correspondingly larger. When the former employee later becomes eligible for Social Security, the deferred income will often drop so that he or she continues to receive approximately the same amount through the combined sources. Sometimes, the combined sources will give the employee an amount slightly more than the original amount in contemplation of the additional needs that may occur as one gets older.

One must remember that both the employee and employer presently pay substantial Social Security taxes. By tying the deferred income to the Social Security payments, the employer is able to provide a fund from which the employee gets the most benefit possible. Thus, one can retire early with an adequate income for as much as ten years before starting to draw Social Security. If the plan was not tied to Social Security, the deferred-income fund would have to be substantially larger and probably beyond the ability of the employer and employee.

Plans often include provisions for continuing payments to the wife in case the husband was the employee and he dies before her. Sometimes such payments are smaller, and sometimes they are made only if the husband elects to receive a smaller amount when his payments start. Deferred-income plans can be flexible and provide considerable security to the employee, particularly when they are combined with Social Security payments.

A criticism of many of the deferred-income plans is that if an employee leaves an employer before retirement, all rights in such a plan are lost. If the next employer has a similar plan, the employee must start all over. The result is usually a lower amount on retirement. Plans are under discussion now by which an employee would acquire early vesting rights; that is, the employee would have a property right in the fund, and if one changed employers, one would either take the accumulated benefits to the next employer or be able to draw on the original plan on retirement.

An additional criticism of some of the present plans stems from the lack of proper funding. In too many cases the funds are not placed on a sound financial base, and if the company falls on hard times, the existing funds are inadequate to meet the withdrawals by employees. This has occurred a sufficient number of times to generate concern by state and federal governments.

Insurance

Insurance is playing an increasingly important part in employee plans. Some plans are designed to provide basic protection for employees and their families while the employees are still employed; others provide employees with an income on retirement.

Life Insurance

The average person finds that life insurance obtained individually through an agent is costly. However, insurance plans available through the employer may be considerably lower if they represent *group insurance*. The employer may be able to negotiate a policy that costs substantially less, because the agent's commission does not have to be paid and much of the paperwork in connection with the policy is done by the employer. Usually a master policy is issued to the employer, and the company issues individual certificates to the employees. Another important reason for the reduced cost to the employee is that the employer often pays as much as half of the premium. The underwriting costs to the insurance company are absorbed by the company since the insurance carrier accepts the insurability of the employee. Through group insurance plans, employees can afford considerably more life insurance than if they were required to secure individual policies.

The insurance under most group policies is *term insurance*. This means that the policyholder does not develop any cash value in such policies. If the employee leaves the company, the insurance is terminated. However, the next employer may be able to grant a similar policy.

On retirement, the arrangement may include a provision to give the employee a reduced amount of paid-up insurance. Thus, if the employee carried $10,000 while employed, the employer may provide a $5,000 paid-up policy that would be payable to the heirs of the employee.

Health and Accident Insurance

A life insurance policy is intended to help the family to adjust to the new situation caused by the death of the breadwinner. However, illnesses and disabilities of long duration can be substantially more serious to the family. Not only does the incapacity disrupt the family and eliminate the breadwinner, it can also produce astronomical hospital expenses. Many families experience hospital bills in excess of $10,000. Meanwhile the income has been cut off even if medical expenses are covered by private or national insurance. To protect the wage earner from such a calamity, insurance companies have offered catastrophe insurance in amounts of $15,000 or more. More recently, a wage protection plan has been added that pays a percentage, usually 75 percent, of the employee's salary during disability.

Other Benefits

Companies often are able to make other special plans available to their employees. Some may arrange for special discounts on merchandise. Appliances, clothing, furniture, and other "big ticket" items may be made available through special outlets. Catalogs of available merchandise are distributed to the employee families. Although the discounts may be small, savings of 5 to 10 percent provide the employee with additional employment benefits.

EMPLOYER RESPONSIBILITIES

The early law dealing with employer-employee relations was extremely harsh toward the employee and the apparent callous indifference of the employer toward the employee's calamities caused great bitterness. Eventually public indignation and pressure brought about fairer treatment of an employee injured in the course of employment. The defense of contributory negligence was eliminated, and laws were enacted that forced the employer to develop safer working conditions. In addition, if the employer wanted to escape legal liability, he had to provide a form of insurance that would compensate the employee, regardless of liability, for work-related injuries without the costly and protracted remedies following a lawsuit. Employers soon found that the workmen's compensation laws turned out to be cheaper to the employer than litigation and eminently fairer to the employee than the harsh treatment under the older laws.

Workmen's Compensation

A major change in terms of liability resulted from enactment of the workmen's compensation laws. These eliminated the problem of finding fault unless the employee deliberately injured himself. Theoretically, if a product is useful to society but its manufacture or production is harmful to the people who produce it, the price of the product should include the cost of compensating the workers for injury. Thus, there is no crushing burden upon either the employer or the employee. Assuming that the accident resulting in injury occurred in the course of the business without gross fault on the part of the injured person, compensation would be payable. Only cases of intoxication, intentional self-injury, and gross fault (for example, ignoring a flashing red light or walking in front of a moving train) or carelessness of the employee would bar recovery of damages.

Usually the employee no longer needs to go to the trouble or expense of hiring a lawyer to prove a case as was true in the days before the workmen's compensation statutes became law. Now one just reports a claim to the board designated by the relevant state statute. Many times there will be no dispute, and payment out of the state or private insurance fund will be reasonably prompt. Claims contested by the employer will be heard by an informal commission. There is a right of appeal from its decision to the courts; however, this appeal measurably increases the cost of the proceedings.

Not all cases are honestly presented. Some injured employees have tried to claim to be unable to work longer than was true, and then they claimed compensation. Consequently, short periods of incapacity (like one or two weeks) are excluded from coverage in some states. Thereafter, the state statute will specify when, how much, and for how long benefit payments are to be made. The amount to be paid will depend on the degree of disability and the amount of the claimant's average weekly earnings. Only occasionally will it be received in a lump sum, because an installment system is usually more convenient.

The Occupational Safety and Health Act passed in 1970 is concerned with employee safety, and it is hoped that through enforcement of this act employee injuries will be further reduced.

Unemployment Compensation

The employer is also responsible in other respects for the workers' welfare and will be expected to make payments to the unemployment insurance plan of that state. Such payments, which operate as a tax and represent a percentage of the employee's wages, go into a fund, part of which is deposited with the federal treasury and part with the individual states. From this fund, benefits are distributed to those who become unemployed.

Social Security

An employee is also entitled to the protection of Social Security. Part is paid by the employer, and part is deducted from the worker's weekly or monthly salary. Social Security payments do not come from a special pension fund but from the general U.S. Treasury. At the age of sixty-two for men or sixty for women, the employee will be entitled to collect benefits unless he or she is earning more than the maximum sum specified by the Social Security statute. Other features of Social Security legislation which are designed to benefit workers or former workers are Medicare, death benefits, and aid to those who are physically handicapped or disabled. Such legislation alleviates much of the uncertainty and hardship which could once overwhelm even the most industrious, foresighted laborer.

These are certainly not the only laws designed to protect the employee. Based on the power of the interstate commerce clause of the U.S. Constitution, the federal government has passed numerous acts since the Fair Labor Standards Act of 1938 which control conditions in industries which produce goods for shipment from one state to another. This covers an unexpectedly large proportion of the products used in the modern American economy. Thus, by this device inhuman child labor has been abolished, and wages and hours are regulated. In short, much has been accomplished in this century within the sphere of social legislation.

EFFECTS OF COLLECTIVE BARGAINING

Although some employers voluntarily introduced many of these benefits, many strongly resisted any inroads into their power. Early union activity concentrated on shorter work hours and better wages. At the end of the Great Depression and the conclusion of World War II, wages were driven up by a shortage of labor as well as steep inflation. Labor union leaders discovered that wages alone were not the best approach to improving the lot of their members. Thus union demands changed, and suddenly union leaders were talking about profit sharing plans, group insurance, purchasing discounts, and other benefits. Many benefits have been won for employees by these collective efforts.

Some observers of the labor scene feel that many of the benefits would have come regardless of union pressure merely because the American public has become familiar with many of the plans advanced by farsighted companies. Nevertheless, at the very least, union activity was responsible for a more rapid advance in these areas.

It can be expected that union pressure will now be directed toward employing people throughout the year, not just seasonally; more leisure; professional care such as legal and dental insurance; and some type of guaranteed annual wage. Present state and federal unemployment compensation plans are not entirely satisfactory for long-term unemployment. Anything that disrupts the income of a large number of employees damages the economy, and others are affected. For this reason many of the causes espoused by labor unions may find support in our legislatures, even while other methods of achieving their goals (such as strikes and collective bargaining) are no longer so popular.

INVOLVEMENT AND STUDY MATERIAL

Understanding Terms

Periodic job appraisal (page 268)
Employee grievances (page 269)
Profit sharing (page 271)
Stock option plan (page 271)
Bonuses (page 272)
Deferred-income plans (page 273)

Group insurance (page 274)
Term insurance (page 274)
Workmen's compensation acts (page 276)
Unemployment compensation (page 276)
Social Security benefits (page 277)

Questions and Problem Solving

1. Describe the principal needs of employees and how these needs are met by employers.
2. Describe the important of a clearly stated job description and job classification.
3. How does the discontent of one employee affect the morale of coworkers and their goodwill to their employer?

4. What is the reason that insurance can be obtained at lower cost from the employer rather than directly from the insurance company?

5. Discuss the standard channels for hearing employee grievances and appealing adverse decisions.

6. Why does serious injury or long disability pose a greater threat to a family than death?

7. How can a profit sharing plan be funded?

8. How do present income tax laws make stock option plans desirable?

9. Why are bonuses not the most attractive method of compensating conscientious and able employees?

10. What legislation discussed in this chapter has improved the condition of employees? Give at least three examples.

11. Why are most deferred-income and pension plans often tied to Social Security payments?

12. When an employee is injured or disabled, what private plans or government programs can assist in meeting expenses and providing for the family?

Cases for Discussion

1. Mrs. George owned an apartment building from which she received rents. She sold the apartment to her son in 1965 for the nominal sum of $20, which he never paid. The son formed a limited partnership with his wife and employed his mother to manage the apartment building for five years. She was to collect the rents and pay the bills on the apartment. In return, she was to receive free rent and an amount equal to the net profit from the operation of the apartment building. In January 1970, the building was transferred back to Mrs. George, and then she sold it to another party. Mrs. George now sues the Secretary of Health, Education, and Welfare to obtain Social Security benefits. The Secretary of H.E.W. claims that Mrs. George is not entitled to benefits under the Social Security Act, since she has not worked at least one quarter of the year and received wages, nor was she self-employed during at least one quarter from 1951 to the year she became sixty-two years old. The Secretary acknowledges that Mrs. George owned the apartment and received rentals from 1951 to 1965 but contends that this did not qualify as self-employment income and that the deal with her

son from 1965 to 1970 was not an employee-employer relationship. Judgment for whom? Why?

2. Ludwig was employed by the Electric Corporation of America at its Lancaster, Pennsylvania, plant. On December 26, 1966, while walking from the company parking lot into the plant, she slipped and fell on the ice- and snow-covered sidewalk, sustaining injuries. She maintained that the company was negligent in failing to clean the sidewalks in front of the plant, that this sidewalk was owned and controlled by the company, and therefore that she was injured on the premises of the company. Thus, she claims, the company is liable for her injuries. The company claims that Ludwig's only remedy is workmen's compensation benefits. Under Pennsylvania law, the sidewalk in question must be owned, controlled, or leased by the employer and must be connected with the business of the employer in order for the injured employee to qualify for workmen's compensation benefits. Judgment for whom? Why?

3. Galvan and Torres were employed in the state of New York. They were citizens of the United States born in Puerto Rico. In 1968, they both lost their jobs, making them eligible for New York's unemployment insurance benefits. The New York law contains various interstate agreements that allow a claimant to collect benefits in another state. Galvan and Torres went back to Puerto Rico and filed for their unemployment benefits. The policy of New York has been not to pay unemployment benefits to a claimant who moves to another labor market where there are depressed conditions creating high unemployment. At the time Galvan and Torres moved back to Puerto Rico there was very high unemployment there, and consequently no work was available for them. New York denied their application for unemployment benefits due to the high rate of unemployment in Puerto Rico, alleging that the claimants were not ready, willing, and able to work as required by the law. Galvan and Torres maintain that the decision by New York infringes on their right to travel and violates their right of due process, since the policy of New York is arbitrary and vague. Section 2 of the law, which is titled "availability and capability," states that claimants who are not capable to work or who are not ready, willing, and able to work in their usual employment or any other for which they are reasonably qualified by training or experience, are not entitled to benefits. This rule is spelled out in the booklet given to every claimant who applies for benefits. Judgment for whom? Why?

Chapter Nineteen

Employee Relations

Many efforts have been made to improve the lot of the worker, but forces such as greed, absentee corporate ownership, competition, monopolistic powers, and problems inherent in large industry tend to frustrate change. Even where sincere efforts are made for improvement, employers often become as frustrated as the employees over the results.

Although many employers have been pictured as greedy, evil people determined to make tremendous profits at terrible cost to the employees, the fact is that there are employers with good intentions toward their employees. Despite their efforts to meet employees' needs, the results are frequently far from satisfactory. The employee often fails to realize that the employer is concerned with both providing the employees with work and keeping the plant operating. If the employer fails in the second, there will be no jobs. The employer's major concern has to be to stay in business.

EMPLOYEE RELATIONS AS A SCIENCE

In the late 1920s, a series of studies was undertaken to determine what the employer could do to improve the situation of the employee. The studies were interrupted by the Depression and World War II, but afterward they were resumed. Although much has been learned about employee behavior and many excellent books have been written on the subject, no positive solutions have been advanced.

Studies have also been conducted about the part management plays in the employer-employee situation. What type of boss does the best job? Who gets along best with other people? What can be done to create a desirable environment for employees? Employers throughout the country have studied the results. Seminars have been conducted for interested groups, and some real progress has been made. Whether the progress can be attributed to the studies or simply to the desire to make working conditions better is not certain.

Employee Needs

Each employee is an individual, and therefore, although basic needs may be identical to those of other employees, everyone will not necessarily have the same priorities. Employers cannot satisfy the needs of every employee, but by dealing with a group rather than an individual, they can act more effectively and incur less displeasure. When management negotiates with a group, it often leaves some areas for self-determination so that the group is given an opportunity to create job conditions.

Unfortunately, despite the best intentions of an employer, there is no assurance that good working conditions will continue. The employees want to feel that they have a right to satisfactory conditions. No one wants to accept the charity of another, particularly when it may be withdrawn without warning.

Company Unions

In the early years of this century there was growing labor unrest and there were drives toward unionization. To discourage the intrusion of outside independent unions, many companies encouraged the formation of *company unions*, which enjoyed some success. In many cases the arrangement proved satisfactory for handling management problems, because it was easier to deal with employees as a group. But in many situations there is no doubt that employee interests were of secondary importance and the main objective of the company union was to prevent independent union organization.

Company unions frequently gave genuine employee representation. Nevertheless, they became dominated by members whose first loyalty was to the company; only rarely were they really independent. Therefore, it can be questioned whether an employee could honestly discuss personal problems with a company-dominated union representative. A union representative who served with divided loyalties would have difficulty giving advice that conflicted with the company's best interests. Thus, employees felt that many problems were never handled adequately or even fairly. An employee who felt strongly about a problem had no one to turn to and often became frustrated. Much dissatisfaction arose with this type of arrangement.

Employee Grievances

Although some employers were genuinely interested in solving employee problems, other employers had a callous disregard for grievances. Employees were subjected to favoritism, sweatshops, intolerable sanitation conditions, harsh discipline, arbitrary firing, discrimination, indifference to the plight of injured or unemployed workers, and in some cases blacklisting of disobedient employees so that they could not find other work. Company reprisals against union members were equally severe. When a union went on strike, nonunion "scab" labor was used. Many times strikers were never rehired. The Ford Motor Company followed hotly contested labor practices. In the late 1930s Republic Steel, whose employment practices were typical, experienced a strike that led to serious bloodshed and brought about a public outcry. The result was substantial public sympathy for unionization.

Whether such conditions were widespread is of little importance. Labor resented the domination by management and demanded a voice in company affairs. Widespread labor disputes led Congress to enact federal labor legislation to enhance the free flow of interstate commerce by reduction of employer-employee disorders.

RISE OF UNIONS

The concept of a union is not new. Early craft guilds originated in the Middle Ages. Still, the idea of a group of workers joining together to present a common front was anathema to employers, many of whom tried to perpetuate the feudal system in the industrial environment. Employers, generally, reacted violently to any outside effort to organize their work force. At first, unions were deemed illegal. Nevertheless, unions were organized shortly after the formation of our republic, although early union strength was limited to skilled workers such as printers and shoemakers.

The Knights of Labor

The Knights of Labor arose from the populist movement in the late nineteenth century. In an effort to build its strength, it accepted all workers, skilled and unskilled. To avoid harsh reprisals, it was secret. The organization became involved in radical politics and lost support. After some unsuccessful strikes, it declined and eventually disappeared.

The Growth of Labor

The labor movement did not die with the Knights of Labor. New organizations appeared, and some survived.

The American Federation of Labor

Contemporary with the Knights of Labor, the American Federation of Labor (AFL) was formed in 1886. Under the leadership of Samuel Gompers, it was organized on a federalist plan of different business unions. Each union enjoyed autonomy, and dualism (the organization of the same workers by two unions) was not permitted. The union was committed to improving the lot of its members and was generally not politically oriented. The AFL remained aloof from the rank-and-file factory worker, representing instead the craft unions, like the machinists.

The Congress of Industrial Organizations

Under the colorful leadership of John L. Lewis, president of the United Mine Workers, the Congress of Industrial Organizations (CIO) was formed within the AFL. William Green, while president of the AFL, opposed industrial unions. The new association welcomed workers according to industry, regardless of their particular trades. Thus any worker in the auto industry was eligible for membership.

After some serious policy disputes, the CIO seceded from the AFL in 1933 and did not rejoin until 1955.

Early Legislation

Early labor legislation was hostile to unions. The Sherman Anti-Trust Act, which was passed to curb big business, was turned against labor unions. Any activity which could be construed as conspiracy in restraint of trade subjected the union to triple damages and its leaders to criminal prosecution. Some lawsuits resulted in injunctions, civil and criminal liabilities, and the ruinous imposition of damages.

Samuel Gompers led the labor movement in securing the enactment of the Clayton Act in 1914. This statute was intended to curb the use of injunctions in connection with disputes over terms of employment that did no irreparable harm to property. However, the courts construed the statute very narrowly to permit injunctions against strikers; thus, the Clayton Act did not prove to be the magna charta which labor leaders had anticipated. Despite the success of the Railroad Labor Board in the peaceful settlement of disputes by collective bargaining, labor made few legislative gains until the mid-thirties.

The Norris–La Guardia Act

During the Depression beginning in 1929, the lot of labor was not a happy one. At least one-fourth of the total work force was out of work. There was little opportunity for the average factory worker to be heard. Yet, many labor abuses were brought to light. As a result, Congress passed the Norris–La Guardia Act (1932) designed to eliminate the shortcomings of the Clayton Act. Strikes and picketing became a legitimate weapon of labor, and the use of the injunction was limited. The yellow-dog contract, requiring employees to agree not to join a union when they were hired, was outlawed. Nevertheless, organization of labor did not begin on a large scale until the New Deal.

New Deal Legislation

Despite the growth of unions, the labor movement made slow progress until the start of President Franklin Roosevelt's New Deal. His administration took a vigorous lead in sponsoring labor legislation.

The Wagner Act

The Wagner Act, or the National Labor Relations Act, was passed in 1935. The right to form labor unions now became a matter of national policy. Once a union was formed, it could engage in all normal union functions, especially collective bargaining. In the future, courts would play a lesser role in labor disputes. The principle of nonintervention was adopted.

Because workers now had a right to organize themselves into unions, employers could not intervene without incurring heavy penalties. Statutory provisions which were intended to curtail management's domination of unions were to be enforced by a National Labor Relations Board (NLRB), set up under this statute. The pendulum had now swung to the side of labor.

The Taft-Hartley Act

Nothing infuriates labor leaders more than the words "Taft-Hartley." This expression is just a popular reference to the Labor Management Relations Act of 1947, which amended the National Labor Relations Act. It was passed in a period of conservatism after American industry had been disrupted by a series of strikes and when prices were rising after the end of World War II.

Of all its provisions, the best known is the concept of a *cooling-off period*. The act provides that if a strike would affect national health and safety, the President of the United States can, through the Attorney General, seek an injunction in federal court to prevent the strike from starting or continuing. The injunction is good for only eighty days. At the end of the eighty-day period the injunction is dissolved and the strike can begin or be resumed. This act can be used to prevent strikes in vital defense industries, such as the manufacture of steel or transportation of goods.

The Taft-Hartley Act abolished the closed shop, but permits the union shop to exist if the union can negotiate it and the state does not have a law that forbids such action. In a *union shop* all employees are required to join unions soon after they are hired. In a *closed shop* only those persons who were members of the union while seeking employment can be hired. Thus, the closed-shop provision cuts deeper than does the union-shop clause, because it requires union membership even before one applies for a job.

Unions are now made liable for the acts of their agents. Membership in the union does not make the member an agent of the union unless the member is acting in some representative capacity. Certain unfair practices by labor are barred: refusing to bargain; using coercion, boycotts, or illegal strikes to achieve goals; conducting strikes which endanger the national safety; featherbedding (that is, requiring the hiring of people for whom there is really no work); failing to administer welfare funds for the union members properly; or not filing data about finances, contributions, elections, and officers.

The act expands the NLRB and grants it more clearly defined powers. The Board is given broad powers in union-management affairs. It can issue orders to compel compliance with the National Labor Relations Act. Board orders are not self-enforcing. In practice, if either side disagrees with the ruling of the NLRB, it can file a suit in federal court and seek to have the order set aside. As can be expected, most of the charges complaining of violations are brought before the NLRB by the unions and most of the appeals to the courts are by the companies. Moreover, a General Council is set up having the authority to issue complaints that bring violations of the act before the Board.

Significantly, employers are guaranteed the right of free speech under the Taft-Hartley Act in order to permit them to tell their side of various issues to union members. This important right can also be utilized by employers in connection with union elections.

Landrum-Griffin Act

Subsequent legislation has not been as bitterly contested as the Taft-Hartley Act. Thus, the 1959 Congress could pass the Landrum-Griffin Act without rousing violent opposition. Also known as the Labor Reform Act, it introduced a system to expose and restrict the corrupt and unscrupulous practices of certain union leaders which had become major flaws in the trade union movement. It also limited the use of picketing and secondary boycotts, which are such important tools of the unions. Nevertheless, this Labor Reform Act was also designed to benefit union members. Specifically, it granted them a "bill of rights."

By the second half of the twentieth century, much progress had been made since the early struggles of the labor unions to establish themselves. However, they are still powerless until they are chosen locally to represent the workers of a given industry by specially held elections. The local union is the body which the NLRB has certified as the legal bargaining agent for the workers of that particular plant following a properly conducted election.

Local unions throughout the country banded together into national unions. Up to half of each member's dues were transmitted to the national headquarters. What did they receive in return? Greater power. A national organization often has more resources and perspective than a purely local one. For example, the national union might send in skilled persons to advise or to assist in particularly tough negotiations. In addition, a strike begun by a local union in New York City might elicit support from locals belonging to the same national union and subject to similar working conditions in San Francisco, Houston, and Chicago. The strike would therefore have more impact and might lead more speedily to the desired result.

UNIONIZATION

When a union becomes established, it becomes jealous of its prerogatives. Leaders are concerned with the loyalty of its members and anxious to reduce the influence of management in areas concerning wages, hours, and working conditions. Thus, at the very outset, there is substantial conflict of interests between the two groups. The employer, who is responsible for the outcome of the enterprise, cannot control the employees, who also have a large stake in the success of the operation.

The Election

The first step in unionizing any company is to hold an election. If the company opposes the formation of a union, its proponents can petition the National Labor Relations Board, alleging that a certain number of employees have indicated a desire to have a union represent them in their relations with the company. They collect signed authorization cards from employees that want the union to be organized. The petition may be challenged by the employer, but if the NLRB feels that there is a genuine request, it will order an election. It should be pointed out that the National Labor Relations Board is bound by the Wagner Act and other congressional pronouncements to support the right of employees to engage in union activity if they desire. The law favors labor organization. When the NLRB rules that an election can be held, certain rules apply to the opposing parties.

Permissible Activity of the Company

Before an election, the company can distribute printed, graphic, or visual representations of its views if these are carefully worded and do not contain any threats of reprisal or promises of benefit. Thus, the employer's freedom of speech is not infringed, but neither is it totally unrestricted. The employee must be allowed to form or join a labor union without intimidation or coercion.

Speeches

Management must be careful about making preelection speeches during working hours on company property. If such a speech is made to what amounts to a captive audience on company property within twenty-four hours of the election, the election can be set aside. If the company engages in such activity, the union has the right to reply under similar circumstances. This means that the reply can be on company property and on company time. Failure to allow union replies can lead to a charge of unfair labor practices, and the NLRB might assess penalties and certainly invalidate an election favorable to the company.

Contents of Communications

Employers need not sit back and ignore the fact that an organization drive is on. They are allowed to make factual, temperate, and non-threatening statements regarding what a union can be expected to bring to the company. Before a scheduled election, they have the right to oppose unionization and request that employees oppose it. They can draw attention to existing company programs, but they cannot offer any new programs during this period even if the programs had been in preparation a long time.

Employers can inform employees about their legal rights and the effect of union dues on their income or even express a preference for another union, but management cannot impair the employees' freedom of choice in the forthcoming election under the guise of freedom of expression.

UNION AND COMPANY ACTIVITIES

Although the formation of a union may be met with hostility, many members of both sides eventually recognize that there are benefits to be obtained by establishing better relations. As a result, many companies have maintained harmonious relations with their union counterparts. On occasion these relationships break down. Then neither side is as completely helpless as some would make it appear.

Rights of Management

The company has access to the courts for relief under the Taft-Hartley Act and the Landrum-Griffin Act. It must bargain in good faith on issues brought by the union. No longer can a company use a yellow-dog contract, but it can employ nonunion workers if it can get them.

Rights of Labor

Many union issues have been resolved by amicable agreement. Should collective bargaining fail, the union retains considerable power to enforce its demands but not without restrictions. The Landrum-Griffin Act of 1959 outlaws secondary boycotts designed to put pressure on one employer because of a dispute with another company. Unions also cannot insist on hot-cargo clauses, which provide that union employees do not have to deal with the goods of a firm whose employees are out on strike. The Taft-Hartley Act discourages featherbedding, which forces an employer to pay workers for services that are not performed. This last provision has not been entirely successful, but people are beginning to recognize that nonproductive activity which imposes an economic burden on a company is wasteful and injurious to all of society.

The Taft-Hartley Act and the Labor Reform Act prohibit numerous strikes that are beyond the legitimate goals of organized labor, for example, a wildcat strike, which has not been authorized by the majority of the union and involves a minority of discontented workers rather than the rank-and-file union member. Wildcat strikers can be discharged since they are not protected by current laws. In practice, companies try to resolve even these strikes since they have large investments in the labor force.

Union Shops

The question of whether or not the company should have a union shop is usually thrashed out in early meetings. Companies often oppose it strongly because they realize that some employees might not wish to become union members or to be forced to pay union dues.

Checkoffs

Should the workers choose to join the union, they might want a *checkoff* to be instituted as a means of paying their dues. In a check-off, the employer deducts the union dues from the individual's pay-check before it is ever received by the employee. The sum collected is transmitted directly to the union, where it becomes part of a special fund. Of course, such a deduction from the paycheck could not be made unless it had first been authorized by the employee.

There is ample evidence that employees are primarily interested in their total take-home pay. They are quite likely to forget their own initial authorization and resent the fact that they are not getting that part of their gross pay. They may even turn some of their irritation against the employer who makes the deduction rather than against the union for which it is made. The checkoff can be a source of employee friction.

Strikes

Many people associate unions primarily with strikes. It is true that a union can, and often does, call a strike which disrupts business. Strikes can be differentiated by motive, which, in turn, has a bearing on their legality.

There are many types of strikes. Most common, perhaps, are the *unfair labor practice strike* and the *economic strike*. The former is a strike by employees who object to the alleged unfair labor practices of the employer. The latter occurs when the negotiations concerning wages or other benefits have reached a stalemate. In both cases, the strikers remain employees and retain their seniority rights even though temporary replacements may be hired. A properly organized strike for the sake of obtaining better wages, hours, or working conditions is legal.

Collective Bargaining

To avert strikes and to settle differences peacefully, collective bar-gaining can be used. Strikes may be more spectacular, but much is accomplished by behind-the-scenes negotiation. One bargaining unit

represents a union, the other the company. The company unit will
have a chief negotiator who will work, perhaps, with a personnel
officer, a plant supervisory officer, and such other persons as the
company chooses to have on its team.

The two units have a duty to meet with each other at reasonable
hours and places. Sometimes such bargaining sessions begin at a
reasonable hour but last through the night. This is not a bad sign,
as some positive results may emerge. Moreover, the negotiators must
confer in good faith about wages, hours, and working conditions,
though neither is obligated to make counterproposals to the other's
offer.

Once an agreement is reached on the various points, it must be
incorporated into their contract and even be written down if one
of the parties insists on it. The agreement reached by the bargaining
representatives must ultimately be approved by the rank-and-file
members of the union before it becomes fully effective. Union members have been known to reject an agreement that took countless
hours of hard negotiations to reach. Then the bargaining units must
begin all over again.

The essence of collective bargaining is good faith. Both sides must
come to the table prepared to negotiate with each other. A company
cannot refuse to negotiate with union representatives if that union
has been certified as the bargaining representative by the NLRB.
Neither side can refuse to discuss bona fide issues (wages, seniority,
hours, fringe benefits, discipline, grievance procedures, and duration
or renewal of the contract) raised by the other representatives.
Issues within the collective bargaining area must be submitted to
negotiation.

In preparing for negotiations, the union will collect data on company earnings, economic trends, industry trends, and the wishes of
its members. It will be prepared to negotiate a contract that will
cover not only wages but employee benefits as well.

The company gathers similar data. The details may not seem
significant standing alone but when assembled can point up undesirable practices. For example, employees may like to work on Saturdays
when they can get overtime, but company data may show that those
who work on Saturdays fail to show up for work on Mondays and
thus that Saturday overtime is unnecessarily expensive.

Every unionized company must be sure that its contract provides
for detailed and effective grievance procedure. Unless adequate precautions are taken, management will have constant strife on its
hands, and so employees must be given an opportunity to be heard,
and there must be machinery for the resolution of this problem.

Union Goals

The union is generally interested in improving the status of its members, and its demands amount to increased benefits for its members. It should recognize that it has to operate within the same economic framework as the company. There is a limit beyond which the company cannot go and stay in business.

Built-in Wage Hikes

A union may attempt to write a built-in wage hike into the contract. This means an automatic increase in salaries each year under a long-term contract. The amount, of course, will vary. Annual wage raises of 3 percent have been rejected by unions; pay boosts of 7 percent or more have often been acceptable.

What is the advantage of such a built-in wage hike? It is an attempt to prevent yearly disruptions of the working schedule by frequent strikes for higher wages as inflation undercuts the earnings of the workers. Annual negotiations would be neither necessary nor possible under the long-term contract.

Escalator Clauses

A "galloping" inflation might make even the built-in wage hike inadequate. Consequently, the contract might also have to include a cost-of-living escalator clause, permitting an additional salary increase of a specified percentage if warranted by a rise in the cost of living. Plans for such built-in increases are growing more sophisticated and comprehensive throughout the labor field. Now there are even open escalator clauses, whereby wage increases keep pace with living costs.

Role of Government

The negotiators have to keep in mind possible federal policy. What will the government do to implement plans for a guaranteed minimum annual wage? To what extent will it control price and wage increases? What is the policy of the government about intervening in crippling strikes and the negotiations to end them?

INVOLVEMENT AND STUDY MATERIAL

Understanding Terms

Company unions	(page 282)	Cooling-off period	(page 286)
Knights of Labor	(page 284)	Closed shop	(page 286)
American Federation of Labor		Union shop	(page 286)
	(page 284)	Coercion	(page 287)
Congress of Industrial		Boycotts	(page 287)
Organizations	(page 284)	Landrum-Griffin Act	(page 287)
Sherman Anti-Trust Act		Hot cargo	(page 290)
	(page 285)	Featherbedding	(page 290)
Clayton Act	(page 285)	Wildcat strike	(page 290)
Norris–La Guardia Act		Checkoff	(page 291)
	(page 285)	Economic strike	(page 291)
Wagner Act	(page 286)	Collective bargaining	(page 291)
National Labor Relations		Cost-of-living	
Board	(page 286)	escalator clause	(page 293)
Taft-Hartley Act	(page 286)		

Questions and Problem Solving

1. Distinguish between a company union and an organized union.
2. Describe the effect of the Sherman Anti-Trust Act on the labor movement.
3. What was the intent and effect of the Norris–La Guardia Act?
4. Distinguish between the Wagner Act and the Taft-Hartley Act.
5. What is the function and purpose of the National Labor Relations Board?
6. Distinguish between closed shops and union shops.
7. List several unfair labor practices on the part of employers and on the part of employees or unions.
8. What did the Landrum-Griffin Act attempt to remedy with regard to the union movement?
9. Outline the steps that a union must take to organize the employees of a company.
10. Describe collective bargaining and outline the rights and duties of both the employer and the employee with respect to collective bargaining.

11. Describe several of the goals of unions, and indicate the success of the unions in attaining these goals.

Cases for Discussion

1. The American Oil Company reduced the size of the crew on a fluid cracking unit at its Neodesha, Kansas, refinery. The Independent Oil Workers Union, Local 117, filed a grievance claiming the reduction meant a change in place of employment and an increase in job duties because three men were used per shift instead of four, which was a violation of past practice and of the contract. The contract provided that questions dealing with the establishment by the company of new policies, practices, customs, or usages during the term of the agreement could be referred to arbitration. It also stated that either party could refuse to submit to arbitration questions not covered by the contract. American Oil Company refused to submit the question to arbitration, and the union brought suit to compel the company to arbitrate the grievance. Judgment for whom? Why?

2. In a meeting held with the union on March 1, 1972, the Budd Company notified employees at its Philadelphia office that the corporate headquarters would move to Troy, Michigan. On March 23, 1972, the company met with the union and discussed how to advise the employees of their rights under the contract. The same day twenty-one members of the company whose jobs were being transferred were given an opportunity to indicate in writing whether or not they wished to transfer to Troy, Michigan. Sometime between March 27 and April 3, all twenty-one members indicated they did not wish to transfer. On June 8, 1972, fourteen of these employees were notified that they would be laid off, effective June 16, 1972. The union had filed a grievance protesting this corporate move, and the grievance was progressing through the normal steps but had not yet reached arbitration; however, both parties stated that they intended to place the grievance in arbitration as soon as possible. Local 757 of the Technical, Office and Professional Workers Union sought an injunction to stop the Budd Company from moving to Troy pending the outcome of the arbitration hearing. The union claimed the action by the company was a violation of its contract, which stated that employees not covered by this agreement shall not perform any work regularly done by covered employees. The company claimed it had the right to move its operations under

the contract and that at no time did the union challenge the right of the company to move the corporate functions to Troy. In order for the court to issue a preliminary injunction, the union had to show that irreparable harm would befall the workers that would overshadow any inconvenience that might befall the company. The union claims that the loss of jobs by these fourteen people constitutes irreparable harm. Judgment for whom? Why?

3. Iodice was a member of the Teamsters and Chauffeurs Union, Local 456, as an owner-driver. In 1949, the union called a meeting and informed Iodice and others who owned their own trucks that they could no longer retain their owner-operator status and be union members but that they could sign a contract with the union as truck owners. Iodice and others did not sign a new contract, and were thrown out of the local union. Iodice went to work for another company as a truck driver at the same time that Local 456 was conducting a strike against this company. Iodice on occasion drove through the picket lines of the union. He was then not allowed to work on construction jobs with other union members; contractors who hired him suffered work interruptions and losses; and Local 456 levied a fine against contractors who hired him to work for them. This trouble existed from 1949 through 1966, during which time Iodice lost much business as a result of the pressure that Local 456 exerted on his customers.

Iodice claims this union activity amounted to a secondary boycott and an unfair labor practice, both of which are against the Landrum-Griffin Act. The act states that it is unlawful for any labor organization to engage in any activity or conduct defined as an unfair labor practice in an industry or activity affecting commerce and that it shall be an unfair labor practice for a labor organization or its agents to threaten, coerce, or restrain any person engaged in commerce or an industry affecting commerce, with the object of forcing that person to stop doing business with another person. The union claims its actions are justified and lawful, as it is only enforcing a valid contract between the union and the various contractors. All the contractors had contracts with Local 456 stating that the union has the right to impose fines on contractors whenever the union decides that a contractor has breached his contract with the union. The contract provisions in question dealt with preserving work for union members, and the hiring of Iodice by the contractors to haul their equipment was a threat to the job security of union members. Iodice brought a lawsuit against the union and its agents for damages from the illegal secondary boycott and the violation of the unfair labor practices rules. Judgment for whom? Why?

4. The labor contract between the United Electrical Radio and Machine Workers of America, Local 123, and the Westinghouse Electric Corporation contained a clause allowing the union dues to be deducted from the first paycheck each month and to be turned over to the union. The employees had to sign an authorization to permit this, and the company could stop the dues checkoff upon written notice from the union, or upon written notice from the union member during a period from October 24 to October 31 after the effective date of the authorization, or at the end of the contract period. During 1970 and 1971, eleven members of Local 123 resigned their membership in the union, and they notified Westinghouse in writing of their intention to revoke their authorizations for the checkoff of the dues. They did not submit the notice of revocation between October 24 and 31 nor had the national contract expired. Westinghouse honored the request of these eleven workers and stopped making deductions from their pay for union dues. The union now brought suit against Westinghouse to force the company to comply with the terms of the collective bargaining contract and continue the checkoff of dues for these eleven former members. Judgment for whom? Why?

PART
FOUR

PROPERTY

Chapter Twenty

Locating the Business

BUYING VERSUS LEASING PROPERTY

Every business operation is confronted with the problems posed by owning real property and the alternatives to ownership. *Ownership* has to do with the extent of a person's right in property; it is synonymous with title. The major alternative to ownership is *leasing*, or renting. Instead of transferring the ownership of property, for example, a right to possession and use of it in a specified manner and for a certain time period may be created by a *lease*.

The idea that either method is superior is a myth. Inasmuch as business is governed by economics, the selection of one alternative over the other should be based on a rational analysis of the circumstances of the case.

Considerations in Leasing Property

Possession by lease may be more economical for the small business than ownership. This is particularly true if the new business is unable to locate the type of premises that will accommodate its long-term needs. The same logic applies when the proprietor does not know the size of future needs. Further, a large investment in plant, equipment, or land may be untimely. Renting offers an opportunity to make careful investigation and gives time to develop experience in order that a more informed decision can be made.

Leasing Real Property

Leased premises offer the advantage of minimum outlay at a time when capital requirements are highest. Although the monthly rent becomes a charge on the business, just as interest would be if there were a mortgage, it does not carry the same connotation on the balance sheet. Returns from real estate investments, after the payment of taxes, depreciation, and maintenance, run around 10 percent. A successful business needs to plan for earnings of 15 percent or more for every dollar invested. Under these circumstances, only a mature business can afford to own real property.

All the rent paid by the business is tax deductible. This may represent a substantial benefit to the business. It eliminates the problem of depreciation and obsolescence.

Rented property can be just as suitable as owned property. All that is required is that the location be secured with the same care as if the land were to be purchased.

Leasing Personal Property

Leases of personal property are undertaken for many similar reasons. Lack of resources may dictate either that the business cannot do certain work if it has to buy the machines or that it has to find some way of getting the machines without a large initial investment. Equipment involving large sums of money can be leased on a long-term basis for a rental similar to its installment purchase price. Frequently, an arrangement in the form of a *lease-purchase agreement* provides that the property is acquired by the lessee at the end of the payment period.

For example, assume a company wants calculators for its office but feels it cannot afford to purchase them outright. Instead of arranging separate financing for each piece of equipment, which would necessitate filing certified financial statements with each creditor under the Uniform Commercial Code, it arranges a lease-purchase agreement with the supplier. If the business should encounter financial difficulties, the lessor simply acquires the equipment without the formal foreclosure procedures required by the code. A lease-purchase agreement is a method by which a company can acquire equipment quickly. The final cost of the leased object should be carefully compared with its sale price.

Leasing of equipment offers tax advantages that are also attractive to business. All rent is tax deductible as an item of expense. Meanwhile the lessor-owner of the equipment has the problem of maintenance, depreciation, and obsolescence. For this reason many business and professional people lease a wide range of services, tools, and equipment.

Ground Leases

If a small business finds that purchasing land is inadvisable, its objective can be accomplished by leasing the land for a long term and constructing suitable buildings on it. If the title to the building goes to the landowner at the conclusion of the lease, such a lease is called a *ground lease*. Provisions may be made for an option to renew or an option to purchase the land at the conclusion of the lease. A ground lease can benefit both the landlord and the tenant. Tenants get the buildings they need even though they cannot yet buy land. Landowners get buildings on their land which they could not or would not build themselves and which they can lease to others when the leases expire. Meanwhile, a business that constructs a building will be able to depreciate it for tax purposes during the terms of the lease.

Sale and Leaseback

An alternative to ground leasing is the *sale and leaseback*. The company buys land that suits the needs of the business and builds as necessary. After the building has been completed, it is sold to an investor in exchange for a long-term lease. Rights to repurchase can be reserved for the company. Lease terms often provide that the tenant will assume the expense of maintenance and repairs. A long-term lease is beneficial to the purchaser of such a building, particularly if the lessee is a successful business, because it helps the buyer secure adequate financing. Meanwhile, the company has the best of two worlds. It has the building, location, and facilities it wants without being tied down with a large investment when it needs operating capital. Moreover, no mortgage will appear on the books of the company.

Considerations in Buying Property

Ownership brings both advantages and disadvantages. The business person will generally be interested in the economic effects of ownership. The greatest advantage from ownership of land or personal property is the relative freedom it gives in the use of the property. There is no landlord to consult in regard to alterations or installation of equipment. Ownership of personal property provides similar freedom. In either case, the total costs may be less because the owner takes care of the maintenance and repairs and does not have to pay outsiders to shoulder the burdens of ownership.

Advantages Associated with Real Property

Ownership provides a permanent location. It encourages long-range planning about the use of the property and offers an identity of location that can become an important business asset. Buildings can be designed for needs of a particular business, and additions can be planned that will minimize costs over the long run. Ownership of the property assures the business person that long-range plans need not be disturbed.

Advantages Associated with Personal Property

Owning equipment offers the same advantages as owning real property. In addition it allows the business to develop machines for its particular needs; generally alterations on a leased machine are prohibited. More importantly, reluctance to own equipment often reflects a lack of permanency.

Disadvantages of Owning Real Property

A starting business must consider the allocation of its resources. It has just so much money which has to be distributed in a manner that will enable the enterprise to function. Land generally involves a large investment for the new business. While it is true that one need not pay the entire purchase price of land in cash, nevertheless a sizable amount of cash will be required. It may be more than the business can afford.

If a large mortgage is taken, it will have to appear on the balance sheet. Interest will be shown on the profit and loss statements. Future borrowings and credit arrangements will be greatly influenced by the amount of debt carried by the business. A mortgage which is large in proportion to the total assets of the business can be a serious burden on the company. The mortgagee may insist on control of the premises in a way that is incompatible with the best interests of the company. The supposed freedom of ownership may thus be largely imaginary.

A beginning business may not be able to afford the ideal location. A less desirable site may be selected if the purchase is made with the available resources. After investments in plant facilities have been made, it becomes more difficult to change to a new location. The resulting situation may present a serious obstacle to efficient operations.

If the company has financial problems, as almost all beginning businesses do, it may be reluctant to buy the amount of real property that it needs for long-range operations. Therefore it may be tempted to buy less property than it ought to. If it cannot purchase land that suits its long-range plans, it probably should not buy land at this point. If a business purchases expensive land for potential expansion and then finds itself in need of operating capital, unused land that does not produce a profit can become a drag on the overall profits of a company. A company which has to utilize all its capital to produce a profit may find it impractical to purchase the amount of property it requires.

Disadvantages of Owning Personal Property

The problems of owning equipment are not as readily apparent. However, ownership of personal property often represents a substantial investment, and so the same considerations apply.

ACQUIRING THE PROPERTY

Finding a choice site is only the beginning. After the location and price are determined, the parties will execute a contract for the sale of the land.

Contracts of Sale

When the buyer and seller have reached a meeting of the minds as to the material terms of the transaction, their agreement will be put in the form of a contract. It is important that the identity of the parties, the location of the land, and its cost be specified. The contract may also state the date of the closing and arrange for financing.

ATLANTA REAL ESTATE BOARD
Commercial Sales Contract
September, 1972

CAMPUS REALTY
Atlanta, Georgia

As a result of the efforts of _____ Campus Realty Co. _____

a licensed Broker, the undersigned Purchaser agrees to buy, and the undersigned Seller agrees to sell, all that tract or parcel of land, with such improvements as are located thereon, described as follows: A strip of land starting 1473.5 feet north of large oak tree at west edge of Ridge Road and the north bank of the Yellow River; thence 3240 feet west to an iron pin next to a fence line owned by Henry George; thence north along said fence 4365 feet to an iron pin an the south edge of Telegraph Road; thence east along the south edge of Telegraph Road to an iron pin on the west side of Ridge Road and on the south edge of Telegraph Road; thence south along the west side of Ridge Road to the point of beginning.

together with all electrical, mechanical, plumbing, air-conditioning, and any other systems or fixtures as are attached thereto and all plants, trees, and shrubbery now on the premises.

The purchase price of said property shall be:
Thirty eight Thousand and no/100 $38,000.00

_____ DOLLARS, $ _____

to be paid as follows: $36,800.00 on day transfer of title

Campus Realty Co.

Purchaser has paid to the undersigned, _____ , as Broker,

$ _1,200_____ ( ) cash ( ) check, receipt whereof is hereby acknowledged by Broker, as earnest money, which earnest

money is to be promptly deposited in Broker's escrow account and is to be applied as part payment of purchase price of said property at the time sale is consummated.

Purchaser's covenants herein, Purchaser shall forthwith pay Broker the full commission; provided that Broker may first apply one-half of the earnest money toward payment of, but not to exceed, the full commission and may pay the balance thereof to seller as liquidated damages of Seller, if Seller claims balance as Seller's liquidated damages in full settlement of any claim for damages, whereupon Broker shall be released from any and all liability for return of earnest money to Purchaser. If this transaction involves exchange of real estate, the full commission shall be paid in respect to the property conveyed by each party to the other and notice of the dual agency is hereby given and accepted by Seller and Purchaser. The commission on an exchange shall be calculated on the amount on the basis of which each property is taken in such exchange, according to the contract between the parties, and if no value is placed on any property exchange, then according to the reasonable value thereof. In the event of an exchange, each party shall be regarded as Seller as to the property conveyed by each party.

Commission to be paid in connection with this transaction has been negotiated between Seller and Broker and shall be _____
10% of the first $10,000 and 5% on balance _____

Time is of essence of this contract.

This contract shall inure to the benefit of, and be binding upon, the parties hereto, their heirs, successors, administrators, executors and assigns.

The interest of the Purchaser in this contract shall not be transferred or assigned without the written consent of Seller.

This contract constitutes the sole and entire agreement between the parties hereto and no modification of this contract shall be binding unless attached hereto and signed by all parties to this agreement. No representation, promise, or inducement not included in this contract shall be binding upon any party hereto.

The following stipulations shall, if conflicting with printed matter, control:

Fig. 20-1. Commercial sales contract.

Real estate contracts usually require a down payment known as *earnest money*. Many contracts are silent concerning the disposition of this money if the sale is not completed. If financing arrangements cannot be obtained on proper terms, the contract should state that the earnest money will be refunded. Otherwise, the earnest money will be forefeited even though the circumstances causing nonperformance were beyond the control of the buyer.

Land Records

After the contract has been negotiated, the seller will usually start a search of the title. *Title search* involves an examination of the records concerning land transactions in the county where the property is located. It requires familiarity with technicalities and forms of recording transactions. Frequently clerks or experienced searchers in the county recorder's office help the beginner.

The Search

The object of a title search is to trace the chain of title or the passage of the property from the first owner through the hands of heirs and successors right down to the present seller. This is harder than it sounds in some states, where land titles have been in relative chaos since colonial times. In other states, however, it is a comparatively easy procedure.

Suppose a man named Jonathan Hill first acquired ownership of the land in the eighteenth century by paying a small sum to the authorities, settling on it, clearing it, and cultivating it for forty years. When he died, it passed by inheritance to his son Nathan, grandson Richard, and so on until a remote descendant named Henry Hill decided to sell it in 1924 to a friend named Jack Araminian for $10,000. Araminian encountered financial problems in the Depression, and so his mortgage on the property was foreclosed in 1931. In 1935, the Fidelity Title Company sold the land to Ruth Kennedy and her husband, who died during the Second World War. Mrs. Kennedy remained in possession as a widow until her own death in 1952, when it passed to her son George Kennedy under the terms of the will. George Kennedy decided to divide the land into three lots and sold them to Levy, Albany, and Cavanagh. Cavanagh had and inside plot and therefore he acquired an easement of neces-

TABLE 20-1

Chain of Title

Grantor	Grantee	Consideration or means of transfer	Instrument book, volume, page, and date	Miscellaneous observations
Jonathan Hill	Nathan Hill	Inheritance	Probate Records, V, 43, 1761	Fee tail male
Nathan Hill	Richard Hill	Inheritance	Probate Records, XIII, 10, 1801	Warranty deed
Henry Hill	Jack Araminian	$10,000	Records of Deeds, CXXV, 103, 1924	Warranty deed
Jack Araminian	Fidelity Title Company	Foreclosure	Mortgage Book, XCV, 12, Aug. 2, 1931	Mortgage foreclosure
Fidelity Title Company	John and Ruth Kennedy	$3,500		Tenants by the entireties
Ruth Kennedy	George Kennedy	Inheritance	Probate Records, XC, 42, 1952	
George Kennedy	L. Levy	$4,000	Records of Deeds, CCX, 15, 1952	One-third of plot; easement to Cavanagh

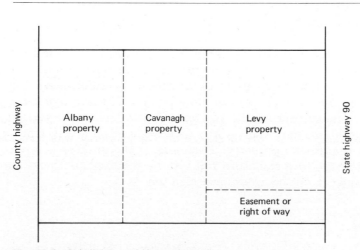

Fig. 20-2. Subdivision of Kennedy land.

sity, or a right of way, over Levy's land to the highway. Now Levy wants to sell his lot and the prospective buyer is searching the title to it.

The passage of the land from Jonathan Hill to Levy is illustrated in Table 20-1. Such a table can make even the complexities of the record book reasonably clear to a relative beginner. Of course, hours of searching lie behind it because generations of land transactions often result in tangled situations.

Transfer of Title

Laws relating to land ownership are complex. Failure to understand them can result in costly mistakes. Once the buyer's lawyer is satisfied by the title search that the grantor has good title, the next step is to close the transaction by securing transferring documents called *deeds*.

Elements of Deeds

The deed itself is a contract or written instrument for the transfer of an interest in land. The seller who conveys property is the *grantor;* the buyer is the *grantee*. The deed is executed and delivered to the grantee at the conclusion of a transaction called the *settlement*. It is at this time that the purchase price has to be paid in accordance with the terms of the original contract of sale. Should the seller refuse to convey the property, the buyer may be able to compel its transfer.

There are certain basic requirements in a deed. It should contain a clear description of the land, references to outstanding liens or mortgages, and descriptions of easements or possible restrictions. It is accepted by the grantee, who may be an adult, a minor, or a corporation. The grantor can be any legal person having the capacity to make such a transfer. Many states give husbands and wives property rights in the other's property. Therefore, if the grantor is a married person, the spouse's signature will also be required. If there is more than one owner, the coowner must sign too.

Types of Deeds

Since there are a great number of deeds differing in important details, it is valuable to be able to recognize certain ones. Such technical details can have a major effect on one's rights and duties under the deed.

Common law Deeds

Originally deeds were long documents incorporating virtually every relevant detail: the names of the parties, the description of the property, the consideration that had been paid, the reservation of any interests or information on any covenants made by the grantor, the words of the grant, the specification of any conditions attached to it, and the fact that the deed had been executed by the grantor.

Statutory Deeds

In order to simplify the transaction and to facilitate recording, laws were passed which permit a mere recital that the named grantor is making the specified conveyance to the named grantee. Five distinct types of statutory deeds are recognizable: deeds of indenture, deeds poll, quitclaim deeds, bargain and sale deeds, and warranty deeds. Only the last three require description here.

Quitclaim Deeds

These deeds are executed generally by people who do not wish to make any promises to the grantee. To depend on a title through such deed may be risky because it conveys only such rights, titles, and interests as the grantor has at the time of the conveyance. In some cases, this may be quite sufficient; in others, it will be far from enough. There are no warranties or guarantees of title in this type of deed. Should title prove to be defective, the buyer bears the loss and has no recourse against the seller.

Bargain and Sale Deeds

These are also called *grant deeds* and are more satisfactory for the buyer. Unlike the quitclaim deed, the bargain and sale deed contains two valuable implied warranties. First, it is a guarantee that the grantor has title and has conveyed no prior interest or title in that property to anyone else at the time the deed is executed. Second, it is an assurance to the buyer that the property is free of any encumbrance (liens, mortgages, etc.) placed on it by the grantor or by anyone else when the deed is executed.

The safest deed of all is warranty deed. In addition to the two warranties of the bargain and sale deed, it guarantees quiet enjoyment. That means that the grantor will defend the title conveyed to the grantee against the lawful claims of a third person. If an outsider has a judgment entered which results in sale of the land by the sheriff, then the grantor of the warranty deed will be responsible for the resultant loss to the grantee. It is the seller's personal promise that the title is valid. The grantee can then make improvements without fear of eviction.

While a warranty deed is not absolute assurance that the title to the land is good, it offers more security to anyone investing in land than do other types of deeds. Additional assurance is provided by a title search, title certificate, and title insurance.

Although it is not necessary to record the deed, it is wise to do so as soon as the settlement has been completed. Recording is done at the county recorder's office. Failure to record the deed gives the seller an opportunity to sell the property a second time. An innocent purchaser could have a title superior to that of the first buyer. An early recording forecloses other subsequent claims, such as mortgages or liens, against the property. If there is a mortgage for the purchase money, the mortgagee will also require recording to preserve a claim against others.

Recording

For increased security the state should provide a good recording system, so that sufficient publicity, or *constructive notice* of the transaction, is given to any future purchasers or mortgagees. The record is there for them to inspect either in person or through an expert before investing in the land. The courts assume that any prudent, reasonable person will have done so. Consequently, only if there has been a failure to record the deed will the courts protect subsequent mortgagees and purchasers against loss.

Particularly effective has been the Torrens system of land registration originating in Australia. It is regarded as conclusive as to the title of the owner and the claims of all other persons. Two certificates of title are issued: one is entered in the register of titles; the other is delivered to the applicant.

The procedure leading to the issuance of these certificates is routine. The owner files a written application stating the names, ages,

WARRANTY DEED (Short Form)

STATE OF GEORGIA, County of Fulton   .

This INDENTURE, Made this 20th day of June   in the

Year of Our Lord One Thousand Nine Hundred and Seventy Three   between

                 Adam Smith and Mildred Smith

of the State of   Georgia   and County of   Fulton   of the first part, and

                 Henry George and Nancy George

of the State of   Georgia   and County of   Fulton   of the second part,

WITNESSETH: That the said part ies of the first part, for and in consideration of the sum of

                 Forty three thousand five hundred   Dollars,

in hand paid, at and before the sealing and delivery of these presents, the receipt of which is hereby acknowledged, have granted, bargained, sold and conveyed, and by these presents do   grant, bargain, sell and convey unto the said part ies of the second part, their heirs and assigns, all that tract or parcel of land lying and being in

Land Lot 6, of the 17th District, Fulton County, Georgia, being Lot 17 of the Roy Carlton Property as per plat by Harold L. Bush, Registered Surveyor, dated July 17, 1952, recorded in Plat Book 47, page 45, Fulton County Records, and being more particularly described as follows:

TO HAVE AND TO HOLD the said tract or parcel of land, with all and singular the rights, members and appurtenances thereof, to the same being, belonging, or in anywise appertaining, to the only proper use, benefit and behoof of the said part ies of the second part, their heirs and assigns, forever, in Fee Simple.

AND THE SAID part ies of the first part, for themselves and their   heirs, executors and administrators, will warrant and forever defend the right and title to the above described property, unto the said part ies of the second part, their heirs and assigns, against the claims of all persons whomsoever.

IN WITNESS WHEREOF, the said part ies of the first part ha ve hereunto set their hand and seal s , the day and year above written.

Signed, sealed and delivered in presence of:

Robert Hale

Peter Horvath   s/Adam Smith   (Seal)

Sena Murrel   s/ Mildred Smith   (Seal)

                                            (Seal)

addresses, and marital status of those claiming to be the owners; the names of the parties known to have an interest in the lands; and whether the property is occupied or subject to any liens and encumbrances. This application is filed in the appropriate court. The fact is noted in the docket book. Also filed is the abstract of title. Then notice is served on every person having an adverse interest to that of the applicant. The documents filed are checked by an examiner, who conducts an informal hearing before handing down a decree respecting the registration of title. Then a certificate can be issued.

Ensuring Clear Title of Property

Once the title search has been completed, an abstract of title can be given to the buyer.

Abstracts and Certificates of Title

An *abstract of title* is a history of all the transactions pertaining to the property with emphasis on any encumbrances, liens, or taxes to which it is subject. It is a formal document drawn up by a lawyer or by a title guarantee company. The lawyer may issue, instead of such an abstract, a *certificate of title* stating that all the records have been examined and there are no known unsatisfied claims against that particular property.

Title Insurance

Even a certificate or abstract of title cannot assure that title to property will be unchallenged. No matter how thorough the title search, there is always a chance of error.

Was a prior document forged? Could any of the parties transferring title possibly have lacked the capacity to enter a contract? Either of these common situations can endanger the validity of title to land. So, too, can invalid divorces, failure of the husband to join in his wife's transfer (in some jurisdictions), false affidavits, fraudulent impersonations, undisclosed heirs, or even mistakes about law.

Suppose the title search does turn up the existence of a judgment but the lawyer erroneously believes it does not constitute a valid lien? If the judgment creditor later forecloses and sells the land at a sheriff's sale, the prior buyer will lose an investment. This is substantially what happened in a little-known Pennsylvania case which was the catalyst for the creation of title insurance in 1876.

Title insurance is now big business. The insurance company engages experts who check on the existence of any outstanding mortgages, judgments, taxes, water-sewer rents, or other potential liens. However, they do not make a physical check of the property; that task is one the buyer can and should do in person. The experts can ascertain the condition of the land's title after a real estate broker has indicated the value of the property. Every possible precaution will be taken. Should an error still occur, then the buyer who has been sufficiently foresighted to take out title insurance no longer needs to bear a loss. It will be covered by the insurance, except losses occasioned by those liens and encumbrances specified in the policy.

Title insurance may not be considered important in small communities where abstracts of title are easily relied upon, but it is quite prevalent in metropolitan areas with complex records. The premiums and rates vary according to the community.

Encumbrances on Property

Title to property may be clear except for mortgages, liens, and certain restrictions in the form of *easements, equitable servitudes*, and *reverters*. Buyers who ignore these at the time of purchase will have to deal with them later. A buyer cannot rely entirely on the title search; one is usually held responsible for knowing of adverse claims which would be readily disclosed upon visiting the property, such as unrecorded visible easements and squatters. One should personally check the property to be sure it is suitable for one's needs as well as to find out whether any encumbrances do exist. Of course, the buyer is said to have legal notice of any encumbrances discovered during the title search and cannot later try to claim the seller attempted to mislead.

Easements

Easements can be defined as interests in land, created by express or implied agreement, which confer some right in their owner to some benefit or use over the property of another. The most common example of an easement is the right to go over someone's property to reach other property. A farmer may grant a neighbor an easement to maintain an irrigation ditch over the farmer's property. Adjoining householders may build a driveway between their houses, granting each other easements to use it. Utility companies often acquire easements over property to run sewer, water, and electric lines.

Negative Easements

Negative easements prohibit the owner of land from doing something. For example, landowner Novak may pay a neighbor, Simon, a sum of money in return for an agreement not to build anything taller than four stories. This is a negative easement on Simon's land in favor of Novak. Negative easements are a less common kind of easement.

Servient and Dominant Tenements

The property that suffers the easement is often called the *servient tenement*. After the easement is created, it burdens the property until it is relinquished by the owner of the easement. The property that benefits from the easement is called the *dominant* or *appurtenant tenement*. When the dominant tenement is sold, the easement goes with it.

The buyer must know what easements, if any, there are across the property being purchased. For example, the district manager of a large department store chain bought property without discovering that an easement to maintain a driveway ran across one edge of the property. Since the easement was owned by a competitor, who refused to sell those rights or cooperate, the district manager was forced to sell the property at a considerable loss.

Equitable Servitudes

An *equitable servitude* results when the owner of property subdivides the land and sells each parcel on some condition, such as forbidding its use for commercial purposes. Each owner can force the other owners to abide by the restriction. This device is commonly used by developers of large tracts of housing who want to ensure that the buyers keep the tract residential.

Possibilities of Reverter

Occasionally an owner in the chain of title will sell property on condition that it not be used in a particular way. The owner provides further that if the condition is violated, the property will revert or return to the original owner. For example, in 1925 someone conveyed land with the provision that if the land were ever used as a tavern or saloon, it would revert to the seller or the estate. The owner died in 1930 and the estate was settled the next year. The property passed through many hands. In 1965, after building a large office building on the property, the owners, ignoring the possibility of reverter, installed a stylish nightclub in the lobby. The previous owner's great-grandchildren, accidentally discovering their property right, began a lawsuit and received a large sum from the careless nightclub owners.

Judgments

If the landowner has been sued, notice of the pending suit may have been filed in the recorder's office. If judgment has been rendered against the landowner, it automatically becomes a lien on the real property. Both judgment and the pending suit have the same effect as a mortgage insofar as transferability of property is concerned.

Taxes and Other Liens

Taxes which have not been paid become a lien on real property. The federal government can file tax liens for failure to pay income taxes. Other liens, such as mechanics' or workmen's liens, may also affect the title of real estate.

USING PROPERTY

It is incorrect to believe that the owner of property has an absolute right to enjoy it. Its use is subject to a number of restrictions of which the person in business should be aware before investing capital in the purchase of land.

Governmental Restraints on Land Use

Regulations may be issued under the powers of the government to promote the general welfare. The government is responsible for the health and safety of its citizens. It has a right to guarantee them a place to live and work.

Zoning

This restraint is a form of government control dividing the community into units which determine the type of building and the nature of activity permitted in each area. For example, limitations may be placed on the size and height of buildings. If an area is zoned for commercial use, it may include retail and wholesale enterprises; if industrial, heavy or light manufacturing may be allowed.

Covenants

Effects similar to zoning also can be achieved by individuals through covenants or express clauses inserted into leases and deeds. Such covenants may "run with the land," and if so, they are transferred to the new owner when the land changes hands. They can become an enduring check on the use of the land. The rule of contractual privity means that only the original parties and their successors are affected by these covenants. To this extent, covenants are not as broad as zoning laws, but to the buyer they may be as binding.

Balancing Public and Private Interests

It has been held that zoning laws must comply with the Fourteenth Amendment. They cannot deprive a citizen of property without due process of law. Yet these laws are changing rapidly. Environmentalists gained such power that zoning requirements in one state now require developers to set aside land for parks and recreation as part of a general scheme. Although there is no formal taking of land without due process, the developer who wants a plan approved will donate some of that land for public use.

Building Codes

Municipal and state zoning laws usually include codes that must be observed. Building plans and specifications must be approved by proper officials before construction can be started. The codes specify the type of material to be used and construction details, such as wiring, plumbing, and fireproofing. If the buildings are for public use, there will be additional requirements for fire protection, exits, and railings. When a building does not conform to the code, the buyer who has to correct this situation may find it alarmingly expensive.

Many states and cities have regulations imposing minimum standards for working conditions. Regulations include matters like ventilation, elevator guards, lighting, and stair rail heights. The federal government has also enacted legislation under the Occupational Health and Safety Act which imposes special requirements on employers in regard to employee safety. The manager must be sure to comply.

Equally important is the community's concern with fire prevention. Fires are destructive to both lives and property; governments enact numerous regulations governing fire exits, fire drills, water hydrants, and distances between structures.

Whether intended to prevent fires, to preserve the value of the land, or to ensure adequate light for the occupants of a house, many authorities have enacted ordinances governing the construction of houses. For example, bay windows and awnings cannot protrude too far, and steps and porches must be situated according to the local regulations. Such regulations protect the passerby, assist the smooth flow of traffic, and may also achieve a desired aesthetic effect. A separate garage on the front lawn is not very attractive in an exclusive neighborhood and may diminish surrounding land values.

In addition, allegedly objectionable uses of property (breweries, boarding houses, etc.) can be banned for ecological reasons, such as pollution control or noise prevention. An injunction can be issued to prevent such uses of the land.

Nonconforming Uses

Buildings and businesses that are in existence when the zoning laws are passed are usually allowed to continue. They are known as *nonconforming uses*. If they should be destroyed or severely damaged (generally over 50 percent), they can usually be rebuilt only in conformity with the zoning laws. Nonconforming buildings cannot be enlarged or used for another business that conforms less to the restrictions than the existing enterprise. Thus a retail establishment could not change to light manufacturing even though it had nonconforming rights. Purchase of such property may not be advisable since the owner will be confined to the existing use.

Use of the Land by the Owner

Rights should never be examined without a consideration of corresponding duties. The right to own or use land is balanced by obligations to other landowners.

Duty of Support

If the buyer plans to modify the land in any way, it will be necessary to check whether this change will hurt the neighbors. Their adjacent land is entitled to *lateral support* and *subjacent support* from the purchased property. Usually this means only that land must support neighboring land in its natural state; there is no duty to support a building which has been built upon the land. An engineer should be consulted to determine whether a proposed excavation will cause the neighbor's land to cave in.

Drainage

When the buyer restructures land, it may lead to liability for damages if water is diverted to an unnatural path or if its flow increases. One owner of land built a shopping center and paved a large parking lot which discharged rainwater as a stream on neighboring property. The neighboring landowner sued and won damages. The developer was required to build a separate drainage system.

Sewage

No modern civilization can afford to overlook the effects of poor sanitation. To prevent major epidemics, every municipality or county

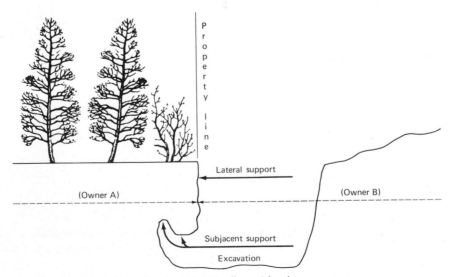

Fig. 20-4. Duty of excavation to support adjacent land.

enacts rules governing sewage disposal practices. These regulations must be strictly adhered to by every property owner. The local government has authority to inspect for violations and to enforce its health and sanitation powers.

The buyer who plans to build should be sure that the plans conform to the local code for water supply and sewage systems. Some industries that require a great deal of water may be forbidden to use community water supplies and forced to develop their own wells. In one case, a developer who planned to install cesspools in a number of houses under construction learned too late that there was not enough land to make the system work and was forced to buy additional land to leave empty as a leaching field.

Subterranean and Riparian Rights

At one time, at least in theory, the landowner enjoyed rights over the use of property down to the center of the earth. However, this doctrine was not too realistic because of the possibility of overlapping claims. It had to be modified. Normally the landowner today can mine the land and sink wells into it, provided that in so doing the duties of subjacent and lateral support owed to neighbors have not been violated, and the well is not used to suck all the oil out of a horizontal oil bed which underlies both properties. In other words, *subterranean rights* must be respected.

A landowner can expect that trees and buildings on the next lot will not extend over the property line. Otherwise, there will be a right of action for trespass or for nuisance giving rise to an injunction and to damages. However, an encroachment that lasts for a specified period of time can become an easement.

The property owner has, in addition, *riparian rights*, that is, the right to enjoy the use of water flowing on or through the property in its natural water course, providing the flow of the water in a stream to which neighbors would also have a right is not unreasonably diminished. One cannot divert the water in such a way as to deprive others of its use. Furthermore, one cannot accumulate or bring onto the land something which would create a hazard to the land of another if it escaped. This last doctrine is commonly known as the rule of *Rylands v. Fletcher*, a famous old case in which the proprietors of a mill constructed a reservoir from which the water escaped into and flooded a nearby colliery that had to be abandoned.

Thus, above, beneath, and on the surface of the land the landowner does not have exclusive rights to use the property. Every landowner must act as a responsible member of the community.

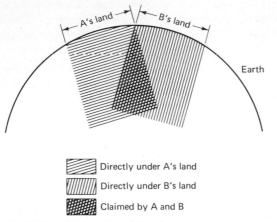

Fig. 20-5. Overlapping claims in space.

Rights in Space

By tradition dating back to ancient Roman law, the property owner owned the land and everything below and above its surface. Since the ancient jurists did not realize the world is round, they could not foresee the problem of overlapping claims of adjacent landowners. The problem arises from the fact that one cannot draw parallel perpendicular lines from a curved surface.

Today yet another consideration has forced modification of the original doctrine. With airplanes flying above the plots of many thousands of landowners and infringing their property rights each day, the old rule could have led to a maze of lawsuits. Now the landowner is entitled only to ownership of such space above the land as one can reasonably control; this may be placed at the height of the tallest structure on the property. Above that height, reasonable use by any vehicles legally aloft is allowed.

Preparing Rental Premises for Occupancy

Few vacant premises are suitable for immediate occupancy. Because the landlord cannot anticipate the needs of all prospective tenants, it may not be advisable to build anything more than the exterior of the building. A new building will frequently have no finished ceilings or floors, minimal safety lighting, and no other facilities. It is left to the tenant to complete the premises. The tenant who does not wish to do so may arrange to have the landlord do it.

Much can be said for having the landlord complete the building for occupancy and absorb the cost. The rental can be adjusted to reflect the landlord's greater investment. If the lease is for a relatively short time, improvements such as glass windows, lighting fixtures, floors, and ceilings involve a comparatively large investment. Occasionally, the building may need power equipment requiring special utility hookups.

Fixtures

Real estate law distinguishes between real property and personal property according to the way it is installed in a building. If an item is movable, it is usually designated as personal property. If an article is built into the building so that it becomes a part of the building or is dug into the ground, that article is permanent and is treated as real property. For example, a furnace system with ducts or pipes fitted into the floors or walls is considered real property, as are windows put in a store front. The matter becomes more complex when stoves, refrigerators, carpeting, bulky machines, and the like are considered.

Trade Fixtures

Equipment or personal property that is attached to the building but used in the tenant's business is called a *trade fixture*. Trade fixtures can be removed at the expiration of the lease if the removal does not cause material damage to the building. In the absence of a specific agreement, it would be foolish for the tenant to affix expensive and valuable items to the building for the benefit of the landlord. The intent of the parties is important. The courts are inclined to support the tenant in permitting removal, but it would be wise to insert the proper provisions into the lease to prevent later disputes.

Mortgaged Fixtures

The tenant may purchase equipment under a mortgage or conditional sale contract. The mortgagee will file a financing statement with the recorder's office and retain a security interest in the property superior to the rights of the landowner. The mortgagee can remove the equipment unless this would substantially damage or destroy the building.

The tenant's right to remove fixtures terminates with the lease. If one wants to remove trade fixtures, one must do so while the lease is in effect. When the lease is terminated, the premises should revert to the landlord. If the tenant fails to make arrangements for the removal of the fixtures, an intent to abandon them is presumed.

A business that must make extensive installations of equipment in a building owned by another should examine the terms of the lease and the formidable problem of removal. Do the costs justify the installation into a leased building? If not, one might reconsider the decision to rent rather than buy the premises.

Whether to own or lease property depends on many factors. The final decision is usually the result of a compromise and may not be ideal. The determination has to be made in a manner that will result in the best operating conditions one can provide for the business. A hasty, ill-conceived decision based on sentiment or opinion gives no assurance that it is economically sound.

INVOLVEMENT AND STUDY MATERIAL

Understanding Terms

Leasing	(page 301)	Abstract of title	(page 312)
Lease-purchase agreement		Easements	(page 313)
	(page 301)	Equitable servitude	(page 314)
Sale and leaseback	(page 302)	Possibilities of reverter	
Title search	(page 306)		(page 314)
Deed	(page 308)	Zoning	(page 315)
Quitclaim deeds	(page 309)	Covenants	(page 316)
Warranty deeds	(page 310)	Building codes	(page 316)
Recording	(page 310)	Nonconforming use	(page 317)

Questions and Problem Solving

1. Explain the purpose of government restraints upon land use and the effect they have on site selection.

2. Define and give an example of nonconforming use. Why is such use allowed?

3. What major advantages are contained in a lease-purchase agreement? How does it affect the debt position of the business?

4. Why is it important to record a deed?

5. Describe how subterranean rights and rights in space of the past differ from those of the present.

6. Describe the circumstances under which a quitclaim deed would be used.

7. Distinguish between a quitclaim deed, a bargain and sale deed, and a warranty deed.

8. Distinguish between a trade fixture and real property.

9. Explain the value of preparing a diagram in tracing a chain of title to a piece of real property.

10. List the considerations that a business person must be concerned with in the selection of a site for a plant.

11. Compare the advantages and disadvantages of owning real estate.

12. Explain the advantages of title insurance.

Cases for Discussion

1. Swenson owned a summer cottage along the seashore. One morning she noticed an oil slick offshore caused by the negligent unloading of oil from a tanker at a neighboring plant. She notified the state's department of human resources and its port authority claiming that the oil polluted the water and harmed wildlife. The state sued the tanker company and the plant for damages because of a public nuisance. The defendants answered that the state had no interest in the water's condition since it did not own it and that the oil slick could not constitute a public nuisance because it was temporary. Judgment for whom? Why?

2. Wang owned a building in a city which was constructing a rapid transit system. As the transit authority began to excavate to prepare a subway which would run beneath Wang's lot, he noticed cracks in his walls. He brought an action to prevent the transit authority from proceeding with its excavation because the removal of the earth and rock was causing serious damage to his property. Judgment for whom? Why?

3. Rockbridge Associates Ltd. owned land in Georgia, part of which was zoned residential and part commercial. The plaintiff applied to the county planning commission to have its property rezoned for apartments. The commission approved, but the county commissioners refused to abide by the report and denied the application. The plaintiff filed a lawsuit claiming the commissioners' decision was capricious and arbitrary and amounted to taking

its property without due process. The plaintiff also claimed that the commissioners' decision discriminated between its property and that of others in the surrounding area. The commissioners stated they denied the plaintiff's application on the grounds that there were insufficient water and sewer facilities as well as inadequate roads, schools were overcrowded, and many undeveloped tracts of land zoned for apartments existed in the immediate area. The zoning laws state the standards and objectives to be used in making decisions. The plaintiff was aware of these standards. Judgment for whom? Why?

4. The Martin Company owned land through which a stream flowed. The stream continued to flow onto the adjacent land, which was owned by the Sikes Building Supply Company. The Martin Company built a parking lot in the rear of the property and installed drain tile through which the stream then flowed. The stream drained onto Sikes's land in different places than formerly. The Sikes Company sustained damage to equipment stored in its basement when water from a nearby drain of the Martin Company flowed in. The Sikes Company brings suit against the Martin Company for damages for unreasonably altering the natural flow of the stream. Judgment for whom? Why?

5. The Hold Copper Corporation sold a piece of land to Jenkins for the purchase price of $10,000. The Hold Company delivered a duly executed deed to Jenkins for the property, but Jenkins did not have the deed recorded, nor did he enter onto the land. Later the Hold Corporation sold the same piece of land to the Budd Wire Company for $15,000 and delivered to it a duly executed deed which the Budd Company recorded. The Budd Company searched the records and found no other deeds; it had no notice of the prior deed to Jenkins. Jenkins then brought suit to recover his property from the Budd Company. The Budd Company claims that it is a bona fide purchaser and that it has the legal right and title to the land. Judgment for whom? Why?

6. La Ferra owned a building in which he wished to install an oil-burning furnace. He contracted with the Smyth Sales Company to sell him the furnace and oil tank. The terms of the contract called for title to the furnace and tank to remain in the Smyth Sales Corporation until La Ferra paid in full for the furnace and tank. The agreement was written up in the form of a conditional sales contract. The tank was buried about five feet in the ground outside the building and was connected to the furnace via pipes through the wall foundation.

La Ferra failed to meet payments on the furnace and tank. The building was mortgaged to the Norfolk Building and Loan Association, which held title to the property. The Smyth Sales Corporation sought to remove the furnace and tank from the building but was stopped from doing so by the Norfolk Association. Smyth now brings suit to recover the furnace and tank. The Norfolk Association maintains that the furnace and tank are now a permanent fixture and part of the building and were originally installed with that intention. To remove them would cause damage to the building. Judgment for whom? Why?

7. Klinger was the owner of the Ajax Hardware Store. He sold the land, buildings, and equipment to the Mooney Supply Company, giving them a quitclaim deed to the property. After acquiring the property, Mooney discovered that there was a lien against the buildings for $4,000. Mooney thereupon brought suit against Klinger, claiming that he had contracted to deliver the property free and clear of any encumbrances and that he warranted the title would be free and clear by giving the quitclaim deed. Klinger denied that he gave any warranty as to the title to the property and that he owed the $4,000 to Mooney Company. Judgment for whom? Why?

Chapter Twenty-one

Landlord-Tenant Relations

Good landlord and tenant relationships depend upon properly drafted lease agreements. The tenant who is preoccupied with the operation of the business may be inclined to ignore the content of the lease despite the fact that the lease will call for monthly payments.

The landlord, too, is interested in the success of the business in order to collect the monthly rent. Anyone in business must recognize that a lease brings obligations and that the terms of the lease determine whether it is burdensome or helpful to the business.

Basically a lease is no different from any other contract. It needs the same elements of offer, acceptance, and consideration. Since it involves an interest in land, certain formalities have to be observed. These will be discussed below.

LEASES

Despite the complex appearance of the typical commercial lease form, there is nothing particularly remarkable about any lease. In actual practice many clauses may be inapplicable to a particular situation. The parties can block out any section they do not like. Each party initials any section that is not to apply. Additional terms can be added with as much detail as the occasion demands.

It is not the purpose of this text to cover all the details of a lease form. Many commercial leases contain four or more pages of provisions in fine print. The introduction to leases contained in this chapter should enable the business person to understand the major provisions.

Selecting a Site

The nature of the business and the space desired, to a large extent, determine the bargaining power of the prospective tenant. For example, the bargaining position of a prospective tenant in a shopping center will depend on the value of the business to the store mix at the center. Unless it is a key business that the center wants, it usually has to take the terms offered. Since the retail business must have a location that is accessible to its customers, many small businesses find their choice of locations and leases limited.

The prospective tenant may improve his or her position by examining locations away from shopping centers where there is less direct competition with large and established merchandisers. Better lease terms may be available away from the centers. Elsewhere landlords may be feeling the effect of competition by the shopping centers and thus may be prepared to make concessions to their tenants.

Terms Providing for Necessary Space

A difficult problem faces many new businesses in regard to the amount of space needed, particularly in long-term leases. The business does not wish to incur obligations for space that it cannot use. Yet it cannot ignore the fact that, if it is successful, it may need more space after it gets started. The problem revolves around the manner in which reserve space can be obtained at minimum cost.

A rental agency is no stranger to the problems faced by the new business. The agency should be sympathetic and may be able to make special arrangements that are helpful to the new tenant. Thus the premises may be in a building occupied by other tenants that are not particularly concerned with location. If the business later requires additional space, the landlord may be able to relocate other

ATLANTA REAL ESTATE BOARD
Commercial Lease Contract
September, 1972

CAMPUS REALTY

Atlanta, Georgia

THIS LEASE, made this 19th day of September , 1973 , by and between John Beaver , first party, (hereinafter called "Landlord"); and Henry George , second party, (hereinafter called "Tenant"); and Campus Realty Co , third party, (hereinafter called "Agent");

WITNESSETH:

Premises 1. The Landlord, for and in consideration of the rents, covenants, agreements, and stipulations hereinafter mentioned, reserved, and contained, to be paid, kept and performed by the Tenant, has leased and rented, and by these presents does lease and rent, unto the said Tenant, and said Tenant hereby agrees to lease and take upon the terms and conditions which hereinafter appear, the following described property (hereinafter called premises), to wit:

and being known as 1234 Maple St., Anytown U.S.A.

No easement for light or air is included in the premises.

Term 2. To have and to hold the same for a term of five years beginning on the 1st day of October , 1973 and ending on the 30th day of Sept. 1973 , at midnight, unless sooner terminated as hereinafter provided.

Rental 3. Tenant agrees to pay Landlord, by payments to Campus Realty Co Agent of Landlord, who negotiated this lease, at office of Agent in Atlanta, Georgia, promptly on the first day of each month in advance, during the term of this lease, a monthly rental of four hundred fifty dollars ($450) or a total of $27,000.

Agent's Commission 4. The commission to be paid in connection with this transaction has been negotiated between Landlord and Agent and Landlord agrees to pay Agent, as compensation for services rendered in procuring this lease, 5% , and Landlord, with consent of Tenant, hereby assigns to Agent aforesaid commission. If the term of this lease is extended, or if new lease is entered into between Landlord and Tenant

Purchase of Property by Tenant 5. In the event that tenant acquires title to the leased premises at any time during the term of this lease, any renewals thereof, or within six months after the expiration of the term hereof or the extended term hereof, then Landlord shall pay Agent a commission on the sale of the property of the Landlord in lieu of any additional rental commissions. Such sales commission, as negotiated between parties, is to be 5%

Utility Bills 6. Tenant shall pay all utility bills, including, but not limited to water, sewer, gas, electricity, fuel, light, and heat bills, for the leased premises and Tenant shall pay all charges for garbage collection services or other sanitary services rendered to the leased premises or used by Tenant in connection therewith. If Tenant fails to pay any of said utility bills or charges for garbage collection or other sanitary services, Landlord may pay the same and such payment may be added to the rental of the premises next due as additional rental.

Use of Premises 7. Premises shall be used for purposes and no other. Premises shall not be used for any illegal purposes; nor in any manner to create any nuisance or trespass; nor in any manner to vitiate the insurance or increase the rate of insurance on premises.

Abandonment of Leased Premises 8. Tenant agrees not to abandon or vacate leased premises during the period of this lease, and agrees to use said premises for purpose herein leased until the expiration hereof.

Repairs by Landlord 9. Landlord agrees to keep in good repair the roof, foundations, and exterior walls of the premises (exclusive of all glass and exclusive of all exterior doors), and underground utility and sewer pipes outside the exterior walls of the Building, except repairs rendered necessary by the negligence of Tenant, its agents, employees, or invitees. Landlord gives to Tenant exclusive control of premises and shall be under no obligation to inspect said premises. Tenant shall promptly report in writing to Landlord any defective condition known to it which Landlord is required to repair, and failure to so report such defects shall make Tenant responsible to Landlord for any liability incurred by Landlord by reason of such defects.

Repairs by Tenant 10. Tenant accepts the leased premises in their present condition and as suited for the uses intended by Tenant. Tenant shall, throughout the initial term of this lease andall renewals thereof, at its expense, maintain in good order and repair the leased premises, including the building and other improvements located thereon, except those repairs expressly required to be made by Landlord. Tenant further agrees to case for the grounds around the building, including the mowing of grass, paving, care of shrubs and general landscaping. Tenant agrees to return said premises to Landlord at the expiration, or prior to termination, of this lease in as good condition and repair as when first received, natural wear and tear, damage by storm, fire, lightning, earthquake or other casualty alone excepted.

assignments or subleases shall be made likewise only on the prior written consent of Landlord. Assignee of Tenant, at option of Landlord, shall become directly liable to Landlord for all obligations of Tenant hereunder, but no sublease or assignment by Tenant shall relieve Tenant of any liability hereunder.

Removal of Fixtures 17. Tenant may (if not in default hereunder) prior to the expiration of this lease, or any extension thereof, remove all fixtures and equipment which he has placed in premises, provided Tenant repairs all damage to premises caused by such removal.

Cancellation of Lease by Landlord 18. It is mutually agreed that in the event the Tenant shall default in the payment of rent, including additional rent, herein reserved, when due, and fails to cure said default within five (5) days after written notice thereof from Landlord; or if Tenant shall be in default in performing any of the terms or provisions of this lease other than the provision requiring the payment of rent, and fails to cure such default within thirty (30) days after the date of receipt of written notice of default from Landlord; or if Tenant is adjudicated bankrupt; or if a permanent receiver is appointed for Tenant's property and such receiver is not removed within sixty days after written notice from Landlord to Tenant to obtain such removal; or if, whether voluntarily or involuntarily, Tenant takes advantage of any debtor relief proceedings under any present or future law, whereby the rent or any part thereof is, or is proposed to be, reduced or payment thereof deferred;

Effect of Termination of Lease 22. No termination of this lease prior to the normal ending thereof, by lapse of time or otherwise, shall affect Landlord's right to collect rent for the period prior to termination thereof.

Mortgagee's Rights 23. Tenant's rights shall be subject to any bona fide mortgage or deed to secure debt which is now, or may hereafter be, placed upon the premises by Landlord.

No Estate in Land 24. This contract shall create the relationship of Landlord and Tenant between the parties hereto; no estate shall pass out of Landlord. Tenant has only a usufruct, not subject to levy and sale, and not assignable by Tenant except by Landlord's consent.

Holding Over 25. If Tenant remains in possession of premises after expiration of the term hereof, with Landlord's acquiescence and without any express agreement of parties, Tenant shall be a tenant at will at rental rate in effect at end of lease; and there shall be no renewal of this lease by operation of law.

Attorney's Fees and Homestead 26. If any rent owing under this lease is collected by or through an attorney at law, Tenant agrees to pay ten percent (10%) thereof as attorneys' fees. Tenant waives all homestead rights and exemptions which he may have under any law as against any obligation owing under this lease. Tenant hereby assigns to Landlord his homestead and exemption.

Rights Cumulative 27. All rights, powers and privileges conferred hereunder upon parties hereto shall be cumulative but not restrictive to those given by law.

Service of Notice 28. Tenant hereby appoints as his agent to receive service of all dispossessory or distraint proceedings and notices hereunder, and all notices required under this lease, the person in charge of leased premises at the time, or occupying said premises; and if no person is in charge of, or occupying said premises, then such service or notice may be made by attaching the same on the main entrance to said premises. A copy of all notices under this lease shall also be sent to Tenant's last known address, if different from said premises.

Waiver of Rights 29. No failure of Landlord to exercise any power given Landlord hereunder, or to insist upon strict compliance by Tenant with his obligation hereunder, and no custom or practice of the parties at variance with the terms hereof shall constitute a waiver of Landlord's right to demand exact compliance with the terms hereof.

Time of Essence 30. Time is of the essence of this agreement.

Definitions 31. "Landlord" as used in this lease shall include first party, his heirs, representatives, assigns and successors in title to premises. "Tenant" shall include second party, his heirs and representatives, and if this lease shall be validly assigned or sublet, shall include also Tenant assignees or sublessees, as to premises covered by such assignment or sublease. "Agent" shall include third party, his successors, assigns, heirs, and representatives. "Landlord", "Tenant", and "Agent", include male and female, singular and plural, corporation, partnership or individual, as may fit the particular parties.

Fig. 21-1. Commercial lease contract. (Used with permission of the Atlanta Real Estate Board. No other reproduction authorized without permission.)

tenants to make more space available. The lease may require adequate notice in order that proper arrangements can be made.

If the building is being built to the tenant's specifications, it can be assumed that plans for expansion will have been included. But most new businesses will find it necessary to secure space in existing locations that may have to be altered to suit the business. Although extra space may be costly, a satisfactory solution can often be found.

No lease should be undertaken without provisions for sufficient space. Mere assurance of availability of additional space is not acceptable to any business. If it prospers, an inadequate location may hamper its operations and expansion plans.

Renewal Provisions

It may be important for a business to retain the location at which it has prospered. Unless the parties recognize that certain enterprises gain business as a result of their location, the lease may not provide for a renewal. If the value of the location rises considerably, the future bargaining power of the lessee may be substantially reduced.

The provisions of the renewal clause need careful attention. If the lease form does not contain such a clause, a section will have to be added. The landlord is well aware of inflation, increased values of property, and the financial situation of the tenant. If the business prospers, there is no reason why the landlord should not share in the prosperity by extending the lease.

Landlord-tenant problems can arise when the renewal terms are vague. The terms for renewal must be workable; an increase in business may be reflected in a proportionate increase in rent, or a rent increase can be related to inflation.

Escalation Clauses

Landlords generally do not want to rely on the potential prosperity and generosity of their new tenants. They know that inflation occurs and taxes rise. Therefore most lease forms have a tax escalation clause and an inflation clause. Figures from the Department of Commerce can be used as a standard.

Notice

Most leases have provisions governing the type of notice that the parties are required to give to each other. For example, the tenant may have to give written notice about certain necessary repairs. If a tenant changes the use of the property or fails to pay rent, the landlord can give written notice that will terminate the lease.

Some leases expire automatically at the end of a given time. Others require that the tenant give written notice, possibly thirty days in advance, when planning to move; otherwise the lease will be considered to have been renewed for another complete term. In some states, a holding-over beyond the specified term creates a tenancy at will which can be terminated in accordance with certain requirements, such as thirty days' notice. We shall discuss tenancy at will shortly.

Re-leasing by Landlord

If the tenant breaches a lease and vacates the premises, the landlord will be legally obligated to minimize damages by finding another tenant. Some leases contain a clause to this effect, but it is not necessary. This requirement may not be of much comfort to the former tenant, since the landlord's efforts will be motivated by self-interest. If the landlord has other vacant property, it is natural to concentrate on these vacancies and be less interested in finding a successor to the former tenant's premises. To avoid paying the amount due for the remaining period of the lease, the tenant should also try to locate another tenant. Of course, if the tenant is insolvent, the landlord will attempt to re-lease the premises.

Requirements of Written and Recorded Leases

Since leases involve interests in land, they generally have to be in writing to be enforced in a court of law if the term runs beyond one year. In a few states, leases are considered special property rights and may be oral for as long as three years.

Occupancy of the premises as a tenant without a lease creates a *tenancy at will*, which is controlled by statutes. Generally it can be terminated by giving thirty days' notice or shorter notice if rent is paid for a shorter period. Thus if rent is being paid by the week, a notice of one week would be adequate.

Many states require recording the lease in the same manner as a mortgage or deed because it involves an interest in land. Thus, before recording, the lease may need an acknowledgment, witnesses, and sometimes a seal. The absence of the necessary formalities may prohibit its recording.

A tenant relying on the leased premises and making any investment in the way of fixtures, improvements, remodeling, or other installations should consider the situation in the same way as any other investment in land. Unless the lease is recorded, the tenant will not be protected against other claimants, encumbrances, and creditors of the landlord.

Hold Harmless Agreements

When people are injured, they frequently look to the owner of the premises where the injury occurred. Yet if the tenant agreed to look after routine maintenance and the injury occurred from a lack of maintenance, the landlord will look to the tenant for any payments that have to be made. For this reason, many leases contain a clause which provides that the tenant shall hold the landlord harmless of any liability resulting from injuries suffered by third parties. If the lease contains this clause, the tenant should make sure that a liability insurance policy makes proper provision to protect the business from such lawsuits.

The hold harmless agreements in leases are not particularly burdensome since liability exposure can readily be transferred to an insurance company. However, they are illegal if the landlord is attempting to transfer to the tenant his own liability for some negligence connected with the building. Violations of building codes, of statutes providing for safety of people on the premises, or of other requirements remain the responsibility of the landlord.

Utility Bills

Generally the landlord rents merely the real estate and the buildings on it. The tenant must make arrangements for lights, water, and other utilities. Hence a provision is often included in the lease that the tenant will pay for the utilities. In cases where the landlord supplies heat, electricity, air conditioning, and water, this clause is eliminated.

Assignment of a Lease

Generally the lease will contain a provision that the tenant must get the permission of the landlord to make an assignment. Assignment is complete substitution of one tenant for another. Whether it releases the original tenant from the rental obligations is another question.

Owners do not like assignments because they have no control over who takes over the property. They know nothing about the assignee's behavior, credit standing, or general desirability as a tenant.

A clause pertaining to assignments may contain a provision that one consent does not apply to subsequent consents. The reason for this is that the courts view the nonassignment clause like a piece of glass; once broken it cannot be mended. By including this provision, the owner can consent once without being bound in regard to a later assignment.

A prohibition against assignments favors the landlord, but fortunately there are courts to see that tenants are not burdened with unconscionable contracts. If the tenant finds that the premises are no longer satisfactory, it may be desirable to find other quarters despite the fact that the lease has a long time to run. A substitute tenant may be willing to take over the lease for the remainder of the term. If the individual is reputable and there is no compelling reason for barring the assignment, the landlord cannot unreasonably refuse to permit it.

Subleasing

Assignment is a transfer of one's rights to another. Subleasing is interposing the tenant as a subordinate landlord. The original landlord still asserts control. If the tenant subleases a part of the building in the course of a regular operation, the premises continue to be used for the purposes for which they were leased. If excess space or a sublease for other purposes is involved, the landlord reserves the right of approval.

Leasing a large space with permission to sublease is one way to answer the problem of the starting business that anticipates future space needs. Such an arrangement has the disadvantage of obligating the business for more rent, but terms can be made to reduce the amount unless the space is occupied. It offers the advantage that the business can control the subleased space for the initial terms of the lease as well as for any renewal periods.

Landlords may not permit subleases since a sublessee's only relationship is with the lessee, the sublessee has no obligation to the owner, and the owner has no right to claim rent from the sublessee. If the lessee disappears, the owner might be in the uncomfortable position of being unable either to collect rent or to force the sublessee to move.

Destruction or Damage to Premises

Leases usually carry a destruction or damage-to-premises clause that can cause difficulty unless the problem is considered beforehand. Most of the clauses are worded in favor of the landlord and provide that if the building is totally destroyed by certain perils, the lease is terminated and the rental adjusted to the date of loss. If the building is only damaged, the landlord has the right to repair "as speedily as practicable" and then the rental is reinstated. The trouble with such a provision is that it leaves the tenant without an opportunity to secure substitute emergency quarters and at the mercy of the landlord. While business interruption insurance is available, a business owner is more interested in the business's survival.

A better clause provides for a survey, evaluation, and opinion by competent engineers or architects. If the building is damaged more than a specified percentage (usually 50 percent), the lease is terminated. The clause also should specify that the decision of the engineer or architect is final. Further provisions should require any repairs to be completed as speedily as possible, and repairs within a specified time period, such as sixty days, should also be considered.

Exterior Signs

A tenant who expects to install advertising signs should make careful review of the sign clause in the contract. If none is included, it should be put in. Landlords have real problems with signs, particularly if they have other tenants in a large building. The landlord will want to maintain some uniformity. Further, it is undesirable to have one tenant outdoing the others by installing larger and brighter signs. The tenant, too, will want to make sure other tenants in the complex will not do that. The signs will also be controlled by the city building codes in regard to size, height, and place of installation.

Government Regulations

The tenant usually pays for adjustments to comply with governmental orders regarding sanitation or pollution problems that come about by reason of the tenant's occupancy. If the violation stems from some defect of the building itself, it is up to the landlord to make the necessary repairs. The problem should be approached with caution, particularly following the enactment of the Occupational Safety and Health Act. Requirements for change may be substantial and involve heavy costs. Most leases protect against such eventualities by stipulating that if the costs of change to either party equal the annual rental, the lease may be terminated.

Eminent Domain

The right of the government to take private property for public use is called *eminent domain.* The government must pay the owner a fair price for the property. If the owner refuses the offered price, the government then begins *condemnation* proceedings to obtain the property through court action. Often a lease stipulates that it terminates on the day public authorities occupy the premises and that the tenant cannot claim a share in any awards made to the landlord by the government. Therefore if the premises are condemned, the tenant may have to find another site with no compensation for the loss of the lease.

LANDLORD'S OBLIGATIONS

A lease is a form of contract. The parties assume certain obligations in exchange for the commitments of the other. Landlords, too, make certain promises to the tenants.

Repairs by the Landlord

Because the landlord owns the building, the tenant generally will not want to perform major repairs involving foundations, roofs, walls, or underground utilities. Yet there may be situations where the use by the tenant necessitates frequent repairs. A manufacturing plant is an example. In such cases the tenant is very likely fully equipped to make the repairs and can treat them as an operating cost. The tenant may be willing to accept this duty of repairs with an appropriate adjustment in rent. In sale-leaseback arrangements, the tenant frequently accepts full maintenance responsibility for the building because the landlord in those situations is an investor rather than an experienced commercial property holder.

Landlord's Right to Enter and Inspect

Most commercial leases require the tenant to notify the lessor of any problems needing the landlord's attention. However, a clause may be inserted to permit inspection by the landlord. This usually occurs with premises occupied by several tenants. Deterioration of the premises because of one tenant will obviously affect the desirability of the site for other tenants.

Almost all leases include a right to enter to make repairs or show premises to prospective buyers. If the current tenant is nearing the end of a lease, the lessor also has a right to show the premises to prospective tenants.

Possession

The landlord must give the tenant possession of the premises—quiet possession undisturbed by other claimants—in order to collect rent. The lessor also cannot engage in activities that would make it impractical for the tenant to conduct the business for which the premises are rented.

Other Requirements

Leases are drawn by the landlord or authorized representatives; thus their clauses often favor the landlord. Many clauses give the landlord control over the premises and who shall occupy them. If a large building with many tenants is leased to a particular type of profession, such as doctors, the landlord may not want to change its character and will exclude other professions or businesses.

TENANT'S OBLIGATIONS

On signing a lease, the tenant can expect certain requirements before the premises can be occupied. The landlord will want to make sure that the tenant understands these obligations.

Proper Use

The lease generally specifies the purpose for which the premises are to be used. Presumably the tenant will not use the premises for any other purpose. The lessor keeps the premises insured, and fire insurance policies reflect the use of the building. If the tenant engages in activity that increases the insurance risk, the insurance company may either declare the policy inapplicable or require installation of special equipment to eliminate or control the risk. Many leases specify that if an insurance company requires changes, the tenant must comply.

Leases also prohibit activity that may involve nuisances or violation of zoning laws. Such activities may be objectionable to other tenants as well as to neighboring businesses. They may adversely affect the value of the neighborhood or reputation of the landlord, who therefore has a genuine interest in controlling the situation.

Rent

The amount of the rental can be given for the entire period divided by the number of months of the lease. Sometimes, instead of saying that the rent is $200 a month for two years, the lease may say that the rent is $4,800, payable $200 a month for twenty-four months. Stating it this way reinforces the landlord's claim for the whole amount if the lessee tries to break the lease and move out of the premises ahead of time.

Lessees are usually required to post a deposit consisting of one month's rent. This amount is included in the above clause as the amount the landlord acknowledges having received. Usually some other clause in the lease specifies what will be done with this amount in various circumstances. If the deposit is considered the last month's rent in advance, one should not forget to include it in describing the remaining rent due. When leasing property, it is wise to read this clause very carefully. It is very easy to make mistakes, and very difficult to persuade someone that a mistake has been made once the lease is signed.

Repairs

It has been shown that certain repairs normally fall to the landlord. Many routine items of daily maintenance are the responsibility of the tenant. Much landlord-tenant conflict can be eliminated if the lease terms are clear about repairs. This can become an area of disagreement if the details are not worked out beforehand.

Normal repairs and maintenance are generally the duty of the tenant. However, the duties will vary, depending on the type of leased premises. The tenant who occupies an office in a large building will probably make few, if any, repairs. Generally the lease will specify that the premises are to be maintained in the same condition as when they were first occupied, but normal wear and tear is expected. The tenant who occupies a complete building with lawns and driveways may be expected to maintain the entire premises. This will include windows and general landscaping. If the totally occupied building includes elevators, the tenant is expected to keep them in a safe condition.

DEFAULTS

Not all leases have a happy ending. The tenant may die, become insolvent, or for other reasons be unable to pay the rent. Then the lessee is in default. The lease terms often contain very stern language about what is likely to happen to this tenant. Some of the language sounds very threatening, but it may be unenforceable at law; landlords cannot always do what the lease provisions say they can do. When the lessee defaults, it is advisable to consult a lawyer to determine the proper course of action.

Insolvency or Bankruptcy

The appcintment of a receiver in bankruptcy presents a different situation because now the ability of the tenant to pay the rent has come into question. Therefore many leases contain a provision that if the tenant becomes bankrupt or otherwise insolvent, the lease shall be terminated within a specified time. The provision is not very harmful to the tenant since it does not come about until the insolvency has occurred. It has greater meaning for the landlord and generally should not be resisted.

CHARACTER OF THE PARTIES

The tenant-landlord relationship is as complex as any family tie. Tenant and landlord take each other for better or worse and either party may have much at stake. Neither can abandon the other without some cost.

As we have seen, the characteristics of reliable contracting parties are character, capability, and capital. Much has been said in the preceding chapter about the condition and the location of the property as well as the legal implications of owning or leasing property. These remain important considerations when leases are being executed, but perhaps none is as important as the character of the landlord. Capability and capital in conducting business can be almost assured through title searches, credit checks, and care in choosing the site. The character of the lessor remains to be tested.

It is wise to check the character of a prospective landlord by inquiring of other tenants, business references, banks, realtors, and brokers. There should be no hesitancy in doing so because experienced landlords are going to inquire about prospective tenants. The business person should always proceed with caution before signing a lease.

INVOLVEMENT AND STUDY MATERIAL

Understanding Terms

Escalation clauses	(page 329)	Subleasing	(page 332)
Tenancy at will	(page 330)	Condemnation	(page 334)
Hold harmless agreement		Eminent domain	(page 334)
	(page 331)	Default	(page 337)
Assignment of lease	(page 331)		

Questions and Problem Solving

1. List some of the important provisions of a lease.

2. What should be done if the parties do not want an escalation clause of the standard lease form to govern their lease?

3. What is the status of a tenant who continues to occupy the premises after the lease has expired?

4. What are the obligations of the landlord after a tenant breaches a lease and vacates the premises?

5. What justification is there for a hold harmless clause in a lease?

6. How can the tenant seek protection from the undesirable consequences of the hold harmless clause?

7. What are the legal consequences of an assignment, if the landlord agrees to substitute the new tenant in place of the original lessee?

8. How can the tenant assure adequate future space when signing

a lease the first time without knowing the amount of space the business will need a few years hence?

9. How does a sign clause protect the tenant?

10. How does condemnation affect the rights of the lessee?

11. Why does the landlord often want the amount of the rent stated in the lease as a lump sum rather than as monthly payments?

12. What are the advantages of a detailed written lease for both the landlord and the tenant?

Cases for Discussion

1. General Motors Corporation had a twenty year lease on a warehouse at 42 cents a square foot. Before the lease expired, the U.S. government condemned the warehouse temporarily for military purposes. General Motors had to remove its bins and fixtures. It estimated the cost of removal to be $46,000 and the loss due to removing the fixtures and bins to be $31,000 more for a total of $77,000. The government allowed 40 cents per square foot, so General Motors seeks to collect the additional 2 cents per square foot rent plus $77,000. Judgment for whom? Why?

2. Freight Terminals Incorporated leased a terminal to Ryder Systems, Inc. The lease required the lessee to keep the property in good condition and return it in the same condition as it was in when rented, less normal wear and tear. It also made allowance for the recovery of attorney's fees in the event of a lawsuit. Although Ryder made some repairs, the property became run down and Ryder eventually moved out. Later Ryder subleased the terminal to Mercury Freight Lines, Inc., for the remainder of the lease. The total deterioration of the property was estimated at $52,500, of which $7,500 occurred during the sublease by Mercury Freight. Upon termination of the lease, Freight Terminals Incorporated sued both Ryder and Mercury Freight for $52,500 in damages and $16,000 in attorney's fees. Ryder claimed Mercury Freight was liable for the entire amount under the sublease because it agreed to return the premises in satisfactory condition in accordance with the original lease. However, Mercury Freight denied that it assumed Ryder's obligations under the lease and that it was liable for damages occurring prior to its sublease. Judgment for whom? Why?

3. The United States government negotiated the sale of a building to the Fullers for $22,500. The contract called for a downpayment of $750 and the balance in monthly installments. The gov-

ernment was to hold the deed until the full purchase price was paid. The government made a complete inspection of the property before the sale and found no defects or hazards. The Fullers were regarded as tenants of the government until the deed was delivered to them and, as such, they sublet a basement apartment to Harris, who ordered some furniture from Canarsie Outlet Sales Corporation. While delivering the furniture, Torres, an employee of Canarsie, slipped on a loose tread on the steps leading down to Harris's apartment. Torres sued the government to recover for his injuries claiming that it was negligent in failing to inspect and maintain the stairway in a reasonably safe condition. The government claimed it parted with possession and control of the property. It had no actual notice of any defective condition. It further maintained that the property was owned by the Fullers since the contract between them merely created a relationship allowing the government a right to enter the property in default of the monthly payments. The law of New York stated that when title to and possession of property was surrendered to another, liability and the duty to maintain the property in good repair rested with the new owner-buyer. Judgment for whom? Why?

4. Durwood American Company leased space for some small theaters on the floor above McCrory Corporation in the Westroads Shopping Center. Durwood hired an independent contractor, A. Borchman & Sons, to build the theaters. The contract between Durwood and Borchman contained a hold harmless agreement protecting Durwood against all claims resulting from that construction. Borchman had a subcontractor, Lewis, install the heating system. The temperature was to be up to 210°F. and the pressure about 100 pounds per square inch. Gates Rubber Company supplied the flexible connectors used by Lewis but was not informed about the operating conditions. Since the plumbing was covered, no visual inspection was possible. Within two years a rubber connector broke flooding the McCrory store and causing damage of $6,600. Durwood was then told what created the problem and warned about periodic inspection but did nothing. A month later, another connector broke and this time the McCrory store suffered damages of $7,900. McCrory sued Durwood, Borchman, Lewis, Gates Rubber Company and the Westroads Corporation. Each party sought reimbursement from the other. Judgment for whom? Why?

Chapter Twenty-two

Risk Management

By necessity rather than by choice, everyone is a risk manager. Risk exists because the future is unknown. People have attempted to minimize risk since the dawn of history. The biblical story of Joseph and the Pharaoh involves the storing of food during the seven rich years to protect against seven lean years. Some feel that insurance is the answer to risk management. However, the manager who depends on insurance to handle risk will soon have little to manage.

A basic cause of economic insecurity is loss of income. There may be a total loss of income or a partial loss leaving an inadequate amount for survival. The income loss may be long- or short-term. What many risk managers fail to recognize is that it often continues far beyond the period of incapacity. A plant that has been destroyed does not regain its regular income as soon as it restarts its manufacturing process.

NATURE OF RISK

Risk may be classified as objective or subjective. It may be different for different people. The poker player who knows odds and considers the chances of drawing an ace compared with the chances of filling an inside straight is dealing with an objective (mathematical) situation. One who is simply playing hunches will be dealing with a subjective risk.

Objectives of a Business

The long-range objective of an enterprise, of course, is to make a profit, but staying in business is the first goal.

Risks Facing a Company

A business can suffer losses of property and of time in many ways. To try to prevent all loss is futile. No one can anticipate every possibility from a falling meteor to a skunk entering the premises. A more logical approach is to examine what needs protection and the general manner in which the enterprise can suffer a loss. The assets that a business must protect generally include its capital, property, and labor. The manner of loss may be

Appropriation: someone else may take the assets
Destruction: direct loss by fires, etc.
Depreciation: equipment wears out
Depletion: source of raw materials is gone
Obsolescence: things are no longer useful

The manager must recognize the production factors essential to the firm and understand that they may be lost in order to consider prevention, retention, transfer, or preservation.

Appropriation

Although appropriation suggests theft, there are many ways in which property can be taken by another. If an employee is careless in driving the company car or in working and injures another, a lawsuit may result in company liability. The owner who is careless about

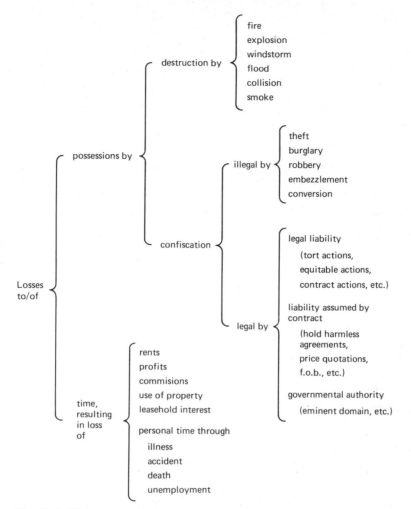

Fig. 22-1. Risk survey chart.

buying property may pay for property without acquiring title. Personnel (labor) can also be hired away.

Destruction

Normally people think of destruction as a risk connected with fire or some natural disaster. However, in business, destruction means simply the elimination of some factor of production. One will be less concerned with how it happened than with the hard fact that it did happen and that one cannot carry on the business.

Depreciation

When the business is being started, depreciation is considered in connection with accounting or tax matters. Nevertheless, physical wear and tear is a prominent factor in risk control and is to be considered and minimized where possible.

Depletion

Loss through depletion figures strongly in mining or oil production. Yet a failure to consider it as a potential loss factor in all business can be disastrous. If the source of raw materials is exhausted, the business cannot function. People may think of depletion as solely a natural phenomenon, but it can also mean interrupted delivery of raw materials because of technological or price changes. Alternative sources must always be identified and placed on the ready list.

Obsolescence

Outgrowing usefulness is a fact of life. Machines become outmoded by technological advances. A handsaw is replaced by a power saw. A person trained in making foundry mouldings is replaced by a die-casting machine. Meanwhile, the manager has to deal with a business stocked with handsaws or with no longer necessary employees. In either event, serious troubles and losses can result for the company.

METHODS OF HANDLING RISK

Successful businesses recognize that not all risks can be handled by insurance. Other methods are available and, on many occasions, more suitable.

Insurance is a transfer mechanism. This simply means that instead of facing a risk of loss alone, the business transfers the risk to a professional risk bearer. The risk bearer, in turn, assesses charges to similar businesses and spreads the loss potential over a large number of policyholders. This appears to be an ideal method of handling losses since the shock to any one business is generally small. Insurance against loss becomes a cost of doing business whereas the loss itself could be ruinous to any particular business.

The trouble with this concept is that insurance is a highly competitive business. Insurance companies are forced to try to give their customers as favorable rates as possible. When a particular customer's losses are higher than the underwriter thinks they should be, the rates are either raised proportionately or insurance is refused or cancelled. The customer may be unable to get insurance or compelled to pay unusually high rates.

Insurance is not a device whereby someone gets something for nothing. On the basis of probabilities, actuaries calculate the number (frequencies) and size (severities) of the losses that can be expected by a particular group. Policyholders with similar risks are grouped together, so that the rates charged that group will reflect the losses sustained by that group. In this way, low-risk businesses pay less for insurance than businesses that suffer proportionately higher losses.

The amount of loss that business suffers is considered by the insurance company to be *pure loss*. The insurance company's own operating expenses determine the *loading factor*. When the actuaries figure how much a policyholder will have to pay in premiums, they take into account both the pure loss and the loading factor. The loading factor may amount to 20 percent or more of the premium dollar.

Thus if the actuaries calculate that ten out of 100 businesses will suffer a loss in a year and that all those losses combined will total $5,000, they will divide the $5,000 among the 100 businesses, and each business will pay for a pure loss of $50. If the loading factor is 20 percent of the premium, then

80 percent of the premium = $50

or

$8/10 \times$ premium = $50

To solve for the amount of the premium

$50 $\div$ 8/10 =

$50 $\times$ 10/8 = $62.50, the amount of the premium

If the business has the facilities for handling its individual losses at a lower cost, it would be foolish to transfer the risk to an insurance company.

The transfer of all losses to an insurance company may not be economical. Therefore, the manager will want to explore all methods of risk management. These include retention, prevention, avoidance, and control and reduction, as well as transfer to an insurance company. All have legitimate places in an analysis of exposure to losses, and we shall consider them in that order.

Retention

Whether or not a business needs insurance will depend in part on its capacity for *retention*, that is, taking the loss itself. Retention of losses that cannot be handled as routine business expenses is not easy for a small business. If anticipated loss reserves are set up, they are not tax deductible until a loss actually occurs. Insurance premiums are deductible, however. Therefore, larger losses may have to be transferred unless the company can afford to tie up large sums of money in loss reserves, even though high losses will generate high insurance company premiums. If the business experiences small losses that can be absorbed as a routine expense, it may want to retain such losses. A business which handles loss replacements anyway will derive little benefit from an insurance transfer. Insurance companies issue policies with deductible amounts. The amount of the deductible represents the amount the policyholder has to pay before the insurance company is required to make payment. To this extent, the deductible amount under the policy is a form of retention.

Risk managers should be guided by three principles:

1. Don't risk a lot for little.
2. Don't risk more than you can afford.
3. Don't ignore the odds.[1]

Prevention

A great many losses may be occurring that need not be sustained by a business. A plant with a high scrap ratio will very likely also have a high loss ratio because the high scrap ratio indicates a lack of respect for property. Perhaps the boss does not know this is happening. Education programs designed to show to the employee that any kind of losses are personally expensive have been very successful. If the business has developed some loss statistics, prevention personnel

[1] Robert Mehr and Bob Hedges, *Risk Management in the Business Enterprise*, Richard D. Irwin, Inc., Homewood, Ill., 1963.

of companies may be able to compare them with those of like businesses. A cooperative manager may discover that small changes in plant operations or layout may bring substantial improvement in loss occurrences and in the premiums asked.

In prevention, every accident is considered important. For example, if a deliveryman backing out of a driveway runs over a child's tricycle, the damage might not run over $10. However, the fact that he did not see the tricycle means that if there had been a child there, he might not have seen it either. The significance should be obvious.

Loss prevention programs can eliminate many potential hazards and make the business a safe place to work. This, in turn, will be reflected in loss rates and loss statistics that should enhance the profits of the business and provide money that may be needed in other areas.

Avoidance

There may be operations that a small enterprise is simply not equipped to handle because the loss prevention mechanism may be too expensive or unavailable. It may require particular skills that the small firm is not justified in developing. Instead, that particular operation will be avoided entirely or assigned to an outside specialist. This practice is common in industry today. Many large companies find it uneconomical to perform high-risk operations. If the operations are necessary to the business, these companies depend on others for performance. Study and experimentation may disclose a different way to accomplish a desired goal and avoid the operation that poses unusually high risk to the business.

Control and Reduction

While prevention is an endeavor to minimize and eliminate practices that lead to loss, control is the method by which a business ensures that preventive practices are being carried out. This may require separating operations by fire walls in order that a loss to a single process does not close the entire business.

Many business people never take the time to analyze what would happen to their business if a loss occurred. What would happen if some raw materials failed to appear? If a particular machine burned out, would it mean the closing of the entire plant? Is the plant so arranged that a sizable fire would close the entire business? Would a sprinkler system control spread of fire and reduce losses? Is stock stored with highly flammable materials? This may become very important if it takes a long time to manufacture the stock.

Control means not merely looking at potential losses but at what those losses would do to the business. The business that anticipates happenings can see alternative courses of action and prepare for them. Standby facilities may be available, or arrangements may be made with friendly competitors for emergency operating space to reduce the impact of loss on the firm. This type of planning will enable business to handle its loss costs. Not only will people in business have an understanding of what loss and insurance are all about, but they will have thought about making preparations to avoid catastrophic situations that might force them out of business.

Transfer

Only after studying the alternatives should one consider transfer of a risk which involves a costly loading factor. It is possible by means of a deductible for a company to retain those losses it is equipped to absorb, thus eliminating part of the loading factor, and to transfer the rest.

If the company does widespread business, and losses occur over a large area, retention may not be feasible. Under these circumstances, an insurance company is better able to handle losses.

A risk management program will probably contain a combination of all the devices discussed above. By recognizing the choices facing a business, it is possible to weigh the advantages and disadvantages of each and make a rational decision ensuring continuity of production and of business itself.

INSURANCE POLICIES

Few policyholders take the time to read an insurance policy. A document with so much print seems overwhelming, yet one can learn a lot about a policy by examining it to see who and what is covered.

An insurance policy is nothing more than a contract. Since the insurance company prepares the contract and the policyholder does not have the privilege of negotiating its terms, it is a contract of adhesion. As we have seen, any ambiguities are generally resolved by the courts in favor of the policyholder.

The principle of indemnity states that an insurance policy pays only the amount of the loss, subject to the total limits of insurance; it does not permit the policyholder to get back more than the loss. The principle of indemnity also requires that the person asking for insurance must have an insurable interest. That is, the insured person must be one who would suffer a financial loss when a particular event happens. Otherwise, insurance policies would be encouraging crime.

Applying for a Policy

The first step in obtaining insurance is an application. An insurance agent usually contacts the applicant to secure information which is entered on a prepared form. It is verified and signed by the applicant. The signing of the application affirms that the information is true and serves as a request to the insurance company to issue a policy. The decision to accept or reject the risk is made by the underwriter, an insurance company employee skilled in evaluating and classifying insurance risks.

Declarations

The statements or declarations made by the applicant are sometimes attached to the policy. In other cases they are transposed to another form. The insurance company relies on the truthfulness of the statements submitted. If they are misrepresentations and materially affect the risk, the policy may be declared null and void. Coverage is cancelled even if a loss has occurred because the company was misled regarding the risk.

The Insuring Agreements

The insuring agreements outline the major terms of the policy, the promises of the company, the losses to be covered, the amounts, and the circumstances under which losses will be covered. For example, an auto liability policy will start with a statement to the effect that the company will pay for all damages that the insured shall become legally obligated to pay because of bodily injury arising out of ownership, maintenance, or use of the automobile. Thus, the policyholder should know from this provision what losses are covered following an automobile accident.

Exclusions

Exclusions specify what is not covered. They are a streamlining device. A family liability policy should not cover a fleet of freight trucks because of its premium limitation. The exclusions in a policy make premium calculations possible. Even an all-risk, or comprehensive, policy has to contain exclusions in order to place some limits on the amount of protection that can be afforded for a given premium.

Conditions

Conditions are the last part of the policy. They spell out the rights and duties of the parties in the event a loss occurs. They provide a method of settling disagreements, cancelling the policy, filing reports, and modifying the policy. Additional requirements cover payments, subrogation rights of the company, apportionment of losses, when other insurance applies, and changes in or assignment of the policy with the company's permission.

CLASSIFICATION OF INSURANCE

To understand insurance, one has to examine what it has to offer the customer. Company underwriters have exhaustive classifications into which they can place a particular line of insurance. It should be helpful to the person in business to know something about these classifications.

Property

Most people think in terms of fire insurance when discussing property. Of course, property is subject to destruction, but as stated earlier, losses are two dimensional and there are many facets of a property loss (see Figure 22-1). Therefore, one should know what a property policy can cover.

The Fire Policy

Basic property protection comes from the fire policy. The New York standard fire policy has been adopted in almost all states as the basis of all property coverages. The basic fire policy covers only fire,

1 **Concealment,** This entire policy shall be void if, whether
2 **fraud.** before or after a loss, the insured has wil-
3 fully concealed or misrepresented any ma-
4 terial fact or circumstance concerning this insurance or the
5 subject thereof, or the interest of the insured therein, or in case
6 of any fraud or false swearing by the insured relating thereto.
7 **Uninsurable** This policy shall not cover accounts, bills,
8 **and** currency, deeds, evidences of debt, money or
9 **excepted property.** securities; nor, unless specifically named
10 herein in writing, bullion or manuscripts.
11 **Perils not** This Company shall not be liable for loss by
12 **included.** fire or other perils insured against in this
13 policy caused, directly or indirectly, by: (a)
14 enemy attack by armed forces, including action taken by mili-
15 tary, naval or air forces in resisting an actual or an immediately
16 impending enemy attack; (b) invasion; (c) insurrection; (d)
17 rebellion; (e) revolution; (f) civil war; (g) usurped power; (h)
18 order of any civil authority except acts of destruction at the time
19 of and for the purpose of preventing the spread of fire, provided
20 that such fire did not originate from any of the perils excluded
21 by this policy; (i) neglect of the insured to use all reasonable
22 means to save and preserve the property at and after a loss, or
23 when the property is endangered by fire in neighboring prem-
24 ises; (j) nor shall this Company be liable for loss by theft.
25 **Other insurance.** Other insurance may be prohibited or the
26 amount of insurance may be limited by en-
27 dorsement attached hereto.
28 **Conditions suspending or restricting insurance. Unless other-**
29 wise provided in writing added hereto this Company shall not
30 be liable for loss occurring
31 (a) while the hazard is increased by any means within the con-
32 trol or knowledge of the insured; or
33 (b) while a described building, whether intended for occupancy
34 by owner or tenant, is vacant or unoccupied beyond a period of
35 sixty consecutive days; or
36 (c) as a result of explosion or riot, unless fire ensue, and in
37 that event for loss by fire only.
38 **Other perils** Any other peril to be insured against or sub-
39 **or subjects.** ject of insurance to be covered in this policy
40 shall be by endorsement in writing hereon or
41 added hereto.
42 **Added provisions.** The extent of the application of insurance
43 under this policy and of the contribution to
44 be made by this Company in case of loss, and any other pro-
45 vision or agreement not inconsistent with the provisions of this
46 policy, may be provided for in writing added hereto, but no pro-
47 vision may be waived except such as by the terms of this policy
48 is subject to change.
49 **Waiver** No permission affecting this insurance shall
50 **provisions.** exist, or waiver of any provision be valid,
51 unless granted herein or expressed in writing
52 added hereto. No provision, stipulation or forfeiture shall be
53 held to be waived by any requirement or proceeding on the part
54 of this Company relating to appraisal or to any examination
55 provided for herein.
56 **Cancellation** This policy shall be cancelled at any time
57 **of policy.** at the request of the insured, in which case
58 this Company shall, upon demand and sur-
59 render of this policy, refund the excess of paid premium above
60 the customary short rates for the expired time. This pol-
61 icy may be cancelled at any time by this Company by giving
62 to the insured a five days' written notice of cancellation with
63 or without tender of the excess of paid premium above the pro
64 rata premium for the expired time, which excess, if not ten-
65 dered, shall be refunded on demand. Notice of cancellation shall
66 state that said excess premium (if not tendered) will be re-
67 funded on demand.
68 **Mortgagee** If loss hereunder is made payable, in whole
69 **interests and** or in part, to a designated mortgagee not
70 **obligations.** named herein as the insured, such interest in
71 this policy may be cancelled by giving to such
72 mortgagee a ten days' written notice of can-
73 cellation.
74 If the insured fails to render proof of loss such mortgagee, upon
75 notice, shall render proof of loss in the form herein specified
76 within sixty (60) days thereafter and shall be subject to the pro-
77 visions hereof relating to appraisal and time of payment and of
78 bringing suit. If this Company shall claim that no liability ex-
79 isted as to the mortgagor or owner, it shall, to the extent of pay-
80 ment of loss to the mortgagee, be subrogated to all the mort-
81 gagee's rights of recovery, but without impairing mortgagee's
82 right to sue; or it may pay off the mortgage debt and require
83 an assignment thereof and of the mortgage. Other provisions

84 relating to the interests and obligations of such mortgagee may
85 be added hereto by agreement in writing.
86 **Pro rata liability.** This Company shall not be liable for a greater
87 proportion of any loss than the amount
88 hereby insured shall bear to the whole insurance covering the
89 property against the peril involved, whether collectible or not.
90 **Requirements in** The insured shall give immediate written
91 **case loss occurs.** notice to this Company of any loss, protect
92 the property from further damage, forthwith
93 separate the damaged and undamaged personal property, put
94 it in the best possible order, furnish a complete inventory of
95 the destroyed, damaged and undamaged property, showing in
96 detail quantities, costs, actual cash value and amount of loss
97 claimed; and within sixty days after the loss, unless such time
98 is extended in writing by this Company, the insured shall render
99 to this Company a proof of loss, signed and sworn to by the
100 insured, stating the knowledge and belief of the insured as to
101 the following: the time and origin of the loss, the interest of the
102 insured and of all others in the property, the actual cash value of
103 each item thereof and the amount of loss thereto, all encum-
104 brances thereon, all other contracts of insurance, whether valid
105 or not, covering any of said property, any changes in the title,
106 use, occupation, location, possession or exposures of said prop-
107 erty since the issuing of this policy, by whom and for what
108 purpose any building herein described and the several parts
109 thereof were occupied at the time of loss and whether or not it
110 then stood on leased ground, and shall furnish a copy of all the
111 descriptions and schedules in all policies and, if required, verified
112 plans and specifications of any building, fixtures or machinery
113 destroyed or damaged. The insured, as often as may be reason-
114 ably required, shall exhibit to any person designated by this
115 Company all that remains of any property herein described, and
116 submit to examinations under oath by any person named by this
117 Company, and subscribe the same; and, as often as may be
118 reasonably required, shall produce for examination all books of
119 account, bills, invoices and other vouchers, or certified copies
120 thereof if originals be lost, at such reasonable time and place as
121 may be designated by this Company or its representative, and
122 shall permit extracts and copies thereof to be made.
123 **Appraisal.** In case the insured and this Company shall
124 fail to agree as to the actual cash value or
125 the amount of loss, then, on the written demand of either, each
126 shall select a competent and disinterested appraiser and notify
127 the other of the appraiser selected within twenty days of such
128 demand. The appraisers shall first select a competent and dis-
129 interested umpire; and failing for fifteen days to agree upon
130 such umpire, then, on request of the insured or this Company,
131 such umpire shall be selected by a judge of a court of record in
132 the state in which the property covered is located. The ap-
133 praisers shall then appraise the loss, stating separately actual
134 cash value and loss to each item; and, failing to agree, shall
135 submit their differences, only, to the umpire. An award in writ-
136 ing, so itemized, of any two when filed with this Company shall
137 determine the amount of actual cash value and loss. Each
138 appraiser shall be paid by the party selecting him and the ex-
139 penses of appraisal and umpire shall be paid by the parties
140 equally.
141 **Company's** It shall be optional with this Company to
142 **options.** take all, or any part, of the property at the
143 agreed or appraised value, and also to re-
144 pair, rebuild or replace the property destroyed or damaged with
145 other of like kind and quality within a reasonable time, on giv-
146 ing notice of its intention so to do within thirty days after the
147 receipt of the proof of loss herein required.
148 **Abandonment.** There can be no abandonment to this Com-
149 pany of any property.
150 **When loss** The amount of loss for which this Company
151 **payable.** may be liable shall be payable sixty days
152 after proof of loss, as herein provided, is
153 received by this Company and ascertainment of the loss is made
154 either by agreement between the insured and this Company ex-
155 pressed in writing or by the filing with this Company of an
156 award as herein provided.
157 **Suit.** No suit or action on this policy for the recov-
158 ery of any claim shall be sustainable in any
159 court of law or equity unless all the requirements of this policy
160 shall have been complied with, and unless commenced within
161 twelve months next after inception of the loss.
162 **Subrogation.** This Company may require from the insured
163 an assignment of all right of recovery against
164 any party for loss to the extent that payment therefor is made
165 by this Company.

SPECIAL STATE PROVISIONS

KANSAS: The words "demand and" in line 58 and "on demand" in lines 65 and 67 are deleted. The word "twelve" in line 161
changed to "sixty".
NORTH DAKOTA: The word "twelve" in line 161 is changed to "thirty-six".
FLORIDA AND WISCONSIN: The word "five" in line 62 is changed to "ten".
VIRGINIA: The words "twelve months" in line 161 of the provisions hereinafter are changed to "two years".

IN WITNESS WHEREOF, this Company has executed and attested these presents; but this policy shall not be valid unless countersigned by the duly authorized Agent of this Company.

Secretary   _President_

Fig. 22-2. The New York standard fire policy.

lightning, and debris removal caused by the two perils. If the property owner wants additional protection, an endorsement can be attached to the fire policy.

Endorsements

Most insurance policies can be tailored to suit the business. Hundreds of endorsements are available to give special coverage.

Replacement-cost insurance. Market value of property may decrease substantially as the building gets old. Meanwhile, zoning and building codes may require that new buildings meet the new code requirements. Buildings destroyed by certain percentages (usually 50 percent) require complete rebuilding. They cannot be repaired. Thus the policyholder will ask for replacement-cost insurance rather than insurance to value. It permits rebuilding without great financial burdens in the event of a loss.

Coinsurance clauses. These are used by insurance companies to provide an equitable insurance rate. Not every fire destroys the building completely; in fact, the average homeowner fire causes less than $500 worth of damage. The frequency of fire losses of over $500 is substantially lower than that of losses under $500. Thus, an average homeowner could insure a home for around $1,000 and have a reasonable chance that the fire loss would not exceed that amount. However, the insurance company would then be paying out close to the maximum provided by the policy on its average fire loss, and the premium rate structure would have to reflect this situation. This would pose a problem for the person who wanted to insure a house for its full value. Since the risk of loss above the average of $500 is comparatively small, insurance rates above this amount should also be relatively low. Insurance is not a gambling device, and partial insurance is bad policy. When a loss occurs that is substantially above the amount covered by the insurance, the owner is inclined to blame the insurance company for refusal to pay the loss, whereas in fact the owner gambled and lost.

The problem is solved by preparing a single rate and providing that an owner who wishes to carry less than a specified percentage of insurance on the property should bear part of the loss in case of fire or other loss. The coinsurance clause encourages adequate insurance protection and eliminates subsequent recrimination in case of loss.

Consequential losses. This coverage endorsement is the least understood by the average business person. The individual can see and feel tangible property. It represents an investment, and so there is a desire to prevent its destruction or to take some alternative action

A L C O **INSURANCE COMPANY**

SECTION I — PROPERTY

STOREKEEPER'S BURGLARY AND ROBBERY FORM

SCHEDULE		
Loc. No.	Location Address	Limits of Insurance
1	1234 Maple St., Anytown, U.S.A.	$20,000
2	1234 Oak St., Anytown, U.S.A.	5,000

Not more than two messengers shall have custody of the insured property outside the premises at one time.

This form is subject to the provisions and stipulations herein and endorsed hereon, the Schedule of this form, the Declarations, the Standard Fire Policy Provisions and the applicable General Provisions of this policy.

INSURING AGREEMENTS

I Robbery Inside the Premises

Alco will pay for loss of money, securities, merchandise, furniture, fixtures and equipment by robbery within the premises.

II Robbery Outside the Premises

Alco will pay for loss of money, securities and merchandise, including the wallet or bag containing such property, by robbery while being conveyed by a messenger outside the premises.

III Kidnapping

Alco will pay for loss of money, securities, merchandise, furniture, fixtures and equipment within the premises by kidnapping.

IV Burglary; Safe Burglary

Alco will pay for loss of money, securities and merchandise by safe burglary within the premises and for loss, not exceeding $50, of money and securities by burglary within the premises.

V Theft - Night Depository or Residence

Alco will pay for loss of money and securities by theft within any night depository in a bank or within the living quarters in the home of a messenger.

VI Burglary; Robbery of Watchman

Alco will pay for loss of merchandise, furniture, fixtures and equipment by burglary or by robbery of a watchman within the premises, while the premises are not open for business. Under this Insuring Agreement, the actual cash value of any one article of jewelry shall be deemed not to exceed $50.

VII Damage

Alco will pay for damages to the premises and to money, securities, merchandise, furniture, fixtures and equipment within the premises, by such robbery, kidnapping, burglary, safe burglary, robbery of a watchman, or attempt thereat, provided with respect to damage to the premises the Insured is the owner thereof or is liable for such damage.

ADDITIONAL CONDITIONS

1. Definitions

"**money**" means currency, coins, bank notes and bullion; and travelers checks, register checks and money orders held for sale to the public.

"**securities**" means all negotiable and non-negotiable instruments or contracts representing either money or other property and includes revenue and other stamps in current use, tokens and tickets, but does not include money.

"**premises**" means the interior of that portion of any building at a location designated in the Schedule which is occupied by the Insured in conducting the business as stated in the Declarations, but shall not include

Fig. 22-3. Storekeeper's burglary and robbery form endorsement. This form is attached to the basic fire insurance policy.

if a loss occurs. However, the consequences of the loss seem to be ignored. A good insurance agent can point out that the business does not own property as a matter of convenience. Business property has been obtained in order to conduct a business. Therefore, one must be able to calculate what the loss means in terms of lost business. Will the business be closed for a week or a year? If one were making Christmas cards, a fire loss in October might be comparatively small, but the consequential loss would be severe.

Crime. Any business is exposed to various crimes. These include embezzlement, theft, robbery, or burglary. A business can take preventive measures, but at some point it must rely upon the protection offered by insurance.

Deductibles. Insurance costs include a loading factor for the operating costs and profits of the insurance company. If the anticipated losses involve numerous small losses, it may be more economical to handle them as an operating expense and transfer only severe losses to the insurance company. This is accomplished by a deductible clause or endorsement.

Specialty Policies

Competitive insurance companies have been sensitive to the needs of their customers and have developed broader coverages. In the 1950s, state insurance departments relaxed their rules and allowed insurance companies to write new lines of insurance in addition to their old lines. Multiline companies began to offer streamlined policies instead of the New York standard fire policy with a large number of endorsements.

Homeowner Policies

The standard homeowner policy contains standard fire coverage and a number of additional coverages. It is a compact policy replacing the cumbersome fire policy with its numerous endorsements. A deluxe all-risk homeowner policy is a comprehensive policy. It covers virtually every kind of loss to the property, and can be supplemented by additional endorsements.

Commercial Policies

Commercial policies cover fire, damage, theft of merchandise, business interruption, and many other losses common to business. Losses can be covered individually with a series of endorsements or with package policies that are very similar to the homeowner policies described above.

Marine Insurance

Insurance is available that deals mainly with transportation. Thus, if a business does a great deal of shipping, one can obtain cargo insurance, which is a form of marine insurance.

Liability Insurance

Whenever one engages in activity that may eventually involve other people, one is exposed to liability losses. Almost everyone is aware of automobile liability insurance. An auto accident can cause staggering losses to a business that is not adequately protected. Recently a manufacturer of a lifting device sold the mechanism to another manufacturer. While the device was being used, the riveting gave way and a heavy load fell upon a worker. The injured worker recovered $3.25 million. When a large batch of canned soup was spoiled and had to be recalled, liability losses were so great that the soup manufacturer was forced into bankruptcy.

No business can afford to omit liability insurance covering all phases of operation. However, it should be used with other risk management devices, such as retention of small losses by use of deductibles. In property insurance it is comparatively easy to calculate potential loss, but this is not so with liability insurance. The insurance agent can be of help here. Rates reflect probable exposure for that particular class of business.

Key-man Insurance

Life insurance on the sole proprietor may make him or her an acceptable credit risk. Creditors will have assurance that their bills will be paid if the proprietor dies. In a partnership, if one of the partners dies key-man insurance keeps the business going by having the proceeds paid to the estate and the deceased partner's share distributed to the remaining partners. Any business, whether a sole proprietorship or a corporation, may have an important employee who would be costly to replace in the event of death. Key-man insurance provides a solution.

RISK MANAGEMENT CAN MEAN SURVIVAL

Protecting the assets of the business is necessary to the survival of the business. Transferring risk to an insurance company is only a partial solution. It may not be economically practical for insurance to absorb all losses, and some matters may not be insurable. After a loss occurs, lost business may never be recovered. Therefore, the business must utilize all the tools of risk management in order to control and minimize losses.

For the new business, there are many sources of aid. Trade associations, police departments, fire departments, safety engineers of insurance companies, and other business organizations are often willing to share their experience and advice. There is some literature that is also helpful. Most large fires are carefully analyzed and suggestions made for improvements to prevent repetition. Regardless of the source of the information, the ability of profit from the mistakes of others is a mark of the successful business.

INVOLVEMENT AND STUDY MATERIAL

Understanding Terms

Questions and Problem Solving

1. What risk factors can produce economic insecurity in a business?
2. Why is risk management fundamental to a business operation?
3. Does insurance eliminate or prevent a business loss? Why?
4. Why is insurance a transfer mechanism?
5. If a piece of property is absolutely certain to be destroyed in the coming year, would it be economically feasible to have it insured? Why?
6. What are the various methods of risk management?
7. What are the functions of an insurance company underwriter?
8. Why does an insurance company deal with financial risk only?
9. What type of misrepresentation in a declaration subjects a policy to a possible cancellation even after a loss has occurred?

Cases for Discussion

1. The Mellon Furniture Company, a sole proprietorship, is located in a two-story wooden-frame building. There are five fire extinguishers on each floor and a water fire hose at each end of the building on each floor. In the last nine months it had five small fires. Each was quickly put out with only minor damage. One was due to defective wiring in a woodworking machine; two were in the paint booth and were caused by electric sparks from an improperly installed exhaust fan; one was in the finished furniture storage area; and one was in a pile of accumulated wastes from discarded packing cases in a room adjoining the supply room. The last two fires were traced to careless employee smoking. When the current insurance policy expired, the insurance company refused to renew the insurance. Mellon contacted other insurance agencies, but all refused to issue a policy of insurance unless he corrected the poor wiring and other fire hazards. What changes can be made in the business to eliminate or control the hazards facing this company? Should the company risk operating without insurance? Why?

2. Assume that the Mellon Furniture Company made adequate corrections in its business operations and an insurance company agreed to issue a policy. The building is thirty-five years old, its actual cash value is $75,000, and insurance is available at $1.20 per $100 of value. The replacement value of the building is

$150,000. Replacement-cost insurance is available at the same cost per $100 of value. What should the company do? Why?

3. The entire business is worth about $200,000. Mellon has earned a profit of $33,600 per year for the past three years in addition to a nominal salary. The insurance agent has pointed out that if a fire got out of control, the entire building could easily be destroyed and business would be halted until the plant could be rebuilt or relocated. Relocation could be completed in about two months, whereas rebuilding would very likely require at least five months. The new city building codes might not permit rebuilding at the present location. The agent strongly recommends consequential-loss insurance. Mellon feels that the agent is trying to get a higher insurance commission. Should this coverage be secured? If not, why not? If it should be obtained, what losses and expenses should be considered? What total amounts?

4. The Mellon Furniture Company uses two trucks in its business. They pick up supplies and make deliveries of finished furniture. One truck is valued at $5,400 and the other $3,100. The trucks are serviced regularly at the local garage. The garage is equipped to make collision repairs. Should the company carry collision insurance on either or both of the trucks? If so, should it provide for a deductible? In what amount? If it should not carry collision insurance, explain why not.

5. The owner of the company, Mellon, is now sixty-two years of age. His wife used to help him in the business but has not done so for over fifteen years. They have a daughter who is married and lives in another city. The only other child is a son, age thirty-five, who is a graduate engineer. He enjoys the production end of the work inside the plant. The father has been particularly good as a salesman, and it is largely due to this that the business has shown such good earnings. The company is too small to employ a second salesman, but the son has done some sales work and shows good aptitude. He will need time to develop into a good salesman if the need should arise. In the event that the father should die or become disabled, the son will have to take his father's place if the business is to continue. Meanwhile there has been no real preparation for such an eventuality. No thought has been given to the possibility of the father's death and what will happen to the business. What steps should be taken to enable the business to continue and to enable the son to succeed the father without impairing the financial position of the company?

Appendix

Uniform Commercial Code

ARTICLE 1: GENERAL PROVISIONS

Part 1

Short Title, Construction, Application and Subject Matter of the Act

§1–101. **Short Title.** This Act shall be known and may be cited as Uniform Commercial Code.

§1–102. **Purposes; Rules of Construction; Variation by Agreement.** (1) This Act shall be liberally construed and applied to promote its underlying purposes and policies.

(2) Underlying purposes and policies of this Act are

(a) to simplify, clarify and modernize the law governing commercial transactions;

(b) to permit the continued expansion of commercial practices through custom, usage and agreement of the parties;

(c) to make uniform the law among the various jurisdictions.

(3) The effect of provisions of this Act may be varied by agreement, except as otherwise provided in this Act and except that the obligations of good faith,

diligence, reasonableness and care prescribed by this Act may not be disclaimed by agreement but the parties may by agreement determine the standards by which the performance of such obligations is to be measured if such standards are not manifestly unreasonable.

(4) The presence in certain provisions of this Act of the words "unless otherwise agreed" or words of similar import does not imply that the effect of other provisions may not be varied by agreement under subsection (3).

(5) In this Act unless the context otherwise requires.

(a) words in the singular number include the plural, and in the plural include the singular;

(b) words of the masculine gender include the feminine and the neuter, and when the sense so indicates words of the neuter gender may refer to any gender.

§1-103. Supplementary General Principles of Law Applicable. Unless displaced by the particular provisions of this Act, the principles of law and equity, including the law merchant and the law relative to capacity to contract, principal and agent, estoppel, fraud, misrepresentation, duress, coercion, mistake, bankruptcy, or other validating or invalidating cause shall supplement its provisions.

§1-104. Construction Against Implicit Repeal. This Act being a general act intended as a unified coverage of its subject matter, no part of it shall be deemed to be impliedly repealed by subsequent legislation if such construction can reasonably be avoided.

§1-105. Territorial Application of the Act; Parties' Power to Choose Applicable Law. (1) Except as provided hereafter in this section, when a transaction bears a reasonable relation to this state and also to another state or nation the parties may agree that the law either of this state or of such other state or nation shall govern their rights and duties. Failing such agreement this Act applies to transactions bearing an appropriate relation to this state.

(2) Where one of the following provisions of this Act specifies the applicable law, that provision governs and a contrary agreement is effective only to the extent permitted by the law (including the conflict of laws rules) so specified:

Rights of creditors against sold goods. Section 2-402.

Applicability of the Article on Bank Deposits and Collections. Section 4-102.

Bulk transfers subject to the Article on Bulk Transfers. Section 6-102.

Applicability of the Article on Investment Securities. Section 8-106.

Policy and scope of the Article on Secured Transactions. Sections 9-102 and 9-103.

§1-106. Remedies to Be Liberally Administered. (1) The remedies provided by this Act shall be liberally administered to the end that the aggrieved party may be put in as good a position as if the other party had fully performed but neither consequential or special nor penal damages may be had except as specifically provided in this Act or by other rule of law.

(2) Any right or obligation declared by this Act is enforceable by action unless the provision declaring it specifies a different and limited effect.

§1-107. Waiver or Renunciation of Claim or Right After Breach. Any claim or right arising out of an alleged breach can be discharged in whole or in part without consideration by a written waiver or renunciation signed and delivered by the aggrieved party.

§1-108. Severability. If any provision or clause of this Act or application thereof to any person or circumstances is held invalid, such invalidity shall not affect other provisions or applications of the Act which can be given effect without the invalid provision or application, and to this end the provisions of this Act are declared to be severable.

§1-109. Section Captions. Section captions are parts of this Act.

Part 2

General Definitions and Principles of Interpretation

§1–201. General Definitions. Subject to additional definitions contained in the subsequent Articles of this Act which are applicable to specific Articles or Parts thereof, and unless the context otherwise requires, in this Act:

(1) "Action" in the sense of a judicial proceeding includes recoupment, counterclaim, set-off, suit in equity and any other proceedings in which rights are determined.

(2) "Aggrieved party" means a party entitled to resort to a remedy.

(3) "Agreement" means the bargain of the parties in fact as found in their language or by implication from other circumstances including course of dealing or usage of trade or course of performance as provided in this Act (Sections 1–205 and 2–208). Whether an agreement has legal consequences is determined by the provisions of this Act, if applicable; otherwise by the law of contracts (Section 1–103). (Compare "Contract".)

(4) "Bank" means any person engaged in the business of banking.

(5) "Bearer" means the person in possession of an instrument, document of title, or security payable to bearer or indorsed in blank.

(6) "Bill of lading" means a document evidencing the receipt of goods for shipment issued by a person engaged in the business of transporting or forwarding goods, and includes an airbill. "Airbill" means a document serving for air transportation as a bill of lading does for marine or rail transportation, and includes an air consignment note or air waybill.

(7) "Branch" includes a separately incorporated foreign branch of a bank.

(8) "Burden of establishing" a fact means the burden of persuading the triers of fact that the existence of the fact is more probable than its nonexistence.

(9) "Buyer in ordinary course of business" means a person who in good faith and without knowledge that the sale to him is in violation of the ownership rights or security interest of a third party in the goods buys in ordinary course from a person in the business of selling goods of that kind but does not include a pawnbroker. "Buying" may be for cash or by exchange of other property or on secured or unsecured credit and includes receiving goods or documents of title under a pre-existing contract for sale but does not include a transfer in bulk or as security for or in total or partial satisfaction of a money debt.

(10) "Conspicuous": A term or clause is conspicuous when it is so written that a reasonable person against whom it is to operate ought to have noticed it. A printed heading in capitals (as: Non-Negotiable Bill of Lading) is "conspicuous." Language in the body of a form is "conspicuous" if it is in larger or other contrasting type or color. But in a telegram any stated term is "conspicuous". Whether a term or clause is "conspicuous" or not is for decision by the court.

(11) "Contract" means the total legal obligation which results from the parties' agreement as affected by this Act and any other applicable rules of law. (Compare "Agreement".)

(12) "Creditor" includes a general creditor, a secured creditor, a lien creditor and any representative of creditors, including an assignee for the benefit of creditors, a trustee in bankruptcy, a receiver in equity and an executor or administrator of an insolvent debtor's or assignor's estate.

(13) "Defendant" includes a person in the position of defendant in a cross-action or counterclaim.

(14) "Delivery" with respect to instruments, documents of title, chattel paper or securities means voluntary transfer of possession.

(15) "Document of title" includes bill of lading, dock warrant, dock receipt, warehouse receipt or order for the delivery of goods, and also any other document which in the regular course of business or financing is treated as adequately evidencing that the person in possession of it is entitled to receive, hold and dispose of the document and the goods it covers. To be a document of title a document must purport to be issued by or addressed to a bailee and purport to cover goods in the bailee's possession which are either identified or are fungible portions of an identified mass.

(16) "Fault" means wrongful act, omission or breach.

(17) "Fungible" with respect to goods or securities means goods or securities of which any unit is, by nature or usage of trade, the equivalent of any other like unit. Goods which are not fungible shall be deemed fungible for the purposes of this Act to the extent that under a particular agreement or document unlike units are treated as equivalents.

(18) "Genuine" means free of forgery or counterfeiting.

(19) "Good faith" means honesty in fact in the conduct or transaction concerned.

(20) "Holder" means a person who is in possession of a document of title or an instrument or an investment security drawn, issued or indorsed to him or to his order or to bearer or in blank.

(21) To "honor" is to pay or to accept and pay, or where a credit so engages to purchase or discount a draft complying with the terms of the credit.

(22) "Insolvency proceedings" includes any assignment for the benefit of creditors or other proceedings intended to liquidate or rehabilitate the estate of the person involved.

(23) A person is "insolvent" who either has ceased to pay his debts in the ordinary course of business or cannot pay his debts as they become due or is insolvent within the meaning of the federal bankruptcy law.

(24) "Money" means a medium of exchange authorized or adopted by a domestic or foreign government as a part of its currency.

(25) A person has "notice" of a fact when

(a) he has actual knowledge of it; or

(b) he has received a notice or notification of it; or

(c) from all the facts and circumstances known to him at the time in question he has reason to know that it exists.

A person "knows" or has "knowledge" of a fact when he has actual knowledge of it. "Discover" or "learn" or a word or phrase of similar import refers to knowledge rather than to reason to know. The time and circumstances under which a notice or notification may cease to be effective are not determined by this Act.

(26) A person "notifies" or "gives" a notice or notification to another by taking such steps as may be reasonably required to inform the other in ordinary course whether or not such other actually comes to know of it. A person "receives" a notice or notification when

(a) it comes to his attention; or

(b) it is duly delivered at the place of business through which the contract was made or at any other place held out by him as the place for receipt of such communications.

(27) Notice, knowledge or a notice or notification received by an organization is effective for a particular transaction from the time when it is brought to the

attention of the individual conducting that transaction, and in any event from the time when it would have been brought to his attention if the organization had exercised due diligence. An organization exercises due diligence if it maintains reasonable routines for communicating significant information to the person conducting the transaction and there is reasonable compliance with the routines. Due diligence does not require an individual acting for the organization to communicate information unless such communication is part of his regular duties or unless he has reason to know of the transaction and that the transaction would be materially affected by the information.

(28) "Organization" includes a corporation, government or governmental subdivision or agency, business trust, estate, trust partnership or association, two or more persons having a joint or common interest, or any other legal or commercial entity.

(29) "Party", as distinct from "third party", means a person who has engaged in a transaction or made an agreement within this Act.

(30) "Person" includes an individual or an organization (see Section 1–102).

(31) "Presumption" or "presumed" means that the trier of fact must find the existence of the fact presumed unless and until evidence is introduced which would support a finding of its non-existence.

(32) "Purchase" includes taking by sale, discount, negotiation, mortgage, pledge, lien, issue or re-issue, gift or any other voluntary transaction creating an interest in property.

(33) "Purchaser" means a person who takes by purchase.

(34) "Remedy" means any remedial right to which an aggrieved party is entitled with or without resort to a tribunal.

(35) "Representative" includes an agent, an officer of a corporation or association, and a trustee, executor or administrator of an estate, or any other person empowered to act for another.

(36) "Rights" includes remedies.

(37) "Security interest" means an interest in personal property or fixtures which secures payment or performance of an obligation. The retention or reservation of title by a seller of goods notwithstanding shipment or delivery to the buyer (Section 2–401) is limited in effect to a reservation of a "security interest". The term also includes any interest of a buyer of accounts, chattel paper, or contract rights which is subject to Article 9. The special property interest of a buyer of goods on identification of such goods to a contract for sale under Section 2–401 is not a "security interest", but a buyer may also acquire a "security interest" by complying with Article 9. Unless a lease or consignment is intended as security, reservation of title thereunder is not a "security interest" but a consignment is in any event subject to the provisions on consignment sales (Section 2–326). Whether a lease is intended as security is to be determined by the facts of each case; however, (a) the inclusion of an option to purchase does not of itself make the lease one intended for security, and (b) an agreement that upon compliance with the terms of the lease the lessee shall become or has the option to become the owner of the property for no additional consideration or for a nominal consideration does make the lease one intended for security.

(38) "Send" in connection with any writing or notice means to deposit in the mail or deliver for transmission by any other usual means of communication with postage or cost of transmission provided for and properly addressed and in the case of an instrument to an address specified thereon or otherwise agreed, or if there be none to any address reasonable under the circumstances. The

receipt of any writing or notice within the time at which it would have arrived if properly sent has the effect of a proper sending.

(39) "Signed" includes any symbol executed or adopted by a party with present intention to authenticate a writing.

(40) "Surety" includes guarantor.

(41) "Telegram" includes a message transmitted by radio, teletype, cable, any mechanical method of transmission, or the like.

(42) "Term" means that portion of an agreement which relates to a particular matter.

(43) "Unauthorized" signature or indorsement means one made without actual, implied or apparent authority and includes a forgery.

(44) "Value". Except as otherwise provided with respect to negotiable instruments and bank collections (Sections 3–303, 4–208 and 4–209) a person gives "value" for rights if he acquires them

(a) in return for a binding commitment to extend credit or for the extension of immediately available credit whether or not drawn upon and whether or not a charge-back is provided for in the event of difficulties in collection; or

(b) as security for or in total or partial satisfaction of a pre-existing claim; or

(c) by accepting delivery pursuant to a pre-existing contract for purchase; or

(d) generally, in return for any consideration sufficient to support a simple contract.

(45) "Warehouse receipt" means a receipt issued by a person engaged in the business of storing goods for hire.

(46) "Written" or "writing" includes printing, typewriting or any other intentional reduction to tangible form.

§1–202. Prima Facie Evidence by Third Party Documents. A document in due form purporting to be a bill of lading, policy or certificate of insurance, official weigher's or inspector's certificate, consular invoice, or any other document authorized or required by the contract to be issued by a third party shall be prima facie evidence of its own authenticity and genuineness and of the facts stated in the document by the third party.

§1–203. Obligation of Good Faith. Every contract or duty within this Act imposes an obligation of good faith in its performance or enforcement.

§1–204. Time; Reasonable Time; "Seasonably". (1) Whenever this Act requires any action to be taken within a reasonable time, any time which is not manifestly unreasonable may be fixed by agreement.

(2) What is a reasonable time for taking any action depends on the nature, purpose and circumstances of such action.

(3) An action is taken "seasonably" when it is taken at or within the time agreed or if no time is agreed at or within a reasonable time.

§1–205. Course of Dealing and Usage of Trade. (1) A course of dealing is a sequence of previous conduct between the parties to a particular transaction which is fairly to be regarded as establishing a common basis of understanding for interpreting their expressions and other conduct.

(2) A usage of trade is any practice or method of dealing having such regularity of observance in a place, vocation or trade as to justify an expectation that it will be observed with respect to the transaction in question. The existence and scope of such a usage are to be proved as facts. If it is established that such a usage is embodied in a written trade code or similar writing the interpretation of the writing is for the court.

(3) A course of dealing between parties and any usage of trade in the vocation or trade in which they are engaged or of which they are or should be

aware give particular meaning to and supplement or qualify terms of an agreement.

(4) The express terms of an agreement and an applicable course of dealing or usage of trade shall be construed wherever reasonable as consistent with each other; but when such construction is unreasonable express terms control both course of dealing and usage of trade and course of dealing controls usage of trade.

(5) An applicable usage of trade in the place where any part of performance is to occur shall be used in interpreting the agreement as to that part of the performance.

(6) Evidence of a relevant usage of trade offered by one party is not admissible unless and until he has given the other party such notice as the court finds sufficient to prevent unfair surprise to the latter.

§1-206. **Statute of Frauds for Kinds of Personal Property Not Otherwise Covered.** (1) Except in the cases described in subsection (2) of this section a contract for the sale of personal property is not enforceable by way of action or defense beyond five thousand dollars in amount or value of remedy unless there is some writing which indicates that a contract for sale has been made between the parties at a defined or stated price, reasonably identifies the subject matter, and is signed by the party against whom enforcement is sought or by his authorized agent.

(2) Subsection (1) of this section does not apply to contracts for the sale of goods (Section 2-201) nor of securities (Section 8-319) nor to security agreements (Section 9-203).

§1-207. **Performance or Acceptance Under Reservation of Rights.** A party who with explicit reservation of rights performs or promises performance or assents to performance in a manner demanded or offered by the other party does not thereby prejudice the rights reserved. Such words as "without prejudice", "under protest" or the like are sufficient.

§1-208. **Option to Accelerate at Will.** A term providing that one party or his successor in interest may accelerate payment or performance or require collateral or additional collateral "at will" or "when he deems himself insecure" or in words of similar import shall be construed to mean that he shall have power to do so only if he in good faith believes that the prospect of payment or performance is impaired. The burden of establishing lack of good faith is on the party against whom the power has been exercised.

ARTICLE 2: SALES

Part 1

Short Title, General Construction and Subject Matter

§2-101. **Short Title.** This Article shall be known and may be cited as Uniform Commercial Code—Sales.

§2-102. **Scope; Certain Security and Other Transactions Excluded From This Article.** Unless the context otherwise requires, this Article applies to transactions in goods; it does not apply to any transaction which although in the form of an unconditional contract to sell or present sale is intended to operate only as a security transaction nor does this Article impair or repeal any statute regulating sales to consumers, farmers or other specified classes of buyers.

§2–103. Definitions and Index of Definitions. (1) In this Article unless the context otherwise requires

(a) "Buyer" means a person who buys or contracts to buy goods.

(b) "Good faith" in the case of a merchant means honesty in fact and the observance of reasonable commercial standards of fair dealing in the trade.

(c) "Receipt" of goods means taking physical possession of them.

(d) "Seller" means a person who sells or contracts to sell goods.

(2) Other definitions applying to this Article or to specified Parts thereof, and the sections in which they appear are:

"Acceptance". Section 2–606.

"Banker's credit". Section 2–325.

"Between merchants". Section 2–104.

"Cancellation". Section 2–106(4).

"Commercial unit". Section 2–105.

"Confirmed credit". Section 2–325.

"Conforming to contract". Section 2–106.

"Contract for sale". Section 2–106.

"Cover". Section 2–712.

"Entrusting". Section 2–403.

"Financing agency". Section 2–104.

"Future goods". Section 2–105.

"Goods". Section 2–105.

"Identification". Section 2–501.

"Installment contract". Section 2–612.

"Letter of Credit". Section 2–325.

"Lot". Section 2–105.

"Merchant". Section 2–104.

"Overseas". Section 2–323.

"Person in position of seller". Section 2–707.

"Present sale". Section 2–106.

"Sale". Section 2–106.

"Sale on approval". Section 2–326.

"Sale or return". Section 2–326.

"Termination". Section 2–106.

(3) The following definitions in other Articles apply to this Article:

"Check". Section 3–104.

"Consignee". Section 7–102.

"Consignor". Section 7–102.

"Consumer goods". Section 9–109.

"Dishonor". Section 3–507.

"Draft". Section 3–104.

(4) In addition Article 1 contains general definitions and principles of construction and interpretation applicable throughout this Article.

§2–104. Definitions: "Merchant"; "Between Merchants"; "Financing Agency". (1) "Merchant" means a person who deals in goods of the kind or otherwise by his occupation holds himself out as having knowledge or skill peculiar to the practices or goods involved in the transaction or to whom such knowledge or skill may be attributed by his employment of an agent or broker or other intermediary who by his occupation holds himself out as having such knowledge or skill.

(2) "Financing agency" means a bank, finance company or other person who in the ordinary course of business makes advances against goods or documents of title or who by arrangement with either the seller or the buyer intervenes in ordinary course to make or collect payment due or claimed under the contract for sale, as by purchasing or paying the seller's draft or making advances against it or by merely taking it for collection whether or not documents of title accompany the draft. "Financing agency" includes also a bank or other person who similarly intervenes between persons who are in the position of seller and buyer in respect to the goods (Section 2–707).

(3) "Between merchants" means in any transaction with respect to which both parties are chargeable with the knowledge or skill of merchants.

§2–105. Definitions: Transferability; "Goods"; "Future" Goods; "Lot"; "Commercial Unit". (1) "Goods" means all things (including specially manufactured goods) which are movable at the time of identification to the contract for sale other than the money in which the price is to be paid, investment securities (Article 8) and things in action. "Goods" also includes the unborn young of animals and growing crops and other identified things attached to realty as described in the section on goods to be severed from realty (Section 2–107).

(2) Goods must be both existing and identified before any interest in them can pass. Goods which are not both existing and identified are "future" goods. A purported present sale of future goods or of any interest therein operates as a contract to sell.

(3) There may be a sale of a part interest in existing identified goods.

(4) An undivided share in an identified bulk of fungible goods is sufficiently identified to be sold although the quantity of the bulk is not determined. Any agreed proportion of such a bulk or any quantity thereof agreed upon by number, weight or other measure may to the extent of the seller's interest in the bulk be sold to the buyer who then becomes an owner in common.

(5) "Lot" means a parcel or a single article which is the subject matter of a separate sale or delivery, whether or not it is sufficient to perform the contract.

(6) "Commercial unit" means such a unit of goods as by commercial usage is a single whole for purposes of sale and division of which materially impairs its character or value on the market or in use. A commercial unit may be a single article (as a machine) or a set of articles (as a suite of furniture or an assortment of sizes) or a quantity (as a bale, gross, or carload) or any other unit treated in use or in the relevant market as a single whole.

§2–106. Definitions: "Contract"; "Agreement"; "Contract for Sales"; "Sale"; "Present Sale"; "Conforming" to Contract; "Termination"; "Cancellation". (1) In this Article unless the context otherwise requires "contract" and "agreement" are limited to those relating to the present or future sale of goods. "Contract for sale" includes both a present sale of goods and a contract to sell goods at a future time. A "sale" consists in the passing of title from the seller to the buyer for a price (Section 2–401). A "present sale" means a sale which is accomplished by the making of the contract.

(2) Goods or conduct including any part of a performance are "conforming" or conform to the contract when they are in accordance with the obligations under the contract.

(3) "Termination" occurs when either party pursuant to a power created by agreement or law puts an end to the contract otherwise than for its breach. On "termination" all obligations which are still executory on both sides are discharged but any right based on prior breach or performance survives.

(4) "Cancellation" occurs when either party puts an end to the contract for

breach by the other and its effect is the same as that of "termination" except that the cancelling party also retains any remedy for breach of the whole contract or any unperformed balance.

§2–107. Goods to Be Severed From Realty: Recording. (1) A contract for the sale of timber, minerals or the like or a structure or its materials to be removed from realty is a contract for the sale of goods within this Article if they are to be severed by the seller but until severance a purported present sale thereof which is not effective as a transfer of an interest in land is effective only as a contract to sell.

(2) A contract for the sale apart from the land of growing crops or other things attached to realty and capable of severance without material harm thereto but not described in subsection (1) is a contract for the sale of goods within this Article whether the subject matter is to be severed by the buyer or by the seller even though it forms part of the realty at the time of contracting, and the parties can by identification effect a present sale before severance.

(3) The provisions of this section are subject to any third party rights provided by the law relating to realty records, and the contract for sale may be executed and recorded as a document transferring an interest in land and shall then constitute notice to third parties of the buyer's rights under the contract for sale.

Part 2

Form, Formation and Readjustment of Contract

§2–201. Formal Requirements; Statute of Frauds. (1) Except as otherwise provided in this section a contract for the sale of goods for the price of $500 or more is not enforceable by way of action or defense unless there is some writing sufficient to indicate that a contract for sale has been made between the parties and signed by the party against whom enforcement is sought or by his authorized agent or broker. A writing is not insufficient because it omits or incorrectly states a term agreed upon but the contract is not enforceable under this paragraph beyond the quantity of goods shown in such writing.

(2) Between merchants if within a reasonable time a writing in confirmation of the contract and sufficient against the sender is received and the party receiving it has reason to know its contents, it satisfies the requirements of subsection (1) against such party unless written notice of objection to its contents is given within ten days after it is received.

(3) A contract which does not satisfy the requirements of subsection (1) but which is valid in other respects is enforceable

(a) if the goods are to be specially manufactured for the buyer and are not suitable for sale to others in the ordinary course of the seller's business and the seller, before notice of repudiation is received and under circumstances which reasonably indicate that the goods are for the buyer, has made either a substantial beginning of their manufacture or commitments for their procurement; or

(b) if the party against whom enforcement is sought admits in his pleading, testimony or otherwise in court that a contract for sale was made, but the contract is not enforceable under this provision beyond the quantity of goods admitted; or

(c) with respect to goods for which payment has been made and accepted or which have been received and accepted (Section 2–606).

§2–202. Final Written Expression: Parol or Extrinsic Evidence. Terms with respect to which the confirmatory memoranda of the parties agree or which are otherwise set forth in a writing intended by the parties as a final expression of their agreement with respect to such terms as are included therein may not be contradicted by evidence of any prior agreement or of a contemporaneous oral agreement but may be explained or supplemented

(a) by course of dealing or usage of trade (Section 1–205) or by course of performance (Section 2–208); and

(b) by evidence of consistent additional terms unless the court finds the writing to have been intended also as a complete and exclusive statement of the terms of the agreement.

§2–203. Seals Inoperative. The affixing of a seal to a writing evidencing a contract for sale or an offer to buy or sell goods does not constitute the writing of a sealed instrument and the law with respect to sealed instruments does not apply to such a contract or offer.

§2–204. Formation in General. (1) A contract for sale of goods may be made in any manner sufficient to show agreement, including conduct by both parties which recognizes the existence of such a contract.

(2) An agreement sufficient to constitute a contract for sale may be found even though the moment of its making is undetermined.

(3) Even though one or more terms are left open a contract for sales does not fail for indefiniteness if the parties have intended to make a contract and there is a reasonably certain basis for giving an appropriate remedy.

§2–205. Firm Offers. An offer by a merchant to buy or sell goods in a signed writing which by its terms gives assurance that it will be held open is not revocable, for lack of consideration, during the time stated or if no time is stated for a reasonable time, but in no event may such period of irrevocability exceed three months; but any such term of assurance on a form supplied by the offeree must be separately signed by the offeror.

§2–206. Offer and Acceptance in Formation of Contract. (1) Unless otherwise unambiguously indicated by the language or circumstances

(a) an offer to make a contract shall be construed as inviting acceptance in any manner and by any medium reasonable in the circumstances;

(b) an order or other offer to buy goods for prompt or current shipment shall be construed as inviting acceptance either by a prompt promise to ship or by the prompt or current shipment of conforming or non-conforming goods, but such a shipment of non-conforming goods does not constitute an acceptance if the seller seasonably notifies the buyer that the shipment is offered only as an accommodation to the buyer.

(2) Where the beginning of a requested performance is a reasonable mode of acceptance an offeror who is not notified of acceptance within a reasonable time may treat the offer as having lapsed before acceptance.

§2–207. Additional Terms in Acceptance or Confirmation. (1) A definite and seasonable expression of acceptance or a written confirmation which is sent within a reasonable time operates as an acceptance even though it states terms additional to or different from those offered or agreed upon, unless acceptance is expressly made conditional on assent to the additional or different terms.

(2) The additional terms are to be construed as proposals for addition to the contract. Between merchants such terms become part of the contract unless:

(a) the offer expressly limits acceptance to the terms of the offer;

(b) they materially alter it; or

(c) notification of objection to them has already been given or is given within a reasonable time after notice of them is received.

(3) Conduct by both parties which recognizes the existence of a contract is sufficient to establish a contract for sale although the writings of the parties do not otherwise establish a contract. In such case the terms of the particular contract consist of those terms on which the writings of the parties agree, together with any supplementary terms incorporated under any other provisions of this Act.

§2–208. Course of Performance or Practical Construction. (1) Where the contract for sale involves repeated occasions for performance by either party with knowledge of the nature of the performance and opportunity for objection to it by the other, any course of performance accepted or acquiesced in without objection shall be relevant to determine the meaning of the agreement.

(2) The express terms of the agreement and any such course of performance, as well as any course of dealing and usage of trade, shall be construed whenever reasonable as consistent with each other; but when such construction is unreasonable, express terms shall control course of performance and course of performance shall control both course of dealing and usage of trade (Section 1–205).

(3) Subject to the provisions of the next section on modification and waiver, such course of performance shall be relevant to show a waiver or modification of any term inconsistent with such course of performance.

§2–209. Modification, Rescission and Waiver. (1) An agreement modifying a contract within this Article needs no consideration to be binding.

(2) A signed agreement which excludes modification or rescission except by a signed writing cannot be otherwise modified or rescinded, but except as between merchants such a requirement on a form supplied by the merchant must be separately signed by the other party.

(3) The requirements of the statute of frauds section of this Article (Section 2–201) must be satisfied if the contract as modified is within its provisions.

(4) Although an attempt at modification or rescission does not satisfy the requirements of subsection (2) or (3) it can operate as a waiver.

(5) A party who has made a waiver affecting an executory portion of the contract may retract the waiver by reasonable notification received by the other party that strict performance will be required of any term waived, unless the retraction would be unjust in view of a material change of position in reliance on the waiver.

§2–210. Delegation of Performance; Assignment of Rights. (1) A party may perform his duty through a delegate unless otherwise agreed or unless the other party has a substantial interest in having his original promisor perform or control the acts required by the contract. No delegation of performance relieves the party delegating of any duty to perform or any liability for breach.

(2) Unless otherwise agreed all rights of either seller or buyer can be assigned except where the assignment would materially change the duty of the other party, or increase materially the burden or risk imposed on him by his contract, or impair materially his chance of obtaining return performance. A right to damages for breach of the whole contract or a right arising out of the assignor's due performance of his entire obligation can be assigned despite agreement otherwise.

(3) Unless the circumstances indicate the contrary a prohibition of assignment of "the contract" is to be construed as barring only the delegation to the assignee of the assignor's performance.

(4) An assignment of "the contract" or of "all my rights under the contract" or an assignment in similar general terms is an assignment of rights and unless the language or the circumstances (as in an assignment for security) indicate the contrary, it is a delegation of performance of the duties of the assignor and its acceptance by the assignee constitutes a promise by him to perform those duties. This promise is enforceable by either the assignor or the other party to the original contract.

(5) The other party may treat any assignment which delegates performance as creating reasonable grounds for insecurity and may without prejudice to his rights against the assignor demand assurances from the assignee (Section 2–609).

Part 3

General Obligation and Construction of Contract

§2–301. General Obligations of Parties. The obligation of the seller is to transfer and deliver and that of the buyer is to accept and pay in accordance with the contract.

§2–302. Unconscionable Contract or Clause. (1) If the court as a matter of law finds the contract or any clause of the contract to have been unconscionable at the time it was made the court may refuse to enforce the contract, or it may enforce the remainder of the contract without the unconscionable clause, or it may so limit the application of any unconscionable clause as to avoid any unconscionable result.

(2) When it is claimed or appears to the court that the contract or any clause thereof may be unconscionable the parties shall be afforded a reasonable opportunity to present evidence as to its commercial setting, purpose and effect to aid the court in making the determination.

§2–303. Allocation or Division of Risks. Where this Article allocates a risk or a burden as between the parties "unless otherwise agreed", the agreement may not only shift the allocation but may also divide the risk or burden.

§2–304. Price Payable in Money, Goods, Realty, or Otherwise. (1) The price can be made payable in money or otherwise. If it is payable in whole or in part in goods each party is a seller of the goods which he is to transfer.

(2) Even though all or part of the price is payable in an interest in realty the transfer of the goods and the seller's obligations with reference to them are subject to this Article, but not the transfer of the interest in realty or the transferor's obligations in connection herewith.

§2–305. Open Price Term. (1) The parties if they so intend can conclude a contract for sale even though the price is not settled. In such a case the price is a reasonable price at the time for delivery if

(a) nothing is said as to price; or

(b) the price is left to be agreed by the parties and they fail to agree; or

(c) the price is to be fixed in terms of some agreed market or other standard as set or recorded by a third person or agency and it is not so set or recorded.

(2) A price to be fixed by the seller or by the buyer means a price for him to fix in good faith.

(3) When a price left to be fixed otherwise than by agreement of the parties fails to be fixed through fault of one party the other may at his option treat the contract as cancelled or himself fix a reasonable price.

(4) Where, however, the parties intend not to be bound unless the price be fixed or agreed and it is not fixed or agreed there is no contract. In such a case the buyer must return any goods already received or if unable so to do must pay their reasonable value at the time of delivery and the seller must return any portion of the price paid on account.

§2–306. Output, Requirements and Exclusive Dealings. (1) A term which measures the quantity by the output of the seller or the requirements of the buyer means such actual output or requirements as may occur in good faith, except that no quantity unreasonably disproportionate to any stated estimate or in the absence of a stated estimate to any normal or otherwise comparable prior output or requirements may be tendered or demanded.

(2) A lawful agreement by either the seller or the buyer for exclusive dealing in the kind of goods concerned imposes unless otherwise agreed an obligation by the seller to use best efforts to supply the goods and by the buyer to use best efforts to promote their sale.

§2–307. Delivery in Single Lot or Several Lots. Unless otherwise agreed all goods called for by a contract for sale must be tendered in a single delivery and payment is due only on such tender but where the circumstances give either party the right to make or demand delivery in lots the price if it can be apportioned may be demanded for each lot.

§2–308. Absence of Specified Place for Delivery. Unless otherwise agreed

(a) the place for delivery of goods is the seller's place of business or if he has none his residence; but

(b) in a contract for sale of identified goods which to the knowledge of the parties at the time of contracting are in some other place, that place is the place for their delivery; and

(c) documents of title may be delivered through customary banking channels.

§2–309. Absence of Specific Time Provisions; Notice of Termination. (1) The time for shipment or delivery or any other action under a contract if not provided in this Article or agreed upon shall be a reasonable time.

(2) Where the contract provides for successive performances but is indefinite in duration it is valid for a reasonable time but unless otherwise agreed may be terminated at any time by either party.

(3) Termination of a contract by one party except on the happening of an agreed event requires that reasonable notification be received by the other party and an agreement dispensing with notification is invalid if its operation would be unconscionable.

§2–310. Open Time for Payment or Running of Credit; Authority to Ship Under Reservation. Unless otherwise agreed

(a) payment is due at the time and place at which the buyer is to receive the goods even though the place of shipment is the place of delivery; and

(b) if the seller is authorized to send the goods he may ship them under reservation, and may tender the documents of title, but the buyer may inspect the goods after their arrival before payment is due unless such inspection is inconsistent with the terms of the contract (Section 2–513); and

(c) if delivery is authorized and made by way of documents of title otherwise than by subsection (b) then payment is due at the time and place at which the buyer is to receive the documents regardless of where the goods are to be received; and

(d) where the seller is required or authorized to ship the goods on credit the credit period runs from the time of shipment but post-dating the invoice or delaying its dispatch will correspondingly delay the starting of the credit period.

§2–311. Options and Cooperative Respecting Performance. (1) An agreement for sale which is otherwise sufficiently definite (subsection (3) of Section 2–204) to be a contract is not made invalid by the fact that it leaves particulars of performance to be specified by one of the parties. Any such specification must be made in good faith and within limits set by commercial reasonableness.

(2) Unless otherwise agreed specifications relating to assortment of the goods are at the buyer's option and except as otherwise provided in subsections (1) (c) and (3) of Section 2–319 specifications or arrangements relating to shipment are at the seller's option.

(3) Where such specification would materially affect the other party's performance but is not seasonably made or where one party's cooperation is necessary to the agreed performance of the other but is not seasonably forthcoming, the other party in addition to all other remedies

(a) is excused for any resulting delay in his own performance; and

(b) may also either proceed to perform in any reasonable manner or after the time for a material part of his own performance treat the failure to specify or to cooperate as a breach by failure to deliver or accept the goods.

§2–312. Warranty of Title and Against Infringement; Buyers Obligation Against Infringement. (1) Subject to subsection (2) there is in a contract for sale a warranty by the seller that

(a) the title conveyed shall be good, and its transfer rightful; and

(b) the goods shall be delivered free from any security interest or other lien or encumbrance of which the buyer at the time of contracting has no knowledge.

(2) A warranty under subsection (1) will be excluded or modified only by specific language or by circumstances which give the buyer reason to know that the person selling does not claim title in himself or that he is purporting to sell only such right or title as he or a third person may have.

(3) Unless otherwise agreed a seller who is a merchant regularly dealing in goods of the kind warrants that the goods shall be delivered free of the rightful claim of any third person by way of infringement or the like but a buyer who furnishes specifications to the seller must hold the seller harmless against any such claim which arises out of compliance with the specifications.

§2–313. Express Warranties by Affirmation, Promise, Description, Sample. (1) Express warranties by the seller are created as follows:

(a) Any affirmation of fact or promise made by the seller to the buyer which relates to the goods and becomes part of the basis of the bargain creates an express warranty that the goods shall conform to the affirmation or promise.

(b) Any description of the goods which is made part of the basis of the bargain creates an express warranty that the goods shall conform to the description.

(c) Any sample or model which is made part of the basis of the bargain creates an express warranty that the whole of the goods shall conform to the sample or model.

(2) It is not necessary to the creation of an express warranty that the seller use formal words such as "warrant" or "guarantee" or that he have a specific intention to make a warranty, but an affirmation merely of the value of the goods or a statement purporting to be merely the seller's opinion or commendation of the goods does not create a warranty.

§2–314. Implied Warranty: Merchantability; Usage of Trade. (1) Unless excluded or modified (Section 2–316), a warranty that the goods shall be merchantable is implied in a contract for their sale if the seller is a merchant with respect to goods of that kind. Under this section the serving for value of food or drink to be consumed either on the premises or elsewhere is a sale.

(2) Goods to be merchantable must be at least such as

(a) pass without objection in the trade under the contract description; and

(b) in the case of fungible goods, are of fair average quality within the description; and

(c) are fit for the ordinary purposes for which such goods are used; and

(d) run, within the variations permitted by the agreement, of even kind, quality and quantity within each unit and among all units involved; and

(e) are adequately contained, packaged, and labeled as the agreement may require; and

(f) conform to the promises or affirmations of fact made on the container or label if any.

(3) Unless excluded or modified (Section 2–316) other implied warranties may arise from course of dealing or usage of trade.

§2–315. Implied Warranty: Fitness for Particular Purpose. Where the seller at the time of contracting has reason to know any particular purpose for which the goods are required and that the buyer is relying on the seller's skill or judgment to select or furnish suitable goods, there is unless excluded or modified under the next section an implied warranty that the goods shall be fit for such purpose.

§2–316. Exclusion or Modification of Warranties. (1) Words or conduct relevant to the creation of an express warranty and words or conduct tending to negate or limit warranty shall be construed wherever reasonable as consistent with each other; but subject to the provisions of this Article on parol or extrinsic evidence (Section 2–202) negation or limitation is inoperative to the extent that such construction is unreasonable.

(2) Subject to subsection (3), to exclude or modify the implied warranty of merchantability or any part of it the language must mention merchantability and in case of a writing must be conspicuous, and to exclude or modify any implied warranty of fitness the exclusion must be by a writing and conspicuous. Language to exclude all implied warranties of fitness is sufficient if it states, for example, that "There are no warranties which extend beyond the description on the face hereof."

(3) Notwithstanding subsection (2)

(a) unless the circumstances indicate otherwise, all implied warranties are excluded by expressions like "as is", "with all faults" or other language which in common understanding calls the buyer's attention to the exclusion of warranties and makes plain that there is no implied warranty; and

(b) when the buyer before entering into the contract has examined the goods or the sample or model as fully as he desired or has refused to examine the goods there is no implied warranty with regard to defects which an examination ought in the circumstances to have revealed to him; and

(c) an implied warranty can also be excluded or modified by course of dealing or course of performance or usage of trade.

(4) Remedies for breach of warranty can be limited in accordance with the provisions of this Article on liquidation or limitation of damages and on contractual modification of remedy (Sections 2–718 and 2–719).

§2–317. Cumulation and Conflict of Warranties Express or Implied. Warranties whether express or implied shall be construed as consistent with each other and as cumulative, but if such construction is unreasonable the intention of the parties shall determine which warranty is dominant. In ascertaining that intention the following rules apply:

(a) Exact or technical specifications displace an inconsistent sample or model or general language of description.

(b) A sample from an existing bulk displaces inconsistent general language of description.

(c) Express warranties displace inconsistent implied warranties other than an implied warranty of fitness for a particular purpose.

§2–318. Third Party Beneficiaries of Warranties Express or Implied. A seller's warranty whether express or implied extends to any natural person who is in the family or household of his buyer or who is a guest in his home if it is reasonable to expect that such person may use, consume or be affected by the goods and who is injured in person by breach of the warranty. A seller may not exclude or limit the operation of this section.

§2–319. F.O.B. and F.A.S. Terms. (1) Unless otherwise agreed the term F.O.B. (which means "free on board") at a named place, even though used only in connection with the stated price, is a delivery term under which

(a) when the term is F.O.B. the place of shipment, the seller must at that place ship the goods in the manner provided in this Article (Section 2–504) and bear the expense and risk of putting them into the possession of the carrier; or

(b) when the term is F.O.B. the place of destination, the seller must at his own expense and risk transport the goods to that place and there tender delivery of them in the manner provided in this Article (Section 2–503);

(c) when under either (a) or (b) the term is also F.O.B. vessel, car or other vehicle, the seller must in addition at his own expense and risk load the goods on board. If the term is F.O.B. vessel the buyer must name the vessel and in an appropriate case the seller must comply with the provisions of this Article on the form of bill of lading (Section 2–323).

(2) Unless otherwise agreed the F.A.S. vessel (which means "free alongside") at a named port, even though used only in connection with the stated price, is a delivery term under which the seller must

(a) at his own expense and risk deliver the goods alongside the vessel in the manner usual in that port or on a dock designated and provided by the buyer; and

(b) obtain and tender a receipt for the goods in exchange for which the carrier is under a duty to issue a bill of lading.

(3) Unless otherwise agreed in any case falling within subsection (1) (a) or (c) or subsection (2) the buyer must seasonably give any needed instructions for making delivery, including when the term is F.A.S. or F.O.B. the loading berth of the vessel and in an appropriate case its name and sailing date. The seller may treat the failure of needed instructions as a failure of cooperation under this Article (Section 2–311). He may also at his option move the goods in any reasonable manner preparatory to delivery or shipment.

(4) Under the term F.O.B. vessel or F.A.S. unless otherwise agreed the buyer must make payment against tender of the required documents and the seller may not tender nor the buyer demand delivery of the goods in substitution for the documents.

§2–320. C.I.F. and C. & F. Terms. (1) The term C.I.F. means that the price includes in a lump sum the cost of the goods and the insurance and freight to the named destination. The term C. & F. or C.F. means that the price so includes cost and freight to the named destination.

(2) Unless otherwise agreed and even though used only in connection with

the stated price and destination, the term C.I.F. destination or its equivalent requires the seller at his own expense and risk to

(a) put the goods into the possession of a carrier at the port for shipment and obtain a negotiable bill or bills of lading covering the entire transportation to the named destination; and

(b) load the goods and obtain a receipt from the carrier (which may be contained in the bill of lading) showing that the freight has been paid or provided for; and

(c) obtain a policy or certificate of insurance, including any war risk insurance, of a kind and on terms then current at the port of shipment in the usual amount, in the currency of the contract, shown to cover the same goods covered by the bill of lading and providing for payment of loss to the order of the buyer or for the account of whom it may concern; but the seller may add to the price the amount of the premium for any such war risk insurance; and

(d) prepare an invoice of the goods and procure any other documents required to effect shipment or to comply with the contract; and

(e) forward and tender with commercial promptness all the documents in due form and with any indorsement necessary to perfect the buyer's rights.

(3) Unless otherwise agreed the term C. & F. or its equivalent has the same effect and imposes upon the seller the same obligations and risks as a C.I.F. term except the obligation as to insurance.

(4) Under the term C.I.F. or C. & F. unless otherwise agreed the buyer must make payment against tender of the required documents and the seller may not tender nor the buyer demand delivery of the goods in substitution for the documents.

§2–321. C.I.F. or C. & F.: "Net Landed Weights"; "Payment on Arrival"; Warranty of Condition on Arrival. Under a contract containing a term C.I.F. or C. & F.

(1) Where the price is based on or is to be adjusted according to "net landed weights", "delivered weights", "out turn" quantity or quality or the like, unless otherwise agreed the seller must reasonably estimate the price. The payment due on tender of the documents called for by the contract is the amount so estimated, but after final adjustment of the price a settlement must be made with commercial promptness.

(2) An agreement described in subsection (1) or any warranty of quality or condition of the goods on arrival places upon the seller the risk of ordinary deterioration, shrinkage and the like in transportation but has no effect on the place or time of identification to the contract for sale or delivery or on the passing of the risk of loss.

(3) Unless otherwise agreed where the contract provides for payment on or after arrival of the goods the seller must before payment allow such preliminary inspection as is feasible; but if the goods are lost delivery of the documents and payment are due when the goods should have arrived.

§2–322. Delivery "Ex-Ship". (1) Unless otherwise agreed a term for delivery of goods "ex-ship" (which means from the carrying vessel) or in equivalent language is not restricted to a particular ship and requires delivery from a ship which has reached a place at the named port of destination where goods of the kind are usually discharged.

(2) Under such a term unless otherwise agreed

(a) the seller must discharge all liens arising out of the carriage and furnish the buyer with a direction which puts the carrier under a duty to deliver the goods; and

(b) the risk of loss does not pass to the buyer until the goods leave the ship's tackle or are otherwise properly unloaded.

§2–323. Form of Bill of Lading Required in Overseas Shipment; "Overseas". (1) Where the contract contemplates overseas shipment and contains a term C.I.F. or C. & F. or F.O.B. vessel, the seller unless otherwise agreed must obtain a negotiable bill of lading stating that the goods have been loaded on board or, in the case of a term C.I.F. or C. & F., received for shipment.

(2) Where in a case within subsection (1) a bill of lading has been issued in a set of parts, unless otherwise agreed if the documents are not to be sent from abroad the buyer may demand tender of the full set; otherwise only one part of the bill of lading need be tendered. Even if the agreement expressly requires a full set

(a) due tender of a single part is acceptable within the provisions of this Article on cure of improper delivery (subsection (1) of Section 2–508); and

(b) even though the full set is demanded, if the documents are sent from abroad the person tendering an incomplete set may nevertheless require payment upon furnishing an indemnity which the buyer in good faith deems adequate.

(3) A shipment by water or by air or a contract contemplating such shipment is "overseas" insofar as by usage of trade or agreement it is subject to the commercial, financing or shipping practices characteristic of international deep water commerce.

§2–324. "No Arrival, No Sale" Term. Under a term "no arrival, no sale" or terms of like meaning, unless otherwise agreed,

(a) the seller must properly ship conforming goods and if they arrive by any means he must tender them on arrival but he assumes no obligation that the goods will arrive unless he has caused the non-arrival; and

(b) where without fault of the seller the goods are in part lost or have so deteriorated as no longer to conform to the contract or arrive after the contract time, the buyer may proceed as if there had been casualty to identified goods (Section 2–613).

§2–325. "Letter of Credit" Term; "Confirmed Credit". (1) Failure of the buyer seasonably to furnish an agreed letter of credit is a breach of the contract for sale.

(2) The delivery to seller of a proper letter of credit suspends the buyer's obligation to pay. If the letter of credit is dishonored, the seller may on seasonable notification to the buyer require payment directly from him.

(3) Unless otherwise agreed the term "letter of credit" or "banker's credit" in a contract for sale means an irrevocable credit issued by a financing agency of good repute and, where the shipment is overseas, of good international repute. The term "confirmed credit" means that the credit must also carry the direct obligation of such an agency which does business in the seller's financial market.

§2–326. Sale on Approval and Sale or Return; Consignment Sales and Rights of Creditors. (1) Unless otherwise agreed, if delivered goods may be returned by the buyer even though they conform to the contract, the transaction is

(a) a "sale on approval" if the goods are delivered primarily for use, and

(b) a "sale or return" if the goods are delivered primarily for resale.

(2) Except as provided in subsection (3), goods held on approval are not subject to the claims of the buyer's creditors until acceptance; goods held on sale or return are subject to such claims while in the buyer's possession.

(3) Where goods are delivered to a person for sale and such person main-

tains a place of business at which he deals in goods of the kind involved, under a name other than the name of the person making delivery, then with respect to claims of creditors of the person conducting the business the goods are deemed to be on sale or return. The provisions of this subsection are applicable even though an agreement purports to reserve title to the person making delivery until payment or resale or uses such words as "on consignment" or "on memorandum". However, this subsection is not applicable if the person making delivery

(a) complies with an applicable law providing for a consignor's interest or the like to be evidence by a sign, or

(b) establishes that the person conducting the business is generally known by his creditors to be substantially engaged in selling the goods of others, or

(c) complies with the filing provisions of the Article on Secured Transactions (Article 9).

(4) Any "or return" term of a contract for sale is to be treated as a separate contract for sale within the statute of frauds section of this Article (Section 2–201) and as contradicting the sale aspect of the contract within the provisions of this Article on parol or extrinsic evidence (Section 2–202).

§2–327. Special Incidents of Sale on Approval and Sale or Return. (1) Under a sale on approval unless otherwise agreed

(a) although the goods are identified to the contract the risk of loss and the title do not pass to the buyer until acceptance; and

(b) use of the goods consistent with the purpose of trial is not acceptance but failure seasonably to notify the seller of election to return the goods is acceptance, and if the goods conform to the contract acceptance of any part is acceptance of the whole; and

(c) after due notification of election to return, the return is at the seller's risk and expense but a merchant buyer must follow any reasonable instructions.

(2) Under a sale or return unless otherwise agreed

(a) the option to return extends to the whole or any commercial unit of the goods while in substantially their original condition, but must be exercised seasonably; and

(b) the return is at the buyer's risk and expense.

§2–328. Sale by Auction. (1) In a sale by auction if goods are put up in lots each lot is the subject of a separate sale.

(2) A sale by auction is complete when the auctioneer so announces by the fall of the hammer or in other customary manner. Where a bid is made while the hammer is falling in acceptance of a prior bid the auctioneer may in his discretion reopen the bidding or declare the goods sold under the bid on which the hammer was falling.

(3) Such a sale is with reserve unless the goods are in explicit terms put up without reserve. In an auction with reserve the auctioneer may withdraw the goods at any time until he announces completion of the sale. In an auction without reserve, after the auctioneer calls for bids on an article or lot, that article or lot cannot be withdrawn unless no bid is made within a reasonable time. In either case a bidder may retract his bid until the auctioneer's announcement of completion of the sale, but a bidder's retraction does not revive any previous bid.

(4) If the auctioneer knowingly receives a bid on the seller's behalf or the seller makes or procures such a bid, and notice has not been given that liberty for such bidding is reserved, the buyer may at his option avoid the sale or take the goods at the price of the last good faith bid prior to the completion of the sale. This subsection shall not apply to any bid at a forced sale.

Part 4

Title, Creditors and Good Faith Purchasers

§2–401. Passing of Title; Reservation for Security; Limited Application of This Section. Each provision of this Article with regard to the rights, obligations and remedies of the seller, the buyer, purchasers or other third parties applies irrespective of title to the goods except where the provision refers to such title. Insofar as situations are not covered by the other provisions of this Article and matters concerning title become material the following rules apply:

(1) Title to goods cannot pass under a contract for sale prior to their identification to the contract (Section 2–501), and unless otherwise explicitly agreed the buyer acquires by their identification a special property as limited by this Act. Any retention or reservation by the seller of the title (property) in goods shipped or delivered to the buyer is limited in effect to a reservation of a security interest. Subject to these provisions and to the provisions of the Article on Secured Transactions (Article 9), title to goods passes from the seller to the buyer in any manner and on any conditions explicitly agreed on by the parties.

(2) Unless otherwise explicitly agreed title passes to the buyer at the time and place at which the seller completes his performance with reference to the physical delivery of the goods, despite any reservation of a security interest and even though a document of title is to be delivered at a different time or place; and in particular and despite any reservation of a security interest by the bill of lading.

(a) if the contract requires or authorizes the seller to send the goods to the buyer but does not require him to deliver them at destination, title passes to the buyer at the time and place of shipment; but

(b) if the contract requires delivery at destination, title passes on tender there.

(3) Unless otherwise explicitly agreed where delivery is to be made without moving the goods,

(a) if the seller is to deliver a document of title, title passes at the time when and the place where he delivers such documents; or

(b) if the goods are at the time of contracting already identified and no documents are to be delivered, title passes at the time and place of contracting.

(4) A rejection or other refusal by the buyer to receive or retain the goods, whether or not justified, or a justified revocation of acceptance revests title to the goods in the seller. Such revesting occurs by operation of law and is not a "sale".

§2–402. Rights of Seller's Creditors Against Sold Goods. (1) Except as provided in subsections (2) and (3), rights of unsecured creditors of the seller with respect to goods which have been identified to a contract for sale are subject to the buyer's rights to recover the goods under this Article (Sections 2–502 and 2–716).

(2) A creditor of the seller may treat a sale or an identification of goods to a contract for sale as void if as against him a retention of possession by the seller is fraudulent under any rule of law of the state where the goods are situated, except that retention of possession in good faith and current course of trade by a merchant-seller for a commercially reasonable time after a sale or identification is not fraudulent.

(3) Nothing in this Article shall be deemed to impair the rights of creditors of the seller

(a) under the provisions of the Article on Secured Transactions (Article 9); or

(b) where identification to the contract or delivery is made not in current course of trade but in satisfaction of or as security for a pre-existing claim for money, security or the like and is made under circumstances which under any rule of law of the state where the goods are situated would apart from this Article constitute the transaction a fraudulent transfer or voidable preference.

§2–403. Power to Transfer; Good Faith Purchase of Goods; "Entrusting". (1) A purchaser of goods acquires all title which his transferor had or had power to transfer except that a purchaser of a limited interest acquires rights only to the extent of the interest purchased. A person with voidable title has power to transfer a good title to a good faith purchaser for value. When goods have been delivered under a transaction of purchase the purchaser has such power even though

(a) the transferor was deceived as to the identity of the purchaser, or

(b) the delivery was in exchange for a check which is later dishonored, or

(c) it was agreed that the transaction was to be a "cash sale", or

(d) the delivery was procured through fraud punishable as larcenous under the criminal law.

(2) Any entrusting of possession of goods to a merchant who deals in goods of that kind gives him power to transfer all rights of the entruster to a buyer in ordinary course of business.

(3) "Entrusting" includes any delivery and any acquiescence in retention of possession regardless of any condition expressed between the parties to the delivery or acquiescence and regardless of whether the procurement of the entrusting or the possessor's disposition of the goods have been such as to be larcenous under the criminal law.

(4) The rights of other purchasers of goods and lien creditors are governed by the Articles on Secured Transactions (Article 9), Bulk Transfers (Article 6) and Documents of Title (Article 7).

Part 5

Performance

§2–501. Insurable Interest in Goods; Manner of Identification of Goods. (1) The buyer obtains a special property and an insurable interest in goods by identification of existing goods as goods to which the contract refers even though the goods so identified are non-conforming and he has an option to return or reject them. Such identification can be made at any time and in any manner explicitly agreed to by the parties. In the absence of explicit agreement identification occurs

(a) when the contract is made if it is for the sale of goods already existing and identified;

(b) if the contract is for the sale of future goods other than those described in paragraph (c), when goods are shipped, marked or otherwise designated by the seller as goods to which the contract refers;

(c) when the crops are planted or otherwise become growing crops or the young are conceived if the contract is for the sale of unborn young to be born within twelve months after contracting or for the sale of crops to be harvested within twelve months or the next normal harvest season after contracting whichever is longer.

(2) The seller retains an insurable interest in goods so long as title to or any security interest in the goods remains in him and where the identification is by the seller alone he may until default or insolvency or notification to the buyer that the identification is final substitute other goods for those identified.

(3) Nothing in this section impairs any insurable interest recognized under any other statute or rule of law.

§2–502. Buyer's Right to Goods on Seller's Insolvency. (1) Subject to subsection (2) and even though the goods have not been shipped a buyer who has paid a part or all of the price of goods in which he has a special property under the provisions of the immediately preceding section may on making and keeping good a tender of any unpaid portion of their price recover them from the seller if the seller becomes insolvent within ten days after receipt of the first installment on their price.

(2) If the identification creating his special property has been made by the buyer he acquires the right to recover the goods only if they conform to the contract for sale.

§2–503. Manner of Seller's Tender of Delivery. (1) Tender of delivery requires that the seller put and hold conforming goods at the buyer's disposition and give the buyer any notification reasonably necessary to enable him to take delivery. The manner, time and place for tender are determined by the agreement and this Article, and in particular

(a) tender must be at a reasonable hour, and if it is of goods they must be kept available for the period reasonably necessary to enable the buyer to take possession; but

(b) unless otherwise agreed the buyer must furnish facilities reasonably suited to the receipt of the goods.

(2) Where the case is within the next section respecting shipment tender requires that the seller comply with its provisions.

(3) Where the seller is required to deliver at a particular destination tender requires that he comply with subsection (1) and also in any appropriate case tender documents as described in subsections (4) and (5) of this section.

(4) Where goods are in the possession of a bailee and are to be delivered without being moved

(a) tender requires that the seller either tender a negotiable document of title covering such goods or procure acknowledgement by the bailee of the buyer's right to possession of the goods; but

(b) tender to the buyer of a non-negotiable document of title or of a written direction to the bailee to deliver is sufficient tender unless the buyer seasonably objects, and receipt by the bailee of notification of the buyer's rights fixes those rights as against the bailee and all third persons; but risk of loss of the goods and of any failure by the bailee to honor the non-negotiable document of title or to obey the direction remains on the seller until the buyer has had a reasonable time to present the document or direction, and a refusal by the bailee to honor the document or to obey the direction defeats the tender.

(5) Where the contract requires the seller to deliver documents

(a) he must tender all such documents in correct form, except as provided in this Article with respect to bills of lading in a set (subsection (2) of Section 2–323); and

(b) tender through customary banking channels is sufficient and dishonor of a draft accompanying the documents constitutes non-acceptance or rejection.

§2–504. Shipment by Seller. Where the seller is required or authorized to send the goods to the buyer and the contract does not require him to deliver them at a particular destination, then unless otherwise agreed he must

(a) put the goods in the possession of such a carrier and make such a contract for their transportation as may be reasonable having regard to the nature of the goods and other circumstances of the case; and

(b) obtain and promptly deliver or tender in due form any document necessary to enable the buyer to obtain possession of the goods or otherwise required by the agreement or by usage of trade; and

(c) promptly notify the buyer of the shipment.

Failure to notify the buyer under paragraph (c) or to make a proper contract under paragraph (a) is a ground for rejection only if material delay or loss ensues.

§2–505. Seller's Shipment Under Reservation. (1) Where the seller has identified goods to the contract by or before shipment:

(a) his procurement of a negotiable bill of lading to his own order or otherwise reserves in him a security interest in the goods. His procurement of the bill to the order of a financing agency or of the buyer indicates in addition only the seller's expectation of transferring that interest to the person named.

(b) a non-negotiable bill of lading to himself or his nominee reserves possession of the goods as security but except in a case of conditional delivery (subsection (2) of Section 2–507) a non-negotiable bill of lading naming the buyer as consignee reserves no security interest even though the seller retains possession of the bill of lading.

(2) When shipment by the seller with reservation of a security interest is in violation of the contract for sale it constitutes an improper contract for transportation within the preceding section but impairs neither the rights given to the buyer by shipment and identification of the goods to the contract nor the seller's powers as a holder of a negotiable document.

§2–506. Rights of Financing Agency. (1) A financing agency by paying or purchasing for value a draft which relates to a shipment of goods acquires to the extent of the payment or purchase and in addition to its own rights under the draft and any document of title securing it any rights of the shipper in the goods including the right to stop delivery and the shipper's right to have the draft honored by the buyer.

(2) The right to reimbursement of a financing agency which has in good faith honored or purchased the draft under commitment to or authority from the buyer is not impaired by subsequent discovery of defects with reference to any relevant document which was apparently regular on its face.

§2–507. Effect of Seller's Tender; Delivery on Condition. (1) Tender of delivery is a condition to the buyer's duty to accept the goods and, unless otherwise agreed, to his duty to pay for them. Tender entitles the seller to acceptance of the goods and to payment according to the contract.

(2) Where payment is due and demanded on the delivery to the buyer of goods or documents of title, his right as against the seller to retain or dispose of them is conditional upon his making the payment due.

§2–508. Cure by Seller of Improper Tender or Delivery; Replacement. (1) Where any tender or delivery by the seller is rejected because non-conforming and the time for performance has not yet expired, the seller may seasonably notify the buyer of his intention to cure and may then within the contract time make a conforming delivery.

(2) Where the buyer rejects a non-conforming tender which the seller had

reasonable grounds to believe would be acceptable with or without money allowance the seller may if he seasonably notifies the buyer have a further reasonable time to substitute a conforming tender.

§2–509. Risk of Loss in the Absence of Breach. (1) Where the contract requires or authorizes the seller to ship the goods by carrier

(a) if it does not require him to deliver them at a particular destination, the risk of loss passes to the buyer when the goods are duly delivered to the carrier even though the shipment is under reservation (Section 2–505); but

(b) if it does require him to deliver them at a particular destination and the goods are there duly tendered while in the possession of the carrier, the risk of loss passes to the buyer when the goods are there duly so tendered as to enable the buyer to take delivery.

(2) Where the goods are held by a bailee to be delivered without being moved, the risk of loss passes to the buyer

(a) on his receipt of a negotiable document of title covering the goods; or

(b) on acknowledgment by the bailee of the buyer's right to possession of the goods; or

(c) after his receipt of a non-negotiable document of title or other written direction to deliver, as provided in subsection (4) (b) of Section 2–503.

(3) In any case not within subsection (1) or (2), the risk of loss passes to the buyer on his receipt of the goods if the seller is a merchant; otherwise the risk passes to the buyer on tender of delivery.

(4) The provisions of this section are subject to contrary agreement of the parties and to the provisions of this Article on sale on approval (Section 2–327) and on effect of breach on risk of loss (Section 2–510).

§2–510. Effect of Breach on Risk of Loss. (1) Where a tender or delivery of goods so fails to conform to the contract as to give a right of rejection the risk of their loss remains on the seller until cure or acceptance.

(2) Where the buyer rightfully revokes acceptance he may to the extent of any deficiency in his effective insurance coverage treat the risk of loss as having rested on the seller from the beginning.

(3) Where the buyer as to conforming goods already identified to the contract for sale repudiates or is otherwise in breach before risk of their loss has passed to him, the seller may to the extent of any deficiency in his effective insurance coverage treat the risk of loss as resting on the buyer for a commercially reasonable time.

§2–511. Tender of Payment by Buyer; Payment by Check. (1) Unless otherwise agreed tender of payment is a condition to the seller's duty to tender and complete any delivery.

(2) Tender of payment is sufficient when made by any means or in any manner current in the ordinary course of business unless the seller demands payment in legal tender and gives any extension of time reasonably necessary to procure it.

(3) Subject to the provisions of this Act on the effect of an instrument on an obligation (Section 3–802), payment by check is conditional and is defeated as between the parties by dishonor of the check on due presentment.

§2–512. Payment by Buyer; Before Inspection. (1) Where the contract requires payment before inspection non-conformity of the goods does not excuse the buyer from so making payment unless

(a) the non-conformity appears without inspection; or

(b) despite tender of the required documents the circumstances would justify injunction against honor under the provisions of this Act (Section 5–114).

(2) Payment pursuant to subsection (1) does not constitute an acceptance of goods or impair the buyer's right to inspect or any of his remedies.

§2–513. Buyer's Right to Inspection of Goods. (1) Unless otherwise agreed and subject to subsection (3), where goods are tendered or delivered or identified to the contract for sale, the buyer has a right before payment or acceptance to inspect them at any reasonable place and time and in any reasonable manner. When the seller is required or authorized to send the goods to the buyer, the inspection may be after their arrival.

(2) Expenses of inspection must be borne by the buyer but may be recovered from the seller if the goods do not conform and are rejected.

(3) Unless otherwise agreed and subject to the provisions of this Article on C.I.F. contracts (subsection (3) of Section 2–321), the buyer is not entitled to inspect the goods before payment of the price when the contract provides

(a) for delivery "C.O.D." or on other like terms; or

(b) for payment against documents of title, except where such payment is due only after the goods are to become available for inspection.

(4) A place or method of inspection fixed by the parties is presumed to be exclusive but unless otherwise expressly agreed it does not postpone identification or shift the place for delivery or for passing the risk of loss. If compliance becomes impossible, inspection shall be as provided in this section unless the place or method fixed was clearly intended as an indispensable condition failure of which avoids the contract.

§2–514. When Documents Deliverable on Acceptance; When on Payment. Unless otherwise agreed documents against which a draft is drawn are to be delivered to the drawee on acceptance of the draft if it is payable more than three days after presentment; otherwise, only on payment.

§2–515. Preserving Evidence of Goods in Dispute. In furtherance of the adjustment of any claim or dispute

(a) either party on reasonable notification to the other and for the purpose of ascertaining the facts and preserving evidence has the right to inspect, test and sample the goods including such of them as may be in the possession or control of the other; and

(b) the parties may agree to a third party inspection or survey to determine the conformity or condition of the goods and may agree that the findings shall be binding upon them in any subsequent litigation or adjustment.

Part 6

Breach, Repudiation and Excuse

§2–601. Buyer's Rights on Improper Delivery. Subject to the provisions of this Article on breach in installment contracts (Section 2–612) and unless otherwise agreed under the sections on contractual limitations of remedy (Sections 2–718 and 2–719), if the goods or the tender of delivery fail in any respect to conform to the contract, the buyer may

(a) reject the whole; or

(b) accept the whole; or

(c) accept any commercial unit or units and reject the rest.

§2–602. Manner and Effect of Rightful Rejection. (1) Rejection of goods must be within a reasonable time after their delivery or tender. It is ineffective unless the buyer seasonably notifies the seller.

(2) Subject to the provisions of the two following sections on rejected goods (Sections 2–603 and 2–604),

(a) after rejection any exercise of ownership by the buyer with respect to any commercial unit is wrongful as against the seller; and

(b) if the buyer has before rejection taken physical possession of goods in which he does not have a security interest under the provisions of this Article (subsection (3) of Section 2–711), he is under a duty after rejection to hold them with reasonable care at the seller's disposition for a time sufficient to permit the seller to remove them; but

(c) the buyer has no further obligations with regard to goods rightfully rejected.

(3) The seller's rights with respect to goods wrongfully rejected are governed by the provisions of this Article on Seller's remedies in general (Section 2–703).

§2–603. Merchant Buyer's Duties as to Rightfully Rejected Goods. (1) Subject to any security interest in the buyer (subsection (3) of Section 2–711), when the seller has no agent or place of business at the market of rejection a merchant buyer is under a duty after rejection of goods in his possession or control to follow any reasonable instructions received from the seller with respect to the goods and in the absence of such instructions to make reasonable efforts to sell them for the seller's account if they are perishable or threaten to decline in value speedily. Instructions are not reasonable if on demand indemnity for expenses is not forthcoming.

(2) When the buyer sells goods under subsection (1), he is entitled to reimbursement from the seller or out of the proceeds for reasonable expenses of caring for and selling them, and if the expenses include no selling commission then to such commission as is usual in the trade or if there is none to a reasonable sum not exceeding ten per cent on the gross proceeds.

(3) In complying with this section the buyer is held only to good faith and good faith conduct hereunder is neither acceptance nor conversion nor the basis of an action for damages.

§2–604. Buyer's Options as to Salvage of Rightfully Rejected Goods. Subject to the provisions of the immediately preceding section on perishables if the seller gives no instructions within a reasonable time after notification of rejection the buyer may store the rejected goods for the seller's account or reship them to him or resell them for the seller's account with reimbursement as provided in the preceding section. Such action is not acceptance or conversion.

§2–605. Waiver of Buyer's Objections by Failure to Particularize. (1) The buyer's failure to state in connection with rejection a particular defect which is ascertainable by reasonable inspection precludes him from relying on the unstated defect to justify rejection or to establish breach

(a) where the seller could have cured it if stated seasonably; or

(b) between merchants when the seller has after rejection made a request in writing for a full and final written statement of all defects on which the buyer proposes to rely.

(2) Payment against documents made without reservation of rights precludes recovery of the payment for defects apparent on the face of the documents.

§2–606. What Constitutes Acceptance of Goods. (1) Acceptance of goods occurs when the buyer

(a) after a reasonable opportunity to inspect the goods signifies to the seller that the goods are conforming or that he will take or retain them in spite of their non-conformity; or

(b) fails to make an effective rejection (subsection (1) of Section 2–602), but such acceptance does not occur until the buyer has had a reasonable opportunity to inspect them; or

(c) does any act inconsistent with the seller's ownership; but if such act is wrongful as against the seller it is an acceptance only if ratified by him.

(2) Acceptance of a part of any commercial unit is acceptance of that entire unit.

§2–607. Effect of Acceptance; Notice of Breach; Burden of Establishing Breach After Acceptance; Notice of Claim or Litigation to Person Answerable Over. (1) The buyer must pay at the contract rate for any goods accepted.

(2) Acceptance of goods by the buyer precludes rejection of the goods accepted and if made with knowledge of a non-conformity cannot be revoked because of it unless the acceptance was on the reasonable assumption that the non-conformity would be seasonably cured but acceptance does not of itself impair any other remedy provided by this Article for non-conformity.

(3) Where a tender has been accepted

(a) the buyer must within a reasonable time after he discovers or should have discovered any breach notify the seller of breach or be barred from any remedy; and

(b) if the claim is one for infringement or the like (subsection (3) of Section 2–312) and the buyer is sued as a result of such a breach he must so notify the seller within a reasonable time after he receives notice of the litigation or be barred from any remedy over for liability established by the litigation.

(4) The burden is on the buyer to establish any breach with respect to the goods accepted.

(5) Where the buyer is sued for breach of a warranty or other obligation for which his seller is answerable over

(a) he may give his seller written notice of the litigation. If the notice states that the seller may come in and defend and that if the seller does not do so he will be bound in any action against him by his buyer by any determination of fact common to the two litigations, then unless the seller after seasonable receipt of the notice does come in and defend he is so bound.

(b) if the claim is one for infringement or the like (subsection (3) of Section 2–312) the original seller may demand in writing that his buyer turn over to him control of the litigation including settlement or else be barred from any remedy over and if he also agrees to bear all expense and to satisfy any adverse judgment, then unless the buyer after seasonable receipt of the demand does turn over control the buyer is so barred.

(6) The provision of subsections (3), (4) and (5) apply to any obligation of a buyer to hold the seller harmless against infringement or the like (subsection (3) of Section 2–312).

§2–608. Revocation of Acceptance in Whole or in Part. (1) The buyer may revoke his acceptance of a lot or commercial unit whose non-conformity substantially impairs its value to him if he has accepted it

(a) on the reasonable assumption that its non-conformity would be cured and it has not been seasonably cured; or

(b) without discovery of such non-conformity if his acceptance was reasonably induced either by the difficulty of discovery before acceptance or by the seller's assurances.

(2) Revocation of acceptance must occur within a reasonable time after the buyer discovers or should have discovered the ground for it and before any substantial change in condition of the goods which is not caused by their own defects. It is not effective until the buyer notifies the seller of it.

(3) A buyer who so revokes has the same rights and duties with regard to the goods involved as if he had rejected them.

§2–609. Right to Adequate Assurance of Performance. (1) A contract for sale imposes an obligation on each party that the other's expectation of receiving due performance will not be impaired. When reasonable grounds for insecurity arise with respect to the performance of either party the other may in writing demand adequate assurance of due performance and until he receives such assurance may if commercially reasonable suspend any performance for which he has not already received the agreed return.

(2) Between merchants the reasonableness of grounds for insecurity and the adequacy of any assurance offered shall be determined according to commercial standards.

(3) Acceptance of any improper delivery or payment does not prejudice the aggrieved party's right to demand adequate assurance of future performance.

(4) After receipt of a justified demand failure to provide within a reasonable time not exceeding thirty days such assurance of due performance as is adequate under the circumstances of the particular case is a repudiation of the contract.

§2–610. Anticipatory Repudiation. When either party repudiates the contract with respect to a performance not yet due the loss of which will substantially impair the value of the contract to the other, the aggrieved party may

(a) for a commercially reasonable time await performance by the repudiating party; or

(b) resort to any remedy for breach (Section 2–703 or Section 2–711), even though he has notified the repudiating party that he would await the latter's performance and has urged retraction; and

(c) in either case suspend his own performance or proceed in accordance with the provisions of this Article on the seller's right to identify goods to the contract notwithstanding breach or to salvage unfinished goods (Section 2–704).

§2–611. Retraction of Anticipatory Repudiation. (1) Until the repudiating party's next performance is due he can retract his repudiation unless the aggrieved party has since the repudiation cancelled or materially changed his position or otherwise indicated that he considers the repudiation final.

(2) Retraction may be by any method which clearly indicates to the aggrieved party that the repudiating party intends to perform, but must include any assurance justifiably demanded under the provisions of this Article (Section 2–609).

(3) Retraction reinstates the repudiating party's rights under the contract with due excuse and allowance to the aggrieved party for any delay occasioned by the repudiation.

§2–612. "Installment Contract"; Breach. (1) An "installment contract" is one which requires or authorizes the delivery of goods in separate lots to be separately accepted, even though the contract contains a clause "each delivery is a separate contract" or its equivalent.

(2) The buyer may reject any installment which is non-conforming if the non-conformity substantially impairs the value of that installment and cannot be cured or if the non-conformity is a defect in the required documents; but if the non-conformity does not fall within subsection (3) and the seller gives adequate assurance of its cure the buyer must accept that installment.

(3) Whenever non-conformity or default with respect to one or more installments substantially impairs the value of the whole contract there is a breach of the whole. But the aggrieved party reinstates the contract if he accepts a

non-conforming installment without seasonably notifying of cancellation or if he brings an action with respect only to past installments or demands performance as to future installments.

§2–613. Casualty to Identified Goods. Where the contract requires for its performance goods identified when the contract is made, and the goods suffer casualty without fault of either party before the risk of loss passes to the buyer, or in a proper case under a "no arrival, no sale" term (Section 2–324) then

   (a) if the loss is total the contract is avoided; and

   (b) if the loss is partial or the goods have so deteriorated as no longer to conform to the contract the buyer may nevertheless demand inspection and at his option either treat the contract as avoided or accept the goods with due allowance from the contract price for the deterioration or the deficiency in quantity but without further right against the seller.

§2–614. Substituted Performance. (1) Where without fault of either party the agreed berthing, loading, or unloading facilities fail or an agreed type of carrier becomes unavailable or the agreed manner of delivery otherwise becomes commercially impracticable but a commercially reasonable substitute is available, such substitute performance must be tendered and accepted.

   (2) If the agreed means or manner of payment fails because of domestic or foreign governmental regulation, the seller may withhold or stop delivery unless the buyer provides a means or manner of payment which is commercially a substantial equivalent. If delivery has already been taken, payment by the means or in the manner provided by the regulation discharges the buyer's obligation unless the regulation is discriminatory, oppressive or predatory.

§2–615. Excuse by Failure of Presupposed Conditions. Except so far as a seller may have assumed a greater obligation and subject to the preceding section on substituted performance:

   (a) Delay in delivery or non-delivery in whole or in part by a seller who complies with paragraphs (b) and (c) is not a breach of his duty under a contract for sale if performance as agreed has been made impracticable by the occurrence of a contingency the non-occurrence of which was a basic assumption on which the contract was made or by compliance in good faith with any applicable foreign or domestic governmental regulation or order whether or not it later proves to be invalid.

   (b) Where the causes mentioned in paragraph (a) affect only a part of the seller's capacity to perform, he must allocate production and deliveries among his customers but may at his option include regular customers not then under contract as well as his own requirements for further manufacture. He may so allocate in any manner which is fair and reasonable.

   (c) The seller must notify the buyer seasonably that there will be delay or non-delivery and, when allocation is required under paragraph (b), of the estimated quota thus made available for the buyer.

§2–616. Procedure on Notice Claiming Excuse. (1) Where the buyer receives notification of a material or indefinite delay, or an allocation justified under the preceding section he may by written notification to the seller as to any delivery concerned, and where the prospective deficiency substantially impairs the value of the whole contract under the provisions of this Article relating to breach of installment contracts (Section 2–612), then also as to the whole,

   (a) terminate and thereby discharge any unexecuted portion of the contract; or

   (b) modify the contract by agreeing to take his available quota in substitution.

(2) If after receipt of such notification from the seller the buyer fails so to modify the contract within a reasonable time not exceeding thirty days the contract lapses with respect to any deliveries affected.

(3) The provisions of this section may not be negated by agreement except in so far as the seller has assumed a greater obligation under the preceding section.

Part 7

Remedies

§2-701. Remedies for Breach of Collateral Contracts Not Impaired. Remedies for breach of any obligation or promise collateral or ancillary to a contract for sale are not impaired by the provisions of this Article.

§2-702. Seller's Remedies on Discovery of Buyer's Insolvency. (1) Where the seller discovers the buyer to be insolvent he may refuse delivery except for cash including payment for all goods theretofore delivered under the contract, and stop delivery under this Article (Section 2-705).

(2) Where the seller discovers that the buyer has received goods on credit while insolvent he may reclaim the goods upon demand made within ten days after the receipt, but if misrepresentation of solvency has been made to the particular seller in writing within three months before delivery the ten day limitation does not apply. Except as provided in this subsection the seller may not base a right to reclaim goods on the buyer's fraudulent or innocent misrepresentation of solvency or of intent to pay.

(3) The seller's right to reclaim under subsection (2) is subject to the rights of a buyer in ordinary course or other good faith purchaser or lien creditor under this Article (Section 2-403). Successful reclamation of goods excludes all other remedies with respect to them.

§2-703. Seller's Remedies in General. Where the buyer wrongfully rejects or revokes acceptance of goods or fails to make a payment due on or before delivery or repudiates with respect to a part or the whole, then with respect to any goods directly affected and, if the breach is of the whole contract (Section 2-612), then also with respect to the whole undelivered balance, the aggrieved seller may

(a) withhold delivery of such goods;

(b) stop delivery by any bailee as hereafter provided (Section 2-705);

(c) proceed under the next section respecting goods still unidentified to the contract;

(d) resell and recover damages as hereafter provided (Section 2-706);

(e) recover damages for non-acceptance (Section 2-708) or in a proper case the price (Section 2-709);

(f) cancel.

§2-704. Seller's Right to Identify Goods to the Contract Notwithstanding Breach or to Salvage Unfinished Goods. (1) An aggrieved seller under the preceding section may

(a) identify to the contract conforming goods not already identified if at the time he learned of the breach they are in his possession or control;

(b) treat as the subject of resale goods which have demonstrably been intended for the particular contract even though those goods are unfinished.

(2) Where the goods are unfinished an aggrieved seller may in the exercise of reasonable commercial judgment for the purposes of avoiding loss and of effective realization either complete the manufacture and wholly identify the goods to the contract or cease manufacture and resell for scrap or salvage value or proceed in any other reasonable manner.

§2-705. Seller's Stoppage of Delivery in Transit or Otherwise. (1) The seller may stop delivery of goods in the possession of a carrier or other bailee when he discovers the buyer to be insolvent (Section 2-702) and may stop delivery of carload, truckload, planeload or larger shipments of express or freight when the buyer repudiates or fails to make a payment due before delivery or if for any other reason the seller has a right to withhold or reclaim the goods.

(2) As against such buyer the seller may stop delivery until

(a) receipt of the goods by the buyer; or

(b) acknowledgment to the buyer by any bailee of the goods except a carrier that the bailee holds the goods for the buyer; or

(c) such acknowledgment to the buyer by a carrier by reshipment or as warehouseman; or

(d) negotiation to the buyer of any negotiable document of title covering the goods.

(3) (a) To stop delivery the seller must so notify as to enable the bailee by reasonable diligence to prevent delivery of the goods.

(b) After such notification the bailee must hold and deliver the goods according to the directions of the seller but the seller is liable to the bailee for any ensuing charges or damages.

(c) If a negotiable document of title has been issued for goods the bailee is not obliged to obey a notification to stop until surrender of the document.

(d) A carrier who has issued a non-negotiable bill of lading is not obliged to obey a notification to stop received from a person other than the consignor.

§2-706. Seller's Resale Including Contract for Resale. (1) Under the conditions stated in Section 2-703 on seller's remedies, the seller may resell the goods concerned or the undelivered balance thereof. Where the resale is made in good faith and in a commercially reasonable manner the seller may recover the difference between the resale price and the contract price together with any incidental damages allowed under the provisions of this Article (Section 2-710), but less expenses saved in consequence of the buyer's breach.

(2) Except as otherwise provided in subsection (3) or unless otherwise agreed resale may be at public or private sale including sale by way of one or more contracts to sell or of identification to an existing contract of the seller. Sale may be as a unit or in parcels and at any time and place and on any terms but every aspect of the sale including the method, manner, time, place and terms must be commercially reasonable. The resale must be reasonably identified as referring to the broken contract, but it is not necessary that the goods be in existence or that any or all of them have been identified to the contract before the breach.

(3) Where the resale is at private sale the seller must give the buyer reasonable notification of his intention to resell.

(4) Where the resale is at public sale

(a) only identified goods can be sold except where there is a recognized market for a public sale of futures in goods of the kind; and

(b) it must be made at a usual place or market for public sale if one is reasonably available and except in the case of goods which are perishable or threaten to decline in value speedily the seller must give the buyer reasonable notice of the time and place of the resale; and

(c) if the goods are not to be within the view of those attending the sale the notification of sale must state the place where the goods are located and provide for their reasonable inspection by prospective bidders; and

(d) the seller may buy.

(5) A purchaser who buys in good faith at a resale takes the goods free of any rights of the original buyer even though the seller fails to comply with one or more of the requirements of this section.

(6) The seller is not accountable to the buyer for any profit made on any resale. A person in the position of a seller (Section 2–707) or a buyer who has rightfully rejected or justifiably revoked acceptance must account for any excess over the amount of his security interest, as hereinafter defined (subsection (3) of Section 2–711).

§2–707. "Person in the Position of a Seller". (1) A "person in the position of a seller" includes as against a principal an agent who has paid or become responsible for the price of goods on behalf of his principal or anyone who otherwise holds a security interest or other right in goods similar to that of a seller.

(2) A person in the position of a seller may as provided in this Article withhold or stop delivery (Section 2–705) and resell (Section 2–706) and recover incidental damages (Section 2–710).

§2–708. Seller's Damages for Non-Acceptance or Repudiation. (1) Subject to subsection (2) and to the provisions of this Article with respect to proof of market price (Section 2–723), the measure of damages for non-acceptance or repudiation by the buyer is the difference between the market price at the time and place for tender and the unpaid contract price together with any incidental damages provided in this Article (Section 2–710), but less expenses saved in consequence of the buyer's breach.

(2) If the measure of damages provided in subsection (1) is inadequate to put the seller in as good a position as performance would have done then the measure of damages is the profit (including reasonable overhead) which the seller would have made from full performance by the buyer, together with any incidental damages provided in this Article (Section 2–710), due allowance for costs reasonably incurred and due credit for payments or proceeds of resale.

§2–709. Action for the Price. (1) When the buyer fails to pay the price as it becomes due the seller may recover, together with any incidental damages under the next section, the price

(a) of goods accepted or of conforming goods lost or damaged within a commercially reasonable time after risk of their loss has passed to the buyer; and

(b) of goods identified to the contract if the seller is unable after reasonable effort to resell them at a reasonable price or the circumstances reasonably indicate that such effort will be unavailing.

(2) Where the seller sues for the price he must hold for the buyer any goods which have been identified to the contract and are still in his control except that if resale becomes possible he may resell them at any time prior to the collection of the judgment. The net proceeds of any such resale must be credited to the buyer and payment of the judgment entitles him to any goods not resold.

(3) After the buyer has wrongfully rejected or revoked acceptance of the goods or has failed to make a payment due or has repudiated (Section 2–610),

a seller who is held not entitled to the price under this section shall nevertheless be awarded damages for non-acceptance under the preceding section.

§2–710. Seller's Incidental Damages. Incidental damages to an aggrieved seller
include any commercially reasonable charges, expenses or commissions incurred
in stopping delivery, in the transportation, care and custody of goods after the
buyer's breach, in connection with return or resale of the goods or otherwise
resulting from the breach.

**§2–711. Buyer's Remedies in General; Buyer's Security Interest in Rejected
Goods.** (1) Where the seller fails to make delivery or repudiates or the buyer
rightfully rejects or justifiably revokes acceptance then with respect to any
goods involved, and with respect to the whole if the breach goes to the whole
contract (Section 2–612), the buyer may cancel and whether or not he has
done so may in addition to recovering so much of the price as has been paid

(a) "cover" and have damages under the next section as to all the goods
affected whether or not they have been identified to the contract; or

(b) recover damages for non-delivery as provided in this Article (Section
2–713).

(2) Where the seller fails to deliver or repudiates the buyer may also

(a) if the goods have been identified recover them as provided in this
Article (Section 2–502); or

(b) in a proper case obtain specific performance or replevy the goods as
provided in this Article (Section 2–716).

(3) On rightful rejection or justifiable revocation of acceptance a buyer has
a security interest in goods in his possession or control for any payments made
on their price and any expenses reasonably incurred in their inspection,
receipt, transportation, care and custody and may hold such goods and resell
them in like manner as an aggrieved seller (Section 2–706).

§2–712. "Cover"; Buyer's Procurement of Substitute Goods. (1) After a breach
within the preceding section the buyer may "cover" by making in good faith
and without unreasonable delay any reasonable purchase of or contract to purchase goods in substitution for those due from the seller.

(2) The buyer may recover from the seller as damages the difference
between the cost of cover and the contract price together with any incidental
or consequential damages as hereinafter defined (Section 2–715), but less
expenses saved in consequence of the seller's breach.

(3) Failure of the buyer to effect cover within this section does not bar
him from any other remedy.

§2–713. Buyer's Damages for Non-Delivery or Repudiation. (1) Subject to the
provisions of this Article with respect to proof of market price (Section 2–723),
the measure of damages for non-delivery or repudiation by the seller is the difference between the market price at the time when the buyer learned of the
breach and the contract price together with any incidental and consequential
damages provided in this Article (Section 2–715), but less expenses saved in
consequence of the seller's breach.

(2) Market price is to be determined as of the place for tender or, in cases
of rejection after arrival or revocation of acceptance, as of the place of arrival.

§2–714. Buyer's Damages for Breach in Regard to Accepted Goods. (1) Where
the buyer has accepted goods and given notification (subsection (3) of Section
2–607) he may recover as damages for any non-conformity of tender the loss
resulting in the ordinary course of events from the seller's breach as determined
in any manner which is reasonable.

(2) The measure of damages for breach of warranty is the difference at the
time and place of acceptance between the value of the goods accepted and the

value they would have had if they had been as warranted, unless special circumstances show proximate damages of a different amount.

(3) In a proper case any incidental and consequential damages under the next section may also be recovered.

§2-715. Buyer's Incidental and Consequential Damages. (1) Incidental damages resulting from the seller's breach include expenses reasonably incurred in inspection, receipt, transportation and care and custody of goods rightfully rejected, any commercially reasonable charges, expenses or commissions in connection with effecting cover and any other reasonable expense incident to the delay or other breach.

(2) Consequential damages resulting from the seller's breach include

(a) any loss resulting from general or particular requirements and needs of which the seller at the time of contracting had reason to know and which could not reasonably be prevented by cover or otherwise; and

(b) injury to person or property proximately resulting from any breach of warranty.

§2-716. Buyer's Right to Specific Performance or Replevin. (1) Specific performance may be decreed where the goods are unique or in other proper circumstances.

(2) The decree for specific performance may include such terms and conditions as to payment of the price, damages, or other relief as the court may deem just.

(3) The buyer has a right of replevin for goods identified to the contract if after reasonable effort he is unable to effect cover for such goods or the circumstances reasonably indicate that such effort will be unavailing or if the goods have been shipped under reservation and satisfaction of the security interest in them has been made or tendered.

§2-717. Deduction of Damages From the Price. The buyer on notifying the seller of his intention to do so may deduct all or any part of the damages resulting from any breach of the contract from any part of the price still due under the same contract.

§2-718. Liquidation or Limitation of Damages; Deposits. (1) Damages for breach by either party may be liquidated in the agreement but only at an amount which is reasonable in the light of the anticipated or actual harm caused by the breach, the difficulties of proof of loss, and the inconvenience or non-feasibility of otherwise obtaining an adequate remedy. A term fixing unreasonably large liquidated damages is void as a penalty.

(2) Where the seller justifiably withholds delivery of goods because of the buyer's breach, the buyer is entitled to restitution of any amount by which the sum of his payment exceeds

(a) the amount to which the seller is entitled by virtue of terms liquidating the seller's damages in accordance with subsection (1), or

(b) in the absence of such terms, twenty per cent of the value of the total performance for which the buyer is obligated under the contract or $500, whichever is smaller.

(3) The buyer's right to restitution under subsection (2) is subject to offset to the extent that the seller establishes

(a) a right to recover damages under the provisions of this Article other than subsection (1), and

(b) the amount or value of any benefits received by the buyer directly or indirectly by reason of the contract.

(4) Where a seller has received payment in goods their reasonable value or the proceeds of their resale shall be treated as payments for the purposes

of subsection (2); but if the seller has notice of the buyer's breach before reselling goods received in part performance, his resale is subject to the conditions laid down in this Article on resale by an aggrieved seller (Section 2–706).

§2–719. Contractual Modification or Limitation of Remedy. (1) Subject to the provisions of subsections (2) and (3) of this section and of the preceding section on liquidation and limitation of damages,

(a) the agreement may provide for remedies in addition to or in substitution for those provided in this Article and may limit or alter the measure of damages recoverable under this Article, as by limiting the buyer's remedies to return of the goods and repayment of the price or to repair and replacement of non-conforming goods or parts; and

(b) resort to a remedy as provided is optional unless the remedy is expressly agreed to be exclusive, in which case it is the sole remedy.

(2) Where circumstances cause an exclusive or limited remedy to fail of its essential purpose, remedy may be had as provided in this Act.

(3) Consequential damages may be limited or excluded unless the limitation or exclusion is unconscionable. Limitation of consequential damages for injury to the person in the case of consumer goods is prima facie unconscionable but limitation of damages where the loss is commercial is not.

§2–720. Effect of "Cancellation" or "Rescission" on Claims for Antecedent Breach. Unless the contrary intention clearly appears, expression of "cancellation" or "rescission" of the contract or the like shall not be construed as a renunciation or discharge of any claim in damages for an antecedent breach.

§2–721. Remedies for Fraud. Remedies for material misrepresentation or fraud include all remedies available under this Article for non-fraudulent breach. Neither rescission or a claim for rescission of the contract for sale nor rejection or return of the goods shall bar or be deemed inconsistent with a claim for damages or other remedy.

§2–722. Who Can Sue Third Parties for Injury to Goods. Where a third party so deals with goods which have been identified to a contract for sale as to cause actionable injury to a party to that contract

(a) a right of action against the third party is in either party to the contract for sale who has title to or a security interest or a special property or an insurable interest in the goods; and if the goods have been destroyed or converted a right of action is also in the party who either bore the risk of loss under the contract for sale or has since the injury assumed that risk is against the other;

(b) if at the time of the injury the party plaintiff did not bear the risk of loss as against the other party to the contract for sale and there is no arrangement between them for disposition of the recovery, his suit or settlement is, subject to his own interest, as a fiduciary for the other party to the contract;

(c) either party may with the consent of the other sue for the benefit of whom it may concern.

§2–723. Proof of Market Price: Time and Place. (1) If an action based on anticipatory repudiation comes to trial before the time for performance with respect to some or all of the goods, any damages based on market price (Section 2–708 or Section 2–713) shall be determined according to the price of such goods prevailing at the time when the aggrieved party learned of the repudiation.

(2) If evidence of a price prevailing at the times or places described in this Article is not readily available the price prevailing within any reasonable time before or after the time described or at any other place which in com-

mercial judgment or under usage of trade would serve as a reasonable substitute for the one described may be used, making any proper allowance for the cost of transporting the goods to or from such other place.

(3) Evidence of a relevant price prevailing at a time or place other than the one described in this Article offered by one party is not admissible unless and until he has given the other party such notice as the court finds sufficient to prevent unfair surprise.

§2–724. Admissibility of Market Quotations. Whenever the prevailing price or value of any goods regularly bought and sold in any established commodity market is in issue, reports in official publications or trade journals or in newspapers or periodicals of general circulation published as the reports of such market shall be admissible in evidence. The circumstances of the preparation of such a report may be shown to affect its weight but not its admissibility.

§2–725. Statute of Limitations in Contracts for Sale. (1) An action for breach of any contract for sale must be commenced within four years after the cause of action has accrued. By the original agreement the parties may reduce the period of limitation to not less than one year but may not extend it.

(2) A cause of action accrues when the breach occurs, regardless of the aggrieved party's lack of knowledge of the breach. A breach of warranty occurs when tender of delivery is made, except that where a warranty explicitly extends to future performance of the goods and discovery of the breach must await the time of such performance the cause of action accrues when the breach is or should have been discovered.

(3) Where an action commenced within the time limited by subsection (1) is so terminated as to leave available a remedy by another action for the same breach such other action may be commenced after the expiration of the time limited and within six months after the termination of the first action unless the termination resulted from voluntary discontinuance or from dismissal for failure or neglect to prosecute.

(4) This section does not alter the law on tolling of the statute of limitations nor does it apply to causes of action which have accrued before this Act becomes effective.

ARTICLE 3: COMMERCIAL PAPER

Part 1

Short Title, Form and Interpretation

§3–101. Short Title. This Article shall be known and may be cited as Uniform Commercial Code—Commercial Paper.

§3–102. Definitions and Index of Definitions. (1) In this Article unless the context otherwise requires

(a) "Issue" means the first delivery of an instrument to a holder or a remitter.

(b) An "order" is a direction to pay and must be more than an authorization or request. It must identify the person to pay with reasonable certainty. It may be addressed to one or more such persons jointly or in the alternative but not in succession.

(c) A "promise" is an undertaking to pay and must be more than an acknowledgment of an obligation.

(d) "Secondary party" means a drawer or endorser.

(e) "Instrument" means a negotiable instrument.

(2) Other definitions applying to this Article and the sections in which they appear are:

"Acceptance". Section 3–410.

"Accommodation party". Section 3–415.

"Alteration". Section 3–407.

"Certificate of deposit". Section 3–104.

"Certification". Section 3–411.

"Check". Section 3–104.

"Definite time". Section 3–109.

"Dishonor". Section 3–507.

"Draft". Section 3–104.

"Holder in due course". Section 3–302.

"Negotiation". Section 3–202.

"Note". Section 3–104.

"Notice of dishonor". Section 3–508.

"On demand". Section 3–108.

"Presentment". Section 3–504.

"Protest". Section 3–509.

"Restrictive Indorsement". Section 3–205.

"Signature". Section 3–401.

(3) The following definitions in other Articles apply to this Article:

"Account". Section 4–104.

"Banking Day". Section 4–104.

"Clearing house". Section 4–104.

"Collecting bank". Section 4–105.

"Customer". Section 4–104.

"Depositary Bank". Section 4–105.

"Documentary Draft". Section 4–104.

"Intermediary Bank". Section 4–105.

"Item". Section 4–104.

"Midnight deadline". Section 4–104.

"Payor bank". Section 4–105.

(4) In addition Article 1 contains general definitions and principles of construction and interpretation applicable throughout this Article.

§3–103. Limitations on Scope of Article. (1) This article does not apply to money, documents of title or investment securities.

(2) The provisions of this Article are subject to the provisions of the Article on Bank Deposits and Collection (Article 4) and Secured Transactions (Article 9).

§3–104. Form of Negotiable Instruments; "Draft"; "Check"; "Certificate of Deposit"; "Note". (1) Any writing to be a negotiable instrument within this Article must

(a) be signed by the maker or drawer; and

(b) contain an unconditional promise or order to pay a sum certain in money and no other promise, order, obligation or power given by the maker or drawer except as authorized by this Article; and

(c) be payable on demand or at a definite time; and

(d) be payable to order or to bearer.

(2) A writing which complies with the requirements of this section is

(a) a "draft" ("bill of exchange") if it is an order;

(b) a "check" if it is a draft drawn on a bank and payable on demand;

(c) a "certificate of deposit" if it is an acknowledgment by a bank of receipt of money with an engagement to repay it;

(d) a "note" if it is a promise other than a certificate of deposit.

(3) As used in other Articles of this Act, and as the context may require, the terms "draft", "check", "certificate of deposit" and "note" may refer to instruments which are not negotiable within this Article as well as to instruments which are so negotiable.

§3–105. When Promise or Order Unconditional. (1) A promise or order otherwise unconditional is not made conditional by the fact that the instrument

(a) is subject to implied or constructive conditions; or

(b) states its consideration, whether performed or promised, or the transaction which gave rise to the instrument, or that the promise or order is made or the instrument matures in accordance with or "as per" such transaction; or

(c) refers to or states that it arises out of a separate agreement or refers to a separate agreement for rights as to prepayment or acceleration; or

(d) states that it is drawn under a letter of credit; or

(e) states that it is secured, whether by mortgage, reservation of title or otherwise; or

(f) indicates a particular account to be debited or any other fund or source from which reimbursement is expected; or

(g) is limited to payment out of a particular fund or the proceeds of a particular source, if the instrument is issued by a government or governmental agency or unit; or

(h) is limited to payment out of the entire assets of a partnership, unincorporated association, trust or estate by or on behalf of which the instrument is issued.

(2) A promise or order is not unconditional if the instrument

(a) states that it is subject to or governed by any other agreement; or

(b) states that it is to be paid only out of a particular fund or source except as provided in this section.

§3–106. Sum Certain. (1) The sum payable is a sum certain even though it is to be paid

(a) with stated interest or by stated installments; or

(b) with stated different rates of interest before and after default or a specified date; or

(c) with a stated discount or addition if paid before or after the date fixed for payment; or

(d) with exchange or less exchange, whether at a fixed rate or at the current rate; or

(e) with costs of collection or an attorney's fee or both upon default.

(2) Nothing in this section shall validate any term which is otherwise illegal.

§3–107. Money. (1) An instrument is payable in money if the medium of exchange in which it is payable is money at the time the instrument is made. An instrument payable in "currency" or "current funds" is payable in money.

(2) A promise or order to pay a sum stated in a foreign currency is for a sum certain in money and, unless a different medium of payment is specified in the instrument, may be satisfied by payment of that number of dollars which the stated foreign currency will purchase at the buying sight rate for that currency on the day on which the instrument is payable or, if payable on

demand, on the day of demand. If such an instrument specifies a foreign currency as the medium of payment the instrument is payable in that currency.

§3–108. Payable on Demand. Instruments payable on demand include those payable at sight or on presentation and those in which no time for payment is stated.

§3–109. Definite Time. (1) An instrument is payable at a definite time if by its terms it is payable

(a) on or before a stated date or at a fixed period after a stated date; or

(b) at a fixed period after sight; or

(c) at a definite time subject to any acceleration; or

(d) at a definite time subject to extension at the option of the holder, or to extension to a further definite time at the option of the maker or acceptor or automatically upon or after a specified act or event.

(2) An instrument which by its terms is otherwise payable only upon an act or event uncertain as to time of occurrence is not payable at a definite time even though the act or event has occurred.

§3–110. Payable to Order. (1) An instrument is payable to order when by its terms it is payable to the order or assigns of any person therein specified with reasonable certainty, or to him or his order, or when it is conspicuously designated on its face as "exchange" or the like and names a payee. It may be payable to the order of

(a) the maker or drawer; or

(b) the drawee; or

(c) a payee who is not maker, drawer or drawee; or

(d) two or more payees together or in the alternative; or

(e) an estate, trust or fund, in which case it is payable to the order of the representative of such estate, trust or fund or his successors; or

(f) an office, or an officer by his title as such in which case it is payable to the principal but the incumbent of the office or his successors may act as if he or they were the holder; or

(g) a partnership or unincorporated association, in which case it is payable to the partnership or association and may be indorsed or transferred by any person thereto authorized.

(2) An instrument not payable to order is not made so payable by such words as "payable upon return of this instrument properly indorsed."

(3) An instrument made payable both to order and to bearer is payable to order unless the bearer words are handwritten or typewritten.

§3–111. Payable to Bearer. An instrument is payable to bearer when by its terms it is payable to

(a) bearer or the order of bearer; or

(b) a specified person or bearer; or

(c) "cash" or the order of "cash", or any other indication which does not purport to designate a specific payee.

§3–112. Terms and Omissions Not Affecting Negotiability. (1) The negotiability of an instrument is not affected by

(a) the omission of a statement of any consideration or of the place where the instrument is drawn or payable; or

(b) a statement that collateral has been given to secure obligations either on the instrument or otherwise of an obligor on the instrument or that in case of default on those obligations the holder may realize on or dispose of the collateral; or

(c) a promise or power to maintain or protect collateral or to give additional collateral; or

(d) a term authorizing a confession of judgment on the instrument if it is not paid when due; or

(e) a term purporting to waive the benefit of any law intended for the advantage or protection of any obligor; or

(f) a term in a draft providing that the payee by indorsing or cashing it acknowledges full satisfaction of an obligation of the drawer; or

(g) a statement in a draft drawn in a set of parts (Section 3–801) to the effect that the order is effective only if no other part has been honored.

(2) Nothing in this section shall validate any term which is otherwise illegal.

§3–113. **Seal.** An instrument otherwise negotiable is within this Article even though it is under a seal.

§3–114. **Date, Antedating, Postdating.** (1) The negotiability of an instrument is not affected by the fact that it is undated, antedated or postdated.

(2) Where an instrument is antedated or postdated the time when it is payable is determined by the stated date if the instrument is payable on demand or at a fixed period after date.

(3) Where the instrument or any signature thereon is dated, the date is presumed to be correct.

§3–115. **Incomplete Instruments.** (1) When a paper whose contents at the time of signing show that it is intended to become an instrument is signed while still incomplete in any necessary respect it cannot be enforced until completed, but when it is completed in accordance with authority given it is effective as completed.

(2) If the completion is unauthorized the rules as to material alteration apply (Section 3–407), even though the paper was not delivered by the maker or drawer; but the burden of establishing that any completion is unauthorized is on the party so asserting.

§3–116. **Instruments Payable to Two or More Persons.** An instrument payable to the order of two or more persons

(a) if in the alternative is payable to any one of them and may be negotiated, discharged or enforced by any of them who has possession of it;

(b) if not in the alternative is payable to all of them and may be negotiated, discharged or enforced only by all of them.

§3–117. **Instruments Payable With Words of Description.** An instrument made payable to a named person with the addition of words describing him

(a) as agent or officer of a specified person is payable to his principal but the agent or officer may act as if he were the holder;

(b) as any other fiduciary for a specified person or purpose is payable to the payee and may be negotiated, discharged or enforced by him;

(c) in any other manner is payable to the payee unconditionally and the additional words are without effect on subsequent parties.

§3–118. **Ambiguous Terms and Rules of Construction.** The following rules apply to every instrument:

(a) Where there is doubt whether the instrument is a draft or a note the holder may treat it as either. A draft drawn on the drawer is effective as a note.

(b) Handwritten terms control typewritten and printed terms, and typewritten control printed.

(c) Words control figures except that if the words are ambiguous figures control.

(d) Unless otherwise specified a provision for interest means interest at the judgment rate at the place of payment from the date of the instrument, or if it is undated from the date of issue.

(e) Unless the instrument otherwise specifies two or more persons who sign as maker, acceptor or drawer or indorser and as a part of the same transaction are jointly and severally liable even though the instrument contains such words as "I promise to pay."

(f) Unless otherwise specified consent to extension authorizes a single extension for not longer than the original period. A consent to extension, expressed in the instrument, is binding on secondary parties and accommodation makers. A holder may not exercise his option to extend an instrument over the objection of a maker or acceptor or other party who in accordance with Section 3–604 tenders full payment when the instrument is due.

§3–119. Other Writings Affecting Instrument. (1) As between the obligor and his immediate obligee or any transferee the terms of an instrument may be modified or affected by any other written agreement executed as a part of the same transaction, except that a holder in due course is not affected by any limitation of his rights arising out of the separate written agreement if he had no notice of the limitation when he took the instrument.

(2) A separate agreement does not affect the negotiability of an instrument.

§3–120. Instruments "Payable Through" Bank. An instrument which states that it is "payable through" a bank or the like designates that bank as a collecting bank to make presentment but does not of itself authorize the bank to pay the instrument.

§3–121. Instruments Payable at Bank. Note: *If this Act is introduced in the Congress of the United States this section should be omitted. (States to select either alternative)*

Alternative A—

A note or acceptance which states that it is payable at a bank is the equivalent of a draft drawn on the bank payable when it falls due out of any funds of the maker or acceptor in current account or otherwise available for such payment.

Alternative B—

A note or acceptance which states that it is payable at a bank is not of itself an order or authorization to the bank to pay it.

§3–122. Accrual of Cause of Action. (1) A cause of action against a maker or an acceptor accrues

(a) in the case of a time instrument on the day after maturity;

(b) in the case of a demand instrument upon its date or, if no date is stated, on the date of issue.

(2) A cause of action against the obligor of a demand or time certificate of deposit accrues upon demand, but demand on a time certificate may not be made until on or after the date of maturity.

(3) A cause of action against a drawer of a draft or an indorser of any instrument accrues upon demand following dishonor of the instrument. Notice of dishonor is a demand.

(4) Unless an instrument provides otherwise, interest runs at the rate provided by law for a judgment

(a) in the case of a maker, acceptor or other primary obligor of a demand instrument, from the date of demand;

(b) in all other cases from the date of accrual of the cause of action.

Part 2

Transfer and Negotiation

§3–201. Transfer: Right to Indorsement. (1) Transfer of an instrument vests in the transferee such rights as the transferor has therein, except that a transferee who has himself been a party to any fraud or illegality affecting the instrument or who as a prior holder had notice of a defense or claim against it cannot improve his position by taking from a later holder in due course.

(2) A transfer of a security interest in an instrument vests the foregoing rights in the transferee to the extent of the interest transferred.

(3) Unless otherwise agreed any transfer for value of an instrument not then payable to bearer gives the transferee the specifically enforceable right to have the unqualified indorsement of the transferor. Negotiation takes effect only when the indorsement is made and until that time there is no presumption that the transferee is the owner.

§3–202. Negotiation. (1) Negotiation is the transfer of an instrument in such form that the transferee becomes a holder. If the instrument is payable to order it is negotiated by delivery with any necessary indorsement; if payable to bearer it is negotiated by delivery.

(2) An indorsement must be written by or on behalf of the holder and on the instrument or on a paper so firmly affixed thereto as to become a part thereof.

(3) An indorsement is effective for negotiation only when it conveys the entire instrument or any unpaid residue. If it purports to be of less it operates only as a partial assignment.

(4) Words of assignment, condition, waiver, guaranty, limitation or disclaimer of liability and the like accompanying an indorsement do not affect its character as an indorsement.

§3–203. Wrong or Misspelled Name. Where an instrument is made payable to a person under a misspelled name or one other than his own he may indorse in that name or his own or both; but signature in both names may be required by a person paying or giving value for the instrument.

§3–204. Special Indorsement; Blank Indorsement. (1) A special indorsement specifies the person to whom or to whose order it makes the instrument payable. Any instrument specially indorsed becomes payable to the order of the special indorsee and may be further negotiated only by his indorsement.

(2) An indorsement in blank specifies no particular indorsee and may consist of a mere signature. An instrument payable to order and indorsed in blank becomes payable to bearer and may be negotiated by delivery alone until specially indorsed.

(3) The holder may convert a blank indorsement into a special indorsement by writing over the signature of the indorser in blank any contract consistent with the character of the indorsement.

§3–205. Restrictive Indorsements. An indorsement is restrictive which either

(a) is conditional; or

(b) purports to prohibit further transfer of the instrument; or

(c) includes the words "for collection", "for deposit", "pay any bank", or like terms signifying a purpose of deposit or collection; or

(d) otherwise states that it is for the benefit or use of the indorser or of another person.

§3–206. Effect of Restrictive Indorsement. (1) No restrictive indorsement prevents further transfer or negotiation of the instrument.

(2) An intermediary bank, or a payor bank which is not the depositary bank, is neither given notice nor otherwise affected by a restrictive indorsement of any person except the bank's immediate transferor or the person presenting for payment.

(3) Except for an intermediary bank, any transferee under an indorsement which is conditional or includes the words "for collection", "for deposit", "pay any bank", or like terms (subparagraphs (a) and (c) of Section 3–205) must pay or apply any value given by him for or on the security of the instrument consistently with the indorsement and to the extent that he does so he becomes a holder for value. In addition such transferee is a holder in due course if he otherwise complies with the requirements of Section 3–302 on what constitutes a holder in due course.

(4) The first taker under an indorsement for the benefit of the indorser or another person (subparagraph (d) of Section 3–205) must pay or apply any value given by him for or on the security of the instrument consistently with the indorsement and to the extent that he does so he becomes a holder for value. In addition such taker is a holder in due course if he otherwise complies with the requirements of Section 3–302 on what constitutes a holder in due course. A later holder for value is neither given notice nor otherwise affected by such restrictive indorsement unless he has knowledge that a fiduciary or other person has negotiated the instrument in any transaction for his own benefit or otherwise in breach of duty (subsection (2) of Section 3–304).

§3–207. Negotiation Effective Although It May Be Rescinded. (1) Negotiation is effective to transfer the instrument although the negotiation is

(a) made by an infant, a corporation exceeding its powers, or any other person without capacity; or

(b) obtained by fraud, duress or mistake of any kind; or

(c) part of an illegal transaction; or

(d) made in breach of duty.

(2) Except as against a subsequent holder in due course such negotiation is in an appropriate case subject to rescission, the declaration of a constructive trust or any other remedy permitted by law.

§3–208. Reacquisition. Where an instrument is returned to or reacquired by a prior party he may cancel any indorsement which is not necessary to his title and reissue or further negotiate the instrument, but any intervening party is discharged as against the reacquiring party and subsequent holders not in due course and if his indorsement has been cancelled is discharged as against subsequent holders in due course as well.

Part 3

Rights of a Holder

§3–301. Rights of a Holder. The holder of an instrument whether or not he is the owner may transfer or negotiate it and, except as otherwise provided in Section 3–603 on payment or satisfaction, discharge it or enforce payment in his own name.

§3–302. Holder in Due Course. (1) A holder in due course is a holder who takes the instrument

(a) for value; and

(b) in good faith; and

(c) without notice that it is overdue or has been dishonored or of any defense against or claim to it on the part of any person.

(2) A payee may be a holder in due course.

(3) A holder does not become a holder in due course of an instrument:

(a) by purchase of it at judicial sale or by taking it under legal process; or

(b) by acquiring it in taking over an estate; or

(c) by purchasing it as part of a bulk transaction not in regular course of business of the transferor.

(4) A purchaser of a limited interest can be a holder in due course only to the extent of the interest purchased.

§3–303. Taking for Value. A holder takes the instrument for value

(a) to the extent that the agreed consideration has been performed or that he acquires a security interest in or a lien on the instrument otherwise than by legal process; or

(b) when he takes the instrument in payment of or as security for an antecedent claim against any person whether or not the claim is due; or

(c) when he gives a negotiable instrument for it or makes an irrevocable commitment to a third person.

§3–304. Notice to Purchaser. (1) The purchaser has notice of a claim or defense if

(a) the instrument is so incomplete, bears such visible evidence of forgery or alteration, or is otherwise so irregular as to call into question its validity, terms or ownership or to create an ambiguity as to the party to pay; or

(b) the purchaser has notice that the obligation of any party is voidable in whole or in part, or that all parties have been discharged.

(2) The purchaser has notice of a claim against the instrument when he has knowledge that a fiduciary has negotiated the instrument in payment of or as security for his own debt or in any transaction for his own benefit or otherwise in breach of duty.

(3) The purchaser has notice that an instrument is overdue if he has reason to know

(a) that any part of the principal amount is overdue or that there is an uncured default in payment of another instrument of the same series; or

(b) that acceleration of the instrument has been made; or

(c) that he is taking a demand instrument after demand has been made or more than a reasonable length of time after its issue. A reasonable time for a check drawn and payable within the states and territories of the United States and the District of Columbia is presumed to be thirty days.

(4) Knowledge of the following facts does not of itself give the purchaser notice of a defense or claim

(a) that the instrument is antedated or postdated;

(b) that it was issued or negotiated in return for an executory promise or accompanied by a separate agreement, unless the purchaser has notice that a defense or claim has arisen from the terms thereof;

(c) that any party has signed for accommodation;

(d) that an incomplete instrument has been completed, unless the purchaser has notice of any improper completion;

(e) that any person negotiating the instrument is or was a fiduciary;

(f) that there has been default in payment of interest on the instrument or in payment of any other instrument, except one of the same series.

(5) The filing or recording of a document does not of itself constitute notice within the provisions of this Article to a person who would otherwise be a holder in due course.

(6) To be effective notice must be received at such time and in such manner as to give a reasonable opportunity to act on it.

§3–305. Rights of a Holder in Due Course. To the extent that a holder is a holder in due course he takes the instrument free from

(1) all claims to it on the part of any person; and

(2) all defenses of any party to the instrument with whom the holder has not dealt except

(a) infancy, to the extent that it is a defense to a simple contract; and

(b) such other incapacity, or duress, or illegality of the transaction, as renders the obligation of the party a nullity; and

(c) such misrepresentation as has induced the party to sign the instrument with neither knowledge nor reasonable opportunity to obtain knowledge of its character or its essential terms; and

(d) discharge in insolvency proceedings; and

(e) any other discharge of which the holder has notice when he takes the instrument.

§3–306. Rights of One Not Holder in Due Course. Unless he has the rights of a holder in due course any person takes the instrument subject to

(a) all valid claims to it on the part of any person; and

(b) all defenses of any party which would be available in an action on a simple contract; and

(c) the defenses of want or failure of consideration, non-performance of any condition precedent, non-delivery, or delivery for a special purpose (Section 3–408); and

(d) the defense that he or a person through whom he holds the instrument acquired it by theft, or that payment or satisfaction to such holder would be inconsistent with the terms of a restrictive indorsement. The claim of any third person to the instrument is not otherwise available as a defense to any party liable thereon unless the third person himself defends the action for such party.

§3–307. Burden of Establishing Signatures, Defenses and Due Course. (1) Unless specifically denied in the pleadings each signature on an instrument is admitted. When the effectiveness of a signature is put in issue

(a) the burden of establishing it is on the party claiming under the signature; but

(b) the signature is presumed to be genuine or authorized except where the action is to enforce the obligation of a purported signer who has died or become incompetent before proof is required.

(2) When signatures are admitted or established, production of the instrument entitles a holder to recover on it unless the defendant establishes a defense.

(3) After it is shown that a defense exists a person claiming the rights of a holder in due course has the burden of establishing that he or some person under whom he claims is in all respects a holder in due course.

Part 4

Liability of Parties

§3–401. Signature. (1) No person is liable on an instrument unless his signature appears thereon.

(2) A signature is made by use of any name, including any trade or assumed name, upon an instrument, or by any word or mark used in lieu of a written signature.

§3–402. Signature in Ambiguous Capacity. Unless the instrument clearly indicates that a signature is made in some other capacity it is an indorsement.

§3–403. Signature by Authorized Representative. (1) A signature may be made by an agent or other representative, and his authority to make it may be established as in other cases of representation. No particular form of appointment is necessary to establish such authority.

(2) An authorized representative who signs his own name to an instrument

(a) is personally obligated if the instrument neither names the person represented nor shows that the representative signed in a representative capacity;

(b) except as otherwise established between the immediate parties, is personally obligated if the instrument names the person represented but does not show that the representative signed in a representative capacity, or if the instrument does not name the person represented but does show that the representative signed in a representative capacity.

(3) Except as otherwise established the name of an organization preceded or followed by the name and office of an authorized individual is a signature made in a representative capacity.

§3–404. Unauthorized Signatures. (1) Any unauthorized signature is wholly inoperative as that of the person whose name is signed unless he ratifies it or is precluded from denying it; but it operates as the signature of the unauthorized signer in favor of any person who in good faith pays the instrument or takes it for value.

(2) Any unauthorized signature may be ratified for all purposes of this Article. Such ratification does not of itself affect any rights of the person ratifying against the actual signer.

§3–405. Impostors; Signature in Name of Payee. (1) An indorsement by any person in the name of a named payee is effective if

(a) an impostor by use of the mails or otherwise has induced the maker or drawer to issue the instrument to him or his confederate in the name of the payee; or

(b) a person signing as or on behalf of a maker or drawer intends the payee to have no interest in the instrument; or

(c) an agent or employee of the maker or drawer has supplied him with the name of the payee intending the latter to have no such interest.

(2) Nothing in this section shall affect the criminal or civil liability of the person so indorsing.

§3–406. Negligence Contributing to Alteration or Unauthorized Signature. Any person who by his negligence substantially contributes to a material alteration of the instrument or to the making of an unauthorized signature is precluded from asserting the alteration or lack of authority against a holder in due course or against a drawee or other payor who pays the instrument in good faith and in accordance with the reasonable commercial standards of the drawee's or payor's business.

§3–407. Alteration. (1) Any alteration of an instrument is material which changes the contract of any party thereto in any respect, including any such change in

(a) the number or relations of the parties; or

(b) an incomplete instrument, by completing it otherwise than as authorized; or

(c) the writing as signed, by adding to it or by removing any part of it.

(2) As against any person other than a subsequent holder in due course

(a) alteration by the holder which is both fraudulent and material discharges any party whose contract is thereby changed unless that party assents or is precluded from asserting the defense;

(b) no other alteration discharges any party and the instrument may be enforced according to its original tenor, or as to incomplete instruments according to the authority given.

(3) A subsequent holder in due course may in all cases enforce the instrument according to its original tenor, and when an incomplete instrument has been completed, he may enforce it as completed.

§3–408. Consideration. Want or failure of consideration is a defense as against any person not having the rights of a holder in due course (Section 3–305), except that no consideration is necessary for an instrument or obligation thereon given in payment of or as security for an antecedent obligation of any kind. Nothing in this section shall be taken to displace any statute outside this Act under which a promise is enforceable notwithstanding lack or failure of consideration. Partial failure of consideration is a defense pro tanto whether or not the failure is in an ascertained or liquidated amount.

§3–409. Draft Not an Assignment. (1) A check or other draft does not of itself operate as an assignment of any funds in the hands of the drawee available for its payment, and the drawee is not liable on the instrument until he accepts it.

(2) Nothing in this section shall affect any liability in contract, tort or otherwise arising from any letter of credit or other obligation or representation which is not an acceptance.

§3–410. Definition and Operation of Acceptance. (1) Acceptance is the drawee's signed engagement to honor the draft as presented. It must be written on the draft, and may consist of his signature alone. It becomes operative when completed by delivery or notification.

(2) A draft may be accepted although it has not been signed by the drawer or is otherwise incomplete or is overdue or has been dishonored.

(3) Where the draft is payable at a fixed period after sight and the acceptor fails to date his acceptance the holder may complete it by supplying a date in good faith.

§3–411. Certification of a Check. (1) Certification of a check is acceptance. Where a holder procures certification the drawer and all prior indorsers are discharged.

(2) Unless otherwise agreed a bank has no obligation to certify a check.

(3) A bank may certify a check before returning it for a lack of proper indorsement. If it does so the drawer is discharged.

§3–412. Acceptance Varying Draft. (1) Where the drawee's proffered acceptance in any manner varies the draft as presented the holder may refuse the acceptance and treat the draft as dishonored in which case the drawee is entitled to have his acceptance cancelled.

(2) The terms of the draft are not varied by an acceptance to pay at any particular bank or place in the United States, unless the acceptance states that the draft is to be paid only at such bank or place.

(3) Where the holder assents to an acceptance varying the terms of the draft each drawer and indorser who does affirmatively assent is discharged.

§3–413. **Contract of Maker, Drawer and Acceptor.** (1) The maker or acceptor engages that he will pay the instrument according to its tenor at the time of his engagement or as completed pursuant to Section 3–115 on incomplete instruments.

(2) The drawer engages that upon dishonor of the draft and any necessary notice of dishonor or protest he will pay the amount of the draft to the holder or to any indorser who takes it up. The drawer may disclaim this liability by drawing without recourse.

(3) By making, drawing or accepting the party admits as against all subsequent parties including the drawee the existence of the payee and his then capacity to indorse.

§3–414. **Contract of Indorser; Order of Liability.** (1) Unless the indorsement otherwise specifies (as by such words as "without recourse") every indorser engages that upon dishonor and any necessary notice of dishonor and protest he will pay the instrument according to its tenor at the time of his indorsement to the holder or to any subsequent indorser who takes it up, even though the indorser who takes it up was not obligated to do so.

(2) Unless they otherwise agree indorsers are liable to one another in the order in which they indorse, which is presumed to be the order in which their signatures appear on the instrument.

§3–415. **Contract of Accommodation Party.** (1) An accommodation party is one who signs the instrument in any capacity for the purpose of lending his name to another party to it.

(2) When the instrument has been taken for value before it is due the accommodation party is liable in the capacity in which he has signed even though the taker knows of the accommodation.

(3) As against a holder in due course and without notice of the accommodation oral proof of the accommodation is not admissible to give the accommodation party the benefit of discharges dependent on his character as such. In other cases the accommodation character may be shown by oral proof.

(4) An indorsement which shows that it is not in the chain of title is notice of its accommodation character.

(5) An accommodation party is not liable to the party accommodated, and if he pays the instrument has a right of recourse on the instrument against such party.

§3–416. **Contract of Guarantor.** (1) "Payment guaranteed" or equivalent words added to a signature mean that the signor engages that if the instrument is not paid when due he will pay it according to its tenor without resort by the holder to any other party.

(2) "Collection guaranteed" or equivalent words added to a signature mean that the signor engages that if the instrument is not paid when due he will pay it according to its tenor, but only after the holder has reduced his claim against the maker or acceptor to judgment and execution has been returned unsatisfied, or after the maker or acceptor has become insolvent or it is otherwise apparent that it is useless to proceed against him.

(3) Words of guaranty which do not otherwise specify guarantee payment.

(4) No words of guaranty added to the signature of a sole maker or

acceptor affect his liability on the instrument. Such words added to the signature of one of two or more makers or acceptors create a presumption that the signature is for the accommodation of the others.

(5) When words of guaranty are used presentment, notice of dishonor and protest are not necessary to charge the user.

(6) Any guaranty written on the instrument is enforceable notwithstanding any statute of frauds.

§3-417. Warranties on Presentment and Transfer. (1) Any person who obtains payment or acceptance and any prior transferor warrants to a person who in good faith pays or accepts that

(a) he has a good title to the instrument or is authorized to obtain payment or acceptance on behalf of one who has a good title; and

(b) he has no knowledge that the signature of the maker or drawer is unauthorized, except that this warranty is not given by a holder in due course acting in good faith

(i) to a maker with respect to the maker's own signature; or

(ii) to a drawer with respect to the drawer's own signature, whether or not the drawer is also the drawee; or

(iii) to an acceptor of a draft if the holder in due course took the draft after the acceptance or obtained the acceptance without knowledge that the drawer's signature was unauthorized; and

(c) the instrument has not been materially altered, except that this warranty is not given by a holder in due course acting in good faith

(i) to the maker of a note; or

(ii) to the drawer of a draft whether or not the drawer is also the drawee; or

(iii) to the acceptor of a draft with respect to an alteration made prior to the acceptance if the holder in due course took the draft after the acceptance, even though the acceptance provided "payable as originally drawn" or equivalent terms; or

(iv) to the acceptor of a draft with respect to an alteration made after the acceptance.

(2) Any person who transfers an instrument and receives consideration warrants to his transferee and if the transfer is by indorsement to any subsequent holder who takes the instrument in good faith that

(a) he has a good title to the instrument or is authorized to obtain payment or acceptance on behalf of one who has a good title and the transfer is otherwise rightful; and

(b) all signatures are genuine or authorized; and

(c) the instrument has not been materially altered; and

(d) no defense of any party is good against him; and

(e) he has no knowledge of any insolvency proceeding instituted with respect to the maker or acceptor or the drawer of an unaccepted instrument.

(3) By transferring "without recourse" the transferor limits the obligation stated in subsection (2) (d) to a warranty that he has no knowledge of such a defense.

(4) A selling agent or broker who does not disclose the fact that he is acting only as such gives the warranties provided in this section, but if he makes such disclosure warrants only his good faith and authority.

§3-418. Finality of Payment or Acceptance. Except for recovery of bank payments as provided in the Article on Bank Deposits and Collections (Article 4) and except for liability for breach of warranty on presentment under the preceding section, payment or acceptance of any instrument is final in favor of a holder in due course, or a person who has in good faith changed his position in reliance on the payment.

§3–419. Conversion of Instrument; Innocent Representative. (1) An instrument is converted when

(a) a drawee to whom it is delivered for acceptance refuses to return it on demand; or

(b) any person to whom it is delivered for payment refuses on demand either to pay or to return it; or

(c) it is paid on a forged indorsement.

(2) In an action against a drawee under subsection (1) the measure of the drawee's liability is the face amount of the instrument. In any other action under subsection (1) the measure of liability is presumed to be the face amount of the instrument.

(3) Subject to the provisions of this Act concerning restrictive indorsements a representative, including a depositary or collecting bank, who has in good faith and in accordance with the reasonable commercial standards applicable to the business of such representative dealt with an instrument or its proceeds on behalf of one who was not the true owner is not liable in conversion or otherwise to the true owner beyond the amount of any proceeds remaining in his hands.

(4) An intermediary bank or payor bank which is not a depositary bank is not liable in conversion solely by reason of the fact that proceeds of an item indorsed restrictively (Sections 3–205 and 3–206) are not paid or applied consistently with the restrictive indorsement of an indorser other than its immediate transferor.

Part 5

Presentment, Notice of Dishonor and Protest

§3–501. When Presentment, Notice of Dishonor, and Protest Necessary or Permissible. (1) Unless excused (Section 3–511) presentment is necessary to charge secondary parties as follows:

(a) presentment for acceptance is necessary to charge the drawer and indorsers of a draft where the draft so provides, or is payable elsewhere than at the residence or place of business of the drawee, or its date of payment depends upon such presentment. The holder may at his option present for acceptance any other draft payable at a stated date;

(b) presentment for payment is necessary to charge any indorser;

(c) in the case of any drawer, the acceptor of a draft payable at a bank or the maker of a note payable at a bank, presentment for payment is necessary, but failure to make presentment discharges such drawer, acceptor or maker only as stated in Section 3–502(1) (b).

(2) Unless excused (Section 3–511)

(a) notice of any dishonor is necessary to charge any indorser;

(b) in the case of any drawer, the acceptor of a draft payable at a bank or the maker of a note payable at a bank, notice of any dishonor is necessary, but failure to give such notice discharges such drawer, acceptor or maker only as stated in Section 3–502(1) (b).

(3) Unless excused (Section 3–511) protest of any dishonor is necessary to charge the drawer and indorsers of any draft which on its face appears to be drawn or payable outside of the states and territories of the United States and the District of Columbia. The holder may at his option make protest of any dishonor of any other instrument and in the case of a foreign draft may on insolvency of the acceptor before maturity make protest for better security.

(4) Notwithstanding any provision of this section, neither presentment nor notice of dishonor nor protest is necessary to charge an indorser who has indorsed an instrument after maturity.

§3–502. Unexcused Delay; Discharge. (1) Where without excuse any necessary presentment or notice of dishonor is delayed beyond the time when it is due

(a) any indorser is discharged; and

(b) any drawer or the acceptor of a draft payable at a bank or the maker of a note payable at a bank who because the drawee or payor bank becomes insolvent during the delay is deprived of funds maintained with the drawee or payor bank to cover the instrument may discharge his liability by written assignment to the holder of his rights against the drawee or payor bank in respect of such funds, but such drawer, acceptor or maker is not otherwise discharged.

(2) Where without excuse a necessary protest is delayed beyond the time when it is due any drawer or indorser is discharged.

§3–503. Time of Presentment. (1) Unless a different time is expressed in the instrument the time for any presentment is determined as follows:

(a) where an instrument is payable at or a fixed period after a stated date any presentment for acceptance must be made on or before the date it is payable;

(b) where an instrument is payable after sight it must either be presented for acceptance or negotiated within a reasonable time after date or issue whichever is later;

(c) where an instrument shows the date on which it is payable presentment for payment is due on that date;

(d) where an instrument is accelerated presentment for payment is due within a reasonable time after the acceleration;

(e) with respect to the liability of any secondary party presentment for acceptance or payment of any other instrument is due within a reasonable time after such party becomes liable thereon.

(2) A reasonable time for presentment is determined by the nature of the instrument, any usage of banking or trade and the facts of the particular case. In the case of an uncertified check which is drawn and payable within the United States and which is not a draft drawn by a bank the following are presumed to be reasonable periods within which to present for payment or to initiate bank collection:

(a) which respect to the liability of the drawer, thirty days after date or issue whichever is later; and

(b) with respect to the liability of an indorser, seven days after his indorsement.

(3) Where any presentment is due on a day which is not a full business day for either the person making presentment or the party to pay or accept, presentment is due on the next following day which is a full business day for both parties.

(4) Presentment to be sufficient must be made at a reasonable hour, and if at a bank during its banking day.

§3–504. How Presentment Made. (1) Presentment is a demand for acceptance or payment made upon the maker, acceptor, drawee or other payor by or on behalf of the holder.

(2) Presentment may be made

(a) by mail, in which event the time of presentment is determined by the time of receipt of the mail; or

(b) through a clearing house; or

(c) at the place of acceptance or payment specified in the instrument or if there be none at the place of business or residence of the party to accept or pay. If neither the party to accept or pay nor any one authorized to act for him is present or accessible at such place presentment is excused.

(3) It may be made

(a) to any one of two or more makers, acceptors, drawees or other payors; or

(b) to any person who has authority to make or refuse the acceptance or payment.

(4) A draft accepted or a note made payable at a bank in the United States must be presented at such bank.

(5) In the cases described in Section 4–210 presentment may be made in the manner and with the result stated in that section.

§3–505. Rights of Party to Whom Presentment Is Made. (1) The party to whom presentment is made may without dishonor require

(a) exhibition of the instrument; and

(b) reasonable identification of the person making presentment and evidence of his authority to make it if made for another; and

(c) that the instrument be produced for acceptance or payment at a place specified in it, or if there be none at any place reasonable in the circumstances; and

(d) a signed receipt on the instrument for any partial or full payment and its surrender upon full payment.

(2) Failure to comply with any such requirement invalidates the presentment but the person presenting has a reasonable time in which to comply and the time for acceptance or payment runs from the time of compliance.

§3–506. Time Allowed for Acceptance or Payment. (1) Acceptance may be deferred without dishonor until the close of the next business day following presentment. The holder may also in a good faith effort to obtain acceptance and without either dishonor of the instrument or discharge of secondary parties allow postponement of acceptance for an additional business day.

(2) Except as a longer time is allowed in the case of documentary drafts drawn under a letter of credit, and unless an earlier time is agreed to by the party to pay, payment of an instrument may be deferred without dishonor pending reasonable examination to determine whether it is properly payable, but payment must be made in any event before the close of business on the day of presentment.

§3–507. Dishonor; Holder's Right of Recourse; Term Allowing Re-Presentment. (1) An instrument is dishonored when

(a) a necessary or optional presentment is duly made and due acceptance or payment is refused or cannot be obtained within the prescribed time or in case of bank collections the instrument is seasonably returned by the midnight deadline (Section 4–301); or

(b) presentment is excused and the instrument is not duly accepted or paid.

(2) Subject to any necessary notice of dishonor and protest, the holder has upon dishonor an immediate right of recourse against the drawers and indorsers.

(3) Return of an instrument for lack of proper indorsement is not dishonor.

(4) A term in a draft or an indorsement thereof allowing a stated time for re-presentment in the event of any dishonor of the draft by non-acceptance if a time draft or by nonpayment if a sight draft gives the holder as against any secondary party bound by the term an option to waive the dishonor without affecting the liability of the secondary party and he may present again up to the end of the stated time.

§3–508. Notice of Dishonor. (1) Notice of dishonor may be given to any person who may be liable on the instrument by or on behalf of the holder or any party who has himself received notice, or any other party who can be compelled to pay the instrument. In addition an agent or bank in whose hands the instrument is dishonored may give notice to his principal or customer or to another agent or bank from which the instrument was received.

(2) Any necessary notice must be given by a bank before its midnight deadline and by any other person before midnight of the third business day after dishonor or receipt of notice of dishonor.

(3) Notice may be given in any reasonable manner. It may be oral or written and in any terms which identify the instrument and state that it has been dishonored. A misdescription which does not mislead the party notified does not vitiate the notice. Sending the instrument bearing a stamp, ticket or writing stating that acceptance or payment has been refused or sending a notice of debit with respect to the instrument is sufficient.

(4) Written notice is given when sent although it is not received.

(5) Notice to one partner is notice to each although the firm has been dissolved.

(6) When any party is in insolvency proceedings instituted after the issue of the instrument notice may be given either to the party or to the representative of his estate.

(7) When any party is dead or incompetent notice may be sent to his last known address or given to his personal representative.

(8) Notice operates for the benefit of all parties who have rights on the instrument against the party notified.

§3–509. Protest; Noting for Protest. (1) A protest is a certificate of dishonor made under the hand and seal of a United States consul or vice consul or a notary public or other person authorized to certify dishonor by the law of the place where dishonor occurs. It may be made upon information satisfactory to such person.

(2) The protest must identify the instrument and certify either that due presentment has been made or the reason why it is excused and that the instrument has been dishonored by nonacceptance or nonpayment.

(3) The protest may also certify that notice of dishonor has been given to all parties or to specified parties.

(4) Subject to subsection (5) any necessary protest is due by the time that notice of dishonor is due.

(5) If, before protest is due, an instrument has been noted for protest by the officer to make protest, the protest may be made at any time thereafter as of the date of the noting.

§3–510. Evidence of Dishonor and Notice of Dishonor. The following are admissible as evidence and create a presumption of dishonor and of any notice of dishonor therein shown:

(a) a document regular in form as provided in the preceding section which purports to be a protest;

(b) the purported stamp or writing of the drawee, payor bank or presenting bank on the instrument or accompanying it stating that acceptance or payment has been refused for reasons consistent with dishonor;

(c) any book or record of the drawee, payor bank, or any collecting bank kept in the usual course of business which shows dishonor, even though there is no evidence of who made the entry.

§3-511. **Waived or Excused Presentment, Protest or Notice of Dishonor or Delay Therein.** (1) Delay in presentment, protest or notice of dishonor is excused when the party is without notice that it is due or when the delay is caused by circumstances beyond his control and he exercises reasonable diligence after the cause of the delay ceases to operate.

(2) Presentment or notice or protest as the case may be is entirely excused when

(a) the party to be charged has waived it expressly or by implication either before or after it is due; or

(b) such party has himself dishonored the instrument or has countermanded payment or otherwise has no reason to expect or right to require that the instrument be accepted or paid; or

(c) by reasonable diligence the presentment or protest cannot be made or the notice given.

(3) Presentment is also entirely excused when

(a) the maker, acceptor or drawee of any instrument except a documentary draft is dead or in insolvency proceedings instituted after the issue of the instrument; or

(b) acceptance or payment is refused but not for want of proper presentment.

(4) Where a draft has been dishonored by non-acceptance a later presentment for payment and any notice of dishonor and protest for non-payment are excused unless in the meantime the instrument has been accepted.

(5) A waiver of protest is also a waiver of presentment and of notice of dishonor even though protest is not required.

(6) Where a waiver of presentment or notice of protest is embodied in the instrument itself it is binding upon all parties; but where it is written above the signature of an indorser it binds him only.

Part 6

Discharge

§3-601. **Discharge of Parties.** (1) The extent of the discharge of any party from liability on an instrument is governed by the sections on

(a) payment or satisfaction (Section 3-603); or

(b) tender of payment (Section 3-604); or

(c) cancellation or renunciation (Section 3-605); or

(d) impairment of right of recourse or of collateral (Section 3-606); or

(e) reacquisition of the instrument by a prior party (Section 3-208); or

(f) fraudulent and material alteration (Section 3-407); or

(g) certification of a check (Section 3-411); or

(h) acceptance varying a draft (Section 3-412); or

(i) unexcused delay in presentment or notice of dishonor or protest (Section 3–502).

(2) Any party is also discharged from his liability on an instrument to another party by any other act or agreement with such party which would discharge his simple contract for the payment of money.

(3) The liability of all parties is discharged when any party who has himself no right of action or recourse on the instrument

(a) reacquires the instrument in his own right; or

(b) is discharged under any provision of this Article, except as otherwise provided with respect to discharge for impairment of recourse or of collateral (Section 3–606).

§3–602. Effect of Discharge Against Holder in Due Course. No discharge of any party provided by this Article is effective against a subsequent holder in due course unless he has notice thereof when he takes the instrument.

§3–603. Payment or Satisfaction. (1) The liability of any party is discharged to the extent of his payment or satisfaction to the holder even though it is made with knowledge of a claim of another person to the instrument unless prior to such payment or satisfaction the person making the claim either supplies indemnity deemed adequate by the party seeking the discharge or enjoins payment or satisfaction by order of a court of competent jurisdiction in an action in which the adverse claimant and the holder are parties. This subsection does not, however, result in the discharge of the liability

(a) of a party who in bad faith pays or satisfies a holder who acquired the instrument by theft or who (unless having the rights of a holder in due course) holds through one who so acquired it; or

(b) of a party (other than an intermediary bank or a payor bank which is not a depositary bank) who pays or satisfies the holder of an instrument which has been restrictively indorsed in a manner not consistent with the terms of such restrictive indorsement.

(2) Payment or satisfaction may be made with the consent of the holder by any person including a stranger to the instrument. Surrender of the instrument to such a person gives him the rights of a transferee (Section 3–201).

§3–604. Tender of Payment. (1) Any party making tender of full payment to a holder when or after it is due is discharged to the extent of all subsequent liability for interest, costs and attorney's fees.

(2) The holder's refusal of such tender wholly discharges any party who has a right of recourse against the party making the tender.

(3) Where the maker or acceptor of an instrument payable otherwise than on demand is able and ready to pay at every place of payment specified in the instrument when it is due, it is equivalent to tender.

§3–605. Cancellation and Renunciation. (1) The holder of an instrument may even without consideration discharge any party

(a) in any manner apparent on the face of the instrument or the indorsement, as by intentionally cancelling the instrument or the party's signature by destruction or mutilation, or by striking out the party's signature; or

(b) by renouncing his rights by a writing signed and delivered or by surrender of the instrument to the party to be discharged.

(2) Neither cancellation nor renunciation without surrender of the instrument affects the title thereto.

§3–606. Impairment of Recourse or of Collateral. (1) The holder discharges any party to the instrument to the extent that without such party's consent the holder

(a) without express reservation of rights releases or agrees not to sue any person against whom the party has to the knowledge of the holder a right of recourse or agrees to suspend the right to enforce against such person the instrument or collateral or otherwise discharges such person, except that failure or delay in effecting any required presentment, protest or notice of dishonor with respect to any such person does not discharge any party as to whom presentment, protest or notice of dishonor is effective or unnecessary; or

(b) unjustifiably impairs any collateral for the instrument given by or on behalf of the party or any person against whom he has a right of recourse.

(2) By express reservation of rights against a party with a right of recourse the holder preserves

(a) all his rights against such party as of the time when the instrument was originally due; and

(b) the right of the party to pay the instrument as of that time; and

(c) all rights of such party to recourse against others.

Part 7

Advice of International Sight Draft

§3–701. Letter of Advice of International Sight Draft. (1) A "letter of advice" is a drawer's communication to the drawee that a described draft has been drawn.

(2) Unless otherwise agreed when a bank receives from another bank a letter of advice of an international sight draft the drawee bank may immediately debit the drawer's account and stop the running of interest pro tanto. Such a debit and any resulting credit to any account covering outstanding drafts leaves in the drawer full power to stop payment or otherwise dispose of the amount and creates no trust or interest in favor of the holder.

(3) Unless otherwise agreed and except where a draft is drawn under a credit issued by the drawee, the drawee of an international sight draft owes the drawer no duty to pay an unadvised draft but if it does so and the draft is genuine, may appropriately debit the drawer's account.

Part 8

Miscellaneous

§3–801. Drafts in a Set. (1) Where a draft is drawn in a set of parts, each of which is numbered and expressed to be an order only if no other part has been honored, the whole of the parts constitutes one draft but a taker of any part may become a holder in due course of the draft.

(2) Any person who negotiates, indorses or accepts a single part of a draft drawn in a set thereby becomes liable to any holder in due course of that part as if it were the whole set, but as between different holders in due course to whom different parts have been negotiated the holder whose title first accrues has all rights to the draft and its proceeds.

(3) As against the drawee the first presented part of a draft drawn in a set is the part entitled to payment, or if a time draft to acceptance and payment. Acceptance of any subsequently presented part renders the drawee liable thereon under subsection (2). With respect both to a holder and to the drawer payment of a subsequently presented part of a draft payable at sight has the same effect as payment of a check notwithstanding an effective stop order (Section 4–407).

(4) Except as otherwise provided in this section, where any part of a draft in a set is discharged by payment or otherwise the whole draft is discharged.

§3–802. Effect of Instrument on Obligation for Which It Is Given. (1) Unless otherwise agreed where an instrument is taken for an underlying obligation

(a) the obligation is pro tanto discharged if a bank is drawer, maker or acceptor of the instrument and there is no recourse on the instrument against the underlying obligor; and

(b) in any other case the obligation is suspended pro tanto until the instrument is due or if it is payable on demand until its presentment. If the instrument is dishonored action may be maintained on either the instrument or the obligation; discharge of the underlying obligor on the instrument also discharges him on the obligation.

(2) The taking in good faith of a check which is not postdated does not of itself so extend the time on the original obligation as to discharge a surety.

§3–803. Notice to Third Party. Where a defendant is sued for breach of an obligation for which a third person is answerable over under this Article he may give the third person written notice of the litigation, and the person notified may then give similar notice to any other person who is answerable over to him under this Article. If the notice states that the person notified may come in and defend and that if the person notified does not do so he will in any action against him by the person giving the notice be bound by any determination of fact common to the two litigations, then unless after seasonable receipt of the notice the person notified does come in and defend he is so bound.

§3–804. Lost, Destroyed or Stolen Instruments. The owner of an instrument which is lost, whether by destruction, theft or otherwise, may maintain an action in his own name and recover from any party liable thereon upon due proof of his ownership, the facts which prevent his production of the instrument and its terms. The court may require security indemnifying the defendant against loss by reason of further claims on the instrument.

§3–805. Instruments Not Payable to Order or to Bearer. This Article applies to any instrument whose terms do not preclude transfer and which is otherwise negotiable within this Article but which is not payable to order or to bearer, except that there can be no holder in due course of such an instrument.

ARTICLE 4: BANK DEPOSITS AND COLLECTIONS

Part 1

General Provisions and Definitions

§4–101. Short Title. This Article shall be known and may be cited as Uniform Commercial Code—Bank Deposits and Collections.

§4–102. Applicability. (1) To the extent that items within this Article are also within the scope of Articles 3 and 8, they are subject to the provisions of those Articles. In the event of conflict the provisions of this Article govern those of Article 3 but the provisions of Article 8 govern those of this Article.

(2) The liability of a bank for action or non-action with respect to any item handled by it for purposes of presentment, payment or collection is governed by the law of the place where the bank is located. In the case of action or non-action by or at a branch or separate office of a bank, its liability is governed by the law of the place where the branch or separate office is located.

§4–103. Variation by Agreement; Measure of Damages; Certain Action Constituting Ordinary Care. (1) The effect of the provisions of this Article may be varied by agreement except that no agreement can disclaim a bank's responsibility for its own lack of good faith or failure to exercise ordinary care or can limit the measure of damages for such lack or failure; but the parties may by agreement determine the standards by which such responsibility is to be measured if such standards are not manifestly unreasonable.

(2) Federal Reserve regulations and operating letters, clearing house rules, and the like, have the effect of agreements under subsection (1), whether or not specifically assented to by all parties interested in items handled.

(3) Action or non-action approved by this Article or pursuant to Federal Reserve regulations or operating letters constitutes the exercise of ordinary care and, in the absence of special instructions, action or non-action consistent with clearing house rules and the like or with a general banking usage not disapproved by this Article, prima facie constitutes the exercise of ordinary care.

(4) The specification or approval of certain procedures by this Article does not constitute disapproval of other procedures which may be reasonable under the circumstances.

(5) The measure of damages for failure to exercise ordinary care in handling an item is the amount of the item reduced by an amount which could not have been realized by the use of ordinary care, and where there is bad faith it includes other damages, if any, suffered by the party as a proximate consequence.

§4–104. Definitions and Index of Definitions. (1) In this Article unless the context otherwise requires

(a) "Account" means any account with a bank and includes a checking, time, interest or savings account;

(b) "Afternoon" means the period of a day between noon and midnight;

(c) "Banking day" means that part of any day on which a bank is open to the public for carrying on substantially all of its banking functions;

(d) "Clearing house" means any association of banks or other payors regularly clearing items;

(e) "Customer" means any person having an account with a bank or for whom a bank has agreed to collect items and includes a bank carrying an account with another bank;

(f) "Documentary draft" means any negotiable or non-negotiable draft with accompanying documents, securities or other papers to be delivered against honor of the draft;

(g) "Item" means any instrument for the payment of money even though it is not negotiable but does not include money;

(h) "Midnight deadline" with respect to a bank is midnight on its next banking day following the banking day on which it receives the relevant item or notice or from which the time for taking action commences to run, whichever is later;

(i) "Properly payable" includes the availability of funds for payment at the time of decision to pay or dishonor;

(j) "Settle" means to pay in cash, by clearing house settlement, in a charge or credit or by remittance, or otherwise as instructed. A settlement may be either provisional or final;

(k) "Suspends payments" with respect to a bank means that it has been closed by order of the supervisory authorities, that a public officer has been appointed to take it over or that it ceases or refuses to make payments in the ordinary course of business.

(2) Other definitions applying to this Article and the sections in which they appear are:

"Collecting bank". Section 4–105.

"Depositary bank". Section 4–105.

"Intermediary bank". Section 4–105.

"Payor bank". Section 4–105.

"Presenting bank". Section 4–105.

"Remitting bank". Section 4–105.

(3) The following definitions in other Articles apply to this Article:

"Acceptance". Section 3–410.

"Certificate of deposit". Section 3–104.

"Certification". Section 3–411.

"Check". Section 3–104.

"Draft". Section 3–104.

"Holder in due course". Section 3–302.

"Notice of dishonor". Section 3–508.

"Presentment". Section 3–504.

"Protest". Section 3–509.

"Secondary party". Section 3–102.

(4) In addition Article 1 contains general definitions and principles of construction and interpretation applicable throughout this Article.

§4–105. "Depositary Bank"; "Intermediary Bank"; "Collecting Bank"; "Payor Bank"; "Presenting Bank"; "Remitting Bank". In this Article unless the context otherwise requires:

(a) "Depositary Bank" means the first bank to which an item is transferred for collection even though it is also the payor bank;

(b) "Payor bank" means a bank by which an item is payable as drawn or accepted;

(c) "Intermediary bank" means any bank to which an item is transferred in course of collection except the depositary or payor bank;

(d) "Collecting bank" means any bank handling the item for collection except the payor bank;

(e) "Presenting bank" means any bank presenting an item except a payor bank;

(f) "Remitting bank" means any payor or intermediary bank remitting for an item.

§4–106. Separate Office of a Bank. A branch or separate office of a bank [maintaining its own deposit ledgers] is a separate bank for the purpose of computing the time within which and determining the place at or to which action may be taken or notices or orders shall be given under this Article and under Article 3.

Note: *The words in brackets are optional.*

§4–107. Time of Receipt of Items. (1) For the purpose of allowing time to process items, prove balances and make the necessary entries on its books to determine its position for the day, a bank may fix an afternoon hour of two P.M. or later as a cut-off hour for the handling of money and items and the making of entries on its books.

(2) Any item or deposit of money received on any day after a cut-off hour so fixed or after the close of the banking day may be treated as being received at the opening of the next banking day.

§4–108. **Delays.** (1) Unless otherwise instructed, a collecting bank in a good faith effort to secure payment may, in the case of specific items and with or without the approval of any person involved, waive, modify or extend time limits imposed or permitted by this Act for a period not in excess of an additional banking day without discharge of secondary parties and without liability to its transferor or any prior party.

(2) Delay by a collecting bank or payor bank beyond time limits prescribed or permitted by this Act or by instructions is excused if caused by interruption of communication facilities, suspension of payments by another bank, war, emergency conditions or other circumstances beyond the control of the bank provided it exercises such diligence as the circumstances require.

§4–109. **Process of Posting.** The "process of posting" means the usual procedure followed by a payor bank in determining to pay an item and in recording the payment including one or more of the following or other steps as determined by the bank:

(a) verification of any signature;

(b) ascertaining that sufficient funds are available;

(c) affixing a "paid" or other stamp;

(d) entering a charge or entry to a customer's account;

(e) correcting or reversing an entry or erroneous action with respect to the item.

Part 2

Collection of Items: Depository and Collecting Banks

§4–201. **Presumption and Duration of Agency Status of Collecting Banks and Provisional Status of Credits; Applicability of Article; Item Indorsed "Pay Any Bank".** (1) Unless a contrary intent clearly appears and prior to the time that a settlement given by a collecting bank for an item is or becomes final (subsection (3) of Section 4–211 and Sections 4–212 and 4–213) the bank is an agent or sub-agent of the owner of the item and any settlement given for the item is provisional. This provision applies regardless of the form of indorsement or lack of indorsement and even though credit given for the item is subject to immediate withdrawal as of right or is in fact withdrawn; but the continuance of ownership of an item by its owner and any rights of the owner to proceeds of the item are subject to rights of a collecting bank such as those resulting from outstanding advances on the item and valid rights of setoff. When an item is handled by banks for purposes of presentment, payment and collection, the relevant provisions of this Article apply even though action of parties clearly establishes that a particular bank has purchased the item and is the owner of it.

(2) After an item has been indorsed with the words "pay any bank" or the like, only a bank may acquire the rights of a holder

(a) until the item has been returned to the customer initiating collection; or

(b) until the item has been specially indorsed by a bank to a person who is not a bank.

§4–202. Responsibility for Collection; When Action Seasonable. (1) A collecting bank must use ordinary care in

(a) presenting an item or sending it for presentment; and

(b) sending notice of dishonor or non-payment or returning an item other than a documentary draft to the bank's transferor [or directly to the depositary bank under subsection (2) of Section 4–212] (*see note to Section 4–212*) after learning that the item has not been paid or accepted, as the case may be; and

(c) settling for an item when the bank receives final settlement; and

(d) making or providing for any necessary protest; and

(e) notifying its transferor of any loss or delay in transit within a reasonable time after discovery thereof.

(2) A collecting bank taking proper action before its midnight deadline following receipt of an item, notice or payment acts seasonably; taking proper action within a reasonably longer time may be seasonable but the bank has the burden of so establishing.

(3) Subject to subsection (1) (a), a bank is not liable for the insolvency, neglect, misconduct, mistake or default of another bank or person or for loss or destruction of an item in transit or in the possession of others.

§4–203. Effect of Instructions. Subject to the provisions of Article 3 concerning conversion of instruments (Section 3–419) and the provisions of both Article 3 and this Article concerning restrictive indorsements only a collecting bank's transferor can give instructions which affect the bank or constitute notice to it and a collecting bank is not liable to prior parties for any action taken pursuant to such instructions or in accordance with any agreement with its transferor.

§4–204. Methods of Sending and Presenting; Sending Direct to Payor Bank. (1) A collecting bank must send items by reasonably prompt method taking into consideration any relevant instructions, the nature of the item, the number of such items on hand, and the cost of collection involved and the method generally used by it or others to present such items.

(2) A collecting bank may send

(a) any item direct to the payor bank;

(b) any item to any non-bank payor if authorized by its transferor; and

(c) any item other than documentary drafts to any non-bank payor, if authorized by Federal Reserve regulation or operating letter, clearing house rule or the like.

(3) Presentment may be made by a presenting bank at a place where the payor bank has requested that presentment be made.

§4–205. Supplying Missing Indorsement; No Notice From Prior Indorsement. (1) A depositary bank which has taken an item for collection may supply any indorsement of the customer which is necessary to title unless the item contains the words "payee's indorsement required" or the like. In the absence of such a requirement a statement placed on the item by the depositary bank to the effect that the item was deposited by a customer or credited to his account is effective as the customer's indorsement.

(2) An intermediary bank, or payor bank which is not a depositary bank, is neither given notice nor otherwise affected by a restrictive indorsement of any person except the bank's immediate transferor.

§4–206. Transfer Between Banks. Any agreed method which identifies the transferor bank is sufficient for the item's further transfer to another bank.

§4–207. Warranties of Customer and Collecting Bank on Transfer or Presentment of Items; Time for Claims. (1) Each customer or collecting bank who obtains payment or acceptance of an item and each prior customer and collecting bank warrants to the payor bank or other payor who in good faith pays or accepts the item that

(a) he has a good title to the item or is authorized to obtain payment or acceptance on behalf of one who has a good title; and

(b) he has no knowledge that the signature of the maker or drawer is unauthorized, except that this warranty is not given by any customer or collecting bank that is a holder in due course and acts in good faith

(i) to a maker with respect to the maker's own signature; or

(ii) to a drawer with respect to the drawer's own signature, whether or not the drawer is also the drawee; or

(iii) to an acceptor of an item if the holder in due course took the item after the acceptance or obtained the acceptance without knowledge that the drawer's signature was unauthorized; and

(c) the item has not been materially altered, except that this warranty is not given by any customer or collecting bank that is a holder in due course and acts in good faith

(i) to the maker of a note; or

(ii) to the drawer of a draft whether or not the drawer is also the drawee; or

(iii) to the acceptor of an item with respect to an alteration made prior to the acceptance if the holder in due course took the item after the acceptance, even though the acceptance provided "payable as originally drawn" or equivalent terms; or

(iv) to the acceptor of an item with respect to an alteration made after the acceptance.

(2) Each customer and collecting bank who transfers an item and receives a settlement or other consideration for it warrants to his transferee and to any subsequent collecting bank who takes the item in good faith that

(a) he has a good title to the item or is authorized to obtain payment or acceptance on behalf of one who has a good title and the transfer is otherwise rightful; and

(b) all signatures are genuine or authorized; and

(c) the item has not been materially altered; and

(d) no defense of any party is good against him; and

(e) he has no knowledge of any insolvency proceeding instituted with respect to the maker or acceptor or the drawer of an unaccepted item.

In addition each customer and collecting bank so transferring an item and receiving a settlement or other consideration engages that upon dishonor and any necessary notice of dishonor and protest he will take up the item.

(3) The warranties and the engagement to honor set forth in the two preceding subsections arise notwithstanding the absence of indorsement or words of guaranty or warranty in the transfer or presentment and a collecting bank remains liable for their breach despite remittance to its transferor. Damages for breach of such warranties or engagement to honor shall not exceed the consideration received by the customer or collecting bank responsible plus finance charges and expenses related to the item, if any.

(4) Unless a claim for breach of warranty under this section is made within a reasonable time after the person claiming learns of the breach, the person liable is discharged to the extent of any loss caused by the delay in making claim.

§4-208. **Security Interest of Collecting Bank in Items, Accompanying Documents and Proceeds.** (1) A bank has a security interest in an item and any accompanying documents or the proceeds of either

(a) in case of an item deposited in an account to the extent to which credit given for the item has been withdrawn or applied;

(b) in case of an item for which it has given credit available for withdrawal as of right, to the extent of the credit given whether or not the credit is drawn upon and whether or not there is a right of charge-back; or

(c) if it makes an advance on or against the item.

(2) When credit which has been given for several items received at one time or pursuant to a single agreement is withdrawn or applied in part the security interest remains upon all the items, any accompanying documents are the proceeds of either. For the purpose of this section, credits first given are first withdrawn.

(3) Receipt by a collecting bank of a final settlement for an item is a realization on its security interest in the item, accompanying documents and proceeds. To the extent and so long as the bank does not receive final settlement for the item or give up possession of the item or accompanying documents for purposes other than collection, the security interest continues and is subject to the provisions of Article 9 except that

(a) no security agreement is necessary to make the security interest enforceable (subsection (1) (b) of Section 9–203); and

(b) no filing is required to perfect the security interest; and

(c) the security interest has priority over conflicting perfected security interests in the item, accompanying documents or proceeds.

§4–209. When Bank Gives Value for Purposes of Holder in Due Course. For purposes of determining its status as a holder in due course, the bank has given value to the extent that it has a security interest in an item provided that the bank otherwise complies with the requirements of Section 3–302 on what constitutes a holder in due course.

§4–210. Presentment by Notice of Item Not Payable by, Through or at a Bank; Liability of Secondary Parties. (1) Unless otherwise instructed, a collecting bank may present an item not payable by, through or at a bank by sending to the party to accept or pay a written notice that the bank holds the item for acceptance or payment. The notice must be sent in time to be received on or before the day when presentment is due and the bank must meet any requirement of the party to accept or pay under Section 3–505 by the close of the bank's next banking day after it knows of the requirement.

(2) Where presentment is made by notice and neither honor nor request for compliance with a requirement under Section 3–505 is received by the close of business on the day after maturity or in the case of demand items by the close of business on the third banking day after notice was sent, the presenting bank may treat the item as dishonored and charge any secondary party by sending him notice of the facts.

§4–211. Media of Remittance; Provisional and Final Settlement in Remittance Cases. (1) A collecting bank may take in settlement of an item

(a) a check of the remitting bank or of another bank on any bank except the remitting bank; or

(b) a cashier's check or similar primary obligation of a remitting bank which is a member of or clears through a member of the same clearing house or group as the collecting bank; or

(c) appropriate authority to charge an account of the remitting bank or of another bank with the collecting bank; or

(d) if the item is drawn upon or payable by a person other than a bank, a cashier's check, certified check or other bank check or obligation.

(2) If before its midnight deadline the collecting bank properly dishonors a remittance check or authorization to charge on itself or presents or forwards for collection a remittance instrument of or on another bank which is of a kind approved by subsection (1) or has not been authorized by it, the collecting bank is not liable to prior parties in the event of the dishonor of such check, instrument or authorization.

(3) A settlement for an item by means of a remittance instrument or authorization to charge is or becomes a final settlement as to both the person making and the person receiving the settlement

(a) if the remittance instrument or authorization to charge is of a kind approved by subsection (1) or has not been authorized by the person receiving the settlement and in either case the person receiving the settlement acts seasonably before its midnight deadline in presenting, forwarding for collection or paying the instrument or authorization,—at the time the remittance instrument or authorization is finally paid by the payor by which it is payable;

(b) if the person receiving the settlement has authorized remittance by a non-bank check or obligation or by a cashier's check or similar primary obligation of or a check upon the payor or other remitting bank which is not of a kind approved by subsection (1) (b),—at the time of the receipt of such remittance check or obligation; or

(c) if in a case not covered by sub-paragraphs (a) or (b) the person receiving the settlement fails to seasonably present, forward for collection, pay or return a remittance instrument or authorization to it to charge before its midnight deadline,—at such midnight deadline.

§4–212. Right of Charge-Back or Refund. (1) If a collecting bank has made provisional settlement with its customer for an item and itself fails by reason of dishonor, suspension of payments by a bank or otherwise to receive a settlement for the item which is or becomes final, the bank may revoke the settlement given by it, charge back the amount of any credit given for the item to its customer's account or obtain refund from its customer whether or not it is able to return the items if by its midnight deadline or within a longer reasonable time after it learns the facts it returns the item or sends notification of the facts. These rights to revoke, charge-back and obtain refund terminate if and when a settlement for the item received by the bank is or becomes final (subsection (3) of Section 4–211 and subsections (2) and (3) of Section 4–213).

[(2) Within the time and manner prescribed by this section and Section 4–301, an intermediary or payor bank, as the case may be, may return an unpaid item directly to the depositary bank and may send for collection a draft on the depositary bank and obtain reimbursement. In such case, if the depositary bank has received provisional settlement for the item, it must reimburse the bank drawing the draft and any provisional credits for the item between banks shall become and remain final.]

Note: *Direct returns is recognized as an innovation that is not yet established bank practice, and therefore, Paragraph 2 has been bracketed. Some lawyers have doubts whether it should be included in legislation or left to development by agreement.*

(3) A depositary bank which is also the payor may charge-back the amount of an item to its customer's account or obtain refund in accordance with the section governing return of an item received by a payor bank for credit on its books (Section 4–301).

(4) The right to charge-back is not affected by

(a) prior use of the credit given for the item; or

(b) failure by any bank to exercise ordinary care with respect to the item but any bank so failing remains liable.

(5) A failure to charge-back or claim refund does not affect other rights of the bank against the customer or any other party.

(6) If credit is given in dollars as the equivalent of the value of an item payable in a foreign currency the dollar amount of any charge-back or refund shall be calculated on the basis of the buying sight rate for the foreign currency prevailing on the day when the person entitled to the charge-back or refund learns that it will not receive payment in ordinary course.

§4–213. Final Payment of Item by Payor Bank; When Provisional Debits and Credits Become Final; When Certain Credits Become Available for Withdrawal. (1) An item is finally paid by a payor bank when the bank has done any of the following, whichever happens first:

(a) paid the item in cash; or

(b) settled for the item without reserving a right to revoke the settlement and without having such right under statute, clearing house rule or agreement; or

(c) completed the process of posting the item to the indicated account of the drawer, maker or other person to be charged therewith; or

(d) made a provisional settlement for the item and failed to revoke the settlement in the time and manner permitted by statute, clearing house rule or agreement.

Upon a final payment under subparagraphs (b), (c) or (d) the payor bank shall be accountable for the amount of the item.

(2) If provisional settlement for an item between the presenting and payor banks is made through a clearing house or by debits or credits in an account between them, then to the extent that provisional debits or credits for the item are entered in accounts between the presenting and payor banks or between the presenting and successive prior collecting banks seriatim, they become final upon final payment of the item by the payor bank.

(3) If a collecting bank receives a settlement for an item which is or becomes final (subsection (3) of Section 4–211, subsection (2) of Section 4–213) the bank is accountable to its customer for the amount of the item and any provisional credit given for the item in an account with its customer becomes final.

(4) Subject to any right of the bank to apply the credit to an obligation of the customer, credit given by a bank for an item in an account with its customer becomes available for withdrawals as of right

(a) in any case where the bank has received a provisional settlement for the item,—when such settlement becomes final and the bank has had a reasonable time to learn that the settlement is final;

(b) in any case where the bank is both a depositary bank and a payor bank and the item is finally paid,—at the opening of the bank's second banking day following receipt of the item.

(5) A deposit of money in a bank is final when made but, subject to any right of the bank to apply the deposit to an obligation of the customer, the deposit becomes available for withdrawal as of right at the opening of the bank's next banking day following receipt of the deposit.

§4–214. Insolvency and Preference. (1) Any item in or coming into the possession of a payor or collecting bank which suspends payment and which item is not finally paid shall be returned by the receiver, trustee or agent in charge of the closed bank to the presenting bank or the closed bank's customer.

(2) If a payor bank finally pays an item and suspends payments without making a settlement for the item with its customer or the presenting bank which settlement is or becomes final, the owner of the item has a preferred claim against the payor bank.

(3) If a payor bank gives or a collecting bank gives or receives a provisional settlement for an item and thereafter suspends payments, the suspension does not prevent or interfere with the settlement becoming final if such finality occurs automatically upon the lapse of certain time or the happening of certain events (subsection (3) of Section 4–211, subsections (1) (d), (2) and (3) of Section 4–213).

(4) If a collecting bank receives from subsequent parties settlement for an item which settlement is or becomes final and suspends payments without making a settlement for the item with its customer which is or becomes final, the owner of the item has a preferred claim against such collecting bank.

Part 3

Collection of Items: Payor Banks

§4–301. Deferred Posting; Recovery of Payment by Return of Items; Time of Dishonor. (1) Where an authorized settlement for a demand item (other than a documentary draft) received by a payor bank otherwise than for immediate payment over the counter has been made before midnight of the banking day of receipt the payor bank may revoke the settlement and recover any payment if before it has made final payment (subsection (1) of Section 4–213) and before its midnight deadline it

(a) returns the item; or

(b) sends written notice of dishonor or non-payment if the item is held for protest or is otherwise unavailable for return.

(2) If a demand item is received by a payor bank for credit on its books it may return such item or send notice of dishonor and may revoke any credit given or recover the amount thereof withdrawn by its customer, if it acts within the time limit and in the manner specified in the preceding subsection.

(3) Unless previous notice of dishonor has been sent an item is dishonored at the time when for purposes of dishonor it is returned or notice sent in accordance with this section.

(4) An item is returned:

(a) as to an item received through a clearing house, when it is delivered to the presenting or last collecting bank or to the clearing house or is sent or delivered in accordance with its rules; or

(b) in all other cases, when it is sent or delivered to the bank's customer or transferor or pursuant to his instructions.

§4–302. Payor Bank's Responsibility for Late Return of Item. In the absence of a valid defense such as breach of a presentment warranty (subsection (1) of Section 4–207), settlement effected or the like, if an item is presented on and received by a payor bank the bank is accountable for the amount of

(a) a demand item other than a documentary draft whether properly payable or not if the bank, in any case where it is not also the depositary bank, retains the item beyond midnight of the banking day of receipt without settling for it or, regardless of whether it is also the depositary bank, does not pay or return the item or send notice of dishonor until after its midnight deadline; or

(b) any other properly payable item unless within the time allowed for acceptance or payment of that item the bank either accepts or pays the item or returns it and accompanying documents.

§4–303. When Items Subject to Notice, Stop-Order, Legal Process or Setoff; Order in Which Items May Be Charged or Certified. (1) Any knowledge, notice or stop-order received by, legal process served upon or setoff exercised by a payor bank, whether or not effective under other rules of law to terminate, suspend or modify the bank's right or duty to pay an item or to charge its customer's account for the item, comes too late to so terminate, suspend or modify such right or duty if the knowledge, notice, stop-order or legal process is received or served and a reasonable time for the bank to act thereon expires or the setoff is exercised after the bank has done any of the following:

(a) accepted or certified the item;

(b) paid the item in cash;

(c) settled for the item without reserving a right to revoke the settlement and without having such right under statute, clearing house rule or agreement;

(d) completed the process of posting the item to the indicated account of the drawer, maker or other person to be charged therewith or otherwise has evidenced by examination of such indicated account and by action its decision to pay the item; or

(e) become accountable for the amount of the item under subsection (1) (d) of Section 4–213 and Section 4–302 dealing with the payor bank's responsibility for late return of items.

(2) Subject to the provisions of subsection (1) items may be accepted, paid, certified or charged to the indicated account of its customer in any order convenient to the bank.

Part 4

Relationship Between Payor Bank and Its Customer

§4–401. When Bank May Charge Customer's Account. (1) As against its customer, a bank may charge against his account any item which is otherwise properly payable from that account even though the charge creates an overdraft.

(2) A bank which in good faith makes payment to a holder may charge the indicated account of its customer according to

(a) the original tenor of his altered item; or

(b) the tenor of his completed item, even though the bank knows the item has been completed unless the bank has notice that the completion was improper.

§4–402. Bank's Liability to Customer for Wrongful Dishonor. A payor bank is liable to its customer for damages proximately caused by the wrongful dishonor of an item. When the dishonor occurs through mistake liability is limited to actual damages proved. If so proximately caused and proved damages may include damages for an arrest or prosecution of the customer or other consequential damages. Whether any consequential damages are proximately caused by the wrongful dishonor is a question of fact to be determined in each case.

§4–403. Customer's Right to Stop Payment; Burden of Proof of Loss. (1) A customer may by order to his bank stop payment of any item payable for his account but the order must be received at such time and in such manner as to afford the bank a reasonable opportunity to act on it prior to any action by the bank with respect to the item described in Section 4–303.

(2) An oral order is binding upon the bank only for fourteen calendar days unless confirmed in writing within that period. A written order is effective for only six months unless renewed in writing.

(3) The burden of establishing the fact and amount of loss resulting from the payment of an item contrary to a binding stop payment order is on the customer.

§4–404. Bank Not Obligated to Pay Check More Than Six Months Old. A bank is under no obligation to a customer having a checking account to pay a check, other than a certified check, which is presented more than six months after its date, but it may charge its customer's account for a payment made thereafter in good faith.

§4–405. Death or Incompetence of Customer. (1) A payor or collecting bank's authority to accept, pay or collect an item or to account for proceeds of its collection if otherwise effective is not rendered ineffective by incompetence of a customer of either bank existing at the time the item is issued or its collection is undertaken if the bank does not know of an adjudication of incompetence. Neither death nor incompetence of a customer revokes such authority to accept, pay, collect or account until the bank knows of the fact of death or of an adjudication of incompetence and has reasonable opportunity to act on it.

(2) Even with knowledge a bank may for ten days after the date of death pay or certify checks drawn on or prior to that date unless ordered to stop payment by a person claiming an interest in the account.

§4–406. Customer's Duty to Discover and Report Unauthorized Signature or Alteration. (1) When a bank sends to its customer a statement of account accompanied by items paid in good faith in support of the debit entries or holds the statement and items pursuant to a request or instructions of its customer or otherwise in a reasonable manner makes the statement and items available to the customer, the customer must exercise reasonable care and promptness to examine the statement and items to discover his unauthorized signature or any alteration on an item and must notify the bank promptly after discovery thereof.

(2) If the bank establishes that the customer failed with respect to an item to comply with the duties imposed on the customer by subsection (1) the customer is precluded from asserting against the bank

(a) his unauthorized signature or any alteration on the item if the bank also establishes that it suffered a loss by reason of such failure; and

(b) an unauthorized signature or alteration by the same wrongdoer on any other item paid in good faith by the bank after the first item and statement was available to the customer for a reasonable period not exceeding fourteen calendar days and before the bank receives notification from the customer of any such unauthorized signature or alteration.

(3) The preclusion under subsection (2) does not apply if the customer establishes lack of ordinary care on the part of the bank in paying the item(s).

(4) Without regard to care or lack of care of either the customer or the bank a customer who does not within one year from the time the statement and items are made available to the customer (subsection (1)) discover and report his unauthorized signature or any alteration on the face or back of the item or does not within three years from that time discover and report any unauthorized indorsement is precluded from asserting against the bank such unauthorized signature or indorsement or such alteration.

(5) If under this section a payor bank has a valid defense against a claim of a customer upon or resulting from payment of an item and waives or fails upon request to assert the defense the bank may not assert against any collecting bank or other prior party presenting or transferring the item a claim based upon the unauthorized signature or alteration giving rise to the customer's claim.

§4–407. Payor Bank's Right to Subrogation on Improper Payment. If a payor bank has paid an item over the stop payment order of the drawer or maker or otherwise under circumstances giving a basis for objection by the drawer or maker, to prevent unjust enrichment and only to the extent necessary to prevent loss to the bank by reason of its payment of the item, the payor bank shall be subrogated to the rights

(a) of any holder in due course on the item against the drawer or maker; and

(b) of the payee or any other holder of the item against the drawer or maker either on the item or under the transaction out of which the item arose; and

(c) of the drawer or maker against the payee or any other holder of the item with respect to the transaction out of which the item arose.

Part 5

Collection of Documentary Drafts

§4–501. Handling of Documentary Drafts; Duty to Send for Presentment and to Notify Customer of Dishonor. A bank which takes a documentary draft for collection must present or send the draft and accompanying documents for presentment and upon learning that the draft has not been paid or accepted in due course must seasonably notify its customer of such fact even though it may have discounted or bought the draft or extended credit available for withdrawal as of right.

§4–502. Presentment of "On Arrival" Drafts. When a draft or the relevant instructions require presentment "on arrival", "when goods arrive" or the like, the collecting bank need not present until in its judgment a reasonable time for arrival of the goods has expired. Refusal to pay or accept because the goods have not arrived is not dishonor; the bank must notify its transferor of such refusal but need not present the draft again until it is instructed to do so or learns of the arrival of the goods.

§4–503. Responsibility of Presenting Bank for Documents and Goods; Report of Reasons for Dishonor; Referee in Case of Need. Unless otherwise instructed and except as provided in Article 5 a bank presenting a documentary draft

(a) must deliver the documents to the drawee on acceptance of the draft if it is payable more than three days after presentment; otherwise, only on payment; and

(b) upon dishonor, either in the case of presentment for acceptance or presentment for payment, may seek and follow instructions from any referee in case of need designated in the draft or if the presenting bank does not choose to utilize his services it must use diligence and good faith to ascertain the reason for dishonor, must notify its transferor of the dishonor and of the results of its effort to ascertain the reasons therefor and must request instructions.

But the presenting bank is under no obligation with respect to goods represented by the documents except to follow any reasonable instructions seasonably received; it has a right to reimbursement for any expense incurred in following instructions and to prepayment of or indemnity for such expenses.

§4–504. Privilege of Presenting Bank to Deal With Goods; Security Interest for Expenses. (1) A presenting bank which, following the dishonor of a documentary draft, has seasonably requested instructions but does not receive them within a reasonable time may store, sell, or otherwise deal with the goods in any reasonable manner.

(2) For its reasonable expenses incurred by action under subsection (1) the presenting bank has a lien upon the goods or their proceeds, which may be foreclosed in the same manner as an unpaid seller's lien.

ARTICLE 5: LETTERS OF CREDIT

§5–101. Short Title. This Article shall be known and may be cited as Uniform Commercial Code—Letters of Credit.

§5–102. Scope. (1) This Article applies

(a) to a credit issued by a bank if the credit requires a documentary draft or a documentary demand for payment; and

(b) to a credit issued by a person other than a bank if the credit requires that the draft or demand for payment be accompanied by a document of title; and

(c) to a credit issued by a bank or other person if the credit is not within subparagraphs (a) or (b) but conspicuously states that it is a letter of credit or is conspicuously so entitled.

(2) Unless the engagement meets the requirements of subsection (1), this Article does not apply to engagements to make advances or to honor drafts or demands for payment, to authorities to pay or purchase, to guarantees or to general agreements.

(3) This Article deals with some but not all of the rules and concepts of letters of credit as such rules or concepts have developed prior to this Act or may hereafter develop. The fact that this Article states a rule does not by itself require, imply or negate application of the same or a converse rule to a situation not provided for or to a person not specified by this Article.

§5–103. Definitions. (1) In this Article unless the context otherwise requires

(a) "Credit" or "letter of credit" means an engagement by a bank or other person made at the request of a customer and of a kind within the scope of this Article (Section 5–102) that the issuer will honor drafts or other demands for payment upon compliance with the conditions specified in the credit. A credit may be either revocable or irrevocable. The engagement may be either an agreement to honor or a statement that the bank or other person is authorized to honor.

(b) A "documentary draft" or a "documentary demand for payment" is one honor of which is conditioned upon the presentation of a document or documents. "Document" means any paper including document of title, security, invoice, certificate, notice of default and the like.

(c) An "issuer" is a bank or other person issuing a credit.

(d) A "beneficiary" of a credit is a person who is entitled under its terms to draw or demand payment.

(e) An "advising bank" is a bank which gives notification of the issuance of a credit by another bank.

(f) A "confirming bank" is a bank which engages either that it will itself honor a credit already issued by another bank or that such a credit will be honored by the issuer or a third bank.

(g) A "customer" is a buyer or other person who causes an issuer to issue a credit. The term also includes a bank which procures issuance or confirmation on behalf of that bank's customer.

(2) Other definitions applying to this Article and the sections in which they appear are:

"Notation of Credit". Section 5–108.

"Presenter". Section 5–112(3).

(3) Definitions in other Articles applying to this Article and the sections in which they appear are:

"Accept" or "Acceptance". Section 3–410.

"Contract for sale". Section 2–106.

"Draft". Section 3–104.

"Holder in due course". Section 3–302.

"Midnight deadline". Section 4–104.

"Security". Section 8–102.

(4) In addition, Article 1 contains general definitions and principles of construction and interpretation applicable throughout this Article.

§5–104. Formal Requirements; Signing. (1) Except as otherwise required in subsection (1) (c) of Section 5–102 on scope, no particular form of phrasing is required for a credit. A credit must be in writing and signed by the issuer and a confirmation must be in writing and signed by the confirming bank. A modification of the terms of a credit or confirmation must be signed by the issuer or confirming bank.

(2) A telegram may be a sufficient signed writing if it identifies its sender by an authorized authentication. The authentication may be in code and the authorized naming of the issuer in an advice of credit is a sufficient signing.

§5–105. Consideration. No consideration is necessary to establish a credit or to enlarge or otherwise modify its terms.

§5–106. Time and Effect of Establishment of Credit. (1) Unless otherwise agreed a credit is established

(a) as regards the customer as soon as a letter of credit is sent to him or the letter of credit or an authorized written advice of its issuance is sent to the beneficiary; and

(b) as regards the beneficiary when he receives a letter of credit or an authorized written advice of its issuance.

(2) Unless otherwise agreed once an irrevocable credit is established as regards the customer it can be modified or revoked only with the consent of the customer and once it is established as regards the beneficiary it can be modified or revoked only with his consent.

(3) Unless otherwise agreed after a revocable credit is established it may be modified or revoked by the issuer without notice to or consent from the customer or beneficiary.

(4) Notwithstanding any modification or revocation of a revocable credit any person authorized to honor or negotiate under the terms of the original credit is entitled to reimbursement for or honor of any draft or demand for payment duly honored or negotiated before receipt of notice of the modification or revocation and the issuer in turn is entitled to reimbursement from its customer.

§5–107. Advice of Credit; Confirmation; Error in Statement of Terms. (1) Unless otherwise specified an advising bank by advising a credit issued by another bank does not assume any obligation to honor drafts drawn or demands for payment made under the credit but it does assume obligation for the accuracy of its own statement.

(2) A confirming bank by confirming a credit becomes directly obligated on the credit to the extent of its confirmation as though it were its issuer and acquires the rights of an issuer.

(3) Even though an advising bank incorrectly advises the terms of a credit it has been authorized to advise the credit is established as against the issuer to the extent of its original terms.

(4) Unless otherwise specified the customer bears as against the issuer all risks of transmission and reasonable translation or interpretation of any message relating to a credit.

§5–108. "Notation Credit"; Exhaustion of Credit. (1) A credit which specifies that any person purchasing or paying drafts drawn or demands for payment made under it must note the amount of the draft or demand on the letter or advice of credit is a "notation of credit".

(2) Under a notation credit

(a) a person paying the beneficiary or purchasing a draft or demand for payment from him acquires a right to honor only if the appropriate notation is made and by transferring or forwarding for honor the documents under the credit such a person warrants to the issuer that the notation has been made; and

(b) unless the credit or a signed statement that an appropriate notation has been made accompanies the draft or demand for payment the issuer may delay honor until evidence of notation has been procured which is satisfactory to it but its obligation and that of its customer continue for a reasonable time not exceeding thirty days to obtain such evidence.

(3) If the credit is not a notation credit

(a) the issuer may honor complying drafts or demands for payment presented to it in the order in which they are presented and is discharged pro tanto by honor of any such draft or demand;

(b) as between competing good faith purchasers of complying drafts or demands the person first purchasing has priority over a subsequent purchaser even though the later purchased draft or demand has been first honored.

§5–109. Issuer's Obligation to Its Customer. (1) An issuer's obligation to its customer includes good faith and observance of any general banking usage but unless otherwise agreed does not include liability or responsibility

(a) for performance of the underlying contract for sale or other transaction between the customer and the beneficiary; or

(b) for any act or omission of any person other than itself or its own branch or for loss or destruction of a draft, demand or document in transit or in the possession of others; or

(c) based on knowledge or lack of knowledge of any usage of any particular trade.

(2) An issuer must examine documents with care so as to ascertain that on their face they appear to comply with the terms of the credit but unless otherwise agreed assumes no liability or responsibility for the genuineness, falsification or effect of any document which appears on such examination to be regular on its face.

(3) A non-bank issuer is not bound by any banking usage of which it has no knowledge.

§5–110. Availability of Credit in Portions; Presenter's Reservation of Lien or Claim. (1) Unless otherwise specified a credit may be used in portions in the discretion of the beneficiary.

(2) Unless otherwise specified a person by presenting a documentary draft or demand for payment under a credit relinquishes upon its honor all claims to the documents and a person by transferring such draft or demand or causing such presentment authorizes such relinquishment. An explicit reservation of claim makes the draft or demand non-complying.

§5–111. Warranties on Transfer and Presentment. (1) Unless otherwise agreed the beneficiary by transferring or presenting a documentary draft or demand for payment warrants to all interested parties that the necessary conditions of the credit have been complied with. This is in addition to any warranties arising under Articles 3, 4, 7 and 8.

(2) Unless otherwise agreed a negotiating, advising, confirming, collecting or issuing bank presenting or transferring a draft or demand for payment under a credit warrants only the matters warranted by a collecting bank under Article 4 and any such bank transferring a document warrants only the matters warranted by an intermediary under Articles 7 and 8.

§5–112. Time Allowed for Honor or Rejection; Withholding Honor or Rejection by Consent; "Presenter". (1) A bank to which a documentary draft or demand for payment is presented under a credit may without dishonor of the draft, demand, or credit

(a) defer honor until the close of the third banking day following receipt of the documents; and

(b) further defer honor if the presenter has expressly or impliedly consented thereto.

Failure to honor within the time here specified constitutes dishonor of the draft or demand and of the credit [except as otherwise provided in subsection (4) of Section 5–114 on conditional payment].

Note: *The bracketed language in the last sentence of subsection (1) should be included only if the optional provisions of Sections 5–114(4) and (5) are included.*

(2) Upon dishonor the bank may unless otherwise instructed fulfill its duty to return the draft or demand and the documents by holding them at the disposal of the presenter and sending him an advice to that effect.

(3) "Presenter" means any person presenting a draft or demand for payment for honor under a credit even though that person is a confirming bank or other correspondent which is acting under an issuer's authorization.

§5–113. Indemnities. (1) A bank seeking to obtain (whether for itself or another) honor, negotiation or reimbursement under a credit may give an indemnity to induce such honor, negotiation or reimbursement.

(2) An indemnity agreement inducing honor, negotiation or reimbursement

(a) unless otherwise explicitly agreed applies to defects in the documents but not in the goods; and

(b) unless a longer time is explicitly agreed expires at the end of ten business days following receipt of the documents by the ultimate customer unless notice of objection is sent before such expiration date. The ultimate customer may send notice of objection to the person from whom he received the documents and any bank receiving such notice is under a duty to send notice to its transferor before its midnight deadline.

§5–114. Issuer's Duty and Privilege to Honor; Right to Reimbursement. (1) An issuer must honor a draft or demand for payment which complies with the terms of the relevant credit regardless of whether the goods or documents conform to the underlying contract for sale or other contract between the customer and the beneficiary. The issuer is not excused from honor of such a draft or demand by reason of an additional general term that all documents must be satisfactory to the issuer, but an issuer may require that specified documents must be satisfactory to it.

(2) Unless otherwise agreed when documents appear on their face to comply with the terms of a credit but a required document does not in fact conform to the warranties made on negotiation or transfer of a document of title (Section 7–507) or of a security (Section 8–306) or is forged or fraudulent or there is fraud in the transaction

(a) the issuer must honor the draft or demand for payment if honor is demanded by a negotiating bank or other holder of the draft or demand which has taken the draft or demand under the credit and under circumstances which would make it a holder in due course (Section 3–302) and in an appropriate case would make it a person to whom a document of title has been duly negotiated (Section 7–502) or a bona fide purchaser of a security (Section 8–302); and

(b) in all other cases as against its customer, an issuer acting in good faith may honor the draft or demand for payment despite notification from the customer of fraud, forgery or other defect not apparent on the face of the documents but a court of appropriate jurisdiction may enjoin such honor.

(3) Unless otherwise agreed an issuer which has duly honored a draft or demand for payment is entitled to immediate reimbursement of any payment made under the credit and to be put in effectively available funds not later than the day before maturity of any acceptance made under the credit.

[(4) When a credit provides for payment by the issuer on receipt of notice that the required documents are in the possession of a correspondent or other agent of the issuer

(a) any payment made on receipt of such notice is conditional; and

(b) the issuer may reject documents which do not comply with the credit if it does so within three banking days following its receipt of the documents; and

(c) in the event of such rejection, the issuer is entitled by charge back or otherwise to return of the payment made.]

[(5) In the case covered by subsection (4) failure to reject documents within the time specified in sub-paragraph (b) constitutes acceptance of the documents and makes the payment final in favor of the beneficiary.]

Note: *Subsections (4) and (5) are bracketed as optional. If they are included the bracketed language in the last sentence of Section 5–112(1) should also be included.*

§5–115. Remedy for Improper Dishonor or Anticipatory Repudiation. (1) When an issuer wrongfully dishonors a draft or demand for payment presented under a credit the person entitled to honor has with respect to any documents the rights of a person in the position of a seller (Section 2–707) and may recover from the issuer the face amount of the draft or demand together with incidental damages under Section 2–710 on seller's incidental damages and interest but less any amount realized by resale or other use or disposition of the subject matter of the transaction. In the event no resale or other utilization is made the documents, goods or other subject matter involved in the transaction must be turned over to the issuer on payment of judgment.

(2) When an issuer wrongfully cancels or otherwise repudiates a credit before presentment of a draft or demand for payment drawn under it the beneficiary has the rights of a seller after anticipatory repudiation by the buyer under Section 2–610 if he learns of the repudiation in time reasonably to avoid procurement of the required documents. Otherwise the beneficiary has an immediate right of action for wrongful dishonor.

§5–116. Transfer and Assignment. (1) The right to draw under a credit can be transferred or assigned only when the credit is expressly designated as transferable or assignable.

(2) Even though the credit specifically states that it is non-transferable or non-assignable the beneficiary may before performance of the conditions of the credit assign his right to proceeds. Such an assignment is an assignment of a contract right under Article 9 on Secured Transactions and is governed by that Article except that

(a) the assignment is ineffective until the letter of credit or advice of credit is delivered to the assignee which delivery constitutes perfection of the security interest under Article 9; and

(b) the issuer may honor drafts or demands for payment drawn under the credit until it receives a notification of the assignment signed by the beneficiary which reasonably identifies the credit involved in the assignment and contains a request to pay the assignee; and

(c) after what reasonably appears to be such a notification has been received the issuer may without dishonor refuse to accept or pay even to a person otherwise entitled to honor until the letter of credit or advice of credit is exhibited to the issuer.

(3) Except where the beneficiary has effectively assigned his right to draw or his right to proceeds, nothing in this section limits his right to transfer or negotiate drafts or demands drawn under the credit.

§5–117. Insolvency of Bank Holding Funds for Documentary Credit. (1) Where an issuer or an advising or confirming bank or a bank which has for a customer procured issuance of a credit by another bank becomes insolvent before final payment under the credit and the credit is one to which this Article is made applicable by paragraphs (a) or (b) of Section 5–102(1) on scope, the receipt or allocation of funds or collateral to secure or meet obligations under the credit shall have the following results:

(a) to the extent of any funds or collateral turned over after or before the insolvency as indemnity against or specifically for the purpose of payment of drafts or demands for payment drawn under the designated credit, the drafts or demands are entitled to payment in preference over depositors or other general creditors of the issuer or bank; and

(b) on expiration of the credit or surrender of the beneficiary's rights under it unused any person who has given such funds or collateral is similarly entitled to return thereof; and

(c) a change to a general or current account with a bank if specifically consented to for the purpose of indemnity against or payment of drafts or demands for payment drawn under the designated credit falls under the same rules as if the funds had been drawn out in cash and then turned over with specific instructions.

(2) After honor or reimbursement under this section the customer or other person for whose account the insolvent bank has acted is entitled to receive the documents involved.

ARTICLE 6: BULK TRANSFERS

§6–101. Short Title. This Article shall be known and may be cited as Uniform Commercial Code—Bulk Transfers.

§6–102. "Bulk Transfers"; Transfers of Equipment; Enterprises Subject to This Article; Bulk Transfers Subject to This Article. (1) A "bulk transfer" is any transfer in bulk and not in the ordinary course of the transferor's business of a major part of the materials, supplies, merchandise or other inventory (Section 9–109) of an enterprise subject to this Article.

(2) A transfer of a substantial part of the equipment (Section 9–109) of such an enterprise is a bulk transfer if it is made in connection with a bulk transfer of inventory, but not otherwise.

(3) The enterprises subject to this Article are all those whose principal business is the sale of merchandise from stock, including those who manufacture what they sell.

(4) Except as limited by the following section all bulk transfers of goods located within this state are subject to this Article.

§6–103. Transfers Excepted From This Article. The following transfers are not subject to this Article:

(1) Those made to give security for the performance of an obligation;

(2) General assignments for the benefit of all the creditors of the transferor, and subsequent transfers by the assignee thereunder;

(3) Transfers in settlement or realization of a lien or other security interest;

(4) Sales by executors, administrators, receivers, trustees in bankruptcy, or any public officer under judicial process;

(5) Sales made in the course of judicial or administrative proceedings for the dissolution or reorganization of a corporation and of which notice is sent to the creditors of the corporation pursuant to order of the court or administrative agency;

(6) Transfers to a person maintaining a known place of business in this State who becomes bound to pay the debts of the transferor in full and gives public notice of that fact, and who is solvent after becoming so bound;

(7) A transfer to a new business enterprise organized to take over and continue the business, if public notice of the transaction is given and the new enterprise assumes the debts of the transferor and he receives nothing from the transaction except an interest in the new enterprise junior to the claims of creditors;

(8) Transfers of property which is exempt from execution. Public notice under subsection (6) or subsection (7) may be given by publishing once a week for two consecutive weeks in a newspaper of general circulation where the transferor had its principal place of business in this state an advertisement including the names and addresses of the transferor and transferee and the effective date of the transfer.

§6–104. Schedule of Property, List of Creditors. (1) Except as provided with respect to auction sales (Section 6–108), a bulk transfer subject to this Article is ineffective against any creditor of the transferor unless:

(a) The transferee requires the transferor to furnish a list of his existing creditors prepared as stated in this section; and

(b) The parties prepare a schedule of the property transferred sufficient to identify it; and

(c) The transferee preserves the list and schedule for six months next following the transfer and permits inspection of either or both and copying therefrom at all reasonable hours by any creditor of the transferor, or files the list and schedule in (a public office to be here identified).

(2) The list of creditors must be signed and sworn to or affirmed by the transferor or his agent. It must contain the names and business addresses of all creditors of the transferor, with the amounts when known, and also the names of all persons who are known to the transferor to assert claims against him even though such claims are disputed. If the transferor is the obligor of an outstanding issue of bonds, debentures or the like as to which there is an indenture trustee, the list of creditors need include only the name and address of the indenture trustee and the aggregate outstanding principal amount of the issue.

(3) Responsibility for the completeness and accuracy of the list of creditors rests on the transferor, and the transfer is not rendered ineffective by errors or omissions therein unless the transferee is shown to have had knowledge.

§6–105. Notice to Creditors. In addition to the requirements of the preceding section, any bulk transfer subject to this Article except one made by auction sale (Section 6–108) is ineffective against any creditor of the transferor unless at least ten days before he takes possession of the goods or pays for them, whichever happens first, the transferee gives notice of the transfer in the manner and to the persons hereafter provided (Section 6–107).

[**§6–106. Application of the Proceeds.** In addition to the requirements of the two preceding sections:

(1) Upon every bulk transfer subject to this Article for which new consideration becomes payable except those made by sale at auction it is the duty of the transferee to assure that such consideration is applied so far as necessary to pay those debts of the transferor which are either shown on the list furnished by the transferor (Section 6–104) or filed in writing in the place stated in the notice (Section 6–107) within thirty days after the mailing of such notice. This duty of the transferee runs to all the holders of such debts, and may be enforced by any of them for the benefit of all.

(2) If any of said debts are in dispute the necessary sum may be withheld from distribution until the dispute is settled or adjudicated.

(3) If the consideration payable is not enough to pay all of the said debts in full distribution shall be made pro rata.]

Note: *This section is bracketed to indicate division of opinion as to whether or not it is a wise provision, and to suggest that this is a point on which State enactments may differ without serious damage to the principle of uniformity.*

In any State where this section is omitted, the following parts of sections, also bracketed in the text, should be omitted, namely:

Section 6–107(2)(e).
6–108(3)(c).
6–109(2).

In any State where this section is enacted, these other provisions should be also.

Optional Subsection (4)

[(4) The transferee may within ten days after he takes possession of the goods pay the consideration into the (specify court) in the county where the transferor had its principal place of business in this state and thereafter may discharge his duty under this section by giving notice by registered or certified mail to all the persons to whom the duty runs that the consideration has been paid into that court and that they should file their claims there. On motion of any interested party, the court may order the distribution of the consideration to the persons entitled to it.]

Note: *Optional subsection (4) is recommended for those states which do not have a general statute providing for payment of money into court.*

§6–107. **The Notice.** (1) The notice to creditors (Section 6–105) shall state:

(a) that a bulk transfer is about to be made; and

(b) the names and business addresses of the transferor and transferee, and all other business names and addresses used by the transferor within three years last past so far as known to the transferee; and

(c) whether or not all the debts of the transferor are to be paid in full as they fall due as a result of the transaction, and if so, the address to which creditors should send their bills.

(2) If the debts of the transferor are not to be paid in full as they fall due or if the transferee is in doubt on that point then the notice shall state further:

(a) the location and general description of the property to be transferred and the estimated total of the transferor's debts;

(b) the address where the schedule of property and list of creditors (Section 6–104) may be inspected;

(c) whether the transfer is to pay existing debts and if so the amount of such debts and to whom owing;

(d) whether the transfer is for new consideration and if so the amount of such consideration and the time and place of payment; [and]

[(e) if for new consideration the time and place where creditors of the transferor are to file their claims.]

(3) The notice in any case shall be delivered personally or sent by registered or certified mail to all the persons shown on the list of creditors furnished by the transferor (Section 6–104) and to all other persons who are known to the transferee to hold or assert claims against the transferor.

Note: *The words in brackets are optional.*

§6–108. **Auction Sales; "Auctioneer".** (1) A bulk transfer is subject to this Article even though it is by sale at auction, but only in the manner and with the results stated in this section.

(2) The transferor shall furnish a list of his creditors and assist in the preparation of a schedule of the property to be sold, both prepared as before stated (Section 6–104).

(3) The person or persons other than the transferor who direct, control or are responsible for the auction are collectively called the "auctioneer". The auctioneer shall:

(a) receive and retain the list of creditors and prepare and retain the schedule of property for the period stated in this Article (Section 6–104);

(b) give notice of the auction personally or by registered or certified mail at least ten days before it occurs to all persons shown on the list of creditors and to all other persons who are known to him to hold or assert claims against the transferor; [and]

[(c) assure that the net proceeds of the auction are applied as provided in this Article (Section 6–106).]

(4) Failure of the auctioneer to perform any of these duties does not affect the validity of the sale or the title of the purchasers, but if the auctioneer knows that the auction constitutes a bulk transfer such failure renders the auctioneer liable to the creditors of the transferor as a class for the sums owing to them from the transferor up to but not exceeding the net proceeds of the

auction. If the auctioneer consists of several persons their liability is joint and several.

Note: *The words in brackets are optional.*

§6–109. What Creditors Protected; [Credit for Payment to Particular Creditors]. (1) The creditors of the transferor mentioned in this Article are those holding claims based on transactions or events occurring before the bulk transfer, but creditors who become such after notice to creditors is given (Sections 6–105 and 6–107) are not entitled to notice.

[(2) Against the aggregate obligation imposed by the provisions of this Article concerning the application of the proceeds (Section 6–106 and subsection (3) (c) of 6–108) the transferee or auctioneer is entitled to credit for sums paid to particular creditors of the transferor, not exceeding the sums believed in good faith at the time of the payment to be properly payable to such creditors.]

§6–110. Subsequent Transfers. When the title of a transferee to property is subject to a defect by reason of his non-compliance with requirements of this Article, then:

(1) a purchaser of any of such property from such transferee who pays no value or who takes with notice of such non-compliance takes subject to such defect, but

(2) a purchaser for value in good faith and without such notice takes free of such defect.

§6–111. Limitation of Actions and Levies. No action under this Article shall be brought nor levy made more than six months after the date on which the transferee took possession of the goods unless the transfer has been concealed. If the transfer has been concealed, actions may be brought or levies made within six months after its discovery.

ARTICLE 7: WAREHOUSE RECEIPTS, BILLS OF LADING AND OTHER DOCUMENTS OF TITLE

Part 1

General

§7–101. Short Title. This Article shall be known and may be cited as Uniform Commercial Code—Documents of Title.

§7–102. Definitions and Index of Definitions. (1) In this Article, unless the context otherwise requires:

(a) "Bailee" means the person who by a warehouse receipt, bill of lading or other document of title acknowledges possession of goods and contracts to deliver them.

(b) "Consignee" means the person named in a bill to whom or to whose order the bill promises delivery.

(c) "Consignor" means the person named in a bill as the person from whom the goods have been received for shipment.

(d) "Delivery order" means a written order to deliver goods directed to a warehouseman, carrier or other person who in the ordinary course of business issues warehouse receipts or bills of lading.

(e) "Document" means document of title as defined in the general definitions in Article 1 (Section 1–201).

(f) "Goods" means all things which are treated as movable for the purposes of a contract of storage or transportation.

(g) "Issuer" means a bailee who issues a document except that in relation to an unaccepted delivery order it means the person who orders the possessor of goods to deliver. Issuer includes any person for whom an agent or employee purports to act in issuing a document if the agent or employee has real or apparent authority to issue documents, notwithstanding that the issuer received no goods or that the goods were misdescribed or that in any other respect the agent or employee violated his instructions.

(h) "Warehouseman" is a person engaged in the business of storing goods for hire.

(2) Other definitions applying to this Article or to specified Parts thereof, and the sections in which they appear are:

"Duly negotiate". Section 7–501.

"Person entitled under the document". Section 7–403(4).

(3) Definitions in other Articles applying to this Article and the sections in which they appear are:

"Contract for sale". Section 2–106.

"Overseas". Section 2–323.

"Receipt" of goods. Section 2–103.

(4) In addition Article 1 contains general definitions and principles of construction and interpretation applicable throughout this Article.

§7–103. Relation of Article to Treaty, Statute, Tariff, Classification or Regulation. To the extent that any treaty or statute of the United States, regulatory statute of this State or tariff, classification or regulation filed or issued pursuant thereto is applicable, the provisions of this Article are subject thereto.

§7–104. Negotiable and Non-Negotiable Warehouse Receipt, Bill of Lading or Other Document of Title. (1) A warehouse receipt, bill of lading or other document of title is negotiable

(a) if by its terms the goods are to be delivered to bearer or to the order of a named person; or

(b) where recognized in overseas trade, if it runs to a named person or assigns.

(2) Any other document is non-negotiable. A bill of lading in which it is stated that the goods are consigned to a named person is not made negotiable by a provision that the goods are to be delivered only against a written order signed by the same or another named person.

§7–105. Construction Against Negative Implication. The omission from either Part 2 or Part 3 of this Article of a provision corresponding to a provision made in the other Part does not imply that a corresponding rule of law is not applicable.

Part 2

Warehouse Receipts: Special Provisions

§7–201. Who May Issue a Warehouse Receipt; Storage Under Government Bond. (1) A warehouse receipt may be issued by any warehouseman.

(2) Where goods including distilled spirits and agricultural commodities are stored under a statute requiring a bond against withdrawal or a license for the issuance of receipts in the nature of warehouse receipts, a receipt issued for the goods has like effect as a warehouse receipt even though issued by a person who is the owner of the goods and is not a warehouseman.

§7–202. Form of Warehouse Receipt; Essential Terms; Optional Terms. (1) A warehouse receipt need not be in any particular form.

(2) Unless a warehouse receipt embodies within its written or printed terms each of the following, the warehouseman is liable for damages caused by the omission to a person injured thereby:

(a) the location of the warehouse where the goods are stored;

(b) the date of issue of the receipt;

(c) the consecutive number of the receipt;

(d) a statement whether the goods received will be delivered to the bearer, to a specified person, or to a specified person or his order;

(e) the rate of storage and handling charges, except that where goods are stored under a field warehousing arrangement a statement of that fact is sufficient on a non-negotiable receipt;

(f) a description of the goods or of the packages containing them;

(g) the signature of the warehouseman, which may be made by his authorized agent;

(h) if the receipt is issued for goods of which the warehouseman is owner, either solely or jointly or in common with others, the fact of such ownership; and

(i) a statement of the amount of advances made and of liabilities incurred for which the warehouseman claims a lien or security interest (Section 7–209). If the precise amount of such advances made or of such liabilities incurred is, at the time of the issue of the receipt, unknown to the warehouseman or to his agent who issues it, a statement of the fact that advances have been made or liabilities incurred and the purpose thereof is sufficient.

(3) A warehouseman may insert in his receipt any other terms which are not contrary to the provisions of this Act and do not impair his obligation of delivery (Section 7–403) or his duty of care (Section 7–204). Any contrary provisions shall be ineffective.

§7–203. Liability for Non-Receipt or Misdescription. A party to or purchaser for value in good faith of a document of title other than a bill of lading relying in either case upon the description therein of the goods may recover from the issuer damages caused by the non-receipt or misdescription of the goods, except to the extent that the document conspicuously indicates that the issuer does not know whether any part or all of the goods in fact were received or conform to the description, as where the description is in terms of marks or labels or kind, quantity or condition, or the receipt or description is qualified by "contents, condition and quality unknown", "said to contain" or the like, if such indication be true, or the party or purchaser otherwise has notice.

§7–204. Duty of Care; Contractual Limitation of Warehouseman's Liability. (1) A warehouseman is liable for damages for loss of or injury to the goods caused by his failure to exercise such care in regard to them as a reasonably careful man would exercise under like circumstances but unless otherwise agreed he is not liable for damages which could not have been avoided by the exercise of such care.

(2) Damages may be limited by a term in the warehouse receipt or storage agreement limiting the amount of liability in case of loss or damage, and setting forth a specific liability per article or item, or value per unit of weight,

beyond which the warehouseman shall not be liable; provided, however, that such liability may on written request of the bailor at the time of signing such storage agreement or within a reasonable time after receipt of the warehouse receipt be increased on part or all of the goods thereunder, in which event increased rates may be charged based on such increased valuation, but that no such increase shall be permitted contrary to a lawful limitation of liability contained in the warehouseman's tariff, if any. No such limitation is effective with respect to the warehouseman's liability for conversion to his own use.

(3) Reasonable provisions as to the time and manner of presenting claims and instituting actions based on the bailment may be included in the warehouse receipt or tariff.

(4) This section does not impair or repeal . . .

Note: *Insert in subsection (4) a reference to any statute which imposes a higher responsibility upon the warehouseman or invalidates contractual limitations which would be permissible under this Article.*

§7–205. Title Under Warehouse Receipt Defeated in Certain Cases. A buyer in the ordinary course of business of fungible goods sold and delivered by a warehouseman who is also in the business of buying and selling such goods takes free of any claim under a warehouse receipt even though it has been duly negotiated.

§7–206. Termination of Storage at Warehouseman's Option. (1) A warehouseman may on notifying the person on whose account the goods are held and any other person known to claim an interest in the goods require payment of any charges and removal of the goods from the warehouse at the termination of the period of storage fixed by the document, or, if no period is fixed, within a stated period not less than thirty days after the notification. If the goods are not removed before the date specified in the notification, the warehouseman may sell them in accordance with the provisions of the section on enforcement of a warehouseman's lien (Section 7–210).

(2) If a warehouseman in good faith believes that the goods are about to deteriorate or decline in value to less than the amount of his lien within the time prescribed in subsection (1) for notification, advertisement and sale, the warehouseman may specify in the notification any reasonable shorter time for removal of the goods and in case the goods are not removed, may sell them at public sale held not less than one week after a single advertisement or posting.

(3) If as a result of a quality or condition of the goods of which the warehouseman had no notice at the time of deposit the goods are a hazard to other property or to the warehouse or to persons, the warehouseman may sell the goods at public or private sale without advertisement on reasonable notification to all persons known to claim an interest in the goods. If the warehouseman after a reasonable effort is unable to sell the goods he may dispose of them in any lawful manner and shall incur no liability by reason of such disposition.

(4) The warehouseman must deliver the goods to any person entitled to them under this Article upon due demand made at any time prior to sale or other disposition under this section.

(5) The warehouseman may satisfy his lien from the proceeds of any sale or disposition under this section but must hold the balance for delivery on the demand of any person to whom he would have been bound to deliver the goods.

§7–207. Goods Must Be Kept Separate; Fungible Goods. (1) Unless the warehouse receipt otherwise provides, a warehouseman must keep separate the goods covered by each receipt so as to permit at all times identification and delivery of those goods except that different lots of fungible goods may be commingled.

(2) Fungible goods so commingled are owned in common by the persons

entitled thereto and the warehouseman is severally liable to each owner for that owner's share. Where because of overissue a mass of fungible goods is insufficient to meet all the receipts which the warehouseman has issued against it, the persons entitled include all holders to whom overissued receipts have been duly negotiated.

§7–208. Altered Warehouse Receipts. Where a blank in a negotiable warehouse receipt has been filled in without authority, a purchaser for value and without notice of the want of authority may treat the insertion as authorized. Any other unauthorized alteration leaves any receipt enforceable against the issuer according to its original tenor.

§7–209. Lien of Warehouseman. (1) A warehouseman has a lien against the bailor on the goods covered by a warehouse receipt or on the proceeds thereof in his possession for charges for storage or transportation (including demurrage and terminal charges), insurance, labor, or charges present or future in relation to the goods, and for expenses necessary for preservation of the goods or reasonably incurred in their sale pursuant to law. If the person on whose account the goods are held is liable for like charges or expenses in relation to other goods whenever deposited and it is stated in the receipt that a lien is claimed for charges and expenses in relation to other goods, the warehouseman also has a lien against him for such charges and expenses whether or not the other goods have been delivered by the warehouseman. But against a person to whom a negotiable warehouse receipt is duly negotiated a warehouseman's lien is limited to charges in an amount or at a rate specified on the receipt or if no charges are so specified then to a reasonable charge for storage of the goods covered by the receipt subsequent to the date of the receipt.

(2) The warehouseman may also reserve a security interest against the bailor for a maximum amount specified on the receipt for charges other than those specified in subsection (1), such as for money advanced and interest. Such a security interest is governed by the Article on Secured Transactions (Article 9).

(3) A warehouseman's lien for charges and expenses under subsection (1) or a security interest under subsection (2) is also effective against any person who so entrusted the bailor with possession of the goods that a pledge of them by him to a good faith purchaser for value would have been valid but is not effective against a person as to whom the document confers no right in the goods covered by it under Section 7–503.

(4) A warehouseman loses his lien on any goods which he voluntarily delivers or which he unjustifiably refuses to deliver.

§7–210. Enforcement of Warehouseman's Lien. (1) Except as provided in subsection (2), a warehouseman's lien may be enforced by public or private sale of the goods in bloc or in parcels, at any time or place and on any terms which are commercially reasonable, after notifying all persons known to claim an interest in the goods. Such notification must include a statement of the amount due, the nature of the proposed sale and the time and place of any public sale. The fact that a better price could have been obtained by a sale at a different time or in a different method from that selected by the warehouseman is not of itself sufficient to establish that the sale was not made in a commercially reasonable manner. If the warehouseman either sells the goods in the usual manner in any recognized market therefor, or if he sells at the price current in such market at the time of his sale, or if he has otherwise sold in conformity with commercially reasonable practices among dealers in the type of goods sold, he has sold in a commercially reasonable manner. A sale of more goods than apparently necessary to be offered to insure satisfaction of the obligation is not commercially reasonable except in cases covered by the preceding sentence.

(2) A warehouseman's lien on goods other than goods stored by a merchant in the course of his business may be enforced only as follows:

(a) All persons known to claim an interest in the goods must be notified.

(b) The notification must be delivered in person or sent by registered or certified letter to the last known address of any person to be notified.

(c) The notification must include an itemized statement of the claim, a description of the goods subject to the lien, a demand for payment within a specified time not less than ten days after receipt of the notification, and a conspicuous statement that unless the claim is paid within that time the goods will be advertised for sale and sold by auction at a specified time and place.

(d) The sale must conform to the terms of the notification.

(e) The sale must be held at the nearest suitable place to that where the goods are held or stored.

(f) After the expiration of the time given in the notification, an advertisement of the sale must be published once a week for two weeks consecutively in a newspaper of general circulation where the sale is to be held. The advertisement must include a description of the goods, the name of the person on whose account they are being held, and the time and place of the sale. The sale must take place at least fifteen days after the first publication. If there is no newspaper of general circulation where the sale is to be held, the advertisement must be posted at least ten days before the sale in not less than six conspicuous places in the neighborhood of the proposed sale.

(3) Before any sale pursuant to this section any person claiming a right in the goods may pay the amount necessary to satisfy the lien and the reasonable expenses incurred under this section. In that event the goods must not be sold, but must be retained by the warehouseman subject to the terms of the receipt and this Article.

(4) The warehouseman may buy at any public sale pursuant to this section.

(5) A purchaser in good faith of goods sold to enforce a warehouseman's lien takes the goods free of any rights of persons against whom the lien was valid, despite non-compliance by the warehouseman with the requirements of this section.

(6) The warehouseman may satisfy his lien from the proceeds of any sale pursuant to this section but must hold the balance, if any, for delivery on demand to any person to whom he would have been bound to deliver the goods.

(7) The rights provided by this section shall be in addition to all other rights allowed by law to a creditor against his debtor.

(8) Where a lien is on goods stored by a merchant in the course of his business the lien may be enforced in accordance with either subsection (1) or (2).

(9) The warehouseman is liable for damages caused by failure to comply with the requirements for sale under this section and in case of willful violation is liable for conversion.

Part 3

Bills of Lading: Special Provisions

§7–301. Liability for Non-Receipt or Misdescription; "Said to Contain"; "Shipper's Load and Count"; Improper Handling. (1) A consignee of a non-negotiable bill who has given value in good faith or a holder to whom a negotiable bill has been duly negotiated relying in either case upon the description therein of the goods, or upon the date therein shown, may recover from the issuer damages caused by the misdating of the bill or the non-receipt or misdescription of the goods, except to the extent that the document indicates that the issuer does not know whether any part or all of the goods in fact were received or conform to the description, as where the description is in terms of marks or labels or kind, quantity, or condition or the receipt or description is qualified by "contents or condition of contents of packages unknown", "said to contain", "shipper's weight, load and count" or the like, if such indication be true.

(2) When goods are loaded by an issuer who is a common carrier, the issuer must count the packages of goods if package freight and ascertain the kind and quantity if bulk freight. In such cases "shipper's weight, load and count" or other words indicating that the description was made by the shipper are ineffective except as to freight concealed by packages.

(3) When bulk freight is loaded by a shipper who makes available to the issuer adequate facilities for weighing such freight, an issuer who is a common carrier must ascertain the kind and quantity within a reasonable time after receiving the written request of the shipper to do so. In such cases "shipper's weight" or other words of like purport are ineffective.

(4) The issuer may by inserting in the bill the words "shipper's weight, load and count" or other words of like purport indicate that the goods were loaded by the shipper; and if such statement be true the issuer shall not be liable for damages caused by the improper loading. But their omission does not imply liability for such damages.

(5) The shipper shall be deemed to have guaranteed to the issuer the accuracy at the time of shipment of the description, marks, labels, number, kind, quantity, condition and weight, as furnished by him; and the shipper shall indemnify the issuer against damage caused by inaccuracies in such particulars. The right of the issuer to such indemnity shall in no way limit his responsibility and liability under the contract of carriage to any person other than the shipper.

§7–302. Through Bills of Lading and Similar Documents. (1) The issuer of a through bill of lading or other document embodying an undertaking to be performed in part by persons acting as its agents or by connecting carriers is liable to anyone entitled to recover on the document for any breach by such other persons or by a connecting carrier of its obligation under the document but to the extent that the bill covers an undertaking to be performed overseas or in territory not contiguous to the continental United States or an undertaking including matters other than transportation this liability may be varied by agreement of the parties.

(2) Where goods covered by a through bill of lading or other document embodying an undertaking to be performed in part by persons other than the issuer are received by any such person, he is subject with respect to his own performance while the goods are in his possession to the obligation of the issuer. His obligation is discharged by delivery of the goods to another such person pursuant to the document, and does not include liability for breach by any other such persons or by the issuer.

(3) The issuer of such through bill of lading or other document shall be entitled to recover from the connecting carrier or such other person in possession of the goods when the breach of the obligation under the document occurred, the amount it may be required to pay to anyone entitled to recover on the document therefor, as may be evidenced by any receipt, judgment, or transcript thereof, and the amount of any expense reasonably incurred by it in

defending any action brought by anyone entitled to recover on the document therefor.

§7-303. Diversion; Reconsignment; Change of Instructions. (1) Unless the bill of lading otherwise provides, the carrier may deliver the goods to a person or destination other than that stated in the bill or may otherwise dispose of the goods on instructions from

(a) the holder of a negotiable bill; or

(b) the consignor on a non-negotiable bill notwithstanding contrary instructions from the consignee; or

(c) the consignee on a non-negotiable bill in the absence of contrary instructions from the consignor, if the goods have arrived at the billed destination or if the consignee is in possession of the bill; or

(d) the consignee on a non-negotiable bill if he is entitled as against the consignor to dispose of them.

(2) Unless such instructions are noted on a negotiable bill of lading, a person to whom the bill is duly negotiated can hold the bailee according to the original terms.

§7-304. Bills of Lading in a Set. (1) Except where customary in overseas transportation, a bill of lading must not be issued in a set of parts. The issuer is liable for damages caused by violation of this subsection.

(2) Where a bill of lading is lawfully drawn in a set of parts, each of which is numbered and expressed to be valid only if the goods have not been delivered against any other part, the whole of the parts constitute one bill.

(3) Where a bill of lading is lawfully issued in a set of parts and different parts are negotiated to different persons, the title of the holder to whom the first due negotiation is made prevails as to both the document and the goods even though any later holder may have received the goods from the carrier in good faith and discharged the carrier's obligation by surrender of his part.

(4) Any person who negotiates or transfers a single part of a bill of lading drawn in a set is liable to holders of that part as if it were the whole set.

(5) The bailee is obliged to deliver in accordance with Part 4 of this Article against the first presented part of a bill of lading lawfully drawn in a set. Such delivery discharges the bailee's obligation on the whole bill.

§7-305. Destination Bills. (1) Instead of issuing a bill of lading to the consignor at the place of shipment a carrier may at the request of the consignor procure the bill to be issued at destination or at any other place designated in the request.

(2) Upon request of anyone entitled as against the carrier to control the goods while in transit and on surrender of any outstanding bill of lading or other receipt covering such goods, the issuer may procure a substitute bill to be issued at any place designated in the request.

§7-306. Altered Bills of Lading. An unauthorized alteration or filling in of a blank in a bill of lading leaves the bill enforceable according to its original tenor.

§7-307. Lien of Carrier. (1) A carrier has a lien on the goods covered by a bill of lading for charges subsequent to the date of its receipt of the goods for storage or transportation (including demurrage and terminal charges) and for expenses necessary for preservation of the goods incident to their transportation or reasonably incurred in their sale pursuant to law. But against a purchaser for value of a negotiable bill of lading a carrier's lien is limited to charges stated in the bill or the applicable tariffs, or if no charges are stated then to a reasonable charge.

(2) A lien for charges and expenses under subsection (1) on goods which the carrier was required by law to receive for transportation is effective against the consignor or any person entitled to the goods unless the carrier had notice that the consignor lacked authority to subject the goods to such charges and expenses. Any other lien under subsection (1) is effective against the consignor and any person who permitted the bailor to have control or possession of the goods unless the carrier had notice that the bailor lacked such authority.

(3) A carrier loses his lien on any goods which he voluntarily delivers or which he unjustifiably refuses to deliver.

§7–308. **Enforcement of Carrier's Lien.** (1) A carrier's lien may be enforced by public or private sale of the goods, in bloc or in parcels, at any time or place and on any terms which are commercially reasonable, after notifying all persons known to claim an interest in the goods. Such notification must include a statement of the amount due, the nature of the proposed sale and the time and place of any public sale. The fact that a better price could have been obtained by a sale at a different time or in a different method from that selected by the carrier is not of itself sufficient to establish that the sale was not made in a commercially reasonable manner. If the carrier either sells the goods in the usual manner in any recognized market therefor or if he sells at the price current in such market at the time of his sale or if he has otherwise sold in conformity with commercially reasonable practices among dealers in the type of goods sold he has sold in a commercially reasonable manner. A sale of more goods than apparently necessary to be offered to ensure satisfaction of the obligation is not commercially reasonable except in cases covered by the preceding sentence.

(2) Before any sale pursuant to this section any person claiming a right in the goods may pay the amount necessary to satisfy the lien and the reasonable expenses incurred under this section. In that event the goods must not be sold, but must be retained by the carrier subject to the terms of the bill and this Article.

(3) The carrier may buy at any public sale pursuant to this section.

(4) A purchaser in good faith of goods sold to enforce a carrier's lien takes the goods free of any rights of persons against whom the lien was valid, despite noncompliance by the carrier with the requirements of this section.

(5) The carrier may satisfy his lien from the proceeds of any sale pursuant to this section but must hold the balance, if any, for delivery on demand to any person to whom he would have been bound to deliver the goods.

(6) The rights provided by this section shall be in addition to all other rights allowed by law to a creditor against his debtor.

(7) A carrier's lien may be enforced in accordance with either subsection (1) or the procedure set forth in subsection (2) of Section 7–210.

(8) The carrier is liable for damages caused by failure to comply with the requirements for sale under this section and in case of willful violation is liable for conversion.

§7–309. **Duty of Care; Contractual Limitation of Carrier's Liability.** (1) A carrier who issues a bill of lading whether negotiable or non-negotiable must exercise the degree of care in relation to the goods which a reasonably careful man would exercise under like circumstances. This subsection does not repeal or change any law or rule of law which imposes liability upon a common carrier for damages not caused by its negligence.

(2) Damages may be limited by a provision that the carrier's liability shall not exceed a value stated in the document if the carrier's rates are dependent

upon value and the consignor by the carrier's tariff is afforded an opportunity to declare a higher value or a value as lawfully provided in the tariff, or where no tariff is filed he is otherwise advised of such opportunity; but no such limitation is effective with respect to the carrier's liability for conversion to its own use.

(3) Reasonable provisions as to the time and manner of presenting claims and instituting actions based on the shipment may be included in a bill of lading or tariff.

Part 4

Warehouse Receipts and Bills of Lading: General Obligations

§7–401. Irregularities in Issue of Receipt or Bill or Conduct of Issuer. The obligations imposed by this Article on an issuer apply to a document of title regardless of the fact that

(a) the document may not comply with the requirements of this Article or of any other law or regulation regarding its issue, form or content; or

(b) the issuer may have violated laws regulating the conduct of his business; or

(c) the goods covered by the document were owned by the bailee at the time the document was issued; or

(d) the person issuing the document does not come within the definition of warehouseman if it purports to be a warehouse receipt.

§7–402. Duplicate Receipt or Bill; Overissue. Neither a duplicate nor any other document of title purporting to cover goods already represented by an outstanding document of the same issuer confers any right in the goods, except as provided in the case of bills in a set, overissue of documents for fungible goods and substitutes for lost, stolen or destroyed documents. But the issuer is liable for damages caused by his overissue or failure to identify a duplicate document as such by conspicuous notation on its face.

§7–403. Obligation of Warehouseman or Carrier to Deliver; Excuse. (1) The bailee must deliver the goods to a person entitled under the document who complies with subsections (2) and (3), unless and to the extent that the bailee establishes any of the following:

(a) delivery of the goods to a person whose receipt was rightful as against the claimant;

(b) damage to or delay, loss or destruction of the goods for which the bailee is not liable [, but the burden of establishing negligence in such cases is on the person entitled under the document];

Note: *The brackets in (1)(b) indicate that State enactments may differ on this point without serious damage to the principle of uniformity.*

(c) previous sale or other disposition of the goods in lawful enforcement of a lien or on warehouseman's lawful termination of storage;

(d) the exercise by a seller of his right to stop delivery pursuant to the provisions of the Article on Sales (Section 2–705);

(e) a diversion, reconsignment or other disposition pursuant to the provisions of this Article (Section 7–303) or tariff regulating such right;

(f) release, satisfaction or any other fact affording a personal defense against the claimant;

(g) any other lawful excuse.

(2) A person claiming goods covered by a document of title must satisfy the bailee's lien where the bailee so requests or where the bailee is prohibited by law from delivering the goods until the charges are paid.

(3) Unless the person claiming is one against whom the document confers no right under Sec. 7–503 (1), he must surrender for cancellation or notation of partial deliveries any outstanding negotiable document covering the goods, and the bailee must cancel the document or conspicuously note the partial delivery thereon or be liable to any person to whom the document is duly negotiated.

(4) "Person entitled under the document" means holder in the case of a negotiable document, or the person to whom delivery is to be made by the terms of or pursuant to written instructions under a non-negotiable document.

§7–404. No Liability for Good Faith Delivery Pursuant to Receipt or Bill. A bailee who in good faith including observance of reasonable commercial standards has received goods and delivered or otherwise disposed of them according to the terms of the document of title or pursuant to this Article is not liable therefor. This rule applies even though the person from whom he received the goods had no authority to procure the document or to dispose of the goods and even though the person to whom he delivered the goods had no authority to receive them.

Part 5

Warehouse Receipts and Bills of Lading: Negotiation and Transfer

§7–501. Form of Negotiation and Requirements of "Due Negotiation". (1) A negotiable document of title running to the order of a named person is negotiated by his indorsement and delivery. After his indorsement in blank or to bearer any person can negotiate it by delivery alone.

(2) (a) A negotiable document of title is also negotiated by delivery alone when by its original terms it runs to bearer.

(b) When a document running to the order of a named person is delivered to him the effect is the same as if the document had been negotiated.

(3) Negotiation of a negotiable document of title after it has been indorsed to a specific person requires indorsement by the special indorsee as well as delivery.

(4) A negotiable document of title is "duly negotiated" when it is negotiated in the manner stated in this section to a holder who purchases it in good faith without notice of any defense against or claim to it on the part of any person and for value, unless it is established that the negotiation is not in the regular course of business or financing or involves receiving the document in settlement or payment of a money obligation.

(5) Indorsement of a non-negotiable document neither makes it negotiable nor adds to the transferee's rights.

(6) The naming in a negotiable bill of a person to be notified of the arrival of the goods does not limit the negotiability of the bill nor constitute notice to a purchaser thereof of any interest of such person in the goods.

§7–502. Rights Acquired by Due Negotiation. (1) Subject to the following section and to the provisions of Section 7–205 on fungible goods, a holder to whom a negotiable document of title has been duly negotiated acquires thereby:

(a) title to the document;

(b) title to the goods;

(c) all rights accruing under the law of agency or estoppel, including rights to goods delivered to the bailee after the document was issued; and

(d) the direct obligation of the issuer to hold or deliver the goods according to the terms of the document free of any defense or claim by him except those arising under the terms of the document or under this Article. In the case of a delivery order the bailee's obligation accrues only upon acceptance and the obligation acquired by the holder is that the issuer and any indorser will procure the acceptance of the bailee.

(2) Subject to the following section, title and rights so acquired are not defeated by any stoppage of the goods represented by the document or by surrender of such goods by the bailee, and are not impaired even though the negotiation or any prior negotiation constituted a breach of duty or even though any person has been deprived of possession of the document by misrepresentation, fraud, accident, mistake, duress, loss, theft or conversion, or even though a previous sale or other transfer of the goods or document has been made to a third person.

§7–503. Document of Title to Goods Defeated in Certain Cases. (1) A document of title confers no right in goods against a person who before issuance of the document had a legal interest or a perfected security interest in them and who neither

(a) delivered or entrusted them or any document of title covering them to the bailor or his nominee with actual or apparent authority to ship, store or sell or with power to obtain delivery under this Article (Section 7–403) or with power of disposition under this Act (Sections 2–403 and 9–307) or other statute or rule of law; nor

(b) acquiesced in the procurement by the bailor or his nominee of any document of title.

(2) Title to goods based upon an unaccepted delivery order is subject to the rights of anyone to whom a negotiable warehouse receipt or bill of lading covering the goods has been duly negotiated. Such a title may be defeated under the next section to the same extent as the rights of the issuer or a transferee from the issuer.

(3) Title to goods based upon a bill of lading issued to a freight forwarder is subject to the rights of anyone to whom a bill by the freight forwarder is duly negotiated; but delivery by the carrier in accordance with Part 4 of this Article pursuant to its own bill of lading discharges the carrier's obligation to deliver.

§7–504. Rights Acquired in the Absence of Due Negotiation; Effect of Diversion; Seller's Stoppage of Delivery. (1) A transferee of a document, whether negotiable or non-negotiable, to whom the document has been delivered but not duly negotiated, acquires the title and rights which his transferor had or had actual authority to convey.

(2) In the case of a non-negotiable document, until but not after the bailee receives notification of the transfer, the rights of the transferee may be defeated

(a) by those creditors of the transferor who could treat the sale as void under Section 2–402; or

(b) by a buyer from the transferor in ordinary course of business if the bailee has delivered the goods to the buyer or received notification of his rights; or

(c) as against the bailee by good faith dealings of the bailee with the transferor.

(3) A diversion or other change of shipping instructions by the consignor in a non-negotiable bill of lading which causes the bailee not to deliver to the consignee defeats the consignee's title to the goods if they have been delivered to a buyer in ordinary course of business and in any event defeats the consignee's rights against the bailee.

(4) Delivery pursuant to a non-negotiable document may be stopped by a seller under Section 2–705, and subject to the requirement of due notification there provided. A bailee honoring the seller's instructions is entitled to be indemnified by the seller against any resulting loss or expense.

§7–505. Indorser Not a Guarantor for Other Parties. The indorsement of a document of title issued by a bailee does not make the indorser liable for any default by the bailee or by previous indorsers.

§7–506. Delivery Without Indorsement: Right to Compel Indorsement. The transferee of a negotiable document of title has a specifically enforceable right to have his transferor supply any necessary indorsement but the transfer becomes a negotiation only as of the time the indorsement is supplied.

§7–507. Warranties on Negotiation or Transfer of Receipt or Bill. Where a person negotiates or transfers a document of title for value otherwise than as a mere intermediary under the next following section, then unless otherwise agreed he warrants to his immediate purchaser only in addition to any warranty made in selling the goods

(a) that the document is genuine; and

(b) that he has no knowledge of any fact which would impair its validity or worth; and

(c) that his negotiation or transfer is rightful and fully effective with respect to the title to the document and the goods it represents.

§7–508. Warranties of Collecting Bank as to Documents. A collecting bank or other intermediary known to be entrusted with documents on behalf of another or with collection of a draft or other claim against delivery of documents warrants by such delivery of the documents only its own good faith and authority. This rule applies even though the intermediary has purchased or made advances against the claim or draft to be collected.

§7–509. Receipt or Bill: When Adequate Compliance With Commercial Contract. The question whether a document is adequate to fulfill the obligations of a contract for sale or the conditions of a credit is governed by the Articles on Sales (Article 2) and on Letters of Credit (Article 5).

Part 6

Warehouse Receipts and Bills of Lading: Miscellaneous Provisions

§7–601. Lost and Missing Documents. (1) If a document has been lost, stolen or destroyed, a court may order delivery of the goods or issuance of a substitute document and the bailee may without liability to any person comply with such order. If the document was negotiable the claimant must post security approved by the court to indemnify any person who may suffer loss as a result of non-surrender of the document. If the document was not negotiable, such security may be required at the discretion of the court. The court may also in its discretion order payment of the bailee's reasonable costs and counsel fees.

(2) A bailee who without court order delivers goods to a person claiming under a missing negotiable document is liable to any person injured thereby, and if the delivery is not in good faith becomes liable for conversion. Delivery in good faith is not conversion if made in accordance with a filed classification or tariff or, where no classification or tariff is filed, if the claimant posts security with the bailee in an amount at least double the value of the goods at the time of posting to indemnify any person injured by the delivery who files a notice of claim within one year after the delivery.

§7–602. Attachment of Goods Covered by a Negotiable Document. Except where the document was originally issued upon delivery of the goods by a person who had no power to dispose of them, no lien attaches by virtue of any judicial process to goods in the possession of a bailee for which a negotiable document of title is outstanding unless the document be first surrendered to the bailee or its negotiation enjoined, and the bailee shall not be compelled to deliver the goods pursuant to process until the document is surrendered to him or impounded by the court. One who purchases the document for value without notice of the process or injunction takes free of the lien imposed by judicial process.

§7–603. Conflicting Claims; Interpleader. If more than one person claims title or possession of the goods, the bailee is excused from delivery until he has had a reasonable time to ascertain the validity of the adverse claims or to bring an action to compel all claimants to interplead and may compel such interpleader, either in defending an action for non-delivery of the goods, or by original action, whichever is appropriate.

ARTICLE 8: INVESTMENT SECURITIES

Part 1

Short Title and General Matters

§8–101. Short Title. This Article shall be known and may be cited as Uniform Commercial Code—Investment Securities.

§8–102. Definitions and Index of Definitions. (1) In this Article unless the context otherwise requires

(a) A "security" is an instrument which

(i) is issued in bearer or registered form; and

(ii) is of a type commonly dealt in upon securities exchanges or markets or commonly recognized in any area in which it is issued or dealt in as a medium for investment; and

(iii) is either one of a class or series or by its terms is divisible into a class or series of instruments; and

(iv) evidences a share, participation or other interest in property or in an enterprise or evidences an obligation of the issuer.

(b) A writing which is a security is governed by this Article and not by Uniform Commercial Code—Commercial Paper even though it also meets the requirements of that Article. This Article does not apply to money.

(c) A security is in "registered form" when it specifies a person entitled to the security or to the rights it evidences and when its transfer may be registered upon books maintained for that purpose by or on behalf of an issuer or the security so states.

(d) A security is in "bearer form" when it runs to bearer according to its terms and not by reason of any indorsement.

(2) A "subsequent purchaser" is a person who takes other than by original issue.

(3) A "clearing corporation" is a corporation all of the capital stock of which is held by or for a national securities exchange or association registered under a statute of the United States such as the Securities Exchange Act of 1934.

(4) A "custodian bank" is any bank or trust company which is supervised and examined by state or federal authority having supervision over banks and which is acting as custodian for a clearing corporation.

(5) Other definitions applying to this Article or to specified Parts thereof and the sections in which they appear are:

"Adverse claim". Section 8–301.

"Bona fide purchaser". Section 8–302.

"Broker". Section 8–303.

"Guarantee of the signature". Section 8–402.

"Intermediary bank". Section 4–105.

"Issuer". Section 8–201.

"Overissue". Section 8–104.

(6) In addition Article 1 contains general definitions and principles of construction and interpretation applicable throughout this Article.

§8–103. Issuer's Lien. A lien upon a security in favor of an issuer thereof is valid against a purchaser only if the right of the issuer to such lien is noted conspicuously on the security.

§8–104. Effect of Overissue; "Overissue". (1) The provisions of this Article which validate a security or compel its issue or reissue do not apply to the extent that validation, issue or reissue would result in overissue; but

(a) if an identical security which does not constitute an overissue is reasonably available for purchase, the person entitled to issue or validation may compel the issuer to purchase and deliver such a security to him against surrender of the security, if any, which he holds; or

(b) if a security is not so available for purchase, the person entitled to issue or validation may recover from the issuer the price he or the last purchaser for value paid for it with interest from the date of his demand.

(2) "Overissue" means the issue of securities in excess of the amount which the issuer has corporate power to issue.

§8–105. Securities Negotiable; Presumptions. (1) Securities governed by this Article are negotiable instruments.

(2) In any action on a security

(a) unless specifically denied in the pleadings, each signature on the security or in a necessary indorsement is admitted;

(b) when the effectiveness of a signature is put in issue the burden of establishing it is on the party claiming under the signature but the signature is presumed to be genuine or authorized;

(c) when signatures are admitted or established production of the instrument entitles a holder to recover on it unless the defendant establishes a defense or a defect going to the validity of the security; and

(d) after it is shown that a defense or defect exists the plaintiff has the burden of establishing that he or some person under whom he claims is a person against whom the defense or defect is ineffective (Section 8–202).

§8–106. Applicability. The validity of a security and the rights and duties of the issuer with respect to registration of transfer are governed by the law (including the conflict of laws rules) of the jurisdiction of organization of the issuer.

§8–107. Securities Deliverable; Action for Price. (1) Unless otherwise agreed and subject to any applicable law or regulation respecting short sales, a person obligated to deliver securities may deliver any security of the specified issue in bearer form or registered in the name of the transferee or indorsed to him or in blank.

(2) When the buyer fails to pay the price as it comes due under a contract of sale the seller may recover the price

(a) of securities accepted by the buyer; and

(b) of other securities if efforts at their resale would be unduly burdensome or if there is no readily available market for their resale.

Part 2

Issue—Issuer

§8–201. "Issuer". (1) With respect to obligations on or defenses to a security "issuer" includes a person who

(a) places or authorizes the placing of his name on a security (otherwise than as authenticating trustee, registrar, transfer agent or the like) to evidence that it represents a share, participation or other interest in his property or in an enterprise or to evidence his duty to perform an obligation evidenced by the security; or

(b) directly or indirectly creates fractional interests in his right or property which fractional interests are evidenced by securities; or

(c) becomes responsible for or in place of any other person described as an issuer in this section.

(2) With respect to obligations on or defenses to a security a guarantor is an issuer to the extent of his guaranty whether or not his obligation is noted on the security.

(3) With respect to registration of transfer (Part 4 of this Article) "issuer" means a person on whose behalf transfer books are maintained.

§8–202. Issuer's Responsibility and Defenses; Notice of Defect or Defense. (1) Even against a purchaser for value and without notice, the terms of a security include those stated on the security and those made part of the security by reference to another instrument, indenture or document or to a constitution, statute, ordinance, rule, regulation, order or the like to the extent that the terms so referred to do not conflict with the stated terms. Such a reference does not of itself charge a purchaser for value with notice of a defect going to the validity of the security even though the security expressly states that a person accepting it admits such notice.

(2) (a) A security other than one issued by a government or governmental agency or unit even though issued with a defect going to its validity is valid in the hands of a purchaser for value and without notice of the particular defect

unless the defect involves a violation of constitutional provisions in which case the security is valid in the hands of a subsequent purchaser for value and without notice of the defect.

(b) The rule of subparagraph (a) applies to an issuer which is a government or governmental agency or unit only if either there has been substantial compliance with the legal requirements governing the issue or the issuer has received a substantial consideration for the issue as a whole or for the particular security and a stated purpose of the issue is one for which the issuer has power to borrow money or issue the security.

(3) Except as otherwise provided in the case of certain unauthorized signatures on issue (Section 8–205), lack of genuineness of a security is a complete defense even against a purchaser for value and without notice.

(4) All other defenses of the issuer including non-delivery and conditional delivery of the security are ineffective against a purchaser for value who has taken without notice of the particular defense.

(5) Nothing in this section shall be construed to affect the right of a party to a "when, as and if issued" or a "when distributed" contract to cancel the contract in the event of a material change in the character of the security which is the subject of the contract or in the plan or arrangement pursuant to which such security is to be issued or distributed.

§8–203. Staleness as Notice of Defects or Defenses. (1) After an act or event which creates a right to immediate performance of the principal obligation evidenced by the security or which sets a date on or after which the security is to be presented or surrendered for redemption or exchange, a purchaser is charged with notice of any defect in its issue or defense of the issuer

(a) if the act or event is one requiring the payment of money or the delivery of securities or both on presentation or surrender of the security and such funds or securities are available on the date set for payment or exchange and he takes the security more than one year after that date; and

(b) if the act or event is not covered by paragraph (a) and he takes the security more than two years after the date set for surrender or presentation or the date on which such performance became due.

(2) A call which has been revoked is not within subsection (1).

§8–204. Effect of Issuer's Restrictions on Transfer. Unless noted conspicuously on the security a restriction on transfer imposed by the issuer even though otherwise lawful is ineffective except against a person with actual knowledge of it.

§8–205. Effect of Unauthorized Signature on Issue. An unauthorized signature placed on a security prior to or in the course of issue is ineffective except that the signature is effective in favor of a purchaser for value and without notice of the lack of authority if the signing has been done by

(a) an authenticating trustee, registrar, transfer agent or other person entrusted by the issuer with the signing of the security or of similar securities or their immediate preparation for signing; or

(b) an employee of the issuer or of any of the foregoing entrusted with responsible handling of the security.

§8–206. Completion or Alteration of Instrument. (1) Where a security contains the signatures necessary to its issue or transfer but is incomplete in any other respect

(a) any person may complete it by filling in the blanks as authorized; and

(b) even though the blanks are incorrectly filled in, the security as completed is enforceable by a purchaser who took it for value and without notice of such incorrectness.

(2) A complete security which has been improperly altered even though fraudulently remains enforceable but only according to its original terms.

§8–207. Rights of Issuer With Respect to Registered Owners. (1) Prior to due presentment for registration of transfer of a security in registered form the issuer or indenture trustee may treat the registered owner as the person exclusively entitled to vote, to receive notifications and otherwise to exercise all the rights and powers of an owner.

(2) Nothing in this Article shall be construed to affect the liability of the registered owner of a security for calls, assessments or the like.

§8–208. Effect of Signature of Authenticating Trustee, Registrar or Transfer Agent. (1) A person placing his signature upon a security as authenticating trustee, registrar, transfer agent or the like warrants to a purchaser for value without notice of the particular defect that

(a) the security is genuine; and

(b) his own participation in the issue of the security is within his capacity and within the scope of the authorization received by him from the issuer; and

(c) he has reasonable grounds to believe that the security is in the form and within the amount the issuer is authorized to issue.

(2) Unless otherwise agreed, a person by so placing his signature does not assume responsibility for the validity of the security in other respects.

Part 3

Purchase

§8–301. Rights Acquired by Purchaser; "Adverse Claim"; Title Acquired by Bona Fide Purchaser. (1) Upon delivery of a security the purchaser acquires the rights in the security which his transferor had or had actual authority to convey except that a purchaser who has himself been a party to any fraud or illegality affecting the security or who as a prior holder had notice of an adverse claim cannot improve his position by taking from a later bona fide purchaser. "Adverse claim" includes a claim that a transfer was or would be wrongful or that a particular adverse person is the owner of or has an interest in the security.

(2) A bona fide purchaser in addition to acquiring the rights of a purchaser also acquires the security free of any adverse claim.

(3) A purchaser of a limited interest acquires rights only to the extent of the interest purchased.

§8–302. "Bona Fide Purchaser." A "bona fide purchaser" is a purchaser for value in good faith and without notice of any adverse claim who takes delivery of a security in bearer form or of one in registered form issued to him or indorsed to him or in blank.

§8–303. "Broker." "Broker" means a person engaged for all or part of his time in the business of buying and selling securities, who in the transaction concerned acts for, or buys a security from or sells a security to a customer. Nothing in this Article determines the capacity in which a person acts for purposes of any other statute or rule to which such person is subject.

§8–304. Notice to Purchaser of Adverse Claims. (1) A purchaser (including a broker for the seller or buyer but excluding an intermediary bank) of a security is charged with notice of adverse claims if

(a) the security whether in bearer or registered form has been indorsed "for collection" or "for surrender" or for some other purpose not involving transfer; or

(b) the security is in bearer form and has on it an unambiguous statement that it is the property of a person other than the transferor. The mere writing of a name on a security is not such a statement.

(2) The fact that the purchaser (including a broker for the seller or buyer) has notice that the security is held for a third person or is registered in the name of or indorsed by a fiduciary does not create a duty of inquiry into the rightfulness of the transfer or constitute notice of adverse claims, if, however, the purchaser (excluding an intermediary bank) has knowledge that the proceeds are being used or that the transaction is for the individual benefit of the fiduciary or otherwise in breach of duty, the purchaser is charged with notice of adverse claims.

§8–305. Staleness as Notice of Adverse Claims. An act or event which creates a right to immediate performance of the principal obligation evidenced by the security or which sets a date on or after which the security is to be presented or surrendered for redemption or exchange does not of itself constitute any notice of adverse claims except in the case of a purchase

(a) after one year from any date set for such presentment or surrender for redemption or exchange; or

(b) after six months from any date set for payment of money against presentation or surrender of the security if funds are available for payment on that date.

§8–306. Warranties on Presentment and Transfer. (1) A person who presents a security for registration of transfer or for payment or exchange warrants to the issuer that he is entitled to the registration, payment or exchange. But a purchaser for value without notice of adverse claims who receives a new, reissued or re-registered security on registration of transfer warrants only that he has no knowledge of any unauthorized signature (Section 8–311) in a necessary indorsement.

(2) A person by transferring a security to a purchaser for value warrants only that

(a) his transfer is effective and rightful; and

(b) the security is genuine and has not been materially altered; and

(c) he knows no fact which might impair the validity of the security.

(3) Where a security is delivered by an intermediary known to be entrusted with delivery of the security on behalf of another or with collection of a draft or other claim against such delivery, the intermediary by such delivery warrants only his own good faith and authority even though he has purchased or made advances against the claim to be collected against the delivery.

(4) A pledgee or other holder for security who redelivers the security received, or after payment and on order of the debtor delivers that security to a third person makes only the warranties of an intermediary under subsection (3).

(5) A broker gives to his customer and to the issuer and a purchaser the warranties provided in this section and has the rights and privileges of a purchaser under this section. The warranties of and in favor of the broker acting

as an agent are in addition to applicable warranties given by and in favor of his customer.

§8–307. Effect of Delivery Without Indorsement; Right to Compel Indorsement. Where a security in registered form has been delivered to a purchaser without a necessary indorsement he may become a bona fide purchaser only as of the time the indorsement is supplied, but against the transferor the transfer is complete upon delivery and the purchaser has a specially enforceable right to have any necessary indorsement supplied.

§8–308. Indorsement, How Made; Special Indorsement; Indorser Not a Guarantor; Partial Assignment. (1) An indorsement of a security in registered form is made when an appropriate person signs on it or on a separate document an assignment or transfer of the security or a power to assign or transfer it or when the signature of such person is written without more upon the back of the security.

(2) An indorsement may be in blank or special. An indorsement in blank includes an indorsement to bearer. A special indorsement specifies the person to whom the security is to be transferred, or who has power to transfer it. A holder may convert a blank indorsement into a special indorsement.

(3) "An appropriate person" in subsection (1) means

(a) the person specified by the security or by special indorsement to be entitled to the security; or

(b) where the person so specified is described as a fiduciary but is no longer serving in the described capacity—either that person or his successor; or

(c) where the security or indorsement so specifies more than one person as fiduciaries and one or more are no longer serving in the described capacity,—the remaining fiduciary or fiduciaries, whether or not a successor has been appointed or qualified; or

(d) where the person so specified is an individual and is without capacity to act by virtue of death, incompetence, infancy or otherwise,—his executor, administrator, guardian or like fiduciary; or

(e) where the security or indorsement so specifies more than one person as tenants by the entirety or with right of survivorship and by reason of death all cannot sign,—the survivor or survivors; or

(f) a person having power to sign under applicable law or controlling instrument; or

(g) to the extent that any of the foregoing persons may act through an agent,—his authorized agent.

(4) Unless otherwise agreed the indorser by his indorsement assumes no obligation that the security will be honored by the issuer.

(5) An indorsement purporting to be only of part of a security representing units intended by the issuer to be separately transferable is effective to the extent of the indorsement.

(6) Whether the person signing is appropriate is determined as of the date of signing and an indorsement by such a person does not become unauthorized for the purposes of this Article by virtue of any subsequent change of circumstances.

(7) Failure of a fiduciary to comply with a controlling instrument or with the law of the state having jurisdiction of the fiduciary relationship, including any law requiring the fiduciary to obtain court approval of the transfer, does not render his indorsement unauthorized for the purposes of this Article.

§8–309. Effect of Indorsement Without Delivery. An indorsement of a security whether special or in blank does not constitute a transfer until delivery of the security on which it appears or if the indorsement is on a separate document until delivery of both the document and the security.

§8–310. Indorsement of Security in Bearer Form. An indorsement of a security in bearer form may give notice of adverse claims (Section 8–304) but does not otherwise affect any right to registration the holder may possess.

§8–311. Effect of Unauthorized Indorsement. Unless the owner has ratified an unauthorized indorsement or is otherwise precluded from asserting its ineffectiveness

(a) he may assert its ineffectiveness against the issuer or any purchaser other than a purchaser for value and without notice of adverse claims who has in good faith received a new, reissued or re-registered security on registration of transfer; and

(b) an issuer who registers the transfer of a security upon the unauthorized indorsement is subject to liability for improper registration (Section 8–404).

§8–312. Effect of Guaranteeing Signature or Indorsement. (1) Any person guaranteeing a signature of an indorser of a security warrants that at the time of signing

(a) the signature was genuine; and

(b) the signer was an appropriate person to indorse (Section 8–308); and

(c) the signer had legal capacity to sign.

But the guarantor does not otherwise warrant the rightfulness of the particular transfer.

(2) Any person may guarantee an indorsement of a security and by so doing warrants not only the signature (subsection 1) but also the rightfulness of the particular transfer in all respects. But no issuer may require a guarantee of indorsement as a condition to registration of transfer.

(3) The foregoing warranties are made to any person taking or dealing with the security in reliance on the guarantee and the guarantor is liable to such person for any loss resulting from breach of the warranties.

§8–313. When Delivery to the Purchaser Occurs; Purchaser's Broker as Holder. (1) Delivery to a purchaser occurs when

(a) he or a person designated by him acquires possession of a security; or

(b) his broker acquires possession of a security specially indorsed to or issued in the name of the purchaser; or

(c) his broker sends him confirmation of the purchase and also by book entry or otherwise identifies a specific security in the broker's possession as belonging to the purchaser; or

(d) with respect to an identified security to be delivered while still in the possession of a third person when that person acknowledges that he holds for the purchaser; or

(e) appropriate entries on the books of a clearing corporation are made under Section 8–320.

(2) The purchaser is the owner of a security held for him by his broker, but is not the holder except as specified in subparagraphs (b), (c) and (e) of subsection (1). Where a security is part of a fungible bulk the purchaser is the owner of a proportionate property interest in the fungible bulk.

(3) Notice of an adverse claim received by the broker or by the purchaser after the broker takes delivery as a holder for value is not effective either as to the broker or as to the purchaser. However, as between the broker and the purchaser the purchaser may demand delivery of an equivalent security as to which no notice of an adverse claim has been received.

§8–314. Duty to Deliver, When Completed. (1) Unless otherwise agreed where a sale of a security is made on an exchange or otherwise through brokers

(a) the selling customer fulfills his duty to deliver when he places such a security in the possession of the selling broker or of a person designated by the broker or if requested causes an acknowledgment to be made to the selling broker that it is held for him; and

(b) the selling broker including a correspondent broker acting for a selling customer fulfills his duty to deliver by placing the security or a like security in the possession of the buying broker or a person designated by him or by effecting clearance of the sale in accordance with the rules of the exchange on which the transaction took place.

(2) Except as otherwise provided in this section and unless otherwise agreed, a transferor's duty to deliver a security under a contract of purchase is not fulfilled until he places the security in form to be negotiated by the purchaser in the possession of the purchaser or of a person designated by him or at the purchaser's request causes an acknowledgment to be made to the purchaser that it is held for him. Unless made on an exchange a sale to a broker purchasing for his own account is within this subsection and not within subsection (1).

§8–315. Action Against Purchaser Based Upon Wrongful Transfer. (1) Any person against whom the transfer of a security is wrongful for any reason, including his incapacity, may against anyone except a bona fide purchaser reclaim possession of the security or obtain possession of any new security evidencing all or part of the same rights or have damages.

(2) If the transfer is wrongful because of an unauthorized indorsement, the owner may also reclaim or obtain possession of the security or new security even from a bona fide purchaser if the ineffectiveness of the purported indorsement can be asserted against him under the provisions of this Article on unauthorized indorsements (Section 8–311).

(3) The right to obtain or reclaim possession of a security may be specifically enforced and its transfer enjoined and the security impounded pending the litigation.

§8–316. Purchaser's Right to Requisites for Registration of Transfer on Books. Unless otherwise agreed the transferor must on due demand supply his purchaser with any proof of his authority to transfer or with any other requisite which may be necessary to obtain registration of the transfer of the security but if the transfer is not for value a transferor need not do so unless the purchaser furnishes the necessary expenses. Failure to comply with a demand made within a reasonable time gives the purchaser the right to reject or rescind the transfer.

§8–317. Attachment or Levy Upon Security. (1) No attachment or levy upon a security or any share or other interest evidenced thereby which is outstanding shall be valid until the security is actually seized by the officer making the attachment or levy but a security which has been surrendered to the issuer may be attached or levied upon at the source.

(2) A creditor whose debtor is the owner of a security shall be entitled to such aid from courts of appropriate jurisdiction, by injunction or otherwise, in reaching such security or in satisfying the claim by means thereof as is allowed at law or in equity in regard to property which cannot readily be attached or levied upon by ordinary legal process.

§8–318. No Conversion by Good Faith Delivery. An agent or bailee who in good faith (including observance of reasonable commercial standards if he is in the business of buying, selling or otherwise dealing with securities) has received securities and sold, pledged or delivered them according to the instructions of his principal is not liable for conversion or for participation in breach of fiduciary duty although the principal had no right to dispose of them.

§8–319. Statute of Frauds. A contract for the sale of securities is not enforceable by way of action or defense unless

(a) there is some writing signed by the party against whom enforcement is sought or by his authorized agent or broker sufficient to indicate that a contract has been made for sale of a stated quantity of described securities at a defined or stated price; or

(b) delivery of the security has been accepted or payment has been made but the contract is enforceable under this provision only to the extent of such delivery or payment; or

(c) within a reasonable time a writing in confirmation of the sale or purchase and sufficient against the sender under paragraph (a) has been received by the party against whom enforcement is sought and he has failed to send written objection to its contents within ten days after its receipt; or

(d) the party against whom enforcement is sought admits in his pleading, testimony or otherwise in court that a contract was made for sale of a stated quantity of described securities at a defined or stated price.

§8–320. Transfer or Pledge Within a Central Depository System. (1) If a security

(a) is in the custody of a clearing corporation or of a custodian bank or a nominee of either subject to the instructions of the clearing corporation; and

(b) is in bearer form or indorsed in blank by an appropriate person or registered in the name of the clearing corporation or custodian bank or a nominee of either; and

(c) is shown on the account of a transferor or pledgor on the books of the clearing corporation;

then, in addition to other methods, a transfer or pledge of the security or any interest therein may be effected by the making of appropriate entries on the books of the clearing corporation reducing the account of the transferor or pledgor and increasing the account of the transferee or pledgee by the amount of the obligation or the number of shares or rights transferred or pledged.

(2) Under this section entries may be with respect to like securities or interests therein as a part of a fungible bulk and may refer merely to a quantity of a particular security without reference to the name of the registered owner, certificate or bond number or the like and, in appropriate cases, may be on a net basis taking into account other transfers or pledges of the same security.

(3) A transfer or pledge under this section has the effect of a delivery of a security in bearer form or duly indorsed in blank (Section 8–301) representing the amount of the obligation or the number of shares or rights transferred or pledged. If a pledge or the creation of a security interest is intended, the making of entries has the effect of a taking of delivery by the pledgee or a secured party (Sections 9–304 and 9–305). A transferee or pledgee under this section is a holder.

(4) A transfer or pledge under this section does not constitute a registration of transfer under Part 4 of this Article.

(5) That entries made on the books of the clearing corporation as provided in subsection (1) are not appropriate does not affect the validity or effect of

the entries nor the liabilities or obligations of the clearing corporation to any person adversely affected thereby.

Part 4

Registration

§8–401. Duty of Issuer to Register Transfer. (1) Where a security in registered form is presented to the issuer with a request to register transfer, the issuer is under a duty to register the transfer as requested if

(a) the security is indorsed by the appropriate person or persons (Section 8–308); and

(b) reasonable assurance is given that those indorsements are genuine and effective (Section 8–402); and

(c) the issuer has no duty to inquire into adverse claims or has discharged any such duty (Section 8–403); and

(d) any applicable law relating to the collection of taxes has been complied with; and

(e) the transfer is in fact rightful or is to a bona fide purchaser.

(2) Where an issuer is under a duty to register a transfer of a security the issuer is also liable to the person presenting it for registration or his principal for loss resulting from any unreasonable delay in registration or from failure or refusal to register the transfer.

§8–402. Assurance That Indorsements Are Effective. (1) The issuer may require the following assurance that each necessary indorsement (Section 8–308) is genuine and effective

(a) in all cases, a guarantee of the signature (subsection (1) of Section 8–312) of the person indorsing; and

(b) where the indorsement is by an agent, appropriate assurance of authority to sign;

(c) where the indorsement is by a fiduciary, appropriate evidence of appointment or incumbency;

(d) where there is more than one fiduciary, reasonable assurance that all who are required to sign have done so;

(e) where the indorsement is by a person not covered by any of the foregoing, assurance appropriate to the case corresponding as nearly as may be to the foregoing.

(2) A "guarantee of the signature" in subsection (1) means a guarantee signed by or on behalf of a person reasonably believed by the issuer to be responsible. The issuer may adopt standards with respect to responsibility provided such standards are not manifestly unreasonable.

(3) "Appropriate evidence of appointment or incumbency" in subsection (1) means

(a) in the case of a fiduciary appointed or qualified by a court, a certificate issued by or under the direction or supervision of that court or an officer thereof and dated within sixty days before the date of presentation for transfers; or

(b) in any other case, a copy of a document showing the appointment or a certificate issued by or on behalf of a person reasonably believed by the issuer to be responsible or, in the absence of such a document or certificate, other evidence reasonably deemed by the issuer to be appropriate. The issuer may adopt standards with respect to such evidence provided such standards are not manifestly unreasonable. The issuer is not charged with notice of the contents of any document obtained pursuant to this paragraph (b) except to the extent that the contents relate directly to the appointment or incumbency.

(4) The issuer may elect to require reasonable assurance beyond that specified in this section but if it does so and for a purpose other than that specified in subsection 3(b) both requires and obtains a copy of a will, trust, indenture, articles of co-partnership, by-laws or other controlling instrument it is charged with notice of all matters contained therein affecting the transfer.

§8-403. Limited Duty of Inquiry. (1) An issuer to whom a security is presented for registration is under a duty to inquire into adverse claims if

(a) a written notification of an adverse claim is received at a time and in a manner which affords the issuer a reasonable opportunity to act on it prior to the issuance of a new, reissued or re-registered security and the notification identifies the claimant, the registered owner and the issue of which the security is a part and provides an address for communications directed to the claimant; or

(b) the issuer is charged with notice of an adverse claim from a controlling instrument which it has elected to require under subsection (4) of Section 8-402.

(2) The issuer may discharge any duty of inquiry by any reasonable means, including notifying an adverse claimant by registered or certified mail at the address furnished by him or if there be no such address at his residence or regular place of business that the security has been presented for registration of transfer by a named person, and that the transfer will be registered unless within thirty days from the date of mailing the notification, either

(a) an appropriate restraining order, injunction or other process issues from a court of competent jurisdiction; or

(b) an indemnity bond sufficient in the issuer's judgment to protect the issuer and any transfer agent, registrar or other agent of the issuer involved, from any loss which it or they may suffer by complying with the adverse claim is filed with the issuer.

(3) Unless an issuer is charged with notice of an adverse claim from a controlling instrument which it has elected to require under subsection (4) of Section 8-402 or receives notification of an adverse claim under subsection (1) of this section, where a security presented for registration is indorsed by the appropriate person or persons the issuer is under no duty to inquire into adverse claims. In particular

(a) an issuer registering a security in the name of a person who is a fiduciary or who is described as a fiduciary is not bound to inquire into the existence, extent, or correct description of the fiduciary relationship and thereafter the issuer may assume without inquiry that the newly registered owner continues to be the fiduciary until the issuer receives written notice that the fiduciary is no longer acting as such with respect to the particular security;

(b) an issuer registering transfer on an indorsement by a fiduciary is not bound to inquire whether the transfer is made in compliance with a controlling instrument or with the law of the state having jurisdiction of the fiduciary relationship, including any law requiring the fiduciary to obtain court approval of the transfer; and

(c) the issuer is not charged with notice of the contents of any court record or file or other recorded or unrecorded document even though the document is in its possession and even though the transfer is made on the indorsement of a fiduciary to the fiduciary himself or to his nominee.

§8-404. Liability and Non-Liability for Registration. (1) Except as otherwise provided in any law relating to the collection of taxes, the issuer is not liable to the owner or any other person suffering loss as a result of the registration of a transfer of a security if

(a) there were on or with the security the necessary indorsements (Section 8-308); and

(b) the issuer had no duty to inquire into adverse claims or has discharged any such duty (Section 8-403).

(2) Where an issuer has registered a transfer of a security to a person not entitled to it the issuer on demand must deliver a like security to the true owner unless

(a) the registration was pursuant to subsection (1); or

(b) the owner is precluded from asserting any claim for registering the transfer under subsection (1) of the following section; or

(c) such delivery would result in overissue, in which case the issuer's liability is governed by Section 8-104.

§8-405. Lost, Destroyed and Stolen Securities. (1) Where a security has been lost, apparently destroyed or wrongfully taken and the owner fails to notify the issuer of that fact within a reasonable time after he has notice of it and the issuer registers a transfer of the security before receiving such a notification, the owner is precluded from asserting against the issuer any claim for registering the transfer under the preceding section or any claim to a new security under this section.

(2) Where the owner of a security claims that the security has been lost, destroyed or wrongfully taken, the issuer must issue a new security in place of the original security if the owner

(a) so requests before the issuer has notice that the security has been acquired by a bona fide purchaser; and

(b) files with the issuer a sufficient indemnity bond; and

(c) satisfies any other reasonable requirements imposed by the issuer.

(3) If, after the issue of the new security, a bona fide purchaser of the original security presents it for registration of transfer, the issuer must register the transfer unless registration would result in overissue, in which event the issuer's liability is governed by Section 8-104. In addition to any rights on the indemnity bond, the issuer may recover the new security from the person to whom it was issued or any person taking under him except a bona fide purchaser.

§8-406. Duty of Authenticating Trustee, Transfer Agent or Registrar. (1) Where a person acts as authenticating trustee, transfer agent, registrar, or other agent for an issuer in the registration of transfers of its securities or in the issue of new securities or in the cancellation of surrendered securities

(a) he is under a duty to the issuer to exercise good faith and due diligence in performing his functions; and

(b) he has with regard to the particular functions he performs the same obligation to the holder or owner of the security and has the same rights and privileges as the issuer has in regard to those functions.

(2) Notice to an authenticating trustee, transfer agent, registrar or other such agent is notice to the issuer with respect to the functions performed by the agent.

ARTICLE 9: SECURED TRANSACTIONS; SALES OF ACCOUNTS, CONTRACT RIGHTS AND CHATTEL PAPER

Part 1

Short Title, Applicability and Definitions

§9–101. Short Title. This Article shall be known and may be cited as Uniform Commercial Code—Secured Transactions.

§9–102. Policy and Scope of Article. (1) Except as otherwise provided in Section 9–103 on multiple state transactions and in Section 9–104 on excluded transactions, this Article applies so far as concerns any personal property and fixtures within the jurisdiction of this state

(a) to any transaction (regardless of its form) which is intended to create a security interest in personal property or fixtures including goods, documents, instruments, general intangibles, chattel paper, accounts or contract rights; and also

(b) to any sale of accounts, contract rights or chattel paper.

(2) This Article applies to security interests created by contract including pledge, assignment, chattel mortgage, chattel trust, trust deed, factor's lien, equipment trust, conditional sale, trust receipt, other lien or title retention contract and lease or consignment intended as security. This Article does not apply to statutory liens except as provided in Section 9–310.

(3) The application of this Article to a security interest in a secured obligation is not affected by the fact that the obligation is itself secured by a transaction or interest to which this Article does not apply.

Note: *The adoption of this Article should be accompanied by the repeal of existing statutes dealing with conditional sales, trust receipts, factor's liens where the factor is given a non-possessory lien, chattel mortgages, crop mortgages, mortgages on railroad equipment, assignment of accounts and generally statutes regulating security interests in personal property.*

Where the state has a retail installment selling act or small loan act, that legislation should be carefully examined to determine what changes in those acts are needed to conform them to this Article. This Article primarily sets out rules defining rights of a secured party against persons dealing with the debtor; it does not prescribe regulations and controls which may be necessary to curb abuses arising in the small loan business or in the financing of consumer purchases on credit. Accordingly there is no intention to repeal existing regulatory acts in those fields. See Section 9–203(2) and the Note thereto.

§9–103. Accounts, Contract Rights, General Intangibles and Equipment Relating to Another Jurisdiction; and Incoming Goods Already Subject to a Security Interest. (1) If the office where the assignor of accounts or contract rights keeps his records concerning them is in this state, the validity and perfection of a security interest therein and the possibility and effect of proper filing is governed by this Article; otherwise by the law (including the conflict of laws rules) of the jurisdiction where such office is located.

(2) If the chief place of business of a debtor is in this state, this Article governs the validity and perfection of a security interest and the possibility and effect of proper filing with regard to general intangibles or with regard to goods of a type which are normally used in more than one jurisdiction (such as automotive equipment, rolling stock, airplanes, road building equipment, commercial

harvesting equipment, construction machinery and the like) if such goods are classified as equipment or classified as inventory by reason of their being leased by the debtor to others. Otherwise, the law (including the conflict of laws rules) of the jurisdiction where such chief place of business is located shall govern. If the chief place of business is located in a jurisdiction which does not provide for perfection of the security interest by filing or recording in that jurisdiction, then the security interest may be perfected by filing in this state. For the purpose of determining the validity and perfection of a security interest in an airplane, the chief place of business of a debtor who is a foreign air carrier under the Federal Aviation Act of 1958, as amended, is the designated office of the agent upon whom service of process may be made on behalf of the debtor.

(3) If personal property other than that governed by subsections (1) and (2) is already subject to a security interest when it is brought into this state, the validity of the security interest in this state is to be determined by the law (including the conflict of laws rules) of the jurisdiction where the property was when the security interest attached. However, if the parties to the transaction understood at the time that the security interest attached that the property would be kept in this state and it was brought into this state within 30 days after the security interest attached for purposes other than transportation through this state, then the validity of the security interest in this state is to be determined by the law of this state. If the security interest was already perfected under the law of the jurisdiction where the property was when the security interest attached and before being brought into this state, the security interest continues perfected in this state for four months and also thereafter if within the four month period it is perfected in this state. The security interest may also be perfected in this state after the expiration of the four month period; in such case perfection dates from the time of perfection in this state. If the security interest was not perfected under the law of the jurisdiction where the property was when the security interest attached and before being brought into this state, it may be perfected in this state; in such case perfection dates from the time of perfection in this state.

(4) Notwithstanding subsections (2) and (3), if personal property is covered by a certificate of title issued under a statute of this state or any other jurisdiction which requires indication on a certificate of title of any security interest in the property as a condition of perfection, then the perfection is governed by the law of the jurisdiction which issued the certificate.

[(5) Notwithstanding subsection (1) and Section 9–302, if the office where the assignor of accounts or contract rights keeps his records concerning them is not located in a jurisdiction which is a part of the United States, its territories or possessions, and the accounts or contract rights are within the jurisdiction of this state or the transaction which creates the security interest otherwise bears an appropriate relation to this state, this Article governs the validity and perfection of the security interest and the security interest may only be perfected by notification to the account debtor.]

Note: *The last sentence of subsection (2) and subsection (5) are bracketed to indicate optional enactment. In states engaging in financing of airplanes of foreign carriers and of international open accounts receivable, bracketed language will be of value. In other states not engaging in financing of this type, the bracketed language may not be considered necessary.*

§9–104. **Transactions Excluded From Article.** This Article does not apply

(a) to a security interest subject to any statute of the United States such as the Ship Mortgage Act, 1920, to the extent that such statute governs the rights of parties to and third parties affected by transactions in particular types of property; or

(b) to a landlord's lien; or

(c) to a lien given by statute or other rule of law for services or materials except as provided in Section 9–310 on priority of such liens; or

(d) to a transfer of a claim for wages, salary or other compensation of an employee; or

(e) to an equipment trust covering railway rolling stock; or

(f) to a sale of accounts, contract rights or chattel paper as part of a sale of the business out of which they arose, or an assignment of accounts, contract rights or chattel paper which is for the purpose of collection only, or a transfer of a contract right to an assignee who is also to do the performance under the contract; or

(g) to a transfer of an interest or claim in or under any policy of insurance; or

(h) to a right represented by a judgment; or

(i) to any right of set-off; or

(j) except to the extent that provision is made for fixtures in Section 9–313, to the creation or transfer of an interest in or lien on real estate, including a lease or rents thereunder; or

(k) to a transfer in whole or in part of any of the following: any claim arising out of tort; any deposit, savings, passbook or like account maintained with a bank, savings and loan association, credit union or like organization.

§9–105. Definitions and Index of Definitions. (1) In this Article unless the context otherwise requires:

(a) "Account debtor" means the person who is obligated on an account, chattel paper, contract right or general intangible;

(b) "Chattel paper" means a writing or writings which evidence both a monetary obligation and a security interest in or a lease of specific goods. When a transaction is evidenced both by such a security agreement or a lease and by an instrument or a series of instruments, the group of writings taken together constitutes chattel paper;

(c) "Collateral" means the property subject to a security interest, and includes accounts, contract rights and chattel paper which have been sold;

(d) "Debtor" means the person who owes payment or other performance of the obligation secured, whether or not he owns or has rights in the collateral, and includes the seller of accounts, contract rights or chattel paper. Where the debtor and the owner of the collateral are not the same person, the term "debtor" means the owner of the collateral in any provision of the Article dealing with the collateral, the obligor in any provision dealing with the obligation, and may include both where the context so requires;

(e) "Document" means document of title as defined in the general definitions of Article 1 (Section 1–201);

(f) "Goods" includes all things which are movable at the time the security interest attaches or which are fixtures (Section 9–313), but does not include money, documents, instruments, accounts, chattel paper, general intangibles, contract rights and other things in action. "Goods" also include the unborn young of animals and growing crops;

(g) "Instrument" means a negotiable instrument (defined in Section 3–104), or a security (defined in Section 8–102) or any other writing which evidences a right to the payment of money and is not itself a security agreement or lease and is of a type which is in ordinary course of business transferred by delivery with any necessary indorsement or assignment;

(h) "Security agreement" means an agreement which creates or provides for a security interest;

(i) "Secured party" means a lender, seller or other person in whose favor there is a security interest, including a person to whom accounts, contract rights or chattel paper have been sold. When the holders of obligations issued under an indenture of trust, equipment trust agreement or the like are represented by a trustee or other person, the representative is the secured party.

(2) Other definitions applying to this Article and the sections in which they appear are:

"Account". Section 9–106.

"Consumer goods". Section 9–109(1).

"Contract right". Section 9–106.

"Equipment". Section 9–109(2).

"Farm products". Section 9–109(3).

"General intangible". Section 9–106.

"Inventory". Section 9–109(4).

"Lien creditor". Section 9–301(3).

"Proceeds". Section 9–306(1).

"Purchase money security interest". Section 9–107.

(3) The following definitions in other Articles apply to this Article:

"Check". Section 3–104.

"Contract for sale". Section 2–106.

"Holder in due course". Section 3–302.

"Note". Section 3–104.

"Sale". Section 2–106.

(4) In addition Article 1 contains general definitions and principles of construction and interpretation applicable throughout this Article.

§9–106. Definitions: "Account"; "Contract Right"; "General Intangibles". "Account" means any right to payment for goods sold or leased or for services rendered which is not evidenced by an instrument or chattel paper. "Contract right" means any right to payment under a contract not yet earned by performance and not evidenced by an instrument or chattel paper. "General intangibles" means any personal property (including things in action) other than goods, accounts, contract rights, chattel paper, documents and instruments.

§9–107. Definitions: "Purchase Money Security Interest". A security interest is a "purchase money security interest" to the extent that it is

(a) taken or retained by the seller of the collateral to secure all or part of its price; or

(b) taken by a person who by making advances or incurring an obligation gives value to enable the debtor to acquire rights in or the use of collateral if such value is in fact so used.

§9–108. When After-Acquired Collateral Not Security for Antecedent Debt. Where a secured party makes an advance, incurs an obligation, releases a perfected security interest, or otherwise gives new value which is to be secured in whole or in part by after-acquired property his security interest in the after-acquired collateral shall be deemed to be taken for new value and not as security for an antecedent debt if the debtor acquires his rights in such collateral either in the ordinary course of his business or under a contract of purchase made pursuant to the security agreement within a reasonable time after new value is given.

§9–109. Classification of Goods; "Consumer Goods"; "Equipment"; "Farm Products"; "Inventory". Goods are

(1) "consumer goods" if they are used or bought for use primarily for personal, family or household purposes;

(2) "equipment" if they are used or bought for use primarily in business (including farming or a profession) or by a debtor who is a non-profit organization or a governmental subdivision or agency or if the goods are not included in the definitions of inventory, farm products or consumer goods;

(3) "farm products" if they are crops or livestock or supplies used or produced in farming operations or if they are products of crops or livestock in their unmanufactured states (such as ginned cotton, wool-clip, maple syrup, milk and eggs), and if they are in the possession of a debtor engaged in raising, fattening, grazing or other farming operations. If goods are farm products they are neither equipment nor inventory;

(4) "inventory" if they are held by a person who holds them for sale or lease or to be furnished under contracts of service or if he has so furnished them, or if they are raw materials, work in process or materials used or consumed in a business. Inventory of a person is not to be classified as his equipment.

§9-110. Sufficiency of Description. For the purposes of this Article any description of personal property or real estate is sufficient whether or not it is specific if it reasonably identifies what is described.

§9-111. Applicability of Bulk Transfer Laws. The creation of a security interest is not a bulk transfer under Article 6 (see Section 6-103).

§9-112. Where Collateral Is Not Owned by Debtor. Unless otherwise agreed, when a secured party knows that collateral is owned by a person who is not the debtor, the owner of the collateral is entitled to receive from the secured party any surplus under Section 9-502(2) or under Section 9-504(1), and is not liable for the debt or for any deficiency after resale, and he has the same right as the debtor

(a) to receive statements under Section 9-208;

(b) to receive notice of and to object to a secured party's proposal to retain the collateral in satisfaction of the indebtedness under Section 9-505;

(c) to redeem the collateral under Section 9-506;

(d) to obtain injunctive or other relief under Section 9-507(1); and

(e) to recover losses caused to him under Section 9-208(2).

§9-113. Security Interests Arising Under Article on Sales. A security interest arising solely under the Article on Sales (Article 2) is subject to the provisions of this Article except that to the extent that and so long as the debtor does not have or does not lawfully obtain possession of the goods

(a) no security agreement is necessary to make the security interest enforceable; and

(b) no filing is required to perfect the security interest; and

(c) the rights of the secured party on default by the debtor are governed by the Article on Sales (Article 2).

Part 2

Validity of Security Agreement and Rights of Parties Thereto

§9-201. General Validity of Security Agreement. Except as otherwise provided by this Act a security agreement is effective according to its terms between the parties, against purchasers of the collateral and against creditors. Nothing in this Article validates any charge or practice illegal under any statute or regulation thereunder governing usury, small loans, retail installment sales, or the like, or extends the application of any such statute or regulation to any transaction not otherwise subject thereto.

§9–202. Title to Collateral Immaterial. Each provision of this Article with regard to rights, obligations and remedies applies whether title to collateral is in the secured party or in the debtor.

§9–203. Enforceability of Security Interest; Proceeds, Formal Requisites. (1) Subject to the provisions of Section 4–208 on the security interest of a collecting bank and Section 9–113 on a security interest arising under the Article on Sales, a security interest is not enforceable against the debtor or third parties unless

(a) the collateral is in the possession of the secured party; or

(b) the debtor has signed a security agreement which contains a description of the collateral and in addition, when the security interest covers crops or oil, gas or minerals to be extracted or timber to be cut, a description of the land concerned. In describing collateral, the word "proceeds" is sufficient without further description to cover proceeds of any character.

(2) A transaction, although subject to this Article, is also subject to ....*, and in the case of conflict between the provisions of this Article and any such statute, the provisions of such statute control. Failure to comply with any applicable statute has only the effect which is specified therein. **Note:** *At * in subsection (2) insert reference to any local statute regulating small loans, retail installment sales and the like.*

The foregoing subsection (2) is designed to make it clear that certain transactions, although subject to this Article, must also comply with other applicable legislation.

This Article is designed to regulate all the "security" aspects of transactions within its scope. There is, however, much regulatory legislation, particularly in the consumer field, which supplements this Article and should not be repealed by its enactment. Examples are small loan acts, retail installment selling acts and the like. Such acts may provide for licensing and rate regulation and may prescribe particular forms of contract. Such provisions should remain in force despite the enactment of this Article. On the other hand if a Retail Installment Selling Act contains provisions on filing, rights on default, etc., such provisions should be repealed as inconsistent with this Article.

§9–204. When Security Interest Attaches; After-Acquired Property; Future Advances. (1) A security interest cannot attach until there is agreement (subsection (3) of Section 1–201) that it attach and value is given and the debtor has rights in the collateral. It attaches as soon as all of the events in the preceding sentence have taken place unless explicit agreement postpones the time of attaching.

(2) For the purposes of this section the debtor has no rights

(a) in crops until they are planted or otherwise become growing crops, in the young of livestock until they are conceived;

(b) in fish until caught, in oil, gas or minerals until they are extracted, in timber until it is cut;

(c) in a contract right until the contract has been made;

(d) in an account until it comes into existence.

(3) Except as provided in subsection (4) a security agreement may provide that collateral, whenever acquired, shall secure all obligations covered by the security agreement.

(4) No security interest attaches under an after-acquired property clause

(a) to crops which become such more than one year after the security agreement is executed except that a security interest in crops which is given in conjunction with a lease or a land purchase or improvement transaction evidenced by a contract, mortgage or deed of trust may if so agreed attach to crops to be grown on the land concerned during the period of such real estate transaction;

(b) to consumer goods other than accessions (Section 9–314) when given as additional security unless the debtor acquires rights in them within ten days after the secured party gives value.

(5) Obligations covered by a security agreement may include future advances or other value whether or not the advances or value are given pursuant to commitment.

§9–205. Use or Disposition of Collateral Without Accounting Permissible. A security interest is not invalid or fraudulent against creditors by reason of liberty in the debtor to use, commingle or dispose of all or part of the collateral (including returned or repossessed goods) or to collect or compromise accounts, contract rights or chattel paper, or to accept the return of goods or make repossessions, or to use, commingle or dispose of proceeds, or by reason of the failure of the secured party to require the debtor to account for proceeds or replace collateral. This section does not relax the requirements of possession where perfection of a security interest depends upon possession of the collateral by the secured party or by a bailee.

§9–206. Agreement Not to Assert Defenses Against Assignee; Modification of Sales Warranties Where Security Agreement Exists. (1) Subject to any statute or decision which establishes a different rule for buyers or lessees of consumer goods, an agreement by a buyer or lessee that he will not assert against an assignee any claim or defense which he may have against the seller or lessor is enforceable by an assignee who takes his assignment for value, in good faith and without notice of a claim or defense, except as to defenses of a type which may be asserted against a holder in due course of a negotiable instrument under the Article on Commercial Paper (Article 3). A buyer who as part of one transaction signs both a negotiable instrument and a security agreement makes such an agreement.

(2) When a seller retains a purchase money security interest in goods the Article on Sales (Article 2) governs the sale and any disclaimer, limitation or modification of the seller's warranties.

§9–207. Rights and Duties When Collateral Is in Secured Party's Possession. (1) A secured party must use reasonable care in the custody and preservation of collateral in his possession. In the case of an instrument or chattel paper reasonable care includes taking necessary steps to preserve rights against prior parties unless otherwise agreed.

(2) Unless otherwise agreed, when collateral is in the secured party's possession

(a) reasonable expenses (including the cost of any insurance and payment of taxes or other charges) incurred in the custody, preservation, use or operation of the collateral are chargeable to the debtor and are secured by the collateral;

(b) the risk of accidental loss or damage is on the debtor to the extent of any deficiency in any effective insurance coverage;

(c) the secured party may hold as additional security any increase or profits (except money) received from the collateral, but money so received, unless remitted to the debtor, shall be applied in reduction of the secured obligation;

(d) the secured party must keep the collateral identifiable but fungible collateral may be commingled;

(e) the secured party may repledge the collateral upon terms which do not impair the debtor's right to redeem it.

(3) A secured party is liable for any loss caused by his failure to meet any obligation imposed by the preceding subsections but does not lose his security interest.

(4) A secured party may use or operate the collateral for the purpose of preserving the collateral or its value or pursuant to the order of a court of appropriate jurisdiction or, except in the case of consumer goods, in the manner and to the extent provided in the security agreement.

§9–208. Request for Statement of Account or List of Collateral. (1) A debtor may sign a statement indicating what he believes to be the aggregate amount of unpaid indebtedness as of a specified date and may send it to the secured party with a request that the statement be approved or corrected and returned to the debtor. When the security agreement or any other record kept by the secured party identifies the collateral a debtor may similarly request the secured party to approve or correct a list of the collateral.

(2) The secured party must comply with such a request within two weeks after receipt by sending a written correction or approval. If the secured party claims a security interest in all of a particular type of collateral owned by the debtor he may indicate that fact in his reply and need not approve or correct an itemized list of such collateral. If the secured party without reasonable excuse fails to comply he is liable for any loss caused to the debtor thereby; and if the debtor has properly included in his request a good faith statement of the obligation or a list of the collateral or both the secured party may claim a security interest only as shown in the statement against persons misled by his failure to comply. If he no longer has an interest in the obligation or collateral at the time the request is received he must disclose the name and address of any successor in interest known to him and he is liable for any loss caused to the debtor as a result of failure to disclose. A successor in interest is not subject to this section until a request is received by him.

(3) A debtor is entitled to such a statement once every six months without charge. The secured party may require payment of a charge not exceeding $10 for each additional statement furnished.

Part 3

Rights of Third Parties; Perfected and Unperfected Security Interests; Rules of Priority

§9–301. Persons Who Take Priority Over Unperfected Security Interests; "Lien Creditor". (1) Except as otherwise provided in subsection (2), an unperfected security interest is subordinate to the rights of

(a) persons entitled to priority under Section 9–312;

(b) a person who becomes a lien creditor without knowledge of the security interest and before it is perfected;

(c) in the case of goods, instruments, documents, and chattel paper, a person who is not a secured party and who is a transferee in bulk or other buyer not in ordinary course of business to the extent that he gives value and receives delivery of the collateral without knowledge of the security interest and before it is perfected;

(d) in the case of accounts, contract rights, and general intangibles, a person who is not a secured party and who is a transferee to the extent that he gives value without knowledge of the security interest and before it is perfected.

(2) If the secured party files with respect to a purchase money security interest before or within ten days after the collateral comes into possession of the debtor, he takes priority over the rights of a transferee in bulk or of a lien creditor which arise between the time the security interest attaches and the time of filing.

(3) A "lien creditor" means a creditor who has acquired a lien on the property involved by attachment, levy or the like and includes an assignee for benefit of creditors from the time of assignment, and a trustee in bankruptcy from the date of the filing of the petition or a receiver in equity from the time of appointment. Unless all the creditors represented had knowledge of the security interest such a representative of creditors is a lien creditor without knowledge even though he personally has knowledge of the security interest.

§9–302. When Filing Is Required to Perfect Security Interest; Security Interests to Which Filing Provisions of This Article Do Not Apply. (1) A financing statement must be filed to perfect all security interests except the following:

(a) a security interest in collateral in possession of the secured party under Section 9–305;

(b) a security interest temporarily perfected in instruments or documents without delivery under Section 9–304 or in proceeds for a 10 day period under Section 9–306;

(c) a purchase money security interest in farm equipment having a purchase price not in excess of $2500; but filing is required for a fixture under Section 9–313 or for a motor vehicle required to be licensed;

(d) a purchase money security interest in consumer goods; but filing is required for a fixture under Section 9–313 or for a motor vehicle required to be licensed;

(e) an assignment of accounts or contract rights which does not alone or in conjunction with other assignments to the same assignee transfer a significant part of the outstanding accounts or contract rights of the assignor;

(f) a security interest of a collecting bank (Section 4–208) or arising under the Article on Sales (see Section 9–113) or covered in subsection (3) of this section.

(2) If a secured party assigns a perfected security interest, no filing under this Article is required in order to continue the perfected status of the security interest against creditors of and transferees from the original debtor.

(3) The filing provisions of this Article do not apply to a security interest in property subject to a statute

(a) of the United States which provides for a national registration or filing of all security interests in such property; or

Note: *States to select either Alternative A or Alternative B.*

Alternative A—

(b) of this state which provides for central filing of, or which requires indication on a certificate of title of, such security interests in such property.

Alternative B—

(b) of this state which provides for central filing of security interests in such property, or in a motor vehicle which is not inventory held for sale for which a certificate of title is required under the statutes of this state if a notation of such a security interest can be indicated by a public official on a certificate or a duplicate thereof.

(4) A security interest in property covered by a statute described in subsection (3) can be perfected only by registration or filing under that statute or by indication of the security interest on a certificate of title or a duplicate thereof by a public official.

§9–303. When Security Interest Is Perfected; Continuity of Perfection. (1) A security interest is perfected when it has attached and when all of the applicable steps required for perfection have been taken. Such steps are specified in Sections 9–302, 9–304, 9–305 and 9–306. If such steps are taken before the security interest attaches, it is perfected at the time when it attaches.

(2) If a security interest is originally perfected in any way permitted under this Article and is subsequently perfected in some other way under this Article, without an intermediate period when it was unperfected, the security interest shall be deemed to be perfected continuously for the purposes of this Article.

§9–304. Perfection of Security Interest in Instruments, Documents, and Goods Covered by Documents; Perfection by Permissive Filing; Temporary Perfection Without Filing or Transfer of Possession. (1) A security interest in chattel paper or negotiable documents may be perfected by filing. A security interest in instruments (other than instruments which constitute part of chattel paper) can be perfected only by the secured party's taking possession, except as provided in subsections (4) and (5).

(2) During the period that goods are in the possession of the issuer of a negotiable document therefor, a security interest in the goods is perfected by perfecting a security interest in the document, and any security interest in the goods otherwise perfected during such period is subject thereto.

(3) A security interest in goods in the possession of a bailee other than one who has issued a negotiable document therefore is perfected by issuance of a document in the name of the secured party or by the bailee's receipt of notification of the secured party's interest or by filing as to the goods.

(4) A security interest in instruments or negotiable documents is perfected without filing or the taking of possession for a period of 21 days from the time it attaches to the extent that it arises for new value given under a written security agreement.

(5) A security interest remains perfected for a period of 21 days without filing where a secured party having a perfected security interest in an instrument, a negotiable document or goods in possession of a bailee other than one who has issued a negotiable document therefor

(a) makes available to the debtor the goods or documents representing the goods for the purpose of ultimate sale or exchange or for the purpose of loading, unloading, storing, shipping, transshipping, manufacturing, processing or otherwise dealing with them in a manner preliminary to their sale or exchange; or

(b) delivers the instrument to the debtor for the purpose of ultimate sale or exchange or of presentation, collection, renewal or registration of transfer.

(6) After the 21 day period in subsections (4) and (5) perfection depends upon compliance with applicable provisions of this Article.

§9–305. When Possession by Secured Party Perfects Security Interest Without Filing. A security interest in letters of credit and advices of credit (subsection (2) (a) of Section 5–116), goods, instruments, negotiable documents or chattel paper may be perfected by the secured party's taking possession of the collateral. If such collateral other than goods covered by a negotiable document is held by a bailee, the secured party is deemed to have possession from the time the bailee receives notification of the secured party's interest. A security interest is perfected by possession from the time possession is taken without relation back and continues only so long as possession is retained, unless otherwise specified in this Article. The security interest may be otherwise perfected as provided in this Article before or after the period of possession by the secured party.

§9–306. "Proceeds"; Secured Party's Rights on Disposition of Collateral. (1) "Proceeds" includes whatever is received when collateral or proceeds is sold, exchanged, collected or otherwise disposed of. The term also includes the account arising when the right to payment is earned under a contract right. Money, checks and the like are "cash proceeds". All other proceeds are "non-cash proceeds".

(2) Except where this Article otherwise provides, a security interest continues in collateral notwithstanding sale, exchange or other disposition thereof by the debtor unless his action was authorized by the secured party in the security agreement or otherwise, and also continues in any identifiable proceeds including collections received by the debtor.

(3) The security interest in proceeds is a continuously perfected security interest if the interest in the original collateral was perfected but it ceases to be a perfected security interest and becomes unperfected ten days after receipt of the proceeds by the debtor unless

(a) a filed financing statement covering the original collateral also covers proceeds; or

(b) the security interest in the proceeds is perfected before the expiration of the ten day period.

(4) In the event of insolvency proceedings instituted by or against a debtor, a secured party with a perfected security interest in proceeds has a perfected security interest

(a) in identifiable non-cash proceeds;

(b) in identifiable cash proceeds in the form of money which is not commingled with other money or deposited in a bank account prior to the insolvency proceedings;

(c) in identifiable cash proceeds in the form of checks and the like which are not deposited in a bank account prior to the insolvency proceedings; and

(d) in all cash and bank accounts of the debtor, if other cash proceeds have been commingled or deposited in a bank account, but the perfected security interest under this paragraph (d) is

(i) subject to any right of set-off; and

(ii) limited to an amount not greater than the amount of any cash proceeds received by the debtor within ten days before the institution of the insolvency proceedings and commingled or deposited in a bank account prior to the insolvency proceedings less the amount of cash proceeds received by the debtor and paid over to the secured party during the ten day period.

(5) If a sale of goods results in an account or chattel paper which is transferred by the seller to a secured party, and if the goods are returned to or are repossessed by the seller or the secured party, the following rules determine priorities:

(a) If the goods were collateral at the time of sale for an indebtedness of the seller which is still unpaid, the original security interest attaches again to the goods and continues as a perfected security interest if it was perfected at the time when the goods were sold. If the security interest was originally perfected by a filing which is still effective, nothing further is required to continue the perfected status; in any other case, the secured party must take possession of the returned or repossessed goods or must file.

(b) An unpaid transferee of the chattel paper has a security interest in the goods against the transferor. Such security interest is prior to a security interest asserted under paragraph (a) to the extent that the transferee of the chattel paper was entitled to priority under Section 9–308.

(c) An unpaid transferee of the account has a security interest in the goods against the transferor. Such security interest is subordinate to a security interest asserted under paragraph (a).

(d) A security interest of an unpaid transferee asserted under paragraph (b) or (c) must be perfected for protection against creditors of the transferor and purchasers of the returned or repossessed goods.

§9–307. Protection of Buyers of Goods. (1) A buyer in ordinary course of business (subsection (9) of Section 1–201) other than a person buying farm products from a person engaged in farming operations takes free of a security interest created by his seller even though the security interest is perfected and even though the buyer knows of its existence.

(2) In the case of consumer goods and in the case of farm equipment having an original purchase price not in excess of $2500 (other than fixtures, see Section 9–313), a buyer takes free of a security interest even though perfected if he buys without knowledge of the security interest, for value and for his own personal, family or household purposes or his own farming operations unless prior to the purchase the secured party has filed a financing statement covering such goods.

§9–308. Purchase of Chattel Paper and Non-Negotiable Instruments. A purchaser of chattel paper or a non-negotiable instrument who gives new value and takes possession of it in the ordinary course of his business and without knowledge that the specific paper or instrument is subject to a security interest has priority over a security interest which is perfected under Section 9–304 (permissive filing and temporary perfection). A purchaser of chattel paper who gives new value and takes possession of it in the ordinary course of his business has priority over a security interest in chattel paper which is claimed merely as proceeds of inventory subject to a security interest (Section 9–306), even though he knows that the specific paper is subject to the security interest.

§9–309. Protection of Purchasers of Instruments and Documents. Nothing in this Article limits the rights of a holder in due course of a negotiable instrument (Section 3–302) or a holder to whom a negotiable document of title has been duly negotiated (Section 7–501) or a bona fide purchaser of a security (Section 8–301) and such holders or purchasers take priority over an earlier security interest even though perfected. Filing under this Article does not constitute notice of the security interest to such holders or purchasers.

§9–310. Priority of Certain Liens Arising by Operation of Law. When a person in the ordinary course of his business furnishes services or materials with respect to goods subject to a security interest, a lien upon goods in the possession of such person given by statute or rule of law for such materials or services takes priority over a perfected security interest unless the lien is statutory and the statute expressly provides otherwise.

§9–311. Alienability of Debtor's Rights: Judicial Process. The debtor's rights in collateral may be voluntarily or involuntarily transferred (by way of sale, creation of a security interest, attachment, levy, garnishment or other judicial process) notwithstanding a provision in the security agreement prohibiting any transfer or making the transfer constitute a default.

§9–312. Priorities Among Conflicting Security Interests in the Same Collateral.
(1) The rules of priority stated in the following sections shall govern where applicable: Section 4–208 with respect to the security interest of collecting banks in items being collected, accompanying documents and proceeds; Section 9–301 on certain priorities; Section 9–304 on goods covered by documents; Section 9–306 on proceeds and repossessions; Section 9–307 on buyers of goods; Section 9–308 on possessory against non-possessory interests in chattel paper or non-negotiable instruments; Section 9–309 on security interests in negotiable instruments, documents or securities; Section 9–310 on priorities between perfected security interests and liens by operation of law; Section 9–313 on security interests in fixtures as against interests in real estate; Section 9–314 on security interests in accessions as against interest in goods; Section 9–315 on conflicting security interests where goods lose their identity or become part of a product; and Section 9–316 on contractual subordination.

(2) A perfected security interest in crops for new value given to enable the debtor to produce the crops during the production season and given not more than three months before the crops become growing crops by planting or otherwise takes priority over an earlier perfected security interest to the extent that such earlier interest secures obligations due more than six months before the crops become growing crops by planting or otherwise, even though the person giving new value had knowledge of the earlier security interest.

(3) A purchase money security interest in inventory collateral has priority over a conflicting security interest in the same collateral if

(a) the purchase money security interest is perfected at the time the debtor receives possession of the collateral; and

(b) any secured party whose security interest is known to the holder of the purchase money security interest or who, prior to the date of the filing made by the holder of the purchase money security interest, had filed a financing statement covering the same items or type of inventory, has received notification of the purchase money security interest before the debtor receives possession of the collateral covered by the purchase money security interest; and

(c) such notification states that the person giving the notice has or expects to acquire a purchase money security interest in inventory of the debtor, describing such inventory by item or type.

(4) A purchase money security interest in collateral other than inventory has priority over a conflicting security interest in the same collateral if the purchase money security interest is perfected at the time the debtor receives possession of the collateral or within ten days thereafter.

(5) In all cases not governed by other rules stated in this section (including cases of purchase money security interests which do not qualify for the special priorities set forth in subsections (3) and (4) of this section), priority between conflicting security interests in the same collateral shall be determined as follows:

(a) in the order of filing if both are perfected by filing, regardless of which security interest attached first under Section 9–204(1) and whether it attached before or after filing;

(b) in the order of perfection unless both are perfected by filing, regardless of which security interest attached first under Section 9–204(1) and, in the case of a filed security interest, whether it attached before or after filing; and

(c) in the order of attachment under Section 9–204(1) so long as neither is perfected.

(6) For the purpose of the priority rules of the immediately preceding sub-

section, a continuously perfected security interest shall be treated at all times as if perfected by filing if it was originally so perfected and it shall be treated at all times as if perfected otherwise than by filing if it was originally perfected otherwise than by filing.

§9–313. Priority of Security Interests in Fixtures. (1) The rules of this section do not apply to goods incorporated into a structure in the manner of lumber, bricks, tile, cement, glass, metal work and the like and no security interest in them exists under this Article unless the structure remains personal property under applicable law. The law of this state other than this Act determines whether and when other goods become fixtures. This Act does not prevent creation of an encumbrance upon fixtures or real estate pursuant to the law applicable to real estate.

(2) A security interest which attaches to goods before they become fixtures takes priority as to the goods over the claims of all persons who have an interest in the real estate except as stated in subsection (4).

(3) A security interest which attaches to goods after they become fixtures is valid against all persons subsequently acquiring interests in the real estate except as stated in subsection (4) but is invalid against any person with an interest in the real estate at the time the security interest attaches to the goods who has not in writing consented to the security interest or disclaimed an interest in the goods as fixtures.

(4) The security interests described in subsections (2) and (3) do not take priority over

(a) a subsequent purchaser for value of any interest in the real estate; or

(b) a creditor with a lien on the real estate subsequently obtained by judicial proceedings; or

(c) a creditor with a prior encumbrance of record on the real estate to the extent that he makes subsequent advances

if the subsequent purchase is made, the lien by judicial proceedings is obtained, or the subsequent advance under the prior encumbrance is made or contracted for without knowledge of the security interest and before it is perfected. A purchaser of the real estate at a foreclosure sale other than an encumbrancer purchasing at his own foreclosure sale is a subsequent purchaser within this section.

(5) When under subsections (2) or (3) and (4) a secured party has priority over the claims of all persons who have interests in the real estate, he may, on default, subject to the provisions of Part 5, remove his collateral from the real estate but he must reimburse any encumbrancer or owner of the real estate who is not the debtor and who has not otherwise agreed for the cost of repair of any physical injury, but not for any diminution in value of the real estate caused by the absence of the goods removed or by any necessity for replacing them. A person entitled to reimbursement may refuse permission to remove until the secured party gives adequate security for the performance of this obligation.

§9–314. Accessions. (1) A security interest in goods which attaches before they are installed in or affixed to other goods takes priority as to the goods installed or affixed (called in this section "accessions") over the claims of all persons to the whole except as stated in subsection (3) and subject to Section 9–315(1).

(2) A security interest which attaches to goods after they become part of a whole is valid against all persons subsequently acquiring interests in the whole except as stated in subsection (3) but is invalid against any person with an interest in the whole at the time the security interest attaches to the goods

who has not in writing consented to the security interest or disclaimed an interest in the goods as part of the whole.

(3) The security interests described in subsections (1) and (2) do not take priority over

(a) a subsequent purchaser for value of any interest in the whole; or

(b) a creditor with a lien on the whole subsequently obtained by judicial proceedings; or

(c) a creditor with a prior perfected security interest in the whole to the extent that he makes subsequent advances

if the subsequent purchase is made, the lien by judicial proceedings obtained or the subsequent advance under the prior perfected security interest is made or contracted for without knowledge of the security interest and before it is perfected. A purchaser of the whole at a foreclosure sale other than the holder of a perfected security interest purchasing at his own foreclosure sale is a subsequent purchaser within this section.

(4) When under subsections (1) or (2) and (3) a secured party has an interest in accessions which has priority over the claims of all persons who have interests in the whole, he may on default subject to the provisions of Part 5 remove his collateral from the whole but he must reimburse any encumbrancer or owner of the whole who is not the debtor and who has not otherwise agreed for the cost of repair of any physical injury but not for any diminution in value of the whole caused by the absence of the goods removed or by any necessity for replacing them. A person entitled to reimbursement may refuse permission to remove until the secured party gives adequate security for the performance of this obligation.

§9–315. Priority When Goods Are Commingled or Processed. (1) If a security interest in goods was perfected and subsequently the goods or a part thereof have become part of a product or mass, the security interest continues in the product or mass if

(a) the goods are so manufactured, processed, assembled or commingled that their identity is lost in the product or mass; or

(b) a financing statement covering the original goods also covers the product into which the goods have been manufactured, processed or assembled.

In a case to which paragraph (b) applies, no separate security interest in that part of the original goods which has been manufactured, processed or assembled into the product may be claimed under Section 9–314.

(2) When under subsection (1) more than one security interest attaches to the product or mass, they rank equally according to the ratio that the cost of the goods to which each interest originally attached bears to the cost of the total product or mass.

§9–316. Priority Subject to Subordination. Nothing in this Article prevents subordination by agreement by any person entitled to priority.

§9–317. Secured Party Not Obligated on Contract of Debtor. The mere existence of a security interest or authority given to the debtor to dispose of or use collateral does not impose contract or tort liability upon the secured party for the debtor's acts or omissions.

§9–318. Defenses Against Assignee; Modification of Contract After Notification of Assignment; Term Prohibiting Assignment Ineffective; Identification and Proof of Assignment. (1) Unless an account debtor has made an enforceable agreement not to assert defenses or claims arising out of a sale as provided in Section 9–206 the rights of an assignee are subject to

(a) all the terms of the contract between the account debtor and assignor and any defense or claim arising therefrom; and

(b) any other defense or claim of the account debtor against the assignor which accrues before the account debtor receives notification of the assignment.

(2) So far as the right to payment under an assigned contract right has not already become an account, and notwithstanding notification of the assignment, any modification of or substitution for the contract made in good faith and in accordance with reasonable commercial standards is effective against an assignee unless the account debtor has otherwise agreed but the assignee acquires corresponding rights under the modified or substituted contract. The assignment may provide that such modification or substitution is a breach by the assignor.

(3) The account debtor is authorized to pay the assignor until the account debtor receives notification that the account has been assigned and that payment is to be made to the assignee. A notification which does not reasonably identify the rights assigned is ineffective. If requested by the account debtor, the assignee must seasonably furnish reasonable proof that the assignment has been made and unless he does so the account debtor may pay the assignor.

(4) A term in any contract between an account debtor and an assignor which prohibits assignment of an account or contract right to which they are parties is ineffective.

Part 4

Filing

§9-401. Place of Filing; Erroneous Filing; Removal of Collateral

First Alternative Subsection (1)

(1) The proper place to file in order to perfect a security interest is as follows:

(a) when the collateral is goods which at the time the security interest attaches are or are to become fixtures, then in the office where a mortgage on the real estate concerned would be filed or recorded;

(b) in all other cases, in the office of the [Secretary of State].

Second Alternative Subsection (1)

(1) The proper place to file in order to perfect a security interest is as follows:

(a) when the collateral is equipment used in farming operations, or farm products, or accounts, contract rights or general intangibles arising from or relating to the sale of farm products by a farmer, or consumer goods, then in the office of the . . . in the county of the debtor's residence or if the debtor is not a resident of this state then in the office of the . . . in the county where the goods are kept, and in addition when the collateral is crops in the office of the . . . in the county where the land on which the crops are growing or to be grown is located;

(b) when the collateral is goods which at the time the security interest attaches are or are to become fixtures, then in the office where a mortgage on the real estate concerned would be filed or recorded;

(c) in all other cases, in the office of the [Secretary of State].

Third Alternative Subsection (1)

(1) The proper place to file in order to perfect a security interest is as follows:

(a) when the collateral is equipment used in farming operations, or farm products, or accounts, contract rights or general intangibles arising from or relating to the sale of farm products by a farmer, or consumer goods, then in the office of the . . . in the county of the debtor's residence or if the debtor is not a resident of this state then in the office of the . . . in the county where the goods are kept, and in addition when the collateral is crops in the office of the . . . in the county where the land on which the crops are growing or to be grown is located;

(b) when the collateral is goods which at the time of the security interest attaches are or are to become fixtures, then in the office where a mortgage on the real estate concerned would be filed or recorded;

(c) in all other cases, in the office of the [Secretary of State] and in addition, if the debtor has a place of business in only one county of this state, also in the office of . . . of such county, or, if the debtor has no place of business in this state, but resides in the state, also in the office of . . . of the county in which he resides.

Note: *One of the three alternatives should be selected as subsection (1).*

(2) A filing which is made in good faith in an improper place or not in all of the places required by this section is nevertheless effective with regard to any collateral as to which the filing complied with the requirements of this Article and is also effective with regard to collateral covered by the financing statement against any person who has knowledge of the contents of such financing statement.

(3) A filing which is made in the proper place in this state continues effective even though the debtor's residence or place of business or the location of the collateral or its use, whichever controlled the original filing, is thereafter changed.

Alternative Subsection (3)

[(3) A filing which is made in the proper county continues effective for four months after a change to another county of the debtor's residence or place of business or the location of the collateral, whichever controlled the original filing. It becomes ineffective thereafter unless a copy of the financing statement signed by the secured party is filed in the new county within said period. The security interest may also be perfected in the new county after the expiration of the four-month period; in such case perfection dates from the time of perfection in the new county. A change in the use of the collateral does not impair the effectiveness of the original filing.]

(4) If collateral is brought into this state from another jurisdiction, the rules stated in Section 9–103 determine whether filing is necessary in this state.

§9–402. **Formal Requisites of Financing Statement; Amendments.** (1) A financing statement is sufficient if it is signed by the debtor and the secured party, gives an address of the secured party from which information concerning the security interest may be obtained, gives a mailing address of the debtor and contains a statement indicating the types, or describing the items, of collateral. A financing statement may be filed before a security agreement is made or a security interest otherwise attaches. When the financing statement covers crops growing or to be grown or goods which are or are to become fixtures, the statement must also contain a description of the real estate concerned. A copy of the security agreement is sufficient as a financing statement if it contains the above information and is signed by both parties.

(2) A financing statement which otherwise complies with subsection (1) is sufficient although it is signed only by the secured party when it is filed to perfect a security interest in

(a) collateral already subject to a security interest in another jurisdiction when it is brought into this state. Such a financing statement must state that the collateral was brought into this state under such circumstances.

(b) proceeds under Section 9–306 if the security interest in the original collateral was perfected. Such a financing statement must describe the original collateral.

(3) A form substantially as follows is sufficient to comply with subsection (1):

Name of debtor (or assignor) ....

Address ....

Name of secured party (or assignee) ....

Address ....

1. This financing statement covers the following types (or items) of property: (Describe) ....

2. (If collateral is crops) The above described crops are growing or are to be grown on:
   (Describe Real Estate) ....

3. (If collateral is goods which are or are to become fixtures) The above described goods are affixed or are to be affixed to:
   (Describe Real Estate) ....

4. (If proceeds or products of collateral are claimed) Proceeds—Products of the collateral are also covered.
   Signature of Debtor (or Assignor) ....
   Signature of Secured Party (or Assignee) ....

(4) The term "financing statement" as used in this Article means the original financing statement and any amendments but if any amendment adds collateral, it is effective as to the added collateral only from the filing date of the amendment.

(5) A financing statement substantially complying with the requirements of this section is effective even though it contains minor errors which are not seriously misleading.

§9–403. What Constitutes Filing; Duration of Filing; Effect of Lapsed Filing; Duties of Filing Officer. (1) Presentation for filing of a financing statement and tender of the filing fee or acceptance of the statement by the filing officer constitutes filing under this Article.

(2) A filed financing statement which states a maturity date of the obligation secured of five years or less is effective until such maturity date and thereafter for a period of sixty days. Any other filed financing statement is effective for a period of five years from the date of filing. The effectiveness of a filed financing statement lapses on the expiration of such sixty day period after a stated maturity date or on the expiration of such five year period, as the case may be, unless a continuation statement is filed prior to the lapse. Upon such lapse the security interest becomes unperfected. A filed financing statement which states that the obligation secured is payable on demand is effective for five years from the date of filing.

(3) A continuation statement may be filed by the secured party (i) within six months before and sixty days after a stated maturity date of five years or less, and (ii) otherwise within six months prior to the expiration of the five year period specified in subsection (2). Any such continuation statement must be signed by the secured party, identify the original statement by file number and state that the original statement is still effective. Upon timely filing of the continuation statement, the effectiveness of the original statement is continued for five years after the last date to which the filing was effective whereupon it lapses in the same manner as provided in subsection (2) unless another continuation statement is filed prior to such lapse. Succeeding continuation statements may be filed in the same manner to continue the effectiveness of the original statement. Unless a statute on disposition of public records provides otherwise, the filing officer may remove a lapsed statement from the files and destroy it.

(4) A filing officer shall mark each statement with a consecutive file number and with the date and hour of filing and shall hold the statement for public inspection. In addition the filing officer shall index the statements according to the name of the debtor and shall note in the index the file number and the address of the debtor given in the statement.

(5) The uniform fee for filing, indexing and furnishing filing data for an original or a continuation statement shall be $..........................

§9-404. Termination Statement. (1) Whenever there is no outstanding secured obligation and no commitment to make advances, incur obligations or otherwise give value, the secured party must on written demand by the debtor send the debtor a statement that he no longer claims a security interest under the financing statement, which shall be identified by file number. A termination statement signed by a person other than the secured party of record must include or be accompanied by the assignment or a statement by the secured party of record that he has assigned the security interest to the signer of the termination statement. The uniform fee for filing and indexing such an assignment or statement thereof shall be $.......................... If the affected secured party fails to send such a termination statement within ten days after proper demand therefor he shall be liable to the debtor for one hundred dollars, and in addition for any loss caused to the debtor by such failure.

(2) On presentation to the filing officer of such a termination statement he must note it in the index. The filing officer shall remove from the files, mark "terminated" and send or deliver to the secured party the financing statement and any continuation statement, statement of assignment or statement of release pertaining thereto.

(3) The uniform fee for filing and indexing a termination statement including sending or delivering the financing statement shall be $..........................

§9-405. Assignment of Security Interest; Duties of Filing Officer; Fees. (1) A financing statement may disclose an assignment of a security interest in the collateral described in the statement by indication in the statement of the name and address of the assignee or by an assignment itself or a copy thereof on the face or back of the statement. Either the original secured party or the assignee may sign this statement as the secured party. On presentation to the filing officer of such a financing statement the filing officer shall mark the same as provided in Section 9-403(4). The uniform fee for filing, indexing and furnishing filing data for a financing statement so indicating an assignment shall be $..........................

(2) A secured party may assign of record all or a part of his rights under

a financing statement by the filing of a separate written statement of assignment signed by the secured party of record and setting forth the name of the secured party of record and the debtor, the file number and the date of filing of the financing statement and the name and address of the assignee and containing a description of the collateral assigned. A copy of the assignment is sufficient as a separate statement if it complies with the preceding sentence. On presentation to the filing officer of such a separate statement, the filing officer shall mark such separate statement with the date and hour of the filing. He shall note the assignment on the index of the financing statement. The uniform fee for filing, indexing and furnishing filing data about such a separate statement of assignment shall be $............................

(3) After the disclosure or filing of an assignment under this section, the assignee is the secured party of record.

§9–406. Release of Collateral; Duties of Filing Officer; Fees. A secured party of record may by his signed statement release all or a part of any collateral described in a filed financing statement. The statement of release is sufficient if it contains a description of the collateral being released, the name and address of the debtor, the name and address of the secured party, and the file number of the financing statement. Upon presentation of such a statement to the filing officer he shall mark the statement with the hour and date of filing and shall note the same upon the margin of the index of the filing of the financing statement. The uniform fee for filing and noting such a statement of release shall be $..........................

[**§9–407. Information From Filing Officer.** (1) If the person filing any financing statement, termination statement, statement of assignment, or statement of release, furnishes the filing officer a copy thereof, the filing officer shall upon request note upon the copy the file number and date and hour of the filing of the original and deliver or send the copy to such person.

(2) Upon request of any person, the filing officer shall issue his certificate showing whether there is on file on the date and hour stated therein, any presently effective financing statement naming a particular debtor and any statement of assignment thereof and if there is, giving the date and hour of filing of each such statement and the names and addresses of each secured party therein. The uniform fee for such a certificate shall be $...................... plus $...................... for each financing statement and for each statement of assignment reported therein. Upon request the filing officer shall furnish a copy of any filed financing statement or statement of assignment for a uniform fee of $........................ per page.]

Note: *This new section is proposed as an optional provision to require filing officers to furnish certificates. Local law and practices should be consulted with regard to the advisability of adoption.*

Part 5

Default

§9–501. Default; Procedure When Security Agreement Covers Both Real and Personal Property. (1) When a debtor is in default under a security agreement, a secured party has the rights and remedies provided in this Part and except as limited by subsection (3) those provided in the security agreement. He may reduce his claim to judgment, foreclose or otherwise enforce the security interest by any available judicial procedure. If the collateral is documents the secured party may proceed either as to the documents or as to the goods covered thereby. A secured party in possession has the rights, remedies and duties provided in Section 9–207. The rights and remedies referred to in this subsection are cumulative.

(2) After default, the debtor has the rights and remedies provided in this Part, those provided in the security agreement and those provided in Section 9–207.

(3) To the extent that they give rights to the debtor and impose duties on the secured party, the rules stated in the subsections referred to below may not be waived or varied except as provided with respect to compulsory disposition of collateral (subsection (1) of Section 9–505) and with respect to redemption of collateral (Section 9–506) but the parties may by agreement determine the standards by which the fulfillment of these rights and duties is to be measured if such standards are not manifestly unreasonable:

(a) subsection (2) of Section 9–502 and subsection (2) of Section 9–504 insofar as they require accounting for surplus proceeds of collateral;

(b) subsection (3) of Section 9–504 and subsection (1) of Section 9–505 which deal with disposition of collateral;

(c) subsection (2) of Section 9–505 which deals with acceptance of collateral as discharge of obligation;

(d) Section 9–506 which deals with redemption of collateral; and

(e) subsection (1) of Section 9–507 which deals with the secured party's liability for failure to comply with this Part.

(4) If the security agreement covers both real and personal property, the secured party may proceed under this Part as to the personal property or he may proceed as to both the real and the personal property in accordance with his rights and remedies in respect of the real property in which case the provisions of this Part do not apply.

(5) When a secured party has reduced his claim to judgment the lien of any levy which may be made upon his collateral by virtue of any execution based upon the judgment shall relate back to the date of the perfection of the security interest in such collateral. A judicial sale, pursuant to such execution, is a foreclosure of the security interest by judicial procedure within the meaning of this section, and the secured party may purchase at the sale and thereafter hold the collateral free of any other requirements of this Article.

§9–502. Collection Rights of Secured Party. (1) When so agreed and in any event on default the secured party is entitled to notify an account debtor or the obligor on an instrument to make payment to him whether or not the assignor was theretofore making collections on the collateral, and also to take control of any proceeds to which he is entitled under Section 9–306.

(2) A secured party who by agreement is entitled to charge back uncollected collateral or otherwise to full or limited recourse against the debtor and who undertakes to collect from the account debtors or obligors must proceed in a commercially reasonable manner and may deduct his reasonable expenses of realization from the collections. If the security agreement secures an indebtedness, the secured party must account to the debtor for any surplus, and unless otherwise agreed, the debtor is liable for any deficiency. But, if the underlying transaction was a sale of accounts, contract rights, or chattel paper, the debtor is entitled to any surplus or is liable for any deficiency only if the security agreement so provides.

§9–503. Secured Party's Right to Take Possession After Default. Unless otherwise agreed a secured party has on default the right to take possession of the collateral. In taking possession a secured party may proceed without judicial process if this can be done without breach of the peace or may proceed by action. If the security agreement so provides the secured party may require the debtor to assemble the collateral and make it available to the secured party at a place to be designated by the secured party which is reasonably convenient to both parties. Without removal a secured party may render equipment unusable, and may dispose of collateral on the debtor's premises under Section 9–504.

§9–504. Secured Party's Right to Dispose of Collateral After Default; Effect of Disposition. (1) A secured party after default may sell, lease or otherwise dispose of any or all of the collateral in its then condition or following any commercially reasonable preparation or processing. Any sale of goods is subject to the Article on Sales (Article 2). The proceeds of disposition shall be applied in the order following to

(a) the reasonable expenses of retaking, holding, preparing for sale, selling and the like and, to the extent provided for in the agreement and not prohibited by law, the reasonable attorneys' fees and legal expenses incurred by the secured party;

(b) the satisfaction of indebtedness secured by the security interest under which the disposition is made;

(c) the satisfaction of indebtedness secured by any subordinate security interest in the collateral if written notification of demand therefor is received before distribution of the proceeds is completed. If requested by the secured party, the holder of a subordinate security interest must seasonably furnish reasonable proof of his interest, and unless he does so, the secured party need not comply with his demand.

(2) If the security interest secures an indebtedness, the secured party must account to the debtor for any surplus, and, unless otherwise agreed, the debtor is liable for any deficiency. But if the underlying transaction was a sale of accounts, contract rights, or chattel paper, the debtor is entitled to any surplus or is liable for any deficiency only if the security agreement so provides.

(3) Disposition of the collateral may be by public or private proceedings and may be made by way of one or more contracts. Sale or other disposition may be as a unit or in parcels and at any time and place and on any terms but every aspect of the disposition including the method, manner, time, place and terms must be commercially reasonable. Unless collateral is perishable or threatens to decline speedily in value or is of a type customarily sold on a recognized market, reasonable notification of the time and place of any public sale or reasonable notification of the time after which any private sale or other intended disposition is to be made shall be sent by the secured party to the debtor, and except in the case of consumer goods to any other person who has a security interest in the collateral and who has duly filed a financing statement indexed in the name of the debtor in this state or who is known by the secured party to have a security interest in the collateral. The secured party may buy at any public sale and if the collateral is of a type customarily sold in a recognized market or is of a type which is the subject of widely distributed standard price quotations he may buy at private sale.

(4) When collateral is disposed of by a secured party after default, the disposition transfers to a purchaser for value all of the debtor's rights therein, discharges the security interest under which it is made and any security interest

or lien subordinate thereto. The purchaser takes free of all such rights and interests even though the secured party fails to comply with the requirements of this Part or of any judicial proceedings

(a) in the case of a public sale, if the purchaser has no knowledge of any defects in the sale and if he does not buy in collusion with the secured party, other bidders or the person conducting the sale; or

(b) in any other case, if the purchaser acts in good faith.

(5) A person who is liable to a secured party under a guaranty, indorsement, repurchase agreement or the like and who receives a transfer of collateral from the secured party or is subrogated to his rights has thereafter the rights and duties of the secured party. Such a transfer of collateral is not a sale or disposition of the collateral under this Article.

§9–505. Compulsory Disposition of Collateral; Acceptance of the Collateral as Discharge of Obligation. (1) If the debtor has paid sixty per cent of the cash price in the case of a purchase money security interest in consumer goods or sixty per cent of the loan in the case of another security interest in consumer goods, and has not signed after default a statement renouncing or modifying his rights under this Part a secured party who has taken possession of collateral must dispose of it under Section 9–504 and if he fails to do so within ninety days after he takes possession the debtor at his option may recover in conversion or under Section 9–507(1) on secured party's liability.

(2) In any other case involving consumer goods or any other collateral a secured party in possession may, after default, propose to retain the collateral in satisfaction of the obligation. Written notice of such proposal shall be sent to the debtor and except in the case of consumer goods to any other secured party who has a security interest in the collateral and who has duly filed a financing statement indexed in the name of the debtor in this state or is known by the secured party in possession to have a security interest in it. If the debtor or other person entitled to receive notification objects in writing within thirty days from the receipt of the notification or if any other secured party objects in writing within thirty days after the secured party obtains possession the secured party must dispose of the collateral under Section 9–504. In the absence of such written objection the secured party may retain the collateral in satisfaction of the debtor's obligation.

§9–506. Debtor's Right to Redeem Collateral. At any time before the secured party has disposed of collateral or entered into a contract for its disposition under Section 9–504 or before the obligation has been discharged under Section 9–505(2) the debtor or any other secured party may unless otherwise agreed in writing after default redeem the collateral by tendering fulfillment of all obligations secured by the collateral as well as the expenses reasonably incurred by the secured party in retaking, holding and preparing the collateral for disposition, in arranging for the sale, and to the extent provided in the agreement and not prohibited by law, his reasonable attorneys' fees and legal expenses.

§9–507. Secured Party's Liability for Failure to Comply With This Part. (1) If it is established that the secured party is not proceeding in accordance with the provisions of this Part disposition may be ordered or restrained on appropriate terms and conditions. If the disposition has occurred the debtor or any person entitled to notification or whose security interest has been made known to the secured party prior to the disposition has a right to recover from the secured party any loss caused by a failure to comply with the provisions of this Part. If the collateral is consumer goods, the debtor has a right to recover in any event an amount not less than the credit service charge plus ten per cent of the principal amount of the debt or the time price differential plus ten per cent of the cash price.

(2) The fact that a better price could have been obtained by a sale at a different time or in a different method from that selected by the secured party is not of itself sufficient to establish that the sale was not made in a commercially reasonable manner. If the secured party either sells the collateral in the usual manner in any recognized market therefor or if he sells at the price current in such market at the time of his sale or if he has otherwise sold in conformity with reasonable commercial practices among dealers in the type of property sold he has sold in a commercially reasonable manner. The principles stated in the two preceding sentences with respect to sales also apply as may be appropriate to other types of disposition. A disposition which has been approved in any judicial proceeding or by any bona fide creditors' committee or representative of creditors shall conclusively be deemed to be commercially reasonable, but this sentence does not indicate that any such approval must be obtained in any case nor does it indicate that any disposition not so approved is not commercially reasonable.

ARTICLE 10: EFFECTIVE DATE AND REPEALER

§10–101. Effective Date. This Act shall become effective at midnight on December 31st following its enactment. It applies to transactions entered into and events occurring after that date.

§10–102. Specific Repealer; Provision for Transition. (1) The following acts and all other acts and parts of acts inconsistent herewith are hereby repealed:

(Here should follow the acts to be specifically repealed including the following:

Uniform Negotiable Instruments Act
Uniform Warehouse Receipts Act
Uniform Sales Act
Uniform Bills of Lading Act
Uniform Stock Transfer Act
Uniform Conditional Sales Act
Uniform Trust Receipts Act

Also any acts regulating:

Bank collections
Bulk sales
Chattel mortgages
Conditional sales
Factor's lien acts
Farm storage of grain and similar acts
Assignment of accounts receivable)

(2) Transactions validly entered into before the effective date specified in Section 10–101 and the rights, duties and interests flowing from them remain valid thereafter and may be terminated, completed, consummated or enforced as required or permitted by any statute or other law amended or repealed by this Act as though such repeal or amendment had not occurred.

§10–103. General Repealer. Except as provided in the following section, all acts and parts of acts inconsistent with this Act are hereby repealed.

§10–104. Laws Not Repealed. [(1)] The Article on Documents of Title (Article

7) does not repeal or modify any laws prescribing the form or contents of documents of title or the services or facilities to be afforded by bailees, or otherwise regulating bailees' businesses in respects not specifically dealt with herein; but the fact that such laws are violated does not affect the status of a document of title which otherwise complies with the definition of a document of title (Section 1–201).

[(2) This Act does not repeal ....*,
cited as the Uniform Act for the Simplification of Fiduciary Security Transfers, and if in any respect there is any inconsistency between that Act and the Article of this Act on investment securities (Article 8) the provisions of the former Act shall control.]

Note: *At * in subsection (2) insert the statutory reference to the Uniform Act for the Simplification of Fiduciary Security Transfers if such Act has previously been enacted. If it has not been enacted, omit subsection (2).*

Index